Proclaiming Presence from the Washington Stage

Previously Published Books by Blair A. Ruble

Soviet Trade Unions
Leningrad
Money Sings
Second Metropolis
Creating Diversity Capital
Washington's U Street
The Muse of Urban Delirium

Proclaiming Presence
from
the Washington Stage

Blair A. Ruble

NEW ACADEMIA
PUBLISHING

Washington, DC

Library of Congress Control Number: 2021913734
ISBN 978-1-7348659-8-1 paperback (alk. paper)

NEW ACADEMIA
PUBLISHING

New Academia Publishing, 4401-A Connecticut Ave. NW, #236,
Washington, DC 20008
info@newacademia.com - www.newacademia.com

For Philip Arnoult

Contents

Acknowledgments   ix
Previously Published Materials   xi

Introduction: City and Stage   1
1. Proclaiming Racial Presence   17
2. Proclaiming Confessional Presence   85
3. Proclaiming Regional Presence   131
4. Proclaiming Community Presence   211
5. Curtain Call: The Stage Is Set   267

Notes   276
About the Author   335
Index   337

*The creation of beauty in the face of malice
is a radical act*

Acknowledgments

Research is a solitary endeavor, in that scholars must gather materials, formulate the story, and write more or less on their own. Such notions of writerly seclusion are greatly exaggerated. Multitudes of folks help along the way. I am especially aware of how dependent writers are on others from working at an institution that regularly supports researchers on their individual journeys to convert piles of notes and flashes of intellectual insight into products that someone else will want to read. I owe this work—and so much more—to the Woodrow Wilson International Center for Scholars, which has provided a supportive institutional and intellectual home for much of my career.

Among the many other colleagues, friends, and interlopers who have helped me along this particular journey have been Joseph Brinley, Rock Brynner, Sandra Butler-Truesdale, Stephen Deane, Lyn Dyson, Donatella Galella, Allison Garland, Jane Harman, Derek Hyra, Allison Irvin, Barbara Lanciers, Amarilis Lugo de Fabritz, Maurice Jackson, Hope Le Gro, Rob Litwak, Marvin McAllister, Mark Medish, Richard Mennen, Ibrahim Mumin, Neal Pierce, Mike Sfraga, Howard Shalwitz, John Stanley, S. Frederick Starr, Lorraine Treanor, and Paata Tsiurkashvili. The always-gracious Sheila Thomas, the youngest daughter of Howard Players' founder Thomas Montgomery Gregory, has been an especially generous enthusiast for this project. Maurice Jackson has offered insight and wisdom at important moments along this journey. Conversations with Mayhill C. Fowler after the publication of her masterful *Beau Monde on Empire's Edge* helped me clarify my thinking about the interaction between the performing arts and community. Expert editor Alfred F. Imhoff improved the manuscript immeasurably, as have thoughtful interventions by several anonymous reviewers.

Countless professionals have labored to make my research a success. I would like to thank the staffs of the Wilson Center Library (in particular, Janet Spikes, Michelle Kamalich, and Katherine Wahler); the Moorland-Spingarn Research Center and Founders Library at Howard University (in particular, Curator Joellen ElBashir, Archivist Sonja N. Woods, Executive Director of the Howard University Libraries Rhea Ballard-Thrower, Theatre Arts Librarian Celia Daniel, and their staff); the Library Special Collections Research Center at George Mason University (in particular, Brittney Falter, research services coordinator, and her staff), and the Catholic University of America Libraries Special Collection (in particular Brandi Marulli). Wilson Center interns Georgia Eisenmann and Jeanne Torp have provided invaluable support at various stages in the preparation of this work.

Over the course of too many summers to count, Baltimore theater doyen Philip Arnoult and I have sat on muggy evenings in the stands of Camden Yards watching our beloved Orioles. As is typical of life's most enduring experiences, various patterns developed. Early on, when hope ran high, Philip would verbally joust with the legendary vendor Fancy Clancy Haskett, from whom Philip has bought beer for some four decades. By the middle innings, Baltimore's maladroit relief pitchers began to make their appearances (the Orioles consistently have maintained among the worst bullpen records in major league baseball). Faith would slip away. As their pitch counts grew, we redirected our conversations toward theater in Saint Petersburg, Moscow, Yekaterinburg, and Washington. These leisurely chats—punctuated by the confident crack of an opponent's bat—prompted me to understand that Washington has a venerable and intriguing theater history full of stories worthy of attention.

—*Blair A. Ruble*
Washington, D.C.
April 2021

Previously Published Materials

Some materials appearing in this volume have appeared in part in these previous publications:

Blair A. Ruble. *Washington's U Street: A Biography*. Washington and Baltimore: Johns Hopkins University Press and Woodrow Wilson Center Press, 2010.

Blair A. Ruble. *The Muse of Urban Delirium: How the Performing Arts Paradoxically Transform Conflict-Ridden Cities into Centers of Cultural Innovation.* Washington: New Academia Publishing, 2017.

Blair A. Ruble. *Performing Community 3: Short Essays on Community, Diversity, Inclusion, and the Performing Arts*. Washington: Woodrow Wilson Center, 2018.

Blair A. Ruble. *Performing Community 4: Short Essays on Community, Diversity, Inclusion, and the Performing Arts.* Washington: Woodrow Wilson Center, 2020.

Blair A. Ruble. *Portraying the Soul of a People: African Americans Confront Wilson's Legacy from the Washington Stage* (Washington: Woodrow Wilson Center, 2020).

Blair A. Ruble. "Is a Black Actor Capable of Playing Hamlet? That Was a Raging Question in DC in 1951." DC Theatre Scene website, January 15, 2019.

Blair A. Ruble. "Robert Hooks and the Pioneering DC Black Repertory Company," DC Theatre Scene website, September 27, 2019.

Blair A. Ruble. "How 1970's Culture Clashes Played Out on Two Washington DC Stages," DC Theatre Scene website, November 8, 2019.

Blair A. Ruble. "A 'Spiritual Happening' When Morgan Freeman Preached The Gospel at Colonus at Arena Stage," DC Theatre Scene website, December 4, 2019.

Blair A. Ruble. "Father Gilbert Hartke: The Unlikely Story of a Catholic University Priest and James Cagney," DC Theatre Scene website, March 26, 2020.

Blair A. Ruble. "Director Alan Schneider: Beckett and Others Trusted Him with Their World Premieres," DC Theatre Scene website, April 28, 2020.

Blair A. Ruble. "Samuel Beckett's Literary Agent Tried to Close Joy

Zinoman's 1998 Waiting for Godot; How She Prevailed," DC Theatre Scene website, June 19, 2020.

Blair A. Ruble. "Howard University Players' First in the Nation Scandinavian Tour Earns Standing Ovations," DC Theatre Scene website, July 16, 2020.

Blair A. Ruble. "How Indian Ink Connected Tom Stoppard and Joy Zinoman to Their Lives in Asia," DC Theatre Scene website, September 17, 2020.

Blair A. Ruble. "DC Police Shut Down Tennessee Williams' Play at Washington Theatre Club," DC Theatre Scene website, October 9, 2020.

Blair A. Ruble. "After Wounded Knee, Washington Theatre Club Presents Chief Dan George in 'The Ecstasy of Rita Joe,'" DC Theatre Scene website, October 12, 2020.

Blair A. Ruble. "Since Bob Brown Puppets arrived, DC has become a welcoming home for puppets," DC Theatre Scene website, December 23, 2020.

---

1 Mayhill C. Fowler, *Beau Monde on Empire's Edge: State and Stage in Soviet Ukraine* (Toronto: University of Toronto Press, 2017).

Howard Theater, Washington, DC July 2013
(Photo by Blair A. Ruble)

Introduction

City and Stage

It's a mass of irony
For all the world to see.
It's the nation's capital,
It's Washington, DC.
—Gil Scott-Heron, 1982[1]

Cities appear, at times, as faces in a crowd. From a distance, they often look the same. Individual characteristics present themselves on closer inspection. Some cities—like some faces—are so striking that they immediately stand out as beautiful, full of life, or troubled. Other cities reveal their true character with time. Washington is one such city.

Since its founding, three unsettled tensions have beleaguered Washington with little sign of resolution: those between (1) national capital and hometown; (2) north and south; and (3) Black and White. Washington shares the first strains with capital cities around the world. Much of the local culture has been shaped by the ebb and flow of northern and southern influences that are evident in other "border" cities such as Baltimore, Louisville, and Saint Louis, to name a few. Every American urban community with a significant multiracial population daily confronts challenges about the question of race. In many ways, the Washington approached through these lenses remains one more face among the urban crowd. Its singularity lies elsewhere.

Washington, uniquely among American cities, has remained disenfranchised since its founding as a federal enclave. Somewhat independent municipal governance existed in Georgetown, Alexandria (while it was still in the District of Columbia), and Washington City before the Civil War. Congress nonetheless wielded considerable power over local officials even then. With the abolition of home rule in 1874, the city entered just under a century of direct subjugation to Congress. Washington residents had no political outlet for grievance during this period, and frequently turned to cultural expression as a surrogate. The result has been a local urban culture that retains a bent towards resistance.

In the absence of an overarching political life, the very meaning of "local" became contested. Residents and communities seeking to establish their presence in the city—and, because of its capital status, the nation—confronted prohibitions against the sort of political action evident elsewhere throughout the country. For much of the twentieth century, the local life of the theater offered an alternative path to recognition as a step toward acceptance.

Energetic theater leaders representing various communities pursued social and artistic acceptance by proclaiming presence from Washington stages. This book recounts four such efforts: those of African American cognoscente to establish a national Negro theater; those of Roman Catholic clerics to nurture a theater for the nation reflecting their values; those of theater enthusiasts to demonstrate the power of regional theater in an American stage community preoccupied with Manhattan; and, those of community activists to assert the legitimacy of the disenfranchised to establish their own civic presence.

Together, these efforts fostered a theater scene by century's end that would emerge as the second most attended in the country behind only New York. This industry, in turn, propelled an exploding cultural community that transformed a once sleepy, Southern, provincial town into a vibrant international arts center.

Proclaiming Racial Presence

In 1916, the writer Edward Christopher Williams and the activist playwright Carrie Clifford organized a "drama committee" within the local branch of the National Association for the Advancement of Colored People (NAACP).[2] The committee's members included Williams and Clifford, Anna Julia Cooper, together with Howard University professors Alain Leroy Locke, Ernest E. Just, and T. Montgomery Gregory.[3] Beyond promoting theater, the committee set about countering the impact of D. W. Griffith's scurrilous glorification of the Ku Klux Klan in the film *The Birth of a Nation*.[4] In doing so, they wanted to transform theater from the mask of burnt-cork Blackface to a mirror reflecting the realities of African American community life.

Several prominent Washingtonians participated in the founding of the NAACP in 1909 and, by 1913, in establishing a semiautonomous District of Columbia chapter.[5] Intense struggles over control of the Washington-based chapter broke out almost immediately.[6] With easy access to the federal government and to the city's prosperous African American community, the Washington NAACP chapter represented a potential alternative power base to the national NAACP headquarters in New York. Struggles over control of the DC chapter would continue until a bitter 1942 court battle definitively resolved the chapter's status as subordinate to the national organization.

This conflict for control of the NAACP in Washington was more than just a struggle over internal funds, rights, and privileges. The organization was caught up in skirmishes touched off by a rising professional class within the city's African American community as it sought to seize community leadership away from well-entrenched pastor-politicians. Ambassador Archibald Grimké took control of DC's NAACP chapter and built it into the largest and strongest of all the organization's local affiliates. Williams's and Clifford's drama committee was but one component of these larger struggles.

Archibald Grimké, former US consul in Santo Domingo, and his brother, the Reverend Francis Grimké of the prestigious Fifteenth Street Presbyterian Church, had long been intellectual and moral leaders of Washington's African American community. Born slaves in Charleston—and nephews of the famed abolitionists and suffragettes Sara and Angelina Grimké—Archibald and Francis fled slavery to fight with the Union Army. After the Civil War, they attended Lincoln University in Pennsylvania before, respectively, entering Harvard Law School and Princeton Theological Seminary.

Archibald's daughter, Angelina Weld Grimké, attended DC public schools and taught English at Armstrong Technical High School and Dunbar High School. Her essays, short stories, and poems would be included in such anthologies of the New Negro (Harlem) Renaissance as *The New Negro, Carolina Dusk,* and *Negro Poets and Their Poems.* Working closely with the DC NAACP chapter's Drama Committee, the young English teacher penned *Rachel,* which has come to be considered the first "propaganda" play to counter the pernicious impact of Griffith's film and other's racist films and plays.[7]

Rachel premiered under the Drama Committee's auspices at the Myrtilla Miner Normal School on March 3–6, 1916. Directed by Nathaniel Guy, the production, as its playbill noted, was a "race play in three acts" representing "the first attempt to use the stage for race propaganda in order to enlighten the American people relative to the lamentable condition of tens of millions of colored citizens in this Free Republic."[8]

Grimké's script responded to the heightened racism of the era, and to the southern White barbarism underlying an accelerating rate of lynching. Her characters proclaim African American personhood and citizenship by focusing on African American domesticity and the damage inflicted on it by White mob violence.[9] They use theater to proclaim their fundamental humanity—to stake their claim to Washington, and to the United States.

These efforts were not without controversy. Divisions over staging *Rachel* brought focus to what had been often inchoate differences in sensibility. Two distinct schools of thought emerged, driven by the writings of W. E. B. Du Bois and Locke, throughout the 1920s. Over time, their positions became reduced to differences between "propaganda," as advocated by DuBois; and "art," as promoted by Locke's approach to aesthetics.[10] In the end, Du Bois and Locke agreed to disagree. As Henry D. Miller observes, "In both men's cases, the depth of their education and intellect alerted them to the fact that Negro culture could produce art that was beyond the precepts of the White middle class."[11]

Their proponents and admirers continued their argument over what constituted Black theater—and who was in and who was out. Did one accept Du Bois's four principles of African American drama and theater as being "about us, by us, for us, and near us"— or not?[12] This disagreement animated African American—and Washington's—theater for the remainder of the twentieth century.[13]

Locke and Gregory eventually supported the Drama Committee's production of Angelina Weld Grimké's *Rachel* with the expectation that the committee subsequently would support the folk dramas they favored. Locke resigned when the committee failed to back such productions.[14] He and Gregory returned to campus with a dream of establishing a National Negro Theatre similar to the Irish National Theater, founded in 1904 by W. B. Yeats, Lady Gregory, George Moore, and Edward Martyn.[15] This pair of Howard professors sought to create a theater that would allow for racial expression directly through the pens and performances of group members unimpeded, as in Dublin, by the interference of others.

Through these battles, Locke and Gregory discovered a common belief in the power of realistic portraiture of lower-class life, together with a style of storytelling, stage direction, and set and costume design that was coming to define modernist drama.[16] This mutual preference animated Gregory's attempts to transmute Howard University's drama club into the more ambitious Howard Players as a step toward creating a National Negro Theatre based on the Irish model. That evolution forms the core of this volume's first chapter.

Acrimony was guaranteed when Williams, Clifford, Cooper, Locke, Gregory, and Just gathered in 1916 as the NAACP Drama Committee to discuss whether to present Angelina Weld Grimké's new play *Rachel*. Each of the participants embraced differing calculations of the appropriate balance between education, aesthetics, and commerce for constituting the value of theater. These cleavages defined the contours of African American theater more generally throughout the century. The challenge of mediating between such seemingly divergent values continues.

Lost within the resulting tensions stands the deeper reality of shared distress over the condition of African American communities in the capital and the nation. The egos of many committee members trembled before no one. Their phenomenally successful subsequent careers reveal a firm belief in oneself held by all. Nonetheless, all shared the belief that theater could confront the American denial of full citizenship on the basis of skin color.

Proclaiming Confessional Presence

Father Gilbert V. Hartke, OP—like Gregory and Locke a decade and a half previously—sought to transform the American theater by bringing a new sensibility to mainstream productions.[17] Similarly to their colleagues at Howard, Father Hartke and the Catholic University faculty eventually defined their mission as injecting a distinctive spiritual energy into a universal theater.

As a young priest in the Dominican order, Hartke became a prime mover within the movement to create a "National Catholic Theater." He and his colleagues drew on the model of the Irish National Theater to stake their claim to Washington's and the American stage, as had Gregory and Locke before.

Catholic theater in America before World War I remained primarily associated with the Irish traditions and performers that had accompanied the arrival of mass immigration from the Emerald Isle. This is hardly surprising, because traditional anti-Catholic sentiment prompted Catholics to organize their own separate community of institutions, hospitals, schools, settlement houses, orphanages, and every other kind of necessary social support structure. American Catholic culture was, in the words of the theater historian Matthew Donald Powell, a "ghetto" culture still in search of new ways to break into the American mainstream.[18] The popularity of Irish comedy and musical theater helped to erode such restrictions. After the war, a new generation of lay and religious (i.e., those who were members of religious orders) Catholic theater lovers arose, intent on transcending the stereotypes that had dominated the American stage.

Building on networks from his Chicago youth, Hartke recruited Northwestern University speech professor Josephine Callan to his team, together with one of her prize students, another young Midwesterner, Walter Kerr. Long before Kerr became the Pulitzer Prize–winning theater critic for the *New York Herald-Tribune* and the *New York Times*, he taught, penned successful plays, and directed them on stage at Catholic University. Alan Schneider, a recent graduate of Cornell University's graduate program in fine arts, also signed on. Schneider would go on to become the legendary director of plays by such midcentury masters as Samuel Beckett, Edward Albee, Harold Pinter, and Joe Orton.

The original Hartke team stayed together from the late 1930s into the mid-1950s. They mounted productions of classics and experimental plays, as well as nearly two dozen original works (about a quarter of which were subsequently produced professionally).[19] Nine department productions before 1950 went on to Broadway, including six original plays (five of which were penned by Kerr).[20] The department's students—such as Phillip Bosco, Pat Carroll, Henry Gibson, George Herman, Jean Kerr, John McGiver, Ed McMahon, Susan Sarandon, Frances Sternhagen, and Jon Voight—thrived, winning Tony Awards, Pulitzer Prizes, and other accolades throughout distinguished careers.[21] The creative team's talent, energy, and quality of effort animated the program into the 1960s.[22]

Father Hartke and his Catholic University colleagues vigorously opposed Jim Crow segregation in the city and its theaters. By the late 1940s, Actors' Equity and the Dramatists' Guild began picketing Washington productions. Helen Hayes, Oscar Hammerstein II, Cornelia Otis Skinner, and twenty other theater luminaries declared a boycott of both the National Theatre and George Washington University's Lisner Auditorium until they granted African American audiences equal access to their productions.[23] Rather than give in to such pressure, the National Theatre closed in 1948 and tried to make a go as a movie house. The theater remained dark after the collapse of its movie escapade, only to reopen in 1952 under new management as an integrated auditorium.[24]

Catholic University, meanwhile, pursued a different path to proclaim its presence in the city and nation. Father Hartke joined civic efforts to build a municipal theater that would be open to all and lent his own voice to the growing chorus of protests against segregation. As so often is the case in Washington, what seemed focused around the city often proved to be not so local in execution. The drive to create a municipal theater eventually led to the establishment and construction of the national John F. Kennedy Center for the Performing Arts, on whose founding board Father Hartke sat. Father Hartke similarly integrated audiences at the nearby Olney Summer Theater in Maryland, which was becoming ever more strongly associated with Catholic University's drama program.

Father Hartke grew into a formidable presence in Washington—

Washingtonian Magazine named the priest as one of the city's most powerful men in 1981—and used his position to advance the place of the arts in the city. "The show-biz priest" remained a steadfast supporter of civil rights and actively fought to end Jim Crow segregation and racial discrimination in Washington until his death in 1986. Together with his students and colleagues, he expanded the American stage and screen while moving Washington toward a more inclusive cultural life.[25] They did so by proclaiming their values and their presence to stake their claims to the Washington stage.

Proclaiming Regional Presence

Zelda Diamond Fichandler was in her early twenties as the 1940s turned into the 1950s. She and her husband Tom joined up with her George Washington University graduate school drama professor Edward Mangum to launch a local theater company. None of the company's founding troika appear to have been motivated particularly by a social justice agenda. Instead, they wanted to bring theater to a city where virtually none existed, thereby proclaiming a presence as a national institution from the Washington stage.

The absence of a vibrant homegrown theater community in Washington was not as distinguishing as it might have seemed. As the playwright Arthur Miller wrote in 1955, "The American theater occupies five side streets, Forty-Fourth to Forty-Ninth, between Eighth Avenue and Broadway, with a few additional theaters to the north and south and across Broadway. In these thirty-two buildings, every new play in the United States starts life and ends it."[26]

Even if it might have been objectionable to some at the time, the claim that Broadway was the totality of American theater was a plausible point to argue in the 1950s. The Fichandlers helped ensure that such notion could no longer be entertained a handful of years later.

Professional theater was unlikely to take root in the city at a time when the boycott of the National Theatre and Lisner Auditorium over their Jim Crow policies showed no sign of abating. With the help of Father Hartke, the Fichandlers and Mangum succeeded in leasing the Hippodrome, an abandoned movie and burlesque house on the edge of downtown.[27] The building's physical arrangement prevented the construction of a proscenium stage. Taken with Margo Jones's experiments in Dallas with theater-in-the-round, the new company built a central stage reminiscent of a boxing ring. Arena Stage was born.[28]

Arena, from the very beginning, was committed to opening its stage and audience to all races. The company allowed White and African American patrons to sit together from its first performances. These arrangements produced none of the acrimony predicted by White defenders of segregation, and the company went on to extend efforts to integrate the Washington stage. Arena's quiet advocacy for interracial audiences and performances took on ever greater significance as the company became a permanent fixture on the Washington scene.[29]

Arena's engagement with the city's racial politics both shaped and was shaped by profound postwar changes in Washington's demographic structure.[30] Pent-up consumer demand from the harsh years of the Great Depression and World War II combined with new highways and accessible housing to lure middle-class city dwellers to the suburbs around Washington, as was also happening in other metropolitan areas across the United States.[31] Easing racially restrictive real estate practices enabled the African American middle class to move to neighborhoods where they previously had been unwelcome (including some of the very same areas of the city left behind by the suburbanizing White middle class). By 1957, Washington had become the first major US city with a majority African American population.[32]

Arena was not alone among the White arts community in its concern about racial equity. The city's local theater increasingly engaged in disputes over what it meant to be an American in the 1960s and 1970s. Hazel and John Wentworth, for example, opened the Washington Theater Club during the 1950s in a cozy carriage house at 1632 O Street NW.[33] Zoning regulations impinged on the club's attempts to grow into a dramatic arts center and school. The enterprise eventually moved in 1970 to an abandoned church in the traditionally African American, working-class West End neighborhood (the present site of a Ritz-Carlton Hotel). Despite sustained popularity among Washington theatergoers, the club's ambiguous legal status provided scant protection from the city's rapacious tax collectors. The company liquidated its assets in 1974 to cover back real estate taxes.[34]

In her 1990 introductory essay to Arena Stage's fortieth-anniversary celebration of itself—*The Arena Adventure: The First Forty Years*—Zelda Fichandler observes that "the community ringed around the theater circles a community within the theater. The people without, as well as the people within, constitute the theater in its fullest sense." Embracing the community without, those outside the theater, led Zelda and her Arena Stage to engage Washington's vibrant and energetic African American community on the challenges of race.

Simultaneously, their success led them to imagine an American theater spread out across the nation. As they became leaders of an expanding regional theater movement during the 1960s, 1970s, and 1980s, the Fichandlers proclaimed a regional presence on an American stage unbound by Arthur Miller's thirty-two buildings in midtown Manhattan.

Proclaiming Community Presence

Gregory, Hartke, and the Fichandlers had countrywide agendas as they sought to establish national centers for African American, Catholic, and regional theater. Their ties to different communities within the city grew to be robust; their successes and failures held up mirrors to the city around them. Nevertheless, Washington as a place often provided context rather than impetus. What happened next was something quite different.

Washington—during the 1960s, 1970s, and 1980s—was the center of racial resistance to a White-dominated status quo. Ranging from social protest and civil unrest to economic empowerment and political activism, race dominated every aspect of life in this city that had become majority Black just a few years before.[35] Activists, in response, promoted the concept of community for bringing attention down from abstraction to life on the streets.

All of Washington's worlds crashed violently on the evening of April 4, 1968, when radios throughout the city shared the news that the Reverend Martin Luther King Jr. had been shot in Memphis.

Just over an hour later, the announcement came that King had died. Menacing calm turned to shock, which turned to hot anger in a matter of minutes. Soon the neighborhood around the intersection of U and 14th Streets NW was aflame in an outburst of violence. Civil order collapsed for the next three days, and it was only eventually restored after the city was occupied by more than 13,000 federal troops for a dozen days.[36]

For weeks—even months—those who stayed in the neighborhood had to rely on churches and civic organizations for essentials because the stores that sold food and personal items were gone. "Riot corridors" along U Street, Fourteenth and Seventh Streets NW, and H Street NE remained undeveloped for the next quarter century—and longer.

The question of home rule proved to perhaps be the most painful wound left festering as the city tried to move ahead.[37] City residents had been allowed to vote in presidential elections since the early 1960s. They gained an elected school board in 1968. In 1971, residents secured the right to elect a nonvoting delegate to the US House of Representatives. However, such measures mattered little in light of the absence of local electoral control over the District's government.

Against this backdrop, a search for new understandings of American race relations found expression in the arts. Washington emerged as an especially vibrant center within this quest as the potent Black Arts Movement took shape. The various streams swirling around the movement connected with disenfranchised Black communities and neighborhoods across the city. Many artistic endeavors—including those in theater—became deeply embedded in the search for local power.[38]

At about this time, Topper Carew's New Thing Art and Architecture Center in Adams Morgan sought to integrate the arts with inclusive urban planning.[39] A Boston native, he attended Howard University to study architecture, before earning undergraduate and graduate degrees from Yale. He became a civil rights worker in Mississippi and Maryland, and was one among many imaginative activists attracted to Washington's rebellious Black culture. He later earned a PhD in communications from Union Graduate School and the DC think tank the Institute for Policy

Studies.[40] He established the New Thing in a pregentrified corner of Adams Morgan in 1966 to engage the era's "urban crisis."

Washington native Robert Hooks, the son of blue-collar workers living in the city's then-plebeian Foggy Bottom neighborhood, established the DC Black Repertory Theater (DCBRC) in the early-1970s. Hooks—who in 1967 had established New York's venerable Negro Ensemble Company in collaboration with Douglas Turner Ward—brought theater into this effervescent artistic mix.[41] The company's senior creative staff included Artistic Director Motojicho (Vantile Whitfield), Vocal Director Bernice Reagon, and Choreographers Louis Johnson, Mike Malone, and Charles Augins. Malone and Johnson created numerous new works such as *Black Nativity*, a performance piece drawing on the work of Langston Hughes that has proven a lasting achievement.[42] Augins enjoyed success in New York and London before heading the Dance Department at the DC Public School System's Duke Ellington School of the Arts. Reagon used the opportunity to found the successful vocal group Sweet Honey in the Rock.[43]

The DCBRC's leadership had deep DC roots. Motojicho graduated from Dunbar High School and Howard University before heading to Hollywood. Reagon moved to the city after graduating from Spelman College in Atlanta to pursue a PhD at Howard. She would become a fixture at the Smithsonian Institution. Johnson captured the attention of his teachers in the DC Public Schools while growing up in the U Street NW neighborhood. Encouraged by his early mentors, he headed off to the School of American Ballet in New York City, where he studied with Jerome Robbins and George Balanchine. Malone, who had come to Washington to earn a degree in French at Georgetown University, had tap danced with Josephine Baker while studying at the Sorbonne. Augins grew up in Arlington, Virginia, and studied at DC's Jones-Hayward School of Dance.

Although DCBRC would close after only a handful of seasons, Hooks, Motojicho, Reagon, Johnson, Malone, and Augins continued to have phenomenally successful careers after the demise of the DCBRC in 1976. Hooks is perhaps best known today for his role in the 1960s television drama *NYPD*. Motojicho became a major funder of African American and regional performing arts and eventually returned to Los Angeles, where he continued his film career. Reagon won a MacArthur Foundation Genius Award and became the mainstay of the much-lauded Sweet Honey in the Rock. Johnson enjoyed success as a choreographer working with numerous ballet companies, Broadway shows, and Metropolitan Opera productions, and he participated in the establishment of Howard University's Dance Department. He became an admired figure in the New York and American dance world before succumbing to COVID-19 at the age of ninety years during the 2020 pandemic.[44] Malone similarly taught at Howard and was among the founders of the Ellington School in 1974; while Augins joined the Ellington faculty later.[45]

Carew, Hooks, and their partner activists stimulated Washingtonians to embrace the concept of community as an essential building block of the city. They did so in part by proclaiming their presence from the Washington stage. Over time, their ideas have moved from DC neighborhoods into the mainstream of American dramaturgy. The DCBRC's downfall nonetheless left one of the nation's most vibrant centers of African American culture without a fully professional Black theater company.[46]

The Stage Is Set

In 1982, the George Washington University political scientist Jeffrey Henig published an important study of a neighborhood transition about DC's Adams Morgan (the very area that had been the focal point for Topper Carew's New Thing). Henig began by noting that experts on cities expected urban change to be synonymous with decline until well into the 1970s.[47] Washington now experienced a sense of improvement. Such notions of urban upgrading represented a radical departure from the conventional wisdom in an era of suburban hegemony. Henig noted further that consequent "gentrification" will prove different from "normal change" in the rapidity of divergence from the past, and in the scope of the alterations that take place. All aspects of neighborhood life would be affected in a compressed time.[48] Consequently, the underlying community organization substructure will fragment before most residents and outsiders recognize what is happening.[49] A decade or two later, local residents well understood that urban neighborhoods could upgrade. But for whom?

Henig captured the beginning of dramatic political, social, and economic transformations both in DC and throughout its metropolitan region.[50] Unfortunately, home rule—as granted to Washington in 1974—proved to be a nearly fatally flawed legislative compromise that left local officials constantly running up a down escalator. In the enthusiasm of the moment, many legislative fine points limiting taxation authority and retaining congressional oversight authority were lost on young community activists.

The city's appointed mayor, Walter Washington, retained his office in the city's first municipal elections. Marion S. Barry Jr. eventually emerged as master of the new system, serving four terms as mayor and several more on the City Council. The street "radicals" who appeared during the 1960s were now in charge of the city. The role of the arts in providing a surrogate for local political expression began to fade. Meanwhile, theater grew in the city and throughout the region in response to the new communities that were taking shape.

This study of how Washington's local theater scene evolved over the course of the twentieth century is hardly encyclopedic; and certainly, it makes no claim of comprehensiveness. Many compelling themes not covered here—the power of women on the Washington stage; the influence of companies founded by immigrant artists; the emergence of a robust LGBTQ theater community; the authority of Shakespeare in shaping American political discourse—lie beyond the scope of this volume, even as they deserve careful in-depth studies of their own. Rather, this book explores a few among the many stories that can be told about Washington's vibrant theater scene through the lens of urban history—and the unexpectedly dynamic city nurturing it.

Howard Players, 1922
(Photo, HowardPlayers.org)

Chapter 1

Proclaiming Racial Presence

Washington, the national capital, is the center of what is becoming to be regarded as one of the most interesting as well as significant experiments in the development of native American Drama. . . . Now Howard University has undertaken to build upon the slight foundations thus laid a permanent and determined movement for the establishment of a National Negro Theatre similar in general outline to the Irish Theatre at Dublin.
—T. Montgomery Gregory, 1922[1]

In 1903, a twenty-year-old journalist who would go on to a distinguished career in journalism, diplomacy, and politics—future US minister to Liberia, Lester Aglar Walton—excitedly told the readers of *The Colored American Magazine* of African American successes on stage.[2] "The outlook for the Negro on the stage is particularly bright and encouraging," Walton began. "At no time have colored stage folk been accorded such consideration and loyal support from show managers, the press and the general public. . . . Heretofore, colored shows have only found their way to New York theatres of minor importance; and the crowded houses invariable in evidence where 'coon' shows have played have been occasioned more by reason of the meritorious work of the performers than by the popularity of the playhouses."

To Walton's mind, "catchy music, mirth-provoking dialogue and mannerisms void of serious lines" had ensured the success of recently produced "coon" shows. "The stage," he continued, will be one of the principal factors in ultimately placing the Negro before the public in his true and proper light. Instead of being ridiculed before the foot-lights as has been done for years, a sentiment will be crystallized which will be of an instructive and beneficial nature. It is unfortunate that the members of the White race, generally speaking, do not know the colored man as he is, but merely from impressions formed of him from the observation of a certain element obnoxious—yet usually most conspicuous.

For Walton, "the time for the debut of the colored actor in serious stage work is not far distant."

Walton was correct when recording that the African American musical—often closer to the popular "coon" minstrel show than to the operetta—had been enjoying success for several years. His assessment of the openness of White audiences to serious stage work, however, would prove optimistic; as would his assessment of race relations generally. Nearly a decade later, the country would elect a new president—Woodrow Wilson—who brought many of the beliefs and folkways of his native South with him to the White House.

The first Southern-born president since the Civil War, Wilson launched a devastating attack on African Americans generally, with policies that had a disproportionate impact on the African American community in Washington. His administration segregated the Federal Civil Service, effectively denying all but menial federal employment to African Americans. This action lay waste to a community in which the stability of a government job could mean the difference between respectability and penury.[3] Over half of all twentieth-century legislation restricting the rights of African Americans in the District of Columbia became law during the Wilson presidency. These actions earned Wilson deep enmity among Black Washingtonians for policies that the *Washington Bee* maintained promised the "everlasting damnation to the colored Americans in this country."[4]

In 2020, University of California, Berkeley researchers Abhay Aneja and Guo Xu sought to determine the impact of the Wilson Administration's segregationist personnel policies on Black civil servants. After mining personnel documents for 321,470 unique US federal employees (40,020 Blacks and 281,450 Whites) between 1907 and 1921, Aneja and Xu calculate a "Black wage penalty" of 7 percentage points resulting from the relocation of Black civil servants to lower paying positions.[5]

Aneja and Xu capture the direct detrimental impact of Wilson's policies on Black civil servants. Given a highly structured promotion hierarchy, demotions to a lower rung echo throughout the careers of Black civil servants both serving at the time and entering government service later.

The impacts of this penalty on families and the Washington African American community are incalculable. Secure, well-compensated federal employment provided an important pillar upon which the community and its businesses built further accomplishment. As Black commentators signaled at the time, the introduction of Jim Crow employment practices under President Wilson had devastating effects on Washington's African American community.

In 1915, the president hosted a screening of D. W. Griffith's freshly released epic apologia for the Ku Klux Klan, *The Birth of a Nation*. The viewing—the first time a film had been shown at the White House—was taken by many as an endorsement of a rewriting of post–Civil War history.[6]

Responding on Stage

The Washington African American theater community responded directly to Wilson's policies with works emphasizing the pernicious impact of Jim Crow. In addition to Angelina Grimké's *Rachel*, mentioned in the introduction, other prominent authors of the era's anti-lynching plays included Black women who were living in Washington (including Grimké, Mary Burrill, and Georgia Douglas Johnson), who lived near Washington (Alice Dunbar-Nelson), or who spent time in Washington (Myrtle Smith Livingston).

"As the capital," Koritha Mitchell contends, "Washington, DC, stood for the nation's commitment to protecting American life and liberty, but in the 1920s it was where antilynching bills went to die. . . . The genre's characters become representatives for a national Black population whose concerns are not necessarily shared by their representatives in the Congress and Senate." DC, she con-

tinues, "held in perfect tension all of the promises that were pre-
sumably inherent in the North and the perils that were supposedly
more characteristic of the South."[7]

Theater historians have tended to minimize the artistic achievement of *Rachel* and other antilynching plays. Rather than seek commercial production, their playwrights penned superficially modest one-act works suited for reading and amateur performance in
the intimate spaces of family gatherings, school auditoriums, and
church halls. They reached their audience by publishing their plays
in periodicals with large African American and White activist read-
erships, such as W. E. B. Du Bois's *The Crisis,* and Max Eastman's
The Liberator.[8] Focusing on sympathetic, well-mannered, dignified characters (e.g., loyal soldiers, committed lawyers, and caring
mothers), the plays, according to Mitchell, "did not just need those
who would work to gain Whites' empathy; they also needed individuals who could provide tools for surviving."[9]

Georgia Douglas Johnson, among the most prolific writers of
the genre, disguised creative ambition behind the supposedly sim-
plistic format of such "propaganda" plays. As Mitchell records,
Johnson "wrote two versions of a script that dramatizes the moment when White authorities willfully disregard African American
voices. One version of Johnson's *A Sunday Morning in the South* uses
hymns from a Black church as background to the action; the other
features a White church, but both show that police officers abruptly
reject Black testimony."[10]

The Washington antilynching plays reveal how a number of the
writers and playwrights gathered in the city would contribute to
the emergence of African American theater during the years and
decades ahead. The genre's dramatists responded to the heightened racism of the Wilson era, and to the Southern White barbarism
underlying an accelerating rate of lynching. They proclaimed African American presence, personhood, and citizenship by focusing
on African American domesticity and the damage inflicted on it by
mob violence to assert cultural self-affirmation.[11] As Black writers,
composers, comedians, and performers had done in expanding the
boundaries of American musical theater—and as Black dramatic
playwrights and actors would do throughout the twentieth century—the creators of antilynching plays endeavored to bring a fundamental humanity to the portrayal of African Americans.

Their proponents and admirers continued the argument over what constituted Black theater—and who "was in and who was out." Through their battles, Howard University's Gregory and Locke discovered a shared belief in the power of realistic portraiture of lower-class life, together with a style of storytelling, stage direction, and set and costume design that was coming to define modernist drama.[12] This shared preference, together with the backing of Dean Kelly Miller, drove Gregory's attempts to elevate the university's drama club to the more ambitious Howard Players.

Miller argues in *Theorizing Black Theatre* that this strain began to form much earlier in turn-of-the-century efforts to establish an African American musical theater (as evident in the very first full-length African American written musical comedies—Bob Cole's *A Trip to Coontown*, 1898; and Will Marion Cook's *Jes' Lak White Fo'ks*, 1899). The contrast between Cole and Cook rested, for Miller, in the opposition of a focus on the "Outer Life" (represented by Cole's interest in society) and the "Inner Life" (exemplified by Cook's focus on performance). Those distinctions, he continued, trace their origins back to African performance philosophies as well as to divisions within European tradition and evolved over time into a distinction between "propaganda" and "art" evident in the controversy over Angelina Grimké's *Rachel*.[13] The Washington row brought focus to what had been often inchoate differences in sensibility.

A Child of Howard University Returns

Thomas Montgomery Gregory's appointment in 1910 to Howard University's English Department as an instructor was a homecoming. Gregory—who had just graduated from Harvard as a member of the illustrious Class of 1910, where he studied alongside T. S. Eliot, Walter Lippmann, John Reed, Hsi Yun Feng, and Hamilton Fish Jr.—had grown up on the Howard campus. His father transferred to the university from Oberlin College in 1868, becoming the first student to enroll in the collegiate department. He became valedictorian of the university's three-member initial graduating class.

Upon completing his degree, the elder Gregory joined the faculty and the household moved onto the Howard campus.[14] The family eventually relocated to New Jersey, where Gregory headed the Bordentown Industrial and Manual Training School. Thomas Montgomery's mother, Fannie Emma Hagan, a Howard student of Madagascan descent, was a force of nature in her own right. She mentored students, supported young African American women, and enjoyed recognition as an independent and important partner in various family endeavors at Howard and Bordentown.[15]

The younger Gregory established himself at Howard and in Washington, starting a family and moving through the university ranks. When World War I broke out, Gregory unreservedly lobbied for the Army to accept African Americans into officer training programs. His efforts—which joined with those Joel E. Spingarn, Du Bois, and other prominent leaders—prompted the Army to establish the Seventeenth Provisional Training Regiment for Black officer candidates at Fort Des Moines. After completion of officer training, the Army commissioned Gregory as a lieutenant. He served as an intelligence officer without leaving the country, and he continued to remain active in veterans' groups throughout his life.[16]

Gregory became head of the English Department upon returning to Howard in 1919. His publications and professional interests increasingly focused on the role of the arts in promoting social change. Drawn especially to the theater, Gregory used his position to establish the Howard Players in 1919 and, two years later, he became the first director of the newly established Dramatic Art and Public Speaking Division.

Gregory, as Marvin McAllister has argued, remained troubled that elite African Americans had sought "to un-race" themselves by avoiding any association with their own cultural heritage. Arriving at Howard, he became concerned that a fascination with European classical education remained deeply entrenched. Montgomery considered this devotion to European models to be an obstacle for the development of African American drama in particular.[17]

Having been joined, by this time, by Locke, another Harvard man, Gregory set his sights high. He declared that he sought nothing less than the establishment of the National Negro Theater at Howard. As he wrote at the time, the Howard effort would establish the National Negro Theatre as similar in general outline to the Irish Theatre at Dublin.[18]

Transcending Division

African American Washington emerged as a formidable creative center in part because it was divided and contested within itself. The pressures of segregation exposed and exacerbated fractures that otherwise might have lain dormant. Differences in place of birth, skin tone, economic stature, educational achievement, urban experience, employment status, and congregational affiliation set African Americans against one another.

More generally, a fundamental division between those who felt elite achievement was the most appropriate response to White racism and those who looked to economic advancement and nationalism—a partition personified by the debates between W. E. B. Du Bois and Booker T. Washington—distinguished African Americans in Washington one from the other, as it did throughout the nation. Such divisions not only separated groups and individuals but also often reflected different traits within a single personality.

Howard University and M Street (later Dunbar) High School represented the epitome of Du Bois's "talented tenth." In 1866, the Civil War commander and postwar commissioner of the Freedmen's Bureau Major General Oliver Otis Howard secured a congressional charter and established the university that bears his name to train clergy and other professionals to serve the African American community.[19] M Street High—founded in the basement of the Fifteenth Street Presbyterian Church in 1870—was the nation's first public high school for African American youth; and for many years, was its best. Faculty members included graduates—often with postgraduate degrees—of the country's leading universities.[20] These educational institutions attracted middle-class African American families to the city in search of educational opportunities for their children.[21]

Washington's Black bourgeoisie constructed a cultured cocoon around itself every bit as exclusive as anything found in White Washington. Edward Christopher Williams's epochal social commentary captured their foibles in a series of fictional essays appearing under the title "Letters of Davy Carr: A True Story of Colored Vanity Fair" (this indispensable collection eventually appeared as the novel *When Washington Was in Vogue*).[22]

The world that wealthy Washington African Americans creat-ed for themselves generated both admiration and approbation. In 1901, Paul Dunbar observed that Washington had become a city in which "the colored man's life" has reached its highest develop-ment. "Here exists a society," he wrote, "which is sufficient unto itself—a society which is satisfied with 'its own condition,' and which is not asking for social intercourse with Whites."[23]

In contrast, Langston Hughes bitterly excoriated the absence in Washington African American elites of "real culture, kindness, or good common sense."[24] A few years later, the bluesman Lead Belly (Huddie William Ledbetter) would lament Washington's class ten-sions in his tune "The Bourgeois Blues," recorded for the Library of Congress in December 1938. "Tell all the colored folks to listen to me," Lead Belly sang, "Don't try to find you no home in Washing-ton, DC / 'Cause it's a bourgeois town."[25]

Washington's poor rural migrants and undereducated labor-ers were removed from view, often huddled in alleyways. Charles Frederick Weller described this "city within a city" in his path-breaking report *Neglected Neighbors* by observing that "resourceful people live for years in the attractive residences on the avenues without knowing or affecting in the slightest degree the life of the alley hovels just behind them."[26] Nonetheless, indigent Washing-tonians transcended conditions that could crush human souls. In the words of the historian James Borchert, Washington's poorest of the poor "were able to shape and control their own lives within the economic, social, and political limits imposed by the dominant White society."[27]

Whatever their differences, Washington's African Americans were rooted in a single community that frequently came under siege from the outside. They encountered one another on a dai-ly basis and shared a profound disgust for the White racism that haunted America and its capital. Divisions thus became a source of creative engagement.

Washington's African American Crossroads

The neighborhood in which Howard University is embedded—surrounding the intersection of 7th Street, Florida Avenue, and U Street NW—took shape after the Civil War as a robustly diverse community that included residents of different races and economic classes. Slaves fleeing to Washington as "contrabands of war" sought the protection of Union Army encampments, such as Camp Baker, located on the northern edge of the L'Enfant Plan. Many newly freed African Americans remained in their wartime settlements, giving birth to several historically Black neighborhoods around the city, including the area around 7th Street NW. The Freedman's Bureau was established to help newly emancipated slaves, and it built a hospital to serve the Black community nearby. As noted above, bureau commissioner Major General Oliver Otis Howard established an integrated university just outside the L'Enfant Plan on a hilltop north of Boundary Street (later Florida Avenue) and east of 7th Street NW (Georgia Avenue).

Jim Crow customs attained preeminence in Washington after the Compromise of 1877, which ended the Reconstruction Era. When hard segregation followed, beginning in the mid-1880s, these institutions solidified the neighborhood as an energetic center of African American life. Simultaneously, a middle class and elite developed within the African American community in response to economic opportunities found in the federal workforce as well as the uplifting impact of higher education.[28]

The area surrounding Howard University was a space for interconnection among a variety of groups, making it a vital focal point for the emergence of an energetic, rough-and-tumble cultural scene. Various conflicting forces and groups crisscrossed one another in an urban cultural and social wetlands, a contact zone where "cultures meet, clash, and grapple with each other, often in contexts of highly asymmetrical relations of power, such as colonialism, slavery, or their aftermaths."[29] Such zones are the necessary proving grounds where the diverse becomes transformed into an intercultural resource. They are where accomplished cities become successful.

The complexity of the communities and people colliding with one another inspired some of the most profound and enduring voices of early-twentieth-century America. The neighborhood's contradictions created a tense conflict between norms and attitudes that melded into an explosive creative mix of class and background. A half-dozen local cultural figures in particular—the musical composer and librettist team of Will Marion Cook and Paul Laurence Dunbar, the poet Langston Hughes, the novelist Jean Toomer, the playwright Willis Richardson, and the composer Duke Ellington— personify the area's inventiveness by infusing traditional bourgeois culture with the vibrancy of blue-collar life.

Cook and Dunbar were a bit older and represent a slightly earlier generation of creators. Hughes, Toomer, Richardson, and Ellington, as noted above, were more or less contemporary products of the nation's nascent African American middle class, with personal stories tied by family to the neighborhood as well as to its churches, schools, and community life. Cook and Dunbar's 1903 musical *In Dahomey*, Hughes's 1927 poem "Fine Clothes to the Jew," Toomer's 1923 novel *Cane*, Richardson's 1923 play *The Chip Woman's Fortune*, and Ellington's homage in his memoirs to Holliday's pool hall of the same period bring to life the clash between African American working-class values and classic European-originated literary and melodic formats, creating a powerful mix of so-called low and high culture.[30]

The Howard Players simultaneously reflected, and contributed to, this charged political and creative atmosphere. They constantly engaged in clashes over what it meant to be Black in racist White America, what resistance and accommodation meant, and how African American cultural achievements could remain both distinct from and essential to mainstream White culture.

A Long-Standing Commitment to Drama

Like many universities of the era, students and faculty at Howard had organized a Drama Club in 1907.[31] Any liberal arts student enrolled in a four-year degree path could join the club for a membership fee of 50 cents.[32] Formed under the direction of Ernest Everett Just, Benjamin Brawley, and Marie Moore-Forrest, the club attracted members from across the university community who were interested in presenting the works of Shakespeare.[33] Under their guidance, student and community actors offered several Shakespearean plays at the commercial Howard Theatre just off campus over the next several years.[34]

Just arrived at Howard after graduating from Dartmouth College with highest honors.[35] Finding his career options limited by his race, he joined Howard's English Department in 1907. Howard students already had participated in dramatic ventures for some time, because required training in oratory led to their involvement in competitions and other theatrical events as far back as the 1870s and 1880s.[36]

Howard rhetoric professor Coralie Franklin-Cook, who moved to Washington in 1899 from the National School of Oratory in Philadelphia, transformed public-speaking elocution into mandated courses for graduation. The rigor of these requirements prepared students to take the next step onto the stage as Just began to promote drama and theater activities.[37]

Just's first love, however, was zoology. After collaborating during the summers with Frank R. Lillie—head of the Department of Zoology at the University of Chicago and director of the Marine Biological Laboratory at Woods Hole, Massachusetts—Just earned his PhD from the University of Chicago and, beginning in 1912, served as chair of the new Department of Zoology at Howard.

His research on the role of the cell surface in the development of organisms proved pathbreaking. Because he was prevented by race from securing a position at a major American university, he worked in European research centers as much as his Howard duties would allow (he briefly was a prisoner of war at the outbreak of World War II, after being swept up by the German invasion of France in 1940). Although his increasing involvement in biological and zoological research precluded his continued association with the Howard's burgeoning dramaturgical scene, he retained a lifelong interest in the dramatic arts and connection with theater at Howard.

Enthusiastically launched, the club expanded its repertoire in 1909 with Oliver Goldsmith's *She Stoops to Conquer*, followed between 1910 and 1919 by Richard Brinsley Sheridan's *The Rivals*, R. M. Baker's *For One Night Only*, Stephen Phillips's *Herod*, and Shakespeare's *The Merry Wives of Windsor* and *The Merchant of Venice*, among numerous productions.[38] The university's publication of record at the time—the *Howard University Journal*—proclaimed the premier performance of *She Stoops to Conquer* at the Andrew Rankin Chapel as "the greatest success ever attained on the hill [the community's moniker for the school—BR]. It drew the fullest house of anything that has ever been given and reaped the greatest financial rewards."[39] A year later, the *Journal* eagerly anticipated the club's production of *The Rivals*, noting that the majority of seats had been sold "to people not connected with the university."[40]

Success on campus led the actors to move off campus into the surrounding community, with performances at schools and, eventually, at the new Howard Theatre down the hill at 7th and T streets NW.[41] Inaugurated in 1910, the Howard Theatre was unconnected to the university. It quickly became the premier commercial theater in the country catering to African American audiences.[42] With eclectic programming appealing to multiple tastes, the Howard's management booked a production of *Uncle Tom's Cabin* soon after the theater's opening.[43] Other dramatic productions followed. The newly arrived Gregory, for example, played Lysander in a Washington Dramatic Club production of *Midsummer Night's Dream* directed by Anna Julia Cooper at the Howard Theatre in May 1912; and he played Lorenzo in the club's *Merchant of Venice* a year later.[44] These efforts sought to revolutionize how African Americans would be portrayed on the American stage.

African Americans on American Stages

Theater did not begin to develop in what was to become the United States until the mid–eighteenth century. The New York Harmonic Society sponsored special performances as early as the 1750s to enhance public celebrations, such as the king's birthday; and Nassau Street's New Theater opened even earlier to host touring British actors, bringing the latest hits from London. But such performances remained episodic affairs. Sporadic performances began to appear on stages across the British colonies at about this time, especially in such cities as Boston, Charleston, New York, and the colonies' leading cultural center, Philadelphia.

With the opening of Philadelphia's Chestnut Street Theatre, constructed between 1791 and 1805, the country supported its first auditorium built by private investors as a permanent home for theatrical performances.[45] *Cato* (1749), *The Prince of Parthia* (1767), *The Padlock* (1768), and *The Fall of British Tyranny* (1776) were among the first American plays.[46]

The 1752 arrival of the Covent Garden impresario Lewis Hallam and his company on American shores proved to be a foundational event for American theater.[47] He had been the head of London's Company of Comedians, and now he, his wife, their children, and a troupe of ten adults landed in the American colonies. Their appearance in Williamsburg, Virginia, marked the beginning of professional theater in what would become the United States.

Hallam's company established several customary aspects of American theater that would last into the nineteenth century: managers/producers/directors controlled companies; theatrical performances featured stock companies that offered well-known repertoires of dramatic and comedic works; and financial success depended as much or more on touring as on remaining in one town on a single stage. Additionally, in 1769, Hallam's son, Lewis Jr., became the first White actor known to have performed an African American–styled song in Blackface when he sang "Dear Heart! What a Terrible Life I Am Led" at New York's John Street Theatre.[48] Blacks have been mocked on American stages ever since.

Lewis Jr. appeared in *The Disappointment or The Force of Credulity* (1767), presenting the first Black character drawn from American colonial experience with the racially charged name "Raccoon."[49] Lewis Jr.'s performance was followed by British and American productions such as *Robinson Crusoe and Harlequin Friday* (1786), *The Yorker's Strategem, or Banana's Wedding* (1792), *The Triumph of Love* (1795), and *The Politicians* (1797), mocking African American dialect and speech while Black characters shuffled along for comic effect.[50] At least ten plays written by English and American playwrights before 1800 included Black dialect, to the humorous delight of White audiences.[51] Such sarcastic formulas morphed into the nineteenth century's most popular and lucrative entertainment: the minstrel show.

Minstrelsy was a purely American invention, having nothing to do with the minstrel bards who had wandered across Europe from the time of the Middle Ages. European storytelling crossed the Atlantic with French, British, and Dutch colonizers, blending,

by the beginning of the nineteenth century, into what would become American folk music. But the minstrel show was something
else altogether. American minstrelsy—which remained the country's most popular theatrical form throughout the nineteenth century—assumed an extraordinarily pernicious meaning as it became
inexorably intertwined with American racism.

By the 1840s, a Cincinnati bookkeeper named Stephen Foster
began writing songs for monetary profit. Foster's songs—such as
"Oh! Susanna," "Camptown Races," "Old Folks at Home," "My
Old Kentucky Home," and "Old Black Joe"—entered into the
American musical canon and continue to be sung today. [52] They
proved to be well suited for the "Blackface minstrel" variety shows
that dominated the American stage. Foster soon found an easy alliance with the circus promoter and celebrity clown Dan Rice, who
gained fame and fortune by singing "Negro songs" in Blackface as
the character Jim Crow. Other popular Blackface characters sported
a host of offensive names.[53]

By midcentury, the mask of Blackface cork, shoe polish, and
greasepaint—and the accompanying happy-go-lucky darkies who
filled the stage—defined the place of African Americans on stage—
and beyond. For the dramatic form's White originators, minstrelsy
offered a platform for ridiculing African Americans. For African
Americans, as Eleanor Traylor has argued, the genre's cakewalks,
hoedowns, tap dances, "signify" language, and color-drenched
costumes provided the equivalent of the masking-miming rituals
of the slave quarters, in which the last laugh was on master.[54]

African Americans appeared on American stages from the very
beginning. Black actors performed in *The Padlock*, a 1768 comedy
in which a West Indian slave named Mungo appears as a profane
clown.[55] They would remain trapped in buffoonish roles into the
nineteenth century, until William Alexander Brown, James Hewlett, and Ira Aldridge tried to break the mold. In 1821 (six years
before slavery was abolished in New York), Brown, a free Black
from the West Indies, established the African Grove Theatre in New
York.[56]

That theater's audience primarily included New Yorkers of col-
or from all social classes and represented one of several attempts
to establish African American theater in New York. Tired of being

forced to sit in the balconies at other theaters, the city's Blacks readily supported the new venture. Hewlett, who had been performing as a singer around the city, convinced Brown to hire African American actors. Hewlett gained wide recognition for his performances of *Richard III* and is thought to have been the first Black to perform the role of *Othello*. Ira Aldridge, a young graduate of the New York Manumission Society's African Free School, performed with Brown's company while still a teenager, launching a long and distinguished career.[57]

Faced with police harassment and frequent attacks—one of the African Grove Theatre company's theaters burned to the ground under suspicious circumstances—America's first African American theatrical company disappeared by the mid-1820s, as did its founder, Brown. Hewlett continued to perform, though his career went into decline. He died in 1849.

Aldridge gave up on the United States and sailed to Liverpool in 1824, where he began a madly popular European career. He died in 1867, after having performed across the Continent and having received honors from numerous heads of state. Today, he is the only African American actor to have been honored with a bronze plaque at the Shakespeare Memorial Theatre in Stratford-upon-Avon.[58]

The parameters for the African American on the American stage (and later film and television) were set remarkably early in the history of the American theater. As Sterling A. Brown recorded in his seminal 1933 article "Negro Character as Seen by White Authors," African Americans appearing in American letters are pigeonholed into seven stereotypical character types: the contented slave, the wretched freeman, the comic Negro, the brute Negro, the tragic mulatto, the local color Negro, and the exotic primitive.[59]

Brown, widely known as one of the poets of the New Negro (Harlem) Renaissance, was already teaching at Howard University when he wrote this article. He had become deeply involved in the Howard Players by that time.[60] Building on the legacy of Gregory's earlier work, he and Locke were striving to create an African American theater that empowered African Americans to proclaim their presence by telling their own stories about their own people in their own ways.

Dancing to One's Own Tune

The battle to remove the Blackface mask and reinvent the American stage as a mirror of African American life had begun a generation before Gregory, Locke, and Brown arrived at Howard. Led by composers, writers, and performers, a hearty band of innovators had managed to break the White monopoly over the musical stage and the minstrel show. Black performers appearing in Black shows began to enjoy large-scale success for the first time. The African American comedian Bert Williams became arguably the most popular performer in the country at the time.

A turning point came in 1893 when—after substantial lobbying by African American leaders such as Joseph Douglass, the grandson of Frederick Douglass—the Chicago World's Fair conceded to allot a single day to Black achievement. Scheduled at the Haitian Pavilion on August 24 toward the end of the fair's run, the consequent "Colored American Day" appeared to many African American thought leaders as yet one more example of Jim Crow segregation.[61]

However, the prominent African Americans attending Colored American Day enjoyed unprecedented networking possibilities. The poet Paul Laurence Dunbar, serving as Douglass's clerk, made two especially significant connections that day. The first was with a country schoolteacher from Georgia—James Weldon Johnson—who would go on to become one of the leading poets, songwriters, and writers of the New Negro (Harlem) Renaissance.[62] The second was with a young violinist and composer, Will Marion Cook.[63]

Cook was a native Washingtonian, and the son of the dean of Howard University Law School. He began studying the violin and composition at Oberlin Conservatory, before members of Washington's First Congregational Church, led by Frederick Douglass, raised the money for him to continue his studies at the Hochschule für Musik in Berlin, where he became a student of Joseph Jaochim. Cook returned to the United States and studied with the Czech-born composer and conductor Antonin Dvořák at the short-lived National Conservatory in New York.[64]

Dvořák, much to the condemnation of American arbiters of high musical taste, was convinced that African American music would be the source of a distinctive American musical tradition. At his prodding, as many as 150 of the National Conservatory's 600 students were African American, including such noteworthy prodigies as Cook, Maurice Arnold Strathotte, and Harry Burleigh.

Dunbar and Cook undoubtedly visited many of the Chicago World's Fair's sights, most especially the Midway Plaisance. The lowbrow backyard to the fair's famous "White City," the hugely popular Plaisance featured such less elevated entertainments as George Washington Gale Ferris Jr.'s gigantic wheel, together with "hootchy kootchies" and sideshows, where such masters of the new ragtime piano style as Scott Joplin, Ernest Hogan, and Jessye Picket hung out. In addition, the "Dahomey Village" exhibited people direct from West Africa (present-day Benin) via Paris, who were assigned to a campground, where they displayed their "primitive" way of life to "superior" White visitors.[65]

At the urging of Bert Williams and George Walker, the popular vaudeville comedy team then approaching the apex of the American entertainment industry, Cook and Dunbar collaborated on a new musical comedy. The duo wrote *Clorindy; or the Origin in the Cakewalk*, during an alcohol-fueled all-nighter in Cook's brother John's basement in Washington, just off the Howard campus on Sixth Street NW. Set in the Louisiana of the 1880s, the show purported to tell the story of the beginnings of the faddishly popular cakewalk dance.

Williams and Walker bowed out of the production due to scheduling conflicts, but another famous African American actor, Ernest Hogan, signed on. When the show opened in New York at the Casino Theatre's Roof Garden on July 4, 1898, *Clorindy* became the first Broadway musical with an all-Black cast. The show marked the acting debut of a young Abbie Mitchell, who would marry Cook. Mitchell would gather numerous stage credits, including singing "Summertime" in her fabled final musical role as "Clara" in the original 1935 cast of George Gershwin's *Porgy and Bess*.[66]

An instant hit, *Clorindy* demonstrated that African Americans could carry a Broadway show on their own. However, the production conformed to the stereotypes of African Americans that had dominated the American stage from the very beginning. Cook reported that when his mother first heard what would become the show's hit—"Who Dat Say Chicken in Dis Crowd?"—she broke down in tears of shame.[67]

Cook continued to collaborate with Williams and Walker and, together with Dunbar, wrote several more shows, including *Senegambian Carnival* (1898) and *A Lucky Coon* (1898). Other all-Black shows were making their ways to the Great White Way during these years, including Williams and Walker's *Sons of Ham* (1899) and *Bandana Land* (1908), as well as Bob Cole and Billy Johnson's *A Trip to Coontown* (1898).[68] Williams and Walker performed in Blackface (after Walker's death, Williams continued to put on the paint after he joined the Ziegfeld Follies). As these plays' titles indicate, self-mockery reinforced White audiences' stereotypes of African Americans.[69]

Cook and Dunbar collaborated on one more triumph before Dunbar's premature death at the age of thirty-three in 1906: the smash hit *In Dahomey*.[70] They were joined by Jesse A. Shipp, who wrote the book, with Cook writing the score, and Dunbar the lyrics. Bert Williams, George Walker, and Aida Overton Walker played the lead roles.

Inspired by the African Village at the Chicago World's Fair, the musical told the story of two American conmen who seek to colonize Dahomey. A full-scale operetta, *In Dahomey* is considered "the first full-length musical written and played by Blacks to be performed at a major Broadway house."[71]

In Dahomey enjoyed two New York runs, in 1903 and 1904, before extensive tours of the United States over the next four years. Its original production moved to the Shaftsbury Theatre in London in 1903, after an extensive provincial tour around England. The production's immense popularity was capped by a command performance at Buckingham Palace to celebrate the Prince of Wales's (and future King Edward VIII's) ninth birthday.[72]

After these successes, Cook continued to play a prominent role in nurturing African American music. He famously joined Washington-raised Jim Reese Europe at the celebrated Clef Club concerts, which brought African American music to the concert stage; and he mentored yet another young Washingtonian who sought musical success in New York, Edward "Duke" Ellington. Cook and Mitchell remained close to Washington even as they entered New York's musical world. Their son, Will Mercer Cook, joined the Howard faculty and later became John F. Kennedy's ambassador to Niger.[73]

Other works followed, such as the 1921 smash hit *Shuffle Along*, with Eubie Blake's music, Noble Sissle's lyrics, and Fournoy Miller's and Aubrey Lyles's book. The show's creators wrote the play after an encounter at the annual convention of the NAACP in Philadelphia in 1920, where they joined forces to create "high-class" entertainment.[74]

Shuffle Along, a tale of small-town and small-time political corruption, opened at the Howard Theatre in Washington before traveling around the country and ending up in New York. The show broke all records, and it has been reprised multiple times into the twenty-first century. Blacks were integrated into the audience throughout the theater rather than being relegated to the balcony. For the first time, *Shuffle Along* portrayed a serious love affair between two African Americans on the American stage; brought jazz to Broadway; launched the stage careers of Josephine Baker, Adelaide Hall, Florence Mills, Fredi Washington, and Paul Robeson; and featured what would become Harry Truman's campaign song, "I'm Just Wild about Harry." As Lester Aglar Walton had hoped a decade earlier, the wave of African American musicals appearing on major American and British stages during the quarter century after the Chicago World's Fair transformed the "coon" musical show into operetta.[75] But unlike his hopeful prediction in 1903, such success did not extend to the dramatic stage. Plays written by African Americans about African Americans and performed by African Americans remained extraordinarily rare. Thomas Montgomery Gregory made this second artistic revolution his personal mission as he moved into the chair of Howard University's Department of English.

A Racial Drama Is Born at Howard

In early 1922, the theater critic Leonard Hall told readers of the new local tabloid the *Washington Daily News* that "no more significant or satisfying dramatic endeavor has been visible in Washington this Spring," than the efforts of the Howard Department of Dramatic Arts "to build a structure of native Negro drama, to be interpreted

by people of that race." [76] Hall had just attended a campus performance of two one-act plays—one by a student, and one by an alum-
na of the university—and had become a convert to Gregory's cause.

The authors and performers Hall praised were part of Gregory's new effort to create the Negro National Theater at Howard.
Gregory hoped to train actors and producers who would be able
to organize groups of African American players in larger cities
around the country—companies that would achieve a high level
of artistry sufficient to attract fair-minded members of the white
community. He planned to do so by blending elements from four
models: the Irish National Theater, founded by W. B. Yeats, Lady
Gregory, George Moore, and Edward Martyn in Dublin; George
Pierce Baker's "Workshop 47" Program at Harvard; George Cram
"Jig" Cools' and Susan Glaspell's Provincetown Players; and Frederick Koch and Paul Green's Carolina Playmakers at the University
of North Carolina. [77] Hall's review suggested that the enterprise was
off to a fortuitous start.

Gregory, by this time, had secured an energetic partner for
this initiative in the Howard faculty member and fellow Harvard
alumnus Alain Locke. Locke was born into High Victorian African
American Philadelphia, and he set off for Harvard after graduating
from that city's Central High School. Upon graduation from Harvard in 1907, he was chosen as the first African American Rhodes
Scholar (the selecting officials possibly did not realize that he was
Black as there were no interviews of candidates at the time).

After spending research time in Oxford and Berlin, where he
studied literature and philosophy, Locke joined the Howard English Department in 1912. Four years later, he returned to Harvard,
where he completed his doctoral degree in philosophy. He then
took up the position of chair of Howard's Philosophy Department
in 1918. [78]

Locke and Gregory had hit it off well during Locke's initial stint
at Howard. Both shared the experience of having been among the
very few African Americans at Harvard. Together, they founded
Howard's student literary Stylus Society and its magazine, *The Stylus*, which would come to play an important role in the New Negro
(Harlem) Renaissance, launching, among many, the writing career
of the Howard student Zora Neale Hurston. [79]

Locke was already familiar with the work of the Harvard dramatist George Pierce Baker. As Baker's former student, Gregory wanted to emulate the work of his one-time professor.[80] After establishing the Harvard Dramatic Club in 1908, as they both knew, Baker had founded Workshop 47. The workshop's purpose was to provide a cohesive forum for the performance of plays developed within his English 47 class—an arrangement well suited to the plans of Locke and Gregory.[81]

Locke welcomed the endorsement of Department of Dramatic Arts dean Kelly Miller for Gregory's plans to create a drama program at Howard modeled after Baker's Workshop 47 Program for training playwrights, directors, and performers.[82] With Gregory working on productions at Howard, Locke would oversee student playwriting in his English seminars.[83] Women penned the majority of these plays, as female students seized this unusual opportunity for the era to express themselves publicly.[84]

Gregory set out a clear strategy for building his program in the director's reports he filed with the Howard administration in 1921 and 1922. In 1921, he noted that African Americans had lacked the institutional foundations for permanent and determined progress in developing their own theatrical voice. He argued that the establishment of the National Negro Theatre at Howard could provide the catalyzing effect on African American drama that the establishment of the Irish National Theatre in Dublin had achieved for the Irish people.

This argument expanded on Gregory's earlier writing about the relationship between race and art. In 1915, he published a lengthy and considered reflection on "race attitude" in the Boston-based journal *The Citizen*. "By race attitude," he wrote, "I mean the attitude of the individual members of the Negro race to the race itself. For instead of cultivating a race pride, a race self-respect, a race consciousness, we have sought to un-race ourselves, to avoid whatever might definitely associate us with the Negro race." If art is self-expression, he noted, "it is necessarily race expression." This expression demanded a presentation of African Americans outside any sense of inferiority, without any tendency "to mimic the tone and texture of Euro-Americanism."[85]

For these reasons, Gregory argued, the establishment of the

Howard Players represented a significant development for African Americans throughout the country. Noting that support of original dramatic works by African Americans about African Americans would "considerably influence the development of a real native American drama," he explicitly turned to the experience of the Irish National Theatre in advancing a distinctive Irish drama.[86]

The next year, Gregory stated that the Players were larger than Howard. "The Players," he began, "are not simply a college dramatic club or local institution. They are now recognized as a significant movement in American Drama, and great things are expected and demanded of them."[87] To underscore the national reach of his enterprise, he convened a blue ribbon advisory council to support his efforts, which included Harvard's George Pierce Baker; the playwright and poet Percy Mackaye; the drama critics and actors Robert Benchley and Heywood Broun; the American novelist Winston Churchill (who, at the time, was better known than the British politician of the same name); Smith College's Samuel L. Eliot Jr.; the designer Robert L. Jones; Carolina Players' Frederick H. Koch; *Theater Art Magazine*'s Kenneth Macgowan; the NAACP's Joel Spingarn; and the *New Republic*'s Stark Young—as well as the playwrights Ridgely Torrence and Eugene O'Neill.[88]

This advisory council's impressive membership crossed racial and geographic barriers and demonstrated widespread support among many leaders of the American theater community for Gregory's mission of bringing African Americans to the dramatic stage. Letters of support streamed in from such luminaries as W. E. B. Du Bois; Grace Hegger Lewis, on behalf of herself and her husband Sinclair; and Eugene O'Neill.[89] O'Neill's missive was particularly unambiguous. "I am thoroughly in sympathy with your undertaking," he wrote, "and I believe as strongly as you do that the gifts the Negro can—and will—bring to our native drama are invaluable ones. The possibilities are limitless and, to a dramatist they open up new and intriguing opportunities."[90]

Locke shared Gregory's commitment to the enterprise, similarly emphasizing the importance of a university base for the future development of African American theater. His article "Steps Toward a Negro Theatre," appearing in *Crisis* in 1922, echoed several of Gregory's themes.[91]

Locke began his commentary by observing that "culturally, we are abloom in a new field, but it is yet undecidedly a question as to what we shall reap—a few flowers or a harvest. That depends upon how we cultivate this area of the drama in the next few years." Noting that "the Negro actor without the Negro drama is a sporadic phenomenon," he made the case for a comprehensive approach to cultivating a new drama. Successful actors alone were insufficient, he argued. New actors needed to be cultivated, new plays needed to be written, and new theaters needed to be managed.

Although many were concerned that African American theater favor "professional auspices and a greater metropolitan center like New York or Chicago for the Negro theatre," Locke added, those at Howard "believe a university foundation will assure a greater continuity of effort and insure accordingly a greater permanence of result." This perspective stood in opposition to those who favored connections to commercial theaters in New York or Chicago. Despite such diversity of opinion, Locke counseled that the movement to produce African American dramatic theater must receive "the unanimous sanction of our hearts."

Gregory's and Locke's approach reflected the success of two related organizational strategies in American theater that had developed over the previous decade. Beginning in about 1912, a movement formed to support innovation outside the restrictions of large-scale commercial theaters. First emerging in Chicago, Boston, Seattle, and cities in California, the "Little Theatre Movement," as it became known, encouraged intimate, non-profit-centered and reform-minded theater.[92]

Over the next two decades, some 470 African American little theater groups (including the Scribblers of Baltimore, the Dixwell Players of New Haven, the Gilpins of Cleveland, the Quill Club of Boston, the Shadows of Chicago, and other important companies in Dallas, Philadelphia, and Indianapolis) would come into being and pass out of existence in every major Black community across the country.[93] The movement's experimental character, support of playwrights, reform—often radical—politics, and community orientation appealed to Gregory, as he developed strong ties with the Provincetown Players.

The Provincetown Players had moved from Cape Cod to New

York in 1917 and would continue to feature the work of new playwrights until the company vanished during the mid-1920s.[94] At the time when Gregory and Locke were launching the Howard Players, the Provincetown Players—and the many artists then associated with them (including Theodore Dreiser, Edna St. Vincent Millay, Eugene O'Neill, John Reed, and Wallace Stevens)—were among the most influential theatrical innovators of their era.

The Carolina Playmakers at the University of North Carolina provided an even more appropriate model for what Gregory and Locke wanted to achieve.[95] Established in 1918 by Professor Frederick Koch as an outreach effort for the production of original student plays, the Playmakers, like Baker's Workshop 47, sought to create a cadre of theater artists trained in all aspects of their craft. Its first production featured the playwriting debut of the Carolina undergraduate Thomas Wolfe.

The Playmakers primarily produced "folk plays" reflecting the experiences of marginalized communities around North Carolina and the American South. They toured statewide, often to the most dispossessed communities, and gave voice to the concerns of poor rural communities, Appalachian Whites, African Americans, and Native Americans. In 1925, the Playmakers began publishing *Carolina Folk Plays*, providing a model for achieving the goals articulated by Gregory and Locke for the Howard Players. In addition to Koch, the Carolina student writer—and future Pulitzer Prize–winning playwright—Paul Green developed strong connections to the Howard Players.

Each of the archetypes for the Howard Players—the Irish National Theater, Baker's Workshop 47, the Provincetown Players, and the Carolina Playmakers—embodied several shared characteristics. With the exception of Workshop 47, each theater company sought to give voice to marginalized communities. With the exception of the Irish National Theater and the Provincetown Players, they were connected to universities. They all, in different ways, tried to extend the boundaries of theatrical arts beyond large-scale commercial enterprises. They valued innovation and holistic approaches to the training of theatrical professionals. And they valued the realism, unfettered storytelling, and simplicity of the modernist movement in drama.

Playing before the World

On November 3, 1921, *Life Magazine* published an article by its drama critic, Robert C. Benchley, praising Howard University's efforts to establish a national Negro theater where "the Negro playwright, musician, actor, dancer, and artist in concert shall fashion a drama that shall merit the respect and win the admiration of the world."[96] Benchley's article appeared just as Gregory was putting the final touches on a germinal production that extended beyond the bounds of Howard, the city, and even the United States. A month later, the Howard Players performed for the delegates to the World Disarmament Conference (also known as the Washington Naval Conference).

During his first year in office, Republican president Warren G. Harding invited nine nations under the auspices of the League of Nations to resolve disputes and implement an international regulatory system for naval fleets.[97] This event—the first international conference to be convened in the United States—provided an opportunity for Harding and his imposing secretary of state, Charles Evans Hughes, to establish their diplomatic bona fides while diverging from their predecessors in the Democratic Woodrow Wilson administration. The conference organizers faced the additional challenge of needing to figure out how to keep the delegates contented in a city that they considered a provincial backwater.

Today, Harding regularly appears at the bottom of lists ranking American presidents. The fact that he died of a heart attack halfway through his first term limited his legislative accomplishments. And his presidency was further undermined by ever-unfolding scandals and a pattern of womanizing that tarnished his personal stature. Generally, a go-along-get-along politician, Harding was not known for his strong moral stances. However, though long forgotten, Harding initially sought to moderate Wilson's harsh race policies, both nationally and in the nation's capital.

At a planning session with his staff, Harding evidently suggested that the delegates might enjoy an evening of performance by the newly formed Howard Players.[98] This mention was all Gregory needed to swing into action. Despite the absence of support from other administration officials—and only a tepid endorsement by

Howard officers—Gregory succeeded in organizing an immensely well-received evening of theater and music on December 12, 1921.

The silence of senior State Department bureaucrats conformed to the generally patrician disdain many diplomats displayed at the time toward their compatriots—amplified, no doubt, by an unhealthy measure of racism. Senior members of the US delegation skipped the event, with only a relatively low-ranking State Department official—Charles Lee Cook—and delegation advisory committee member—George W. Wilson of Harvard—showing up for the host country.

Gregory's Howard superiors played a distasteful bureaucratic game of claiming success as their own while casting blame for failure on others. Howard president J. Stanley Durkee and his staff undoubtedly were distracted by preparations for the bestowing of an honorary doctor of science degree on the French World War I hero Marshal Ferdinand Foch a month previously. In the end, Durkee dispatched the university's secretary treasurer, Emmett J. Scott, in his stead.

Such behind-the-scenes bureaucratic scuffles passed unnoticed by those who attended Gregory's evening of entertainment.[99] Gregory viewed the show as an opportunity to be "of tremendous importance to the reputation and staging of the Negro race," given that the delegates "knew nothing of the cultural life of the Negro in this country." Those who attended seem to have agreed.

A larger-than-capacity audience crowded into the university's Rankin Chapel to see a two-part program featuring a performance of Ridgely Torrence's new drama *Simon, the Cyrenian*, followed by a musical program performed by the University Glee Club under the direction of Roy W. Tibbs. Torrence's play told the tale of Simon, whom the Romans compelled to carry the cross of Jesus to Calvary. The Players would perform this play on numerous occasions, using sets and costumes designed by the Provincetown Players' Cleon Throckmorton, who had recently begun teaching in Gregory's new Dramatic Arts program. The cast included the future Michigan politician Harold Bledsoe, the future New Negro (Harlem) Renaissance playwright Ottie Graham, and the future actor Alston Burleigh.

After an intermission, the University Glee Club performed a program designed to show the evolution of Negro music. The musical selections moved from such folk songs as "Roll, Jordan, Roll" and "Steal Away" to compositions of later composers such as Harry T. Burleigh, Samuel Coleridge-Taylor, and Ira Aldridge's daughter, the British composer and opera singer Montague Ring.

The evening's audience was as much a part of the show as the works performed. Diplomats from France, China, Japan, and the Netherlands were joined by delegates from the countries of the British Empire, including Britain, Canada, Australia, and India. The English author H. G. Wells and the journalist Henry Nevinson joined the French writer Pierre Combret de Lanux and many of the most distinguished members of Washington's African American elite.

Gregory used every opportunity to promote his work, together with that of his colleagues Marie Moore-Forrest and Alain Locke, to create the National Negro Theatre modeled after the Irish National Theatre in Dublin. Moore-Forrest was an instrumental figure in this effort, as she served as acting coach. She also was a leading activist in the National Women's Party organized in support of women's suffrage.[100] She was a key figure in bringing together the former Dramatic Club with the Department of Dramatic Art. Outside the university, Gregory took every measure to emphasize the growing relationship between the Howard Players and Provincetown Players; as he announced future performances of plays written by Howard students and Washington high school students.[101]

The Emperor Jones

Gregory was an inveterate collector of playbills. He saved the programs from every production he saw, carefully noting those among onstage and offstage artists who were Black. Others noted this passion. His friends and colleagues—including Langston Hughes and Richard B. Harrison (the Da Lawd in Marc Connelly's hit *Green Pastures*)—dutifully sent their programs along, appropriately identifying any people of color associated with a production. Over his lifetime, Gregory amassed scores of programs from productions in Washington, New York, Philadelphia, Boston, and beyond, including such gems as autographed playbills from the original productions of *Show Boat* (1927) and *Porgy and Bess* (1935).[102] One such program proved to be of great significance for the development of the Howard Players.

In November 1920, Gregory held on to the opening reviews of an ambitious, rising playwright's successful new play: *The Emperor Jones* by Eugene O'Neill. O'Neill, the son of an Irish immigrant actor and his first-generation Irish American wife, was literally born to Broadway at the Barrett House hotel in Times Square. Frequently on tour and suffering from substance abuse, his parents dispatched Eugene to a Catholic boarding school in the Riverdale section of the Bronx.

O'Neill eventually made his way to Princeton, where he dropped out due to various conduct violations. Fighting alcoholism and depression, he associated with radical unionists and their political agendas. By the 1910s, he had landed with the Provincetown Players and begun to write for the theater. O'Neill—who would win the Nobel Prize in Literature in 1936 and four Pulitzer Prizes—ranks at the top of any short list of great American playwrights. Together with Henrik Ibsen and Anton Chekov, O'Neill is considered one of the founding luminaries of the sort of modernist realism so attractive to Gregory and Locke.[103]

The Emperor Jones became O'Neill's first genuine "hit."[104] The play consists of flashbacks telling the story of an African American Pullman porter—the escaped criminal Brutus Jones—who finds refuge on a Caribbean Island. Jones starts swindling his way to the pinnacle of local power. The play heaves toward Jones's inevitable death by silver bullet to the steady beat of drums played by rebellious islanders.

The play won every possible prize of its era, and it has been reprised dozens of times over the past century on stage and screen alike. Its success transpired despite controversies over its racialized representations of Jones and the rebels. Demanding an intimidating range of emotions, from euphoria to terror and insanity, the role of Brutus Jones challenged theatergoers raised on Blackface minstrel show stars to accept the lead character as a human being of Shakespearean dimensions. The role's originator, Charles S. Gilpin, achieved the stature of one of the great American dramatic actors of the day.

Gregory saved reviews from the show's opening in November 1920 (well marked, they remain in his archived papers).[105] The *New York Globe*'s Kenneth Macgowan found *The Emperor Jones* to be "perhaps the most interesting play and production to be seen in New York." Alexander Woollcott of the *New York Times* declared the play to be "an extraordinarily striking and dramatic study of panic fear." Heywood Broun wrote in the *New York Tribune* that "*The Emperor Jones* is so unusual in its technique that it might wait in vain for a production anywhere except in so adventurous a playhouse as the Provincetown Players. . . . If *The Emperor Jones* were taken elsewhere, we have little doubt that the manager would engage a White man with a piece of burnt cork to play Brutus Jones. They have done better in Macdougal Street. The Emperor is played by a Negro actor named Charles S. Gilpin, who gives the most thrilling performance we have seen anyplace this season."[106]

For Gregory, searching for ways to advance his vision of an African American theater worthy of admiration, Gilpin had arrived at just the right moment. A carefully marked playbill from December 6–18, 1920, indicates that Gregory traveled to New York to see the production, was as overwhelmed as the critics, and planned to call or visit the Provincetown Players the next day.[107] The resulting collaboration was well in evidence at the Washington Disarmament Conference gala less than a year later, as O'Neill had joined Gregory's advisory board, while the master designer Cleon Throckmorton had signed on to teach at Howard and to work on the Howard Players' productions. Both companies joined together to bring Gilpin to Washington to perform his iconic role of Brutus Jones.

Gregory arranged for the Howard Players to perform *The Emperor Jones* in Washington with an initial afternoon performance featuring Gilpin at the Belasco Theatre near the White House on March 28, 1921. Performances on the evenings of April 1 and 2 at the Myrtilla Miner Normal School followed, with the Howard student thespian George D. Williams in the lead role.[108] The Howard Players added additional performances with the student cast later in the month.[109]

Given the play's and Gilpin's rousing success in New York, the initial performance was something of an event in White Washington as well as within African American society. *The Evening Star* noted that "the audience, White and colored, packed the Belasco."[110] The venture became a fundraising and reputation-building success.

The *Washington Herald* columnist Earle Dorsey, meanwhile, thanked his African American barber for tipping him off about Gilpin's appearance. Noting that "the Negro, a born mimic, and naturally endowed with Thespic accomplishments of an unusual order, might easily evolve a series of native dramatic groups of no mean order," Dorsey complained that "the arrangement of the affair, in presenting Gilpin, is presenting almost for the exclusive delectation of their own race." He concluded that he hoped Gilpin would return for "the delectation of local White theater-goers."[111]

Others among the city's White press were less generous with praise for the student production. The *Evening Star* critic found the play "a weird and awe-inspiring dramatic treatise on the progress of fear and its accompanying hallucinations."[112] The *Washington Herald*'s counterpart noted that Williams is "a student whose stage experience in amateur theatricals has been limited." More generously, the *Herald* continued, "the acting of Williams reflects a wealth of credit upon the university instructors and as much as for his own talents."[113]

African Americans were more forthcoming in their praise. Despite concern among both New York and Washington African Americans that O'Neill portrayed Black characters as criminals and roustabouts, Black audiences generally took pride in the power of Gilpin's performance and in the quality of the student actors. W. E. B. Du Bois found the play to have been "exceedingly well done and most promising for the future."[114]

The play would take on a life of its own, being performed throughout the twentieth century. The film version starred Paul Robeson, who emerged as a powerful presence in his own right. Robeson, for his part, declined to appear on Washington's Jim Crow stages. He frequently came to town for other reasons, such as to support numerous political causes, to protest segregation, and to speak at major African American venues such as Howard University.[115] For example, he appeared alongside Charles Houston, Mary Church Terrell, E. Franklin Frazier, and others at a large rally held at Turner's Arena in October 1949.[116]

Gregory could not have had a better launch for the Howard Players. Gilpin's appearance, followed by the Washington Disarmament Conference's success, validated Gregory's vision of the players as "not simply a college dramatic club or local institution" but also "recognized as a significant movement in American Drama, and great things are expected and demanded of them."[117] The Players embarked on regular productions of new works by established playwrights—such as Lord Dunsany, Booth Tarkington, and Ridgely Torrence—both on campus and at commercial houses around town and in Baltimore. They similarly performed works by Locke's students and winning submissions in competitions in the city's African American public schools.[118]

Success Breeds Trouble

But storm clouds were beginning to gather. The plays produced by Locke's students were proving disappointing. Underneath collegial goodwill, academic jealousies and competing claims for esteem began to creep into Gregory's and Locke's relationships with one another.[119] Sustaining donor interest remained a constant challenge. Southern congressmen were concerned that Howard might become a hotbed of sedition. The university's increasingly venomous atmosphere, fueled by a menacing president and meddlesome trustees, proved even more malignant.

Howard University president James Stanley Durkee was the latest in a line of White presidents who generally looked down on the school's African American students and faculty. Durkee was a Baptist and Congregationalist minister who grew up in Nova Scotia before immigrating to the United States. He completed his higher divinity training in Boston, where he served as pastor of the First Free Baptist Church and the South Congregational Church before arriving at Howard in 1918. He later would serve as associate pastor of the famous Plymouth Congregational Church in Brooklyn.[120]

Durkee was contemptuous of the Howard community and paranoid about somehow having the school's congressional support undermined by radical activity at the time of the post–World War I Red Scare. His concerns only grew as Howard came under attack from Congress for promoting "Bolshevik" ideas after the outbreak of intense racial violence during the summer of 1919, when the communities around Howard armed themselves to fend off attacks by marauding Whites.[121]

Durkee summoned a newly appointed history professor, Carter G. Woodson, into his office and accused him of disloyalty. Durkee produced a letter from Secret Service agents accusing Woodson of communist tendencies. He then tried to recruit Woodson to spy on his fellow faculty members. Instead, Woodson quit, moving to West Virginia Collegiate Institute (now West Virginia State College). Woodson later returned to Washington to edit the *Journal of Negro History* and tend to the affairs of the Association for the Study of Negro Life and History that he established with Jesse E. Moorland in 1915.[122]

The Woodson saga was emblematic of Durkee's relationship with his faculty, and with the Howard Players. In late 1922, Durkee interfered with Gregory's plans to produce a work by the Washington playwright Willis Richardson.[123] Richardson, who would become the first African American playwright to have a drama produced on Broadway, was achieving recognition with his dramas examining African American life. Well connected to the Washington community of African American intellectuals, he was a natural partner in Gregory's and Locke's crusade to bring plays by Blacks about Blacks to Black theater audiences. Durkee eventually relented, and the Players performed Richardson's family drama *Mortgaged* in 1924.[124]

The master designer Cleon Throckmorton resigned precipitously from Howard in June 1922, forcing Gregory to scramble to find faculty to teach courses on set and stage design. His departure eroded the connection between Howard and the Provincetown Players. The precise circumstances of Throckmorton's departure are murky. He continued to work with the Provincetown Players, enjoyed a highly successful career on Broadway, and eventually became artistic designer for the Columbia Broadcasting System. Perhaps he simply had mounting opportunities outside Washington.

Locally, however, Throckmorton was as well known for his notorious speakeasy, the Krazy Kat Klub, at 3 Green Court off Thomas Circle, as he was for his work at Howard. His illicit sideline would not have pleased Durkee in the least. Throckmorton's blunt and brief June 7, 1922, scrawled resignation letter suggests an unexpected departure. Addressed to Gregory, he wrote: "Kindly accept my resignation from 'the Department of Dramatic Arts,' which you head. I would also like to signify that I do not care to join the Department again in the fall. Very respectfully."[125]

Gregory himself would soon follow. In August 1924, he accepted a position as supervisor of Negro schools, and later principal, in Atlantic City, New Jersey, citing a very considerable salary increase. The story may not have been so straightforward. In 1912, he had resigned after an anonymous letter was sent to the university's president accusing him of a drunken display at a Washington bar. Reinstated after a letter-writing campaign by Booker T. Washington, William A. Sinclair, and others, Gregory might well have put the story behind him.[126]

Those close to him—as well as the record found in his papers at the Moorland-Spingarn Research Center—hint at ongoing conflicts with Howard administrators. Whatever its limitations, Howard offered a more visible base of operations than the Atlantic City schools for pursuing his passionate goal of establishing the National Negro Theater.

Gregory did not give up on his dream. In a seminal review of Jean Toomer's freshly published novel *Cane* appearing in the December 1923 issue of the National Urban League's monthly journal *Opportunity*, Gregory set forth why he believed it so important for Blacks to tell their own stories.[127] "It has been conceded that the varied life of the Negro in America, especially his folk-life, offers almost unparalleled opportunities for the brush of the artist and the pen of the poet," he noted. Unfortunately, he continued, there has been "unqualified opposition" in the Negro community "to the utilization of his mass life in fiction, in music, or in drama. What has this meant? It has robbed the race of its birthright for a mess of pottage. It has damned the possibilities of true artistic expression at its very source. It has enabled the White artist to exploit the Negro race for personal recognition or commercial gain." After praising Toomer for telling the story of Black life with extraordinary power, Gregory goes on to repeat his appeal for a Negro theater that is capable of producing works such as *Cane*. Beyond the "alien exploitation" of Black life, Gregory argued that the vast richness and complexity of the African American community required authors from within—such as Toomer—to write plays. In this spirit, he noted that "Art is *self-expression*" (emphasis in the original).

Shortly after arriving in New Jersey, Gregory lectured at Trenton's Lincoln School Lyceum, arguing that the time had arrived to leave behind "the White actor made up as Blackfaced comedian, particularly in the theatre life of New York City."[128] In 1927, he penned the *Encyclopedia Britannica's* entry "The Negro in Drama.[129] Two years later, he toured community drama programs throughout the South.[130]

His friendship and collaboration with Locke continued. Locke tried to lure Gregory back to Howard on at least two occasions.[131] In 1930, the two former colleagues joined forces to compile *Plays of Negro Life: A Source-Book of Native American Drama.*[132]

Despite strong family connections to Washington, Gregory's life had moved north, where he threw himself into his work in Atlantic City with the same enthusiasm and energy as he had when starting out at Howard. He sustained his interest in theater throughout his life, participated in conferences and on scholarly panels, reviewed works by aspiring writers, and continued to build his extensive collection of playbills.[133]

In addition to Locke, Gregory remained a lifelong close friend of Sterling Brown, and he maintained close ties to the Washington intellectual community and to those around Howard. His daughter, Sheila, was a member of the Howard Players while a student at Howard, and she went on to teach in the DC Public Schools, and also produced an award-winning children's television show, *The Magic Door.*[134] Gregory's great-granddaughter, Aisha Tyler, has continued the family connection with theater as a successful actor, comedian, director, and television talk show host.[135] After his retirement in New Jersey, in 1960 the elder Gregory returned to Washington, where he lived until his death in November 1971.[136]

A little under a year after Gregory's departure from the Howard campus, on June 16, 1925, the university's Board of Trustees informed Locke that they would not renew his contract for the 1925–26 academic year. The letter—signed by the board's secretary treasurer, Emmett J. Scott—informed Locke that "after very full discussion of the matter, in all its phases, your place, among others, it was decided, could be vacated and the work of the University not unduly suffer."[137]

The New Negro

Alain LeRoy Locke was uncommon at Howard and among Washington's middle-class African Americans. He grew up in Philadelphia, spent considerable time abroad (Weimar Berlin was his preferred haunt), and traveled at every opportunity around Europe, the Middle East, and Africa. He was an aesthete, a Bahá'í, a homosexual, and a humanities scholar in a conservative university designed to produce teachers, clergy, lawyers, and doctors. He lived with, cared for, and toured accompanied by his mother until her death in 1922, when he was already well into adulthood. He mastered the as-yet-recent academic game of cobbling together prestigious grants so as to spend as little time on campus as possible. He sought a universal and humanistic appreciation of African American achievement within a global community, while many Blacks simply wanted to remove White people from their lives. Finally, to the dismay of those who become jealous over the achievements of others, he was already on his way to becoming one of the most important American intellectuals of his generation.

Locke could be dismissively arrogant toward his Howard colleagues. In 1923, he wrote to Langston Hughes that Howard was "a cultural backwater, even though at the nation's capital." He wanted to stand at the center of a "literary and art coterie" that could not be found in his current position. "And yet," he continued, "I have always been attracted to Howard and in spite of much disillusionment am still intrigued with its possibilities."[138]

Unsurprisingly, far too many of his associates were not always charmed by his presence. However, today, Alain Locke—who retired in 1953, moved to New York, and died a year later—is revered at Howard, with his personal library carefully preserved in a special room of the university's Founders Library. Locke, it turned out, has been easier to celebrate in his absence than when he was present every day. In 1925, he was surrounded at Howard by numerous colleagues who privately supported the trustees' decision not to renew his contract.

Disappointed though he may have been with Howard, he had few options open to him. No "mainstream" (i.e., White) American university was going to appoint an African American philosopher to their faculty, no matter how stellar his achievements had been. Neither his growing attentiveness to African art and aesthetics—an interest that was becoming a signature for his work—nor his enthusiasm for interdisciplinary perspectives fit into the institutional structures and constraints of American academic life.[139]

Initially feeling liberated after his Howard contract was not renewed, Locke escaped to Harlem. Over time, however, anxiety began to replace feelings of emancipation. Ironically, Locke's dismissal came as he was enjoying unprecedented success. After spending most of the summer of 1923 in Europe, he continued on to Egypt and the eastern Mediterranean, including a visit to the Bahá'í holy places in Haifa.

Locke arrived back in the United States full of enthusiasm for training a cadre of students at Howard who could engage with Africa on multiple levels. He stopped off in New York on his way back to Washington to meet the National Urban League's Charles S. Johnson. Locke and Johnson discussed an ambitious publishing plan in conjunction with *Opportunity* magazine before heading on to Washington for the start of Howard's winter term. He returned to campus with a consolidated vision for an African foundation for African American education and myriad new and solidified personal contacts to support his efforts.[140]

Later in the year, Locke connected (and clashed) with Albert Barnes, who was then compiling his impressive collection of African and European art, as well as with Paul Guillaume and Guillaume Apollinaire, who were bringing new European perspectives to West African art.[141] Together with Johnson, Locke convened a dinner of leading African American intellectuals and writers in March to discuss a literary awakening in Black America—the arrival of "New Negro" authors.[142]

After his usual European sojourn, Locke worked with Johnson to capture the artistic and intellectual explosion recasting Harlem.[143] These efforts eventuated in a landmark issue of *Survey Graphic* dedicated to the dynamism sweeping across New York's premier African American neighborhood—a "Harlem Renaissance." Locke was now at the epicenter of one of America's most seminal cultural explosions. The problem was that Howard University was not.

The New Negro Renaissance was moving from Washington's

U Street to New York's 125th Street. James A. Miller correctly notes that sixteen of the thirty-five contributors to Locke's famous compendium *The New Negro: An Interpretation* had been born, raised, educated, or worked in Washington; but that many of them, like Locke, were increasingly spending time on Manhattan.[144]

Back at Howard, Locke had been assigned the unenviable task of serving as secretary to the faculty committee on salaries. This position brought him into direct conflict with members of the Board of Trustees, who resented his demands for improved faculty compensation, even though he was merely reporting the views of the committee.[145]

Locke's biographer, Jeffrey C. Stewart, captures the moment when he tried to explain how the premier Negro institution of higher education could fire its most-educated faculty member just as that professor was at the center of a major intellectual and cultural explosion. "The answer," Stewart writes,

> while complex, came down to this: the New Negro was not a welcome attitude in all quarters of Negro America, especially among administrators of institutional Negro America who viewed the New Negro and its criticality of racial hegemony as a nuisance to be dismissed or, if that did not suffice, to be crushed. Locke's problem was simple. He was not only the principal chronicler of the New Negro—he was a New Negro himself, an upstart rebel against the kind of paternalistic control that had become the staple of Negro higher education.[146]

The truth was that Locke's success became a target for condemnation rather than approbation.

Closing and Reopening the Door for the New Negro

President Durkee appeared to be the most likely initiator of the move against Locke; Locke certainly thought so. But Durkee was soon heading for the exit himself. Caught up in his own scandals, he resigned in March 1926. As Stewart uncovered while trolling Howard's archives, little was what it had seemed at the time.[147]

Durkee, in fact, had not been particularly hostile toward Locke and had supported him in his various requests for absences and research travel. Instead, Locke had earned the lasting dislike of the Howard trustee Jesse E. Moorland.

Meanwhile, a furious Locke headed to New York, where he spent the autumn putting the final touches on what would become one of the most important compendiums of essays published during the twentieth century: *The New Negro: An Interpretation*. Locke hit the lecture circuit after the anthology's publication in December 1925. As he toured around, the struggle back at Howard moved to a new phase.

The Board of Trustees eventually chose the Baptist minister Mortdecai Johnson as the university's new president. Johnson proved to be an inspired choice, despite being a judgmental and an imperious micromanager. As the university's first Black president, Johnson was on a mission to make his university the equal of any school in the country. During his thirty-four years at the helm, he greatly expanded the school's financial base, increasing its congressional appropriation from $216,000 to $12 million, together with an additional $42 million for buildings and other capital expenditures.[148] In addition, he brought numerous top African American scholars to campus—including the legal scholars Charles Hamilton Houston and William Hastie, the chemist Percy Julian, the poet Sterling Brown, the economist Abram Harris, the sociologist E. Franklin Frazier, the political scientist Ralph Bunche, the medical researcher Charles R. Drew, and the historians Rayford Logan and John Hope Franklin—producing such distinguished graduates as Thurgood Marshall, Zora Neale Hurston, David Dinkins, and Toni Morrison.[149] Locke pursued Johnson across Europe during the summer of 1926. Meanwhile, he secured an appointment at Fisk University for the 1927–28 academic year.

Locke's interest in African American theater hardly waned, despite the turmoil in his professional life. In 1927, he continued to engage in discussions over the African American contribution to the American stage. "One would do well to imagine," he pondered, "what might happen if the art of the Negro actor should really become artistically lifted and liberated. Transpose the possible resources of Negro song and dance and pantomime to the serious stage, envisage an American drama under the galvanizing stimulus of a rich transfusion of essential folk-arts, and you may anticipate what I mean."[150]

Locke continued to balance this interest in elevating African American sensibilities within American culture with a need to be precise about what Black writers could bring to cultural developments. Writing in the University of North Carolina's *Carolina Magazine*, he warned African American poets to consider what their experiences meant: "But what is Negro poetry, admitting all this—after all? Is it a matter of theme and subject matter or a question of spirit and attitude—a distinctive angle on life, or a certain idiom of feeling and emotion? We miss the vital point primarily, I think, because we wish to crowd whatever the Negro elements are into a rigid formula."[151] This warning applied equally to Locke's view about African American drama.

Although Johnson would become an ally, the problem's solution would lie elsewhere. The university's trustees, rather than its president, would need to change their minds in order for Locke to be reappointed to the Howard faculty. As Stewart uncovered in the archives, unbeknownst to Locke, his rival and foremost antagonist W. E. B. Du Bois overcame whatever personal misgivings he had about Locke (which evidently were many).[152] He reached out to Jesse Moorland and urged that Locke be reinstated, writing that "we must have cultured and well-trained men in our institutions."[153] By the autumn of 1928, Locke was back on campus.

There is no evidence that Locke ever knew of Du Bois's intervention on his behalf. Both men could be wearisome; and they remained difficult rivals for one another. In this instance, however, the larger goal of advancing the place of African Americans in society eclipsed personal animus. As Locke's journeys indicate, New York's Harlem was becoming the center of gravity for African American cultural and intellectual life. This creative concentration was as unmistakably manifest in the theater, as in other artistic fields.

Just a few years earlier, Locke had warned against the vicissitudes of depending on commercial theaters in major metropolitan centers to sustain the nascent African American theater.[154] He argued instead that universities could provide greater continuity and permanence for the Negro theater. The sagas surrounding the Howard Players and the company's leaders had proven him wrong. University administrators could be no less obtrusive than private funders and commercial producers.

Harlem's ascendancy came late to the African American stage.[155] Unquestionably, the center of American theater, competition in New York was intense. Although the city's African American theaters had flourished during the 1910s, they were hardly alone among Black stages across the United States.[156] Alternative African American commercial and nonprofit companies could be found around the country, to say nothing of the Washington scene. Among the most active centers were Chicago's Pekin Theatre and Ethiopian Art Players; Cleveland's Gilpin Players of the Karamu Theatre; the Krigwa Players' Little Negro Theatres, promoted by W. E. B. Du Bois and the NAACP, with satellite companies to the primary New York stage in Cleveland, Baltimore, and Philadelphia; and various touring companies in California. Harlem's Lafayette Players were more analogous to these smaller companies than to the commercial houses downtown on Broadway.[157] Collectively, they created a thriving setting for aspiring African American playwrights, directors, and actors.[158]

By the late 1920s, the advantages of consolidation in New York became ever more apparent, especially as the economic collapse of the Great Depression eviscerated the economic well-being of African American communities everywhere. With fewer resources to spend on leisure and entertainment—and with the ever-growing reality of truly inexpensive entertainment on radios, phonograph players, and in Hollywood film—community theaters could not compete. Though true for White theater, these trends proved especially malign for generally disadvantaged African American theaters. African American theater professionals, audiences, and venues—like their White counterparts—concentrated on Manhattan.[159]

A Harlem Renaissance for African American Theater

The Harlem theatrical scene constantly sought a balance between the artistic freedom of nonprofit and community-based theater and the financial gains to be accrued from commercial productions. Apprehension about how to address White audiences in commercial houses was real. As H. L. Mencken mused in 1926, African Americans might do well to poke fun at Whites, as Whites had Blacks: "The White man, it seems to me, is extremely ridiculous. He looks ridiculous even to me, a White man myself. To a Negro he must be a hilarious spectacle indeed."[160]

But how many White theatergoers would pay to see themselves ridiculed? Without White theatergoers in the house, how viable could a commercial production be? New York's nonprofit companies, conversely, received support from municipal partners—especially the New York Public Library's 135th Street Branch / Schomburg Center for Research in Black Culture—as well as from the major New York foundations, whose offices and program officers were only a subway ride away. Would such resources prove sufficient to sustain companies over time? For a brief period between 1935 and 1939, these city-based sponsors had unexpected assistance from the US government.

Roosevelt's New Deal economic recovery programs sponsored cultural activities of various kinds through the Works Progress Administration. They sought to provide employment for artists and public access to artistic creativity for an American public often struggling to put food on the table. Established in 1935, one such program—the Federal Theatre Project—supported theater professionals across the country under the direction of administrator Hallie Flanagan.[161]

The project opened regional centers in New York, Boston, Chicago, Los Angeles, and New Orleans to bring jobs to unemployed theater professionals and theater to impoverished people everywhere. The initiative mounted thousands of productions across the United States and launched the careers of several rising artists, including Arthur Miller, Orson Welles, John Houseman, and Elia Kazan. Over the course of its operations, the project provided jobs for 12,500 professionals in twenty-eight states and the District of Columbia, reaching an estimated 350,000 audience members each week.

Flanagan created special divisions for radio and cinema, children's theater, foreign language productions, theater, and dance, as well as the Negro Theatre Unit.[162] The Negro Unit, in turn, established programs across the country, including Washington as well as a major presence in New York City.[163] Based at Harlem's Lafayette Theatre, New York's Negro Unit was especially active under the direction of the African American Broadway actress Rose McClendon.[164]

Orson Welles's *Voodoo Macbeth*, which relocated Shakespeare's Scottish play to a Caribbean Island, proved to be one of the Negro Theatre Unit's most successful efforts.[165] Staged in 1936, when Welles was twenty, the production featured the established African American actors Jack Carter, Edna Thomas, Eric Burroughs, and Canada Lee, backed by the renowned Sierra Leonean drummer Asadata Dafora. The show enjoyed a sold-out, ten-week run in Harlem and on Broadway before touring the nation. The tour closed with four final performances in Brooklyn. The production's reception was sensational, with sold-out crowds trying to gain entry to the Broadway run shutting down Seventh Avenue for ten blocks surrounding the Adelphi Theatre on 54th Street.

The Federal Theatre Project's most notorious show proved to be Marc Blitzstein's 1937 musical *The Cradle Will Rock*. After the Works Progress Administration shut down the show during previews four days before opening, Blitzstein, the cast (including Howard Da Silva and Will Geer), and six hundred expectant audience members famously gathered outside the Maxine Elliot Theatre, before walking twenty blocks to the Venice Theatre. There, they performed for free before a standing-room-only crowd to the accompaniment of an upright piano.[166]

All this was too much for congressional appropriators fearful of unleashing communist and leftist ideas on an unsuspecting public at taxpayer expense. As the drumbeat of congressional outrage grew ever louder, Flanagan and her colleagues were hauled before congressional committees to explain themselves. Congressional members criticized 81 of the Project's 830 major productions. Conservative newspapers joined in the hunt, with even a production of *Mother Goose Goes to Town* coming under scrutiny for being too left wing.[167] The Federal Theatre Project shut down precipitously in 1938 after Congress failed to appropriate continued funding.[168]

Despite its short existence, the Federal Theatre Project would leave a powerful legacy for American theater. Coming as it did just as African American theater was beginning to flourish, its importance for Black theater proved especially potent. In New York alone, the Negro Theatre Unit spawned a number of important successor companies, including the Rose McClendon Players and the Negro Dramatists' Laboratory.[169] By the late 1930s and early 1940s, several experimental theaters were operating in Harlem, such as the Rose McClendon Players, American Negro Theatre, Negro Playwrights Company, Du Bois's Krigwa Players, and Langston Hughes's Harlem Suitcase Theater.[170] African American plays also began to make their way to Broadway, where Orson Welles directed a production of Richard Wright's *Native Son* that ran for 97 performances in 1941, and, after a tour, an additional 84 performances in 1942.[171]

Abram Hill's American Negro Theater, among all such companies, proved to be perhaps the era's closest to Gregory's earlier vision of the National Negro Theater.[172] Over the course of the 1940s, the American Negro Theater provided a home for numerous leading African American theater artists, trained future stars such as Sidney Poitier and Harry Belafonte, and produced nineteen plays before closing in 1949.[173] The company achieved its greatest success with Philip Yordan's *Anna Lucasta*, which opened in 1944. This play was adapted from a family saga about a Polish American family, and it moved to Broadway after several weeks in Harlem. Starring Hilda Simms, Canada Lee, and Alice Childress, the production continued on to Washington's National Theatre and to London before finally closing in 1947.

Harlem surpassed other centers of African American theater, including Washington. Washington and Howard University nonetheless remained vibrant and significant contributors to the African American stage. The two centers were tightly interconnected, as they had been when Locke moved back and forth between Washington and New York in the 1920s. Washington would continue to shape the destiny of African American theater even as its role evolved.

Portraying the Soul of a People

Shortly after Locke returned to the Howard University campus, Sterling Allen Brown joined the Howard faculty. The son of a former slave who rose to be a professor of divinity at Howard, Brown graduated from Williams College before earning a master's at Harvard University.[174] He had taught at several colleges and had established himself as an important poet and literary critic by the time he joined Locke at Howard.

Brown shared Locke's interest in theater, and together they sponsored the Howard Players for several years. Brown remained at Howard until his retirement, becoming an ethical and intellectual compass for the school beyond his retirement until his death in January 1989 at the age of eighty-eight. Known for poetry that reflected the cadences of African American music, Brown was a major figure both nationally and locally. He became the District of Columbia's first poet laureate, and he was honored in 1979 when the city set aside a day named in his honor to celebrate his achievements.

Under Locke's and Brown's guidance, the Howard Players remained one of the country's top university college groups, even though Gregory's ambition to establish the National Negro Theatre no longer seemed possible. The future National Medal of Arts laureate and Kennedy Center Honors recipient Ossie Davis was but one of the impressive future theater professionals to pass through the Howard Players during these years, where he became one of Locke's most prominent protégés.[175]

The Howard Players were not alone in making Washington a center of African American theater during the 1920s and 1930s. Howard University was embedded in a dynamic and creative community that participated in the development of African American—and American—artistic reinvention in music, dance, the social sciences, and law, to name just a few areas of accomplishment. Activities in each of these areas rested on lively interaction among African Americans across socioeconomic barriers imposed by racial segregation. These creative tensions extended to the stage. Two particularly notable figures—Willis Richardson and Georgia Douglas Johnson—personified the inspiration that was to be found beyond the Howard campus.

Willis Richardson was a seminal figure in the history of African American dramatic theater.[176] Though he is now often overlooked, he was a pathbreaking playwright embedded in the blue-collar workaday of most Washingtonians. Richardson attracted the attention of a biographer, Christine Rauchfuss Gray, who boldly promoted his work.[177]

In 1899, when Richardson was nine, leaders of North Carolina's White Democratic Party conspired to overthrow the legitimately elected Black-and-White city government in his hometown of Wilmington. This revolt became the only successful armed coup d'état against an elected government in US history. Drawing on White anger over the city's growing diversity, local and state leaders vilified local officials, and unleashed "Red Shirts" to terrorize local African Americans and their "sympathizers." On the morning of November 10, White gangs rampaged through the city, burning Black businesses and homes, lynching community leaders, and running duly elected local officials out of town. Many African Americans hid out in the swamps north of the city for days. In the end, up to 300 Blacks were killed and 2,000 Blacks left town for good.[178] After taking some time to consider options, Richardson's family followed. [179]

The Richardsons landed in Washington, where young Willis attended public schools, eventually graduating from the elite M Street (Dunbar) High School (studying English with Angeline Grimké).[180] An excellent student, Richardson won a partial scholarship from Howard University. Requiring additional income to survive, he declined this scholarship, instead taking a job with the US Bureau of Engraving and Printing. He worked at the bureau until he retired forty-three years later, marrying and supporting a family household that included his wife and their three children.[181] He died in 1977, after having spent the final two decades of his life trying unsuccessfully to attract attention to his plays.[182]

Theater remained Richardson's passion, and he looked for every opportunity to be involved with the life surrounding the stage. He continued to be particularly concerned over the absence of serious dramatic works by African American authors. "Is it true," he wrote in 1919 in a questioning that remained central to his suspicions, "that there is coming into existence in America a Negro Drama which at some future day may equal in excellence the American Negro Music? If the signs of the times do not point to such a thing, we must change their direction and make them point the way; we must have a Negro drama."[183]

Richardson became a focal point for productions by the Bureau of Engraving and Printing's drama club. Of greater lasting significance, he wrote prolifically, penning forty-nine plays (largely during the 1920s).[184] When Raymond O'Neill's Ethiopian Art Players brought his *The Chip Woman's Fortune* (1923) to New York, Richardson became the first African American playwright to have a dramatic work performed on Broadway.[185]

Richardson advocated the development of a theatrical repertoire written by African Americans about African Americans and performed by African Americans, so as to portray "the soul of a people, and the soul of this people is truly worth showing."[186] Like Gregory and many others of the era, Richardson saw the Irish National Theater as a model, because it empowered Irish playwrights to tell the story of their people unfiltered through the pens of non-Irish playwrights. He believed that African Americans, like the Irish, had developed their own way of speaking English, which reflected their own spirit. This distinctive elocution could bring new life to the classics written by others.

"Sweetness of the Negro tones," he suggested, "is so well suited to the poetry of Shakespeare." These tenets animated Richardson's plays throughout his career. He prepared the way for later landmark works in Black American drama, such as August Wilson's commanding *Pittsburgh Cycle* (1982–2005) of ten plays tracking the life of African Americans in the Steel City's Hill District.

As his biographer Gray observed, Richardson's plays were different from what was being written at the time by other African American playwrights. For Gray,

> protest plays, such as those written by Richardson's colleagues, validated the structures of oppression. In Richardson's plays, the tension springs from the family and displays the effect on the Black community when Blacks themselves do not work together. . . . In focusing on Black-on-Black relations, Richardson put at the core of his plays characters entangled in conflicts with members of their community or family. Parents, aunts, cousins, visiting relatives, aging neighbors, grandparents, adopted children, boarders and lovers fill his stage.[187]

Portraying Daily Domestic Life

Richardson, over the course of his career, published poems, essays, and plays in both leading White (*Carolina Magazine*) and Black (*Crisis*, *Opportunity*) literary journals. In 1931, his play *Compromise* appeared in Hungary. His works have been included in major anthologies of early African American plays.[188] His first produced play— *The Deacon's Awakening*, in 1921—was reprised in the 2010s in New York and elsewhere.

Richardson struggled to sustain his writing career while holding down his full-time job at the Bureau of Engraving and Printing. He remained perhaps closer to the daily life of many African Americans than his contemporaries at Howard and in Harlem. As Canadian writer Robertson Davies mused in 1989 in an observation that applies to Richardson, "The writer, if he is a serious writer, man or woman, tragedian or comedian, writer on epic themes like Tolstoy or on apparently sight themes, like Jane Austin, is one who brings great and important things for the consideration of his tribe." [189]

The U Street NW Washington community of which Howard is a part is noteworthy for the social propinquity of varied social classes forced to live on top of one another by segregation. The neighborhood's substantial influences on African American and American music, literature, jurisprudence, and political protest often rest on chance encounters among Black residents, whose lives otherwise had little in common. From leading constitutional law authorities encountering angry barbers to conservatory-trained composers hearing the sounds emanating from pool halls, U Street became a vital setting for some of the most far-reaching changes in American life, precisely because it remained a mixing bowl of otherwise disparate inspirations.[190]

Richardson was writing for an African American audience, and his plays generally fall into two categories. Many of his works are seemingly modest educational accounts of meaningful moments in African American history that are crafted to be accessible to community, school, and church theater groups in performances for student audiences. Such plays often appeared in Carter G. Woodson's *The Journal of Negro History*, or were published by Woodson's Association Publishers in concert with the Association for the Study of Negro Life and History. Richardson also published a number of children's plays in W. E. B. Du Bois's youth magazine *The Brownies' Book*. These scripts are more complex than they may at first appear. Richardson purposefully wrote plays about seminal historical events calibrated for classroom and drama club use.

In 1930, Woodson published Richardson's best-known work—the collection *Plays and Pageants from the Life of the Negro*—with an explicit educational purpose in mind. This landmark anthology contained Richardson's introductory essay setting forth his goal of compiling a collection of works written primarily for use in schools. These remarks were followed by the scripts for a dozen plays and pageants, including works by Thelma Myrtle Duncan, Maud Cuney-Hare, John Matheus, May Miller, Inzes M. Burke, Dorothy C. Guinn, Frances Gunner, and Edward J. McCoo, as well as four of his own works. The handsomely produced volume included striking block prints by the Howard University faculty member and master printmaker James Lesesne Wells accompanied by passages from the poetry of Paul Laurence Dunbar and James Weldon Johnson.[191] In 1935, Richardson joined May Miller in editing a second anthology of history plays, *Negro History in Thirteen Plays*.[192]

Richardson's plays examining African American life achieved recognition at the time. He won playwriting awards and prizes, including the *Crisis* journal's Drama Award and the Edith Schwab Cup. His works were included in Locke's *The New Negro*, and they were performed around the country. Four of his more successful plays—*The Chip Woman's Fortune* (1923), *Mortgaged* (1924), *The Broken Banjo* (1925), and *Compromise* (1925)—demonstrate how he sought to bring the lives of ordinary African Americans to theater audiences.[193]

The Chip Woman's Fortune focuses on the everyday challenges facing urban African Americans at the outset of the twentieth century.[194] Aunt Nancy has taken a room in the home of Silas and Liza and their daughter Emma. When Silas loses his job, he and Liza face the prospect of defaulting on a Victrola that they purchased on time payments. The Victrola is their one small pleasure, as it brings music into their world. Suspecting that Nancy—who collects chips of coal off the street so that the family can have heat—is hoarding money, Silas confronts the old woman. Nancy, it turns out, has been saving money as best she can so that her son Jim would have a start on a new life once he is released from prison. Nancy and Jim come up with the funds to pay off Silas and Liza's debt just as the store comes to repossess the Victrola. The play ends with everyone dancing to jazz recordings being played on the saved Victrola.

W. E. B. Du Bois arranged for Raymond O'Neill and Mrs. Sherwood Anderson to produce *The Chip Woman's Fortune* in cooperation with the Ethiopian Art Players.[195] The work moved from Chicago for a two-week run at the Howard Theatre and on to Harlem's Lafayette Theatre.[196] Drawing ever larger audiences, the production transferred to the Frazee Theater on New York's 42nd Street for a two-week run, together with Shakespeare's *The Comedy of Errors* and Oscar Wilde's *Salomé*.[197] Percy Hammond, reviewing the production for the *New York Tribune*, found Richardson's work to be "a deft little comedy, engaging real persons in an honest and sentimental situation."[198] John Corbin similarly praised the work for the *New York Times*.[199] The play may well have enjoyed an extended run if O'Neill had not left town, leaving the actors stranded and angry audience members demanding their money back.[200]

As already noted, this Broadway production enabled Gregory to convince Howard University president J. Stanley Durkee to permit the Howard Players to mount a production of Richardson's *Mortgaged*. His 1924 student production became the first play by an African American author to be staged at Howard.[201] Locke included this play in his landmark 1925 anthology *The New Negro: An Interpretation*.

In this work—which was presented by various professional and nonprofessional groups around the country—Richardson juxtaposed two contrasting brothers representing conflicting aspirations among educated African Americans. John Fields, a widower chemist who is struggling financially to cover his son's tuition at Harvard, is contrasted with his brother Tom, who maintains an inflated life style with lucrative real estate deals. In the end, one of John's discoveries is purchased by a major corporation, thus saving him from penury, while Tom is humiliated as a slum lord. Though contrived, the story exposed tensions within the African American middle class between devotion to racial uplift and avarice.[202]

The Broken Banjo and *Compromise* became staples of W. E. B. Du

Bois's Krigwa Players as they performed in New York and else-where around the country.[203] *The Banjo Player* earned Richardson prestigious prizes and became one of his best-known works. The play tells the story of family betrayal as two impoverished newly-weds, Matt and Emma, fight over Matt's preoccupation with play-ing his banjo.[204] Tensions arise when Emma's brother Sam and cous-in Adam show up. A family fight breaks out when Matt discovers that Sam and Adam had broken his beloved banjo while horsing around with it. Sam announces during the brawl that he knows Matt had murdered old man Shelton years before. Emma retrieves her life savings from underneath the mattress and convinces her husband to escape before the police arrive. Sam shows up with the sheriff before Matt can make his run for it, leaving Emma crying alone as the curtain falls.[205]

Compromise represented one of the few times Richardson brings White characters onstage. In this instance, a Black family's malev-olent White neighbors eventually bring about four tragedies, for which they are never penalized. The action explores the various ways in which Blacks must compromise with Whites as they make their way through the world.[206] Richardson, always protective of the rights to his works, became upset when Locke produced the play without his permission. The resulting falling out may have undercut Richardson's future ability to see his works staged and republished.[207] As already mentioned, *Compromise* was published and performed in Hungary in 1931.[208]

Life's obligations and failing health overtook Richardson's play-writing ambitions by the end of the 1930s. He and his work faded from view.[209] He devoted his retirement years to trying to republish and restage various plays, only to be disappointed by an uninter-ested theater public that found his once pace-setting works now dated. As the years passed, he increasingly became a footnote—the first African American to have a dramatic play staged on Broad-way—until his biographer, Gray, set out to systematically recover his work and bring new recognition to his life and achievements.[210]

Saturday Night Salons

Richardson was a regular member of another Washington insti-tution, albeit informal, that would exert lasting influence over the shape of African American and American culture in the years ahead: Georgia Douglas Johnson's "Saturday Nighters." For a decade or so beginning in 1926 (or perhaps as early as 1922), the playwright, poet, and composer Georgia Douglas Johnson regularly hosted the country's leading African American literati for dinner and discussion at her home at 1461 S Street NW.[211]

Johnson was born in Atlanta in 1880, and spent her childhood in Rome, Georgia. After graduating from Atlanta University's Normal School, she attended the Oberlin Conservatory of Music. In 1903, she married the Atlanta lawyer and local Republican notable Henry Lincoln Johnson. The couple moved to Washington when President William Howard Taft appointed Henry as DC's recorder of deeds in 1910. The couple had two sons, and Henry preferred that Georgia devote her attention to homemaking rather than pursuing her song, short story, play, and poetry writing.

However, despite her husband's misgivings, Georgia taught music, became an organist at a local Congregational church, and began to submit her writing to various newspapers and literary magazines. Beginning in 1916, she published four volumes of poetry, including the well-received *The Heart of a Woman*. When Robert died in 1925, Georgia took a job at the Department of Labor to support herself and her two teenage sons. After losing that position in 1934, she worked as a temporary clerk at various offices around town.

Georgia's wide-ranging interests and passionate activism could not be contained. By the 1930s, she had become an outspoken advocate for the antilynching movement. She regularly published her poetry, plays, and activist essays, and, for several years, she wrote a syndicated weekly newspaper column "Homely Philosophy" for some two dozen African American newspapers around the country. She died in 1966.[212]

Shortly after her husband's death, Johnson began inviting local African American intellectuals over for dinner on Saturday nights. These gatherings became a much-sought-after invitation for anyone who wanted to matter in the world swirling around the New Negro (Harlem) Renaissance. After dinner, the crowd would discuss the latest political and artistic challenges of the previous week. Regulars at this gathering over the next decade included

W. E. B. Du Bois, Langston Hughes, Jean Toomer, Mary Church Terrell, Carter Woodson, James Weldon Johnson, Zora Neale Hurston, Aaron Douglas, and Willis Richardson.[213]

Some evenings, the diners would divide up into smaller groups to focus on specific themes. From time to time, several playwrights went off to a room to discuss how to advance African American theater. These playwrights included Johnson herself, Richardson, Marita Bonner, Eulalie Spence, May Miller, Randolph Edmonds, Carrie Clifford, and Edward Christopher Williams. All were involved to some extent in Du Bois's little theater initiative, the Krigwa Players.[214] Others—such as Zora Neale Hurston and Langston Hughes—might join in if they happened to attend that night. Hughes, in particular, was already setting his sights on Broadway (the first of Hughes's several New York Plays—*Mulatto* (1935)—appeared at the time, setting all records for a drama written by an African American).[215]

As one of this country's most significant literary salons, Johnson's Saturday Nighters shaped her own writing as well as that of Richardson and the other participants. They kept Washington deeply involved in the New Negro Renaissance even as that movement's center of gravity shifted to Harlem. Their influence spread throughout Washington's African American community and, in various ways, shaped the future of the Howard Players.

The Howard Players Move Forward

The poet, folklorist, and critic Sterling A. Brown arrived at Howard in 1929 after teaching appointments at Lincoln and Fisk universities. He would remain on campus for the next four decades—with visiting appointments at some of the country's leading universities along the way.[216]

Brown had strong ties to Washington, having grown up in suburban Maryland and graduated from Dunbar High School before heading off to Williams College for his undergraduate years. He grew to have a powerful influence over Howard's development and mentored some of its most illustrious graduates. His essays on the White reception of Black Americans—such as his 1933 essay "Negro Character as Seen by White Authors," cited above—made

seminal contributions to the redefinition of race in American letters.[217]

Brown teamed up with Locke in working with the Howard Players. His deep philosophical engagement with the African American experience was readily evident in his own poetry and essays.
Like Locke, Brown saw African Americans as essential to defining
the American experience, and he promoted the writing—and staging—of works that told their story. He saw the role of the Players
as preparing Howard students for careers on and around the stage.

James W. Butcher Jr.—another Dunbar graduate, a Howard
student, and a holder of degrees from the universities of Illinois
and Iowa—joined Locke and Brown in their work with the Howard
Players.[218] Arriving on campus in 1934 (and remaining until 1976),
Butcher came to Howard after having led Spelman College's drama
department in Atlanta. He served as director of Howard's Office of
Theatrical Productions and held a number of other positions at the
university, including a term as the associate dean of the College of
Fine Arts. Deeply committed to the development of African American and American theater, Butcher was founder and director of
the Negro Repertory Players of Washington and cofounder of the
Washington Repertory Players. He is credited with directing more
than a hundred plays of various genres during his time at Howard.

Under Locke, Brown, and Butcher, the Howard Players performed between two and four plays each year throughout the
1930s, including works by African Americans about African Americans—such as Willis Richardson's *Compromise* (1932), Eulalie Spence's *Undertow* (1932), Georgia Douglas Johnson's *Blueblood* (1933),
and James Butcher's *Milk and Honey* (1934)—and plays by White
authors about African Americans—such as Paul Green's *In Abraham's Bosom* (1929, 1933) and Ridgely Torrence's *Rider of the Dream*
(1935)—as well as a selection of popular works and classics unre-
lated to American race relations—such as Lord Dunsany's *The Lost
Silk Hat* (1933), Henrik Ibsen's *Hedda Gabler* (1933, 1934), Anton
Chekov's *The Proposal* (1936), and Emlyn Williams's *A Murder Has
Been Arranged* (1938).[219]

The trend toward presenting a mix of African American sub-
jects and works from the classical humanist tradition continued after Owen Dodson joined the faculty in 1940, and he was followed

by Anne Cooke (Reed) in 1944. Dodson and Cooke shared graduate school experiences at the Yale Drama School (Dodson earned an MFA in 1939, and Cooke a PhD in 1944). Both had worked together on various projects in Atlanta while Cooke was teaching at Atlanta University's Spelman College.[220]

Cooke joined Atlanta University's English Department at the end of the 1930s, and she launched that school's six-week summer theater festival. She worked closely with Du Bois and others to promote large-scale pageants about African and African American history and, with her students, she staged several African American plays (including works by Richardson). She frequently chose to produce purposefully difficult theater classics to elevate her students' dramatic craft.

Her efforts caught the attention of John D. Rockefeller's General Education Board, which had been established to improve the qualifications of the faculties of southern Black universities by offering scholarships to leading northern schools. She went off to Yale and, having completed her doctoral studies, joined the faculty of the Hampton Institute before moving to Howard in 1944, where she would remain until her retirement in 1958.

Dodson may be best remembered as a poet, having won wide recognition for his verse (including invitations to the White House, several honorary doctorates of letters, and any number of prestigious grants for his literary achievements). He was a considerable playwright as well, eventually penning thirty-seven plays and operas, of which twenty-seven were produced, including two at the Kennedy Center.[221]

Born to a large and struggling family in Brooklyn on the eve of World War I, Dodson retained a deep connection with New York City throughout his life (dying after his retirement from Howard of a heart attack at the age of sixty-eight while living on Manhattan's Upper West Side).[222] After time at Bates College, Dodson earned his master's in fine arts from Yale in 1939, and in 1940 he joined the Howard faculty, where he would become chair of the Drama Department.[223]

In 1939, Dodson landed a job substituting for Cooke at Spelman while she was on leave. Shocked by southern segregation, he spent his time in Atlanta among the African American intellectuals who had formed a community surrounding Du Bois. Dodson moved to Virginia's Hampton Institute at the end of his appointment in Atlanta, and from there, he went to Howard.[224] Simultaneously, he began directing in New York, primarily with the American Negro Theatre, commencing a pattern of working in New York and elsewhere while based in Washington at Howard.[225]

Dodson steadily established himself in Washington. He rented an apartment from the playwright May Miller that happened to abut Georgia Douglas Johnson's house across a back alley.[226] He started to write theater reviews of shows around Washington and directed for off-campus theater companies.[227]

The proud—perhaps arrogant—Dodson had an at times tetchy relationship with some longtime Howard notables. Gregory, for one, believed that his younger successor had snubbed him unforgivably. The task of mending bridges in such circumstances often fell to Sterling Brown.[228] In 1961, Dodson oversaw the opening of a new campus theater named after Ira Aldridge.[229] As discussed in chapter 4, the Kennedy Center celebrated his career in 1975 with a production of *Owen's Song* based on his poetry.[230]

The Howard Players' production of Dodson's *Bayou Legend* (1948) and Miller's *All My Sons* (1948) caught the attention of Washington's leading White critics (Richard Coe of the *Washington Post*, and Jay Carmody of the *Evening Star*), firmly reestablishing the Players as a major theatrical company for the city.[231] A handful of White graduate students from nearby Catholic University began making their way to Howard at about this time to study with both Dodson and Cooke.

Under Cooke and Dodson's tutelage, well into the late twentieth century, Howard University trained leaders of the American stage, such as Debbie Allen, Richard Wesley, Roxie Roker, Charles Brown, Imamu Amiri Baraka, and Earle Hyman.[232] The Howard Players of the era turned to productions of important new Americana drama—including Tennessee Williams's *The Glass Menagerie* (1947) and Arthur Miller's *All My Sons* (1948)—as well as modern European classics, such as the production of Ibsen's *The Wild Duck* that would catch the attention of Norwegian diplomats in 1948.[233]

Moving in Beauty

Throughout the same period when the Howard Players were defining African American theater, Howard University and Washington were simultaneously centers for the emergence of African American concert dance. Although theater and dance remained distinct enterprises, both quests unfolded simultaneously, at times informing one another, and at other moments, blending into a single enterprise. The story of the university's and city's contributions to the American stage would remain incomplete without an acknowledgment of their rich legacy in the world of dance.

Drawing on the work of Iantha Tucker, the Washington dance scholar Tamara Lizette Brown notes that there are three basic perspectives of Blacks who are practitioners of dance. "Those that support a nationalistic agenda," Brown writes,

> recognize that Black dance has roots in African dance forms; is transferred through various dance genres; and is created and performed by Blacks for a Black audience. An inclusive or integrationist agenda also places African dance as the basis for Black dance. However, this dance does not have to be created or performed by Blacks for a Black audience. Finally, there are those who are in denial about the transferal of culture and state. I am not a Black dancer. I am a dancer who happens to be Black.[234]

The development of African American concert dance in Washington contains practitioners of all three approaches.

Maryrose Reeves Allen was the pivotal figure in the development of African American concert dance at Howard. Allen came to the university in 1925 to direct the physical education program for women. An early advocate of advancing Black females' sense of self through the exploration of the unique aspects of the Black body, Allen viewed rhythmic movement as an essential component of the body aesthetics of African American women. In 1927, she established the Howard University Dance Group, which evolved into the Howard University Dance Ensemble.[235]

Allen was joined at the time by Violet Warfield (who had earned degrees from Brown, Boston, and Columbia universities) together with Leonie Burnett (who had studied at Temple and Columbia). Before coming to Howard, Burnett had taught at the Tuskegee Institute and at Alcorn A&M, where she studied African games and dances. Frances Haddock arrived with degrees from the University of Pittsburgh and Wellesley College, ready to contribute to developing a vibrant African-oriented dance program at Howard.[236]

Working together, Reeves's new dance ensemble merged the physical education aspects of the department's curriculum with fine art objectives. As Brown tells the story, "Most physical education majors even remotely interested in dance participated in the dance club."[237] The program produced professional dancers and dance instructors. Of particular note, Brown adds, the university dancers frequently sought out nonacademic sources of African American dance down the hill at the Howard Theatre and in the clubs along U Street NW, adding a distinctive vitality to their formal performances.[238]

After World War II, the expatriate German dancer and choreographer Erika Thimey joined the Howard faculty. Thimey had participated in some of the earliest efforts in Germany to create a modern dance form that would break through the restrictive boundaries of classical ballet. She came to the United States in the early 1930s, teaching in Chicago and Boston. While in New England, she performed with Arthur Fiedler and the Boston Pops, among many appearances on US stages.[239]

Martha Graham had been teaching at Washington's King-Smith Studio School during the late 1930s. When the commute between New York and Washington became too much, Graham turned the position over to Thimey. Once in Washington, Thimey opened her own studios (first near Dupont Circle, and later in Georgetown), and she taught in the DC Public Schools as well as at parks and recreation centers. She later observed that "being at Howard taught me so much. In the beginning of my time there, the attitude that many Americans had was that a White person who surrounded herself with African Americans must be crazy, or a radical of some sort. I knew that I was not crazy, and I knew I was not a radical. I knew I was having a wonderful experience."[240]

As Allen continued to develop the dance program, her performances became an integral part of various university celebrations and festivals. Her efforts were formalized by the creation of the Modern Dance Group within the Department of Physical Education for Women during the early 1950s.[241] This group began performing up and down the East Coast. In 1952, the ensemble performed a joint concert with dancers from Sarah Lawrence College, Adelphi College, and Bennett College at the Henry Street Playhouse in New York.[242] The group danced locally with the National Symphony, the Jewish Community Program, and the Lafayette Square USO Club.[243] Reviewing the troupe's appearance at an annual National Symphony Orchestra children's concert, *Washington Post* critic Paul Hume exclaimed, "Yesterday was even better than usual. In addition to the juvenile joy that breaks loose when the whole orchestra leaves the stage and moves out into the audience, there was real, live dancing."[244]

In a report to university administrators around 1953, Allen wrote, "The dance became the herald of the ideal of self-realization through fine movement and the dance group the medium through which this idea could be expressed. The dance likewise paved the way for the development of physical movement to such a point of artistic realization that there could be applied to it the criteria and designation of 'Fine Art.'"[245]

Graduates of Allen's program populated dance education programs throughout the Washington area as well as the nation, and included many prominent figures in various forms of dance, such as Debbie Allen, Chuck Davis, Melvin Deal, Ulysses Dove, and George Fainson. Allen promoted the worth of the individual and of being Black. She remained active in the Howard and Washington dance communities after her retirement in 1967, until her death in 1992.[246]

The Howard dance program became more deeply embedded in the wider Washington African American community than the Howard Players were; and dance was even more entrenched than drama. During the 1930s, Mabel Jones Freeman pioneered dance education through the District's Recreation Department, public schools, and the Phyllis Wheatley YMCA. By the 1940s, she choreographed for the National Negro Opera Company based in Washington.[247]

Former Howard dance student Bernice Hammond studied

dance at the Phyllis Wheatley YMCA growing up in Washington, before heading off to New York because no local White instructors would teach African American students in Jim Crow Washington.[248] Once in New York, Hammond sought out Russian teachers who had studied with Mikhail Fokine and Adolph Bolm, and had danced with Anna Pavlova. In 1949, she formed Ballet Africana Americana, and opened her own school in Washington. Those efforts eventually led to the creation of the Northeast Academy of Dance on Benning Road NE, which she continued to direct until 2012. She died in 2016 at the age of ninety-eight.[249]

Doris Jones was another Howard dance student who had a profound influence on both Washington and national African American dance. Jones grew up in Massachusetts and made her way to New York and Washington in the 1930s because she had never seen a Black ballet dancer.[250] After receiving an undergraduate degree from Spelman College, she earned a master's from Howard and completed course work for a PhD at Catholic University. In 1940, she opened the Doris W. Jones School of Dance to offer African American youth in a segregated Washington an opportunity to learn dance. She brought in leading choreographers from New York to teach her pupils, and she took her top students to the School of American Ballet to work with George Balanchine.

The school thrived, changing its name to the Jones Haywood School of Ballet in the 1950s and eventually spawning the semiprofessional Capitol Ballet, which performed for a decade and a half before closing in the early 1980s.[251] The Jones Haywood School continues to train young Washington dance students who are looking to follow in the steps of such illustrious alumnae as Chita Rivera, Louis Johnson, Hinton Battle, Sylvester Campbell, George Faison, Renee Robinson, and Charles Augins. Jones died in 2006 at the age of ninety-two.[252] These achievements in the world of dance – as discussed in chapter 4 -- would meld with efforts to create a Black theater during the 1960s and 1970s.

A Scandinavian Prince

The 1950s were a time of change for Howard University, the city, and African American theater. Desegregation enabled African

American high school students to move into mainstream universities; African American Washingtonians to move from around U Street NW; Howard faculty to move to major research universities; and African American entertainers to move to formerly segregated clubs downtown.[253] Cultural tastes changed. The Howard Theatre booked rhythm & blues, rock & roll, and stand-up comics rather than putting on diverse programming that would include a dramatic play from time to time. Cinema and television shattered the audience for live theater.[254] African American theater was on the brink of a revolutionary radicalization—to be unleashed a few years later by Imamu Amiri Baraka's (LeRoi Jones) *The Dutchman*.[255]

The Howard Players were never marginal to the era's African American theatrical development. Baraka studied theater history and philosophy at Howard in the early 1950s. Robert Hooks, a native Washingtonian with strong ties to the Howard Players, gave a standout lead performance in *The Dutchman*'s premier at New York's Cherry Lane Theater in 1964. In 1955, Dodson produced the first performance of James Baldwin's play *The Amen Corner*.[256] And the future playwright Joseph A. Walker—who became the first African American writer to win a Tony Award for *The River Niger* (others, including Lorraine Hansberry, had been nominated)—played the role of Luke in Baldwin's play.[257]

Dodson later directed one of the early performances of Baldwin's controversial *Blues for Mr. Charlie*.[258] The *Washington Post* reviewer, Geoffrey A. Wolff, found that the "agit-prop mannerisms" of Baldwin's play and Dodson's direction "shout and stamp its untruth."[259] Even Wolff, however, acknowledged that the predominantly African American audience reacted far more enthusiastically than he had, at a time—November 1965—when Washington audiences were becoming ever more polarized by race.

Major figures in late-twentieth-century American theater—such as Walker, Ossie Davis, Debbie Allen, and Phylicia Rashad—made their way through the Howard drama program during these years. The story had not ended; nor would it, as evidenced by such contemporary stage and screen stars who learned their craft at Howard as Anthony Anderson, Marlon Wayans, and Chadwick Boseman.

Thomas Montgomery Gregory's dream of founding the National Negro Theatre at Howard University never came to fruition.

Yet the legacy that he, Alain Locke, Sterling Brown, Owen Dodson, Anne Cooke, Marie Moore-Forrest, and Maryrose Reeves Allen built has had a deep, lasting, and profound impact on American theater. Their achievement is one of a community that lies outside the standard accounts of the American stage.

A summer evening's entertainment in July 1951 captures Dodson's loftier achievements at Howard in an event that should have passed into Washington—and American—theater lore (and certainly would have, if the major protagonists had been White). Dodson had admired the work of Earle Hyman, a teenage actor with New York's American Negro Theater. He seized on the opportunity presented by a scheduled Summer School production to invite Hyman to take a turn with the Howard Players in a production of *Hamlet*. Many White critics questioned the ability of African American performers to master the range of emotions required to stage Shakespeare. Dodson and Hyman set out to prove them wrong.[260]

Dodson pulled out all the stops for the production. He hired David Amram, then a student at George Washington University, to write a ground-breaking musical score for the performance. Amram, who would become one of the leading American composers of the late twentieth century, was performing with top-flight jazz musicians around town even as he was holding down a chair playing the French horn with the National Symphony. The Czech conductor and musical educator George Schick (who would later join the conducting staff of the Metropolitan Opera) served as the production's percussionist. Frederick Wilkerson, the noted voice coach, played the King. American Negro Theater actors Austin Briggs-Hall and Claire Leyba played Polonius and Gertrude, while Carolyn Hill Stewart, who already had Broadway credits to her name, was Ophelia.[261]

Dodson and Hyman reached out to Sir John Gielgud when the British actor was on tour in Washington with a production of Christopher Frye's *The Lady's Not for Burning*. When Gielgud discovered that Washington's Jim Crow segregation prevented him from having lunch at his hotel with Dodson and Hyman, he joined them at the Greyhound Bus Station instead. Gielgud spent a day working with the Howard Players, and he coached Hyman as best he could from a distance throughout the young actor's preparations for the role of the Danish Prince.

Operating with a miniscule budget, Owen spread the word as best he could. Avoiding expensive printing, he made sure that the production was the talk of the African American community. He later complained that, during a number of radio interviews, he was constantly asked whether such a play was too ambitious for African American actors. Owen bitterly complained that "no goddamed body here thinks Negros can do anything but [n-word] parts."[262]

Students made the costumes as best they could and, even at that, still ran out of money. They found a solution by having the men perform almost bare-chested. When a professor from Carnegie Tech complained that the men were "wandering around with their tits hanging out," Dodson responded that "we designed the costumes to make them feel free."[263]

Hyman had perfected the ability to fall straight on his face, or tumble backward without hurting himself. The audience gasped when, after the famous Ghost had left the stage, he simply collapsed. Actors entered anyway they could, given the limitations of the stage, walking in from the back, the sides, and even proclaiming from the top levels of the audience. Hyman changed his costume from black to pink, which reportedly sent a shiver through the audience.

In one memorable moment, Wilkerson tried to flee the stage as Hyman launched into a sword attack with more enthusiasm than caution. Owen pushed him back onstage, where he was able to complete his death scene. The play closed as the extras carrying torches lifted Hamlet's body offstage to the reverberations of Schick's drums. And this was all for a run that lasted only from July 18 until July 21.

The *Washington Post* drama critic Richard L. Coe, writing for the *New York Times*, spotted Gielgud's influence on Hyman and noted that the "nunnery scene" was beautifully played. "While all the voices have that variety of accent common to American classical readings," Coe lamented, "Mr. Hyman's has impressive power and command which stood him well in the long role. Considering the very few opportunities a Negro actor has at this role, he shows surprising mastery of its facets and his ability to put his intellectual concept into action is impressive."[264]

The *Evening Star*'s Jay Carmody was more honest about his

own prejudices.[265] "On the surface," he began, "it is lamentably mismatching play and players when any save the most gifted performers take on 'Hamlet.' It is tradition that in any such case, both the greatest dramas and the most reckless cast shall lose with the audience a third loser. Well, tradition is being pleasurably interrupted at Howard University this week where 'Hamlet' is being played by a company of professional performers under the perceptive and artful direction of Owen Dodson."

After noting the influence of Gielgud on the production, Carmody praised Hyman. "Hyman's Prince is a neurotic with a voice that makes a ranging music of Hamlet's agonized indecision. The Negro actor is a lithe, youthful and dynamic figure who never loses awareness that his distraught prince has a singularly sensitive mind. He moves through the role with an arresting sureness of touch that is the play's best feature." After admiring Stewart's Ophelia, he praised the costumes and lighting. Wrapping up, Carmody noted that "the Howard U. 'Hamlet' will close with tonight's performance but it will be remembered by those fortunate enough to see it as the best production in the school's history."

The production had surpassed any expectation. Sold-out crowds streamed into Spaulding Hall each night, with perhaps as many as five hundred people turned away at the door the last evening. The *Washington Afro-American*'s Lois Taylor speculated that the production might even make its way to Broadway.[266] But this was not to be.

Dodson had many years left at Howard when the curtain came down on his *Hamlet*; and, Hyman had decades of superior performances on stage, film, and television. Best remembered for his role of Cliff Huxtable's father Russell in television's *Bill Cosby Show*, Hyman would have plentiful opportunities over an illustrious career to demonstrate the power that African American actors bring to the emotional range contained within Shakespeare's most magnificent characters. Dodson's *Hamlet* reveals how much Montgomery Gregory—and all his partners along the way—created a national Negro presence on the dramatic stage, even if their national Negro theater never materialized.

Confronting Racist Stage Traditions from Abroad

The Howard Players' success during these years was not limited to the city, or even the nation. On August 31, 1949, former first lady Eleanor Roosevelt made her way to the SS *Stavergerfjord* to see off twenty-one Howard University students and faculty leaving on a European sojourn. All members of the Howard University Players, the group was embarking on a lengthy tour of Norway, Sweden, Denmark, and Germany that would earn them rave reviews from some of Europe's most prominent critics. Their expedition included fifty-nine performances in nine cities as the troupe offered Henrik Ibsen's *The Wild Duck* as well as Dorothy and duBose Heyward's *Mamba's Daughters*.

The tour took shape after an offering of Ibsen's play on campus the previous autumn. Several officials from the Norwegian Embassy who had been in attendance declared—as several critics would during the tour—the performance to rank among the most authentic offered by a non-Norwegian company. The diplomats asked Professor Anne Cooke if the company could make the trip. Cooke, at the time, thought the question a pleasant gesture and was surprised when she realized the offer was a serious one.[267]

The proposed tour caught the rising tensions of the era throughout Europe between West and East, exemplifying an emerging American interest in cultural diplomacy.[268] Embraced by the highest levels of the Truman administration, the Howard thespians received funds from the Norwegian Parliament and the US Department of State, with logistical assistance from the US High Command in Europe. The Howard Players' 1949 tour earned immediate historical significance as the first effort by the US government to send cultural troupes abroad to gain friends in the developing global struggle with the Soviet Union. Their success convinced Washington decisionmakers to invest heavily in such tours throughout the remainder of the Cold War.

Faculty members Cooke, Butcher, and Dodson used the nineday transatlantic crossing to rehearse for the grueling schedule ahead. Immediately after settling in with Norwegian host families upon landing in Bergen, officials whisked the group to the US Embassy for the first of many receptions, this one hosted by Ambassador Charles Ulrick Bay for Crown Prince Olaf, his wife Marta, and their two daughters. The Players quickly hit the stage at Oslo's Det Nye Teater, where the overflowing audience greeted the company's first performance of Ibsen with eight curtain calls.[269]

The tour continued to Denmark, Sweden, and Germany, alternating Ibsen's *The Wild Duck* with the Heywards's *Mamba's Daughters* before sold-out theaters, while receiving curious-to-rave reviews. Christen Fribert told Danish readers that "the young actors have wanted to emphasize that they are not professional actors and this is very sensible because they are not. But they are clever young people who evidently love to play and they devote themselves to their parts with great enthusiasm;" while Paul Gjesdahl reported in Oslo that "the American *Wild Duck* was a solid, intelligent, and cultured performance—one had to admit the assurance and the sensitiveness those Negro amateurs possessed." By contrast, Henrik Neiiendam found it "difficult to judge the Howard Players' performances last night because it is based upon a temperament and a tradition we don't quite understand."[270] The tour came to a close after Thanksgiving dinner at the US Army base in Kitzingen, Germany.

Cast members Graham Brown, Roxie Roker, Zaida Coles, William Brown, Marilyn Berry, and Shauneille Perry went on to enjoy successful theatrical careers.[271] Berry later remarked that "we were treated so dearly by the Norwegians. At that time, meat was rationed; they had it only once a week. They gave up their stamps so we could have meat. The trip and those people saved me from ever being a racist."[272] Within months of the Players' return, the US Congress passed legislation enabling the US Information Service to send American dance, film, art, music, and theater to the world.[273]

The Players' 1949 tour marked the culmination of a three-decade effort to elevate the university's campus drama club into a major force defining the African American presence on stage. Initiated by Gregory, and several others, thirty years before, this process accelerated after Locke's return to campus in 1918.

As the European tour suggests, the story of the Howard Players transcends the boundaries of a single university's grounds. Several of the contributors to the story have become icons of twentieth-century African America—including several whose visages now appear on US postage stamps, such as Anna Julia Cooper, W. E. B. Du Bois, Langston Hughes, Zora Neale Hurston, James Weldon Johnson, Ernest E. Just, and Carter G. Woodson.

Looking back, there should have been no question that the Howard Players were engaged in a seminal effort to redefine American theater. The Washington African American community embraced what they were trying to achieve. White Washingtonians, alas, largely ignored the creative explosion taking place underneath their own noses.

Instead, the major downtown venue serving official Washington—the National Theatre—was busy keeping Black patrons out of its audiences. The National's management hired African American bouncers to spot their racial brethren who were trying "to pass" in order to enter the theater. They even canceled performances of the Pulitzer Prize–winning play *The Green Pastures* about life in a heaven where God is Black rather than allow African Americans into their auditorium.[274] By doing so, the theater perfectly reflected the wishes of its patrons. As one letter writer to the *Washington Post* observed, "The theaters, night clubs, and restaurants in Washington are the only places where we can escape mingling with Negroes. Be sure and keep it that way."[275]

The Players remained part of what the magisterial Washington historian Constance McLaughlin Green accurately called Washington's "Secret City."[276] But there was nothing secret about Washington's vibrant and dynamic African American community for anyone who wanted to know. The community within which Howard University and the Howard Players were embedded produced some of the nation's most influential twentieth-century ideas, events, organizations, and personalities. They demonstrably proclaimed their presence from the Washington stage, and their demand for full citizenship.

Father Gilbert Hartke, George M. Cohan, and Catholic University Students, circa 1940
(Photo, The American Catholic History Research Center and University Archives. Used with Permission from Catholic University)

Chapter 2

Proclaiming Confessional Presence

We may conclude . . . that our art is noble in its myriad reflections of the real life of man, and that the art of drama as the art of successful living, rewards him who gives his best efforts not only for himself, but for the benefit of his neighbor.
—Father Gilbert V. Hartke, OP, 1950[1]

A distance of slightly less than a mile and a half separates Howard University and the Catholic University of America. Both schools claimed vacant lands just beyond the city's original L'Enfant Plan during the post–Civil War era; and both served specialized publics that were beyond the definition of respectability at the time. One might easily imagine synergetic relationships between the two institutions. Alas, in Jim Crow Washington, they might as well have been on opposite sides of the moon from one another. Drawn to the charismatic personality of program founder Father Gilbert V. Hartke, Catholic drama students rarely wandered far from campus.[2]

Catholic University was never among the worst violators of racial comity in the nation's capital. That said, the school could not forever escape the city's pernicious race relations. The university accepted a handful of African American students from its founding in 1889 until 1919, when racial segregation hardened throughout the city after the nasty race riot instigated by White World War I veterans.[3]

For the next twenty years, the Catholic University authorities regularly revisited the issue of admitting African Americans to their programs—going so far as to permit "colored sisters" to enroll in university courses in 1932. The color line nonetheless held, until Pope Pius XI intervened in a Christmas 1937 speech calling on all Church institutions to reject racism. Forty African American students enrolled in a variety of university programs eighteen months later.[4] In other words, Jim Crow had become so deeply embedded in Washington that papal intercession was required to force the smallest of changes in racial customs at an institution within his own domain.

The founder of Catholic University's drama program, Father Gilbert V. Hartke, emerged in time as a stalwart advocate for integrating theater audiences throughout the city and region.[5] Although some stages—as already noted—permitted African Americans into the top balcony, many commercial theaters in the city simply prohibited Blacks in their auditoriums. A combination of economic hardship induced by the Great Depression and the rise of motion pictures and radio, together with growing protests over segregation, eventually shut down nearly every commercial theater in the city by the end of the 1930s. Only the most racist of all— downtown's National Theatre—survived.[6]

First opened in 1835, fire destroyed the National several times before the theater was rebuilt in its current configuration in 1923. Long notorious for its prohibition against non-Whites, the National became a focus of community protest during the 1930s.[7] Productions of all-Black shows—such as *The Green Pastures* and *Porgy and Bess*—amplified the absurdity of theater policies. Performers' and community protests surrounding these productions forced the National to permit a very limited number of performances for African American audiences.

Such timid action hardly assuaged the activists affiliated with the local chapter of the National Association for the Advancement of Colored People (NAACP) and with other hometown civil rights groups.[8] In 1939, the contralto Marian Anderson famously performed in front of the Lincoln Memorial on Easter Sunday, after having been denied a booking at the Daughters of the American Revolution's Constitution Hall. The US Department of the Interior helped arrange concerts performed by the National Symphony at integrated federal venues for the next several years. Nonetheless, Jim Crow endured.

In 1946, Ingrid Bergman and Sam Wanamaker, performing in the pre-Broadway tryout of *Joan of Lorraine*, threatened to walk out in protest over the exclusion of African American patrons at George Washington University's new Lisner Auditorium. The show went on as scheduled so as not to violate contractual obligations, while both Actors' Equity and the Dramatists' Guild began picketing local productions. The next year national theater leaders declared a boycott of both the National Theater and Lisner Auditorium. Three dozen playwrights announced that they would not allow their plays to be performed in Washington, a move that only heightened the intransigence of theater owners and the White theatergoing public.[9]

Rather than give in to such pressure, the National Theatre closed in 1948 and tried to make a go as a movie house. The theater remained dark after the collapse of its movie escapade, only to reopen in 1952 under new management as an integrated auditorium.[10]

Father Hartke joined civic efforts to build a municipal theater that would be open to all and lent his own voice to the growing chorus of protests against segregation. He integrated audiences at the nearby Olney Summer Theater in Maryland, which was becoming ever more closely associated with the Catholic University drama program.[11] And one faculty member, Walter Kerr, took additional action. As Kerr later related to Hartke's biographer, Mary Jo Santo Pietro, that he previously had experienced run-ins with Washington patrons who objected to his putting an African American on stage with White performers as part of a twenty-member chorus. That incident—and others—sensitized Kerr to the depth of Washington's embrace of racial segregation. In 1944, Kerr staged *Sing Out, Sweet Land*, which was built around American folk songs, as a patriotic extravaganza. He found the notion of putting on a show celebrating American music without African Americans to be ludicrous. As he told Santo Pietro,

> I went over to Howard University to talk to the dean. I said, "Look, I'm doing a show on American folk music. How can I do it without Blacks, for God's sake, and still make sense?" Except I didn't say "Blacks" then, I would have said "Ne-

groes." I said, "Could you possibly lend me a group that could represent the Negro aspect of folk music?" The dean was nervous about it at first, but he finally agreed to do it with certain limitations. There couldn't be more than a certain number of hours per week and so on. But we got them on stage and we did it.[12]

Sing Out, Sweet Land attracted an integrated audience, which Catholic University accommodated. As Kerr continued, "If you've got twenty or thirty people from Howard University on the stage, you're going to have friends and family in the audience." Fears of antagonism proved unfounded as full houses enthusiastically embraced the show. The play went on to Broadway success with Alfred Drake in the starring role and a large, energetic cast including Dorothy Baxter, Juanita Hall, and Burl Ives.[13]

Efforts such as those of Hartke, Kerr, and their Catholic University colleagues—modest as they may seem today—felt heroic at the time. Local segregationist customs, policies, and laws profoundly encumbered Catholic University's drama program. Such practices forced the program to forgo a significant potential audience of African American theatergoers and limited what transpired onstage. Catholic University's students and its faculty performances remained isolated from their peers just a few minutes away at Howard University.

To their credit, Catholic University's faculty members tried from time to time to break out of this socially imposed racial quarantine. Their school and program could not escape their own city. Despite various limited contacts with their colleagues at Howard University, historians and chroniclers of the Catholic theater program mistakenly assumed that, for many years, Catholic University offered the only live theater in town.[14] Washington's ingrained racist attitudes rendered invisible the robust Washington African American theater scene just next door.

Such indiscernibility appears particularly poignant in retrospect, given the similarity of both program's missions. Father Hartke sought the creation of a "National Catholic Theater," modeled in part on the Irish National Theater in Dublin—just as T. Montgomery Gregory had pursued a "National Negro Theater" similarly inspired by the experience of Dublin's Abbey Theatre. Like their colleagues at Howard, Father Hartke and the Catholic University faculty eventually defined their goal as injecting a distinctive spiritual energy into a universal theater. Both programs nurtured pathways leading outsiders to center stage while bringing discrete African American and Catholic sensibilities into mainstream American theater and society. They and their colleagues sought to proclaim presence from the Washington stage as well as to claim full standing in American society.

America's Pontifical University

The Catholic University of America is a creation of the Vatican. Roman Catholic–supported universities date back to the founding of the republic, with the Jesuits establishing Georgetown University in 1789. Generally, the relatively small number of Roman Catholic believers in postcolonial America combined with deep anti-Catholic sentiment to inhibit the expansion of Roman Catholic education during the nation's first decades.

The incorporation of Catholic Spanish- and French-controlled territories after the Louisiana Purchase brought a growing network of private schools operated by orders of nuns into the American educational landscape for the first time. The sisters' willingness to educate female African American slaves, free women of color, and Native Americans heightened resistance to separate Catholic schools within Protestant America. Before the Civil War, only a handful of dispersed Catholic higher educational institutions— including Fordham University in New York, founded in 1841; the University of Notre Dame in Indiana, in 1842; the University of Dayton, in 1850; and Saint Mary's University in San Antonio, in 1852—offered Catholic instruction beyond secondary school.[15]

The place of Roman Catholics in American society changed dramatically after the Irish Potato Famine of the late 1840s. A quarter of a million Irish immigrants had arrived in American ports before 1840. The next decade saw three times that number leave Ireland for the United States, with nearly a million to follow in the 1850s. Later in the nineteenth century, Catholic immigrants arrived from Germany, Poland, Lithuania, Italy, and elsewhere. Joined in the twentieth century by Catholic Mexicans and other Catholic immigrants from Central and South America, Roman Catholics now represent around a fifth of all Americans (about 70 million adherents).[16]

The expansion of Catholic education kept pace with this demographic growth. A robust system of primary and secondary schools took root in numerous American urban centers. This network, in turn, fed into an expanding assemblage of Catholic universities and colleges. Nonetheless, among the more than two hundred Catholic institutions granting higher degrees around the United States, only a handful are considered to be Pontifical universities subordinate to the Vatican through the US Conference of Catholic Bishops.[17]

After the Civil War, in 1866, the Catholic bishops of the United States met at the Second Plenary Council of Baltimore and initiated the process for founding a university under their auspices that would teach "all branches of literature and science, both sacred and profane." Nearly a quarter century later, on March 7, 1889, Pope Leo XIII granted final approval for the university's constitution, with full power to confer graduate degrees.[18] In the interim, Bishop John Lancaster Spalding and his colleagues had secured both funds and land to bring the project to fruition.

Gathering 66 acres in Washington, outside the footprint of the original L'Enfant Plan near the Old Soldiers Home (Abraham Lincoln's Summer Cottage), the university's founders put down the base for what would become Washington's "Little Rome," as the Brookland neighborhood came to be known for its numerous Roman Catholic institutions. These include the Neo-Byzantine Basilica of the National Shrine of the Immaculate Conception, constructed between 1920 and 2017 (the largest Roman Catholic church on the continent, and one of the largest in the world).[19] President Grover Cleveland, together with various members of Congress and Cabinet officials, attended the university's cornerstone-laying ceremonies in May 1888.[20]

While Bishop Spalding and his squadron of supporters negotiated their way through the Catholic hierarchy in the United States and in Rome, another transformation in American higher education was under way, in Baltimore. In 1876, the Johns Hopkins University opened there, modeled on the Prussian model of graduate study and research. The innovative concept of a graduate research university aligned with the American Catholic bishops' vision. The Catholic University opened solely as a center for graduate education in 1889. The initial curriculum included mental and moral philosophy, English literature, the sacred scriptures, theology, and canon law. The university was a founding member of the Association of American Universities, established in 1900 by fourteen colleges offering doctorate degrees. The university added undergraduate programs in 1904.[21]

This unique lineage distinguishes Catholic University from its peers in myriad ways. Unlike numerous American public and private institutions of higher learning, the school exists to serve international constituencies. The institution did not necessarily participate in the ebb and flow of Washington urban life. Students and faculty come from elsewhere and, especially when connected to theological concerns, pursue their careers elsewhere. Those in religious orders live in various residences and institutions near campus that have not always been focused on the life of the Brookland neighborhood and the larger city surrounding them. Nonetheless, the university did build ties to a largely Irish White working- and middle-class Catholic community that initially had taken root before the District's establishment.

Washington's Catholic Heritage

Maryland had been a Roman Catholic colony at its founding, and many Roman Catholic landholders, artisans, merchants, farmers, and slaves resided on the land the state ceded to the new federal district in 1790.[22] The tobacco port of Georgetown had supported a Catholic congregation since 1787, while Baltimore bishop John Carroll, SJ, established the Jesuit College there in 1789. In 1795, college president Francis Ignatius Neale, SJ, founded the Basilica of Saint Mary across the Potomac at Alexandria, then in the new federal district's southernmost corner.[23] A year earlier in 1794, Father Anthony Cuffrey emigrated from Ireland and established Saint Patrick's Church in what would become Washington City's downtown.

When the Irish architect James Hoban arrived in town from Charleston to supervise the construction of his design for the White House and to work on various elements of the new Capitol Building, he drew on his networks back home to recruit skilled Irish stonemasons from Dublin.[24] These Irish workers carried out any number of skilled artisanal assignments, and many oversaw the work of the African American slaves laboring on the projects. Thus began tension between the city's Irish and African American workers, who competed for the same jobs at wages many felt were suppressed by the availability of free slave labor.[25] Construction crews recruited more Irish workers to build the Chesapeake and Ohio Canal, which began construction in Georgetown in 1828.[26] Similarly, Irish workers formed the core of the laborers hired to run the city's gas works in Foggy Bottom.

By 1840, the Catholic presence in Washington had grown to support its own archdiocese, with an archbishop based at Saint Matthew's Cathedral.[27] Emancipated slaves attending services in the cathedral's basement broke out on their own in 1858, establishing Saint Martin de Porrer Church, which, by 1876, had grown into the city's largest African American Catholic congregation, Saint Augustine's Church.[28]

Unlike the industrial cities of the American northeast and Midwest, Washington never became a major immigrant destination. Nonetheless, German Catholic and Irish Catholic migrants arrived throughout the nineteenth century.[29] By 1850, the local Irish community had become the city's largest ethnic group, accounting for about 10 percent of the total population.[30]

Italian work crews came in the early twentieth century to work on the expansive project consolidating the city's main rail lines at the magnificent Union Station.[31] One of the primary initiatives launched by the McMillan Project, Union Station served as a new focal point just north of the Capitol Building. The Italians established their own religious community around Holy Rosary Church nearby.[32]

Such long-standing religious communities and institutions solidified a Roman Catholic presence in the city well before Hartke arrived at Catholic University. The robust African American Catholic congregations helped spur the Church's active interest in ending Jim Crow segregation throughout the city, especially after World War II. As a result, Hartke quickly found many Washington Catholics who shared his desire to establish a Catholic presence on the

American stage as a means for advancing the social status of their co-religionists. Hartke understood that their support made Washington a particularly appropriate place for his efforts.

The Show-Biz Priest

Gilbert "Gib" Francis Hartke was the son of an interdenominational love match that transcended the social norms of late-nineteenth-century Chicago.[33] His father, Emil, the offspring of a prominent first-generation German and Lutheran household, left medical school at the University of Illinois to marry his mother, Lillian Ward, a first-generation Irish Catholic. Emil converted to Catholicism over family objections, marrying Lillian in 1892 and settling into a comfortable Rogers Park home on Chicago's North Side. On January 16, 1907, Gilbert arrived weeks early, forcing delivery on the family's dining room table. He enjoyed the sort of comfortable childhood appropriate for the offspring of a well-respected pharmacist.

Emil Hartke's Rogers Park pharmacy was near the Essanay movie studios, an important film center in this pre-Hollywood era.[34] Essanay stars during Gib's childhood years included Charlie Chaplin, Ben Turpin, Gloria Swanson, Wallace Beery, Ben Hecht, Francis X. Bushman, and the screenwriter Louella Parsons. Gib saw them around the neighborhood and befriended a few who frequented his father's drug store. Some of these connections—such as his friendship with Parsons, who became a nationally syndicated newspaper columnist—endured after the moviemakers moved to California and young Gib grew up to become a priest. These childhood experiences dissolved any social distance Hartke may have felt between himself and various entertainment and political "stars."

The camera-friendly Gib tried his hand at acting and modeling as he moved through high school at the Jesuit-run Loyola Academy.[35] Although drawn to athletics, he enjoyed greater success on stage, and he advanced from the school to semiprofessional stages around Chicago's North Side and northern suburbs. His interest in the spiritual life took hold as he approached high school graduation. He arranged to stay at Loyola an extra year as an assistant football coach so that he could pursue more advanced training in

Greek and Latin. He was set on becoming a Jesuit, but chance encounters with the Dominican priests Father Tomony and Father
Lawlor changed his life.

The Order of Preachers (OP), founded by Spanish priest Dom-
inic of Caleruega in 1216, is dedicated to preaching the Gospel.
During the Middle Ages, Dominican preachers became known in
England as "Blackfriars" — in contrast to the Carmelite "Whitefri-
ars" and Franciscan "Greyfriars" — because of the black cloaks they
wear over their white habits.[36] For young Gib Hartke, the Dominicans' commitment to evangelization appeared more congenial than
the scholarship of his intellectual Jesuit high school instructors.

In 1927, he set out for the Dominicans' new — and, at the time,
only — college in the United States: Providence College in Rhode
Island. The city of Providence held the additional attraction of being far from the temptations of the Roaring Twenties country club
parties of his adolescent social life. Providence nonetheless offered
many opportunities to sustain an interest in theater. It would be in
Providence, for example, where he first encountered his lifelong
friend — and the future "First Lady of the American Theater" Helen
Hayes.[37]

Over the course of the next decade, Hartke moved within the
Dominican world, seeking opportunities whenever possible to pursue his interest in theater. He wrote plays, studied drama at DePaul
University in Chicago, and organized performance training for the
Dominican seminaries. These efforts brought him into contact with
the remnants of the fading "Little Theater Movement," which had
similarly captured the attention of Thomas Montgomery Gregory
at Howard a decade earlier. Ordained as a priest in June 1936, Hartke received an assignment to join the Dominican House of Studies in Washington, across the street from the Catholic University
of America, where he was to pursue graduate studies in English.[38]

As he passed through various Dominican institutions, Hartke
increasingly engaged with an intensifying movement to create a
national "Catholic theater" in the United States. Launched by Father Urban E. Nagel, OP, and Father Thomas Carey, OP, such initiatives coalesced to become the "Blackfriars Guild," which sought
the union of Catholic values and the American stage. Father Hartke
arrived at Catholic University just as it was to become a crucial hub
of this crusade.[39]

Irish Players Take to the American Stage

The story of the American theatrical portrayal of Roman Catholics is profoundly connected to the emergence of Irish immigrant typecasts after the arrival of indigent émigrés fleeing the starvation of the Potato Famine. Irish and Irish American stage stereotypes took shape during the mid–nineteenth century, often with more than a touch of self-deprecating humor and ridicule.[40] Following well-established patterns of mockery toward African Americans and rural "rubes," Irish characters were outsiders comically at sea in mainstream Protestant and White America. In one of the era's blockbusters—Benjamin Baker's 1848 hit musical *A Glance at New York*—the Irish fireman Mose became the original vulgar and brawling "b'hoy of the Bowery" as he protected the country greenhorn George and Linda the Cigar Girl from lowlifes in Manhattan's infamous Five Points neighborhood.[41]

At about the same time, the Irish patriot and publicist Thomas D'Arcy McGee advocated the integration of his compatriots into American society. McGee eventually departed for Canada in disillusionment over the harsh anti-Catholicism prevalent in the United States at the time. He emerged as a powerful voice supporting Canadian Confederation and served in the First Canadian Parliament and national government. Radical Irish nationalists with strong ties to the United States assassinated him as he returned to his Ottawa home from parliamentary debates on April 7, 1868.[42]

Irish integration into the American mainstream advanced despite the forces of an anti-Catholic nativism that so disturbed McGee. Irish volunteers fighting on both sides of the Civil War undermined the vindictive hostility of the "Know-Nothingism" that had been on the rise on the eve of the war. The American penchant for degrading typecasts was reflected in the theater, even as a number of talented Irish performers, producers, and playwrights—John Brougham, Dion Boucicault, and Edward Harrigan chief among them—began to claim the stage.[43]

The Irish path through the theater to social respectability bears striking similarities to that of African Americans and Jews later. The alacrity with which the Irish came to enrich the American stage is somewhat surprising, given how relatively underdeveloped theater had been in Ireland, where many considered it an English colonial import. The success of the Irish in the United States reinforced the consolidation of a national Irish theater focused on Dublin, which in turn influenced American theater.[44]

Brougham first appeared on the New York stage in 1842, shortly after his arrival in the United States. His plays featured Irish immigrant categories, which often subverted the "Paddy" stereotype by revealing his characters to be hardworking forerunners of a new Irish middle class.

Boucicault became known for his portrayals of rogue heroes. He began writing and directing a cycle of Irish stories that enjoyed great popularity, including *The Colleen Bawn* (1860), *Arrah-na-Pogue* (1864), and *The Shaughraun* (1874). Eugene O'Neill's father, James — as already noted, another immigrant thespian — made his stage debut at the age of twenty-one in a Cincinnati production of Boucicault's *The Colleen Bawn*.

Boucicault's most lasting work, *The Octoroon* (1859), held a mirror up to the absurdities of race in his new homeland.[45] Tackling the taboo subject of miscegenation at the height of antislavery tensions leading to the Civil War, Boucicault's racial melodrama touched an American nerve. *The Octoroon* became the second-most-popular antebellum drama (behind *Uncle Tom's Cabin*). The play was staged across the United States and in England; and is still being performed in the twenty-first century.[46]

Harrigan's theater career began somewhat by accident. After his parents' divorce, he worked as a ship caulker.[47] He moved around, following ships to Central America and eventually to San Francisco, where, in 1867, he appeared onstage at a local variety theater. He thereupon joined Manning's Minstrels and began a long trek east, including a stop in Chicago, where he met Tony Cannon (later Hart). In 1870, Harrigan and Hart joined forces to become regulars at New York's Theatre Comique. The duo perfected comic skits based on the Irish, German, and African American characters they observed on the streets of New York. Their shows began a transition from variety show to musical theater.

Their 1873 parody of an Irish neighborhood militia, set to the music of David Braham — *The Mulligan Guard* — became a major hit. The team continued to expand on their success with the 1878 play

The Mulligan Guard Picnic. This proved to be the first of seventeen shows over seven years that exposed the gang violence, political corruption, personal animosities, and racial tensions of New York working-class life. Their portrayals of various urban characters often reflected the prejudices of their era. For example, Harrigan, Hart, and other White actors in their productions performed in Blackface. At the same time, they brought realism and tenement grit to popular theater. By the end of *The Mulligan Guard* cycle, Harrigan, Hart, and Braham had set down the broad outlines of a uniquely American musical theater.

The younger Hart died in 1891. Braham, who was also Harrigan's father-in-law, became known as "the American Offenbach." He gradually withdrew from the theater after *The Mulligan Guard* series, and he died in 1905. Harrigan continued from success to success, writing and producing another twenty-three plays, which achieved more than a hundred performances each on Broadway before his death in 1911. The Broadway legend George M. Cohan later recounted that he lived "in the hopes that someday my name may mean half as much to the coming generation of American playwrights as Harrigan's name has meant to me."[48]

Moving beyond Stereotypes

Before World War I, Catholic theater in America remained primarily associated with the Irish traditions and performers that had accompanied the arrival of mass immigration from the Emerald Isle. Anti-Catholic sentiment around the United States generally prompted Catholics to organize their own separate communities and institutions. American Catholic culture remained isolated within itself, searching for new ways to break into American society.[49] The popularity of Irish comedy and musical theater offered one path into the American mainstream.

At the same time, a new generation of Catholic lay and religious (i.e., those who were members of religious orders) theater lovers arose, and they were intent on transcending the stereotypes that had so dominated the American stage. The first tentative step toward cultivating a new Catholic stage presence came with the formation of the Catholic Actors Guild of America in 1914.[50] The guild was an outgrowth of an earlier interdenominational organization, the Actors Church Alliance (ACA), which was established in 1899 by an Episcopal priest, the Reverend Walter Edmund Bentley, to minister to the religious needs of New York's actors. Bringing together Protestant, Catholic, and Jewish clergy, the ACA carried forward good works, advancing the spiritual health of the acting community.

Father John Talbot Smith became the Catholic representative on the ACA's national council in 1912. Two years later, Father Smith convened a group of two dozen actors—including George M. Cohan—at the Astor Hotel to form the Catholic Actors Guild of America. They led the effort to designate Saint Malachy's Church on West 49th Street as the actors' church, which, together with the ACA, provided Catholic theatrical personnel with financial and spiritual aid.

The Catholic Theatre Movement (CTM), founded by Eliza O'Brien Lummis in 1912 with the approval of Archbishop John Farley of New York, advanced the cause of Catholic theater in new directions. Seeking to promote less "objectionable" commercial theater, the CTM published a "white list" of plays approved for their moral content until the end of the 1930s, when the group quietly disbanded.[51]

The CTM's focus on moral certification led many within the Catholic theatrical community to disavow its efforts. Meanwhile, in 1923, Father Mathias Helfen established the Catholic Dramatic Movement in Milwaukee, with the practical aim of developing and promoting plays that were morally suitable for parish and Catholic school drama groups. The Catholic Dramatic Movement eventually grew into an important information exchange, costume rental service, publisher, and organizer of workshops, primarily among Catholic communities in the Midwest.[52]

Numerous national Catholic publications—including the *Catholic Review*, *America*, *Catholic World*, and *Commonweal*—began featuring commentary on American theater at this time. These periodicals' reviews reflected the distinct and varying conservative, moderate, or liberal perspectives of their editors and subscribers.[53]

One article—by the playwright Emmet Lavery, appearing in the Jesuit weekly *America*—proved particularly discerning.[54] Lavery suggested the creation of a national organization integrating Catholic ideals of art and morality with American theatrical culture. Charles Costello, director of Chicago's Loyola Community Theatre, proposed hosting a national gathering to discuss the themes raised in Lavery's article. In June 1937, 416 delegates from 28 states—Father Hartke among them—gathered in Chicago and founded the National Catholic Theatre Conference. The National Conference established a permanent office at the Catholic University of America to operationalize the gathering's proposals, including the establishment of summer theater workshops in Washington. By 1938, the organization had 235 individual and 128 institutional members, and it had become a catalyst for several new theatrical initiatives promoting Catholic values onstage.[55]

Blackfriars on Campus and on Broadway

In 1931, upon their graduation from Providence College and ordination as priests, the Dominican Order dispatched two young members of the order to Catholic University to earn doctoral degrees in psychology. These two priests—Father Urban Nagel, OP, and Brother Fabian Carey, OP—discovered a shared love of theater, and thought of the idea of establishing a local Catholic theatrical group in the nation's capital. Their vision led them to form a loose association of affiliated groups under the umbrella name the Blackfriars Guild, after the private Dominican theaters of sixteenth-century London.[56] The Blackfriars would grow at its height to twenty-two chapters across the country. The guild eventually established an influential New York company, which produced plays under Nagel and Carey continuously between 1940 and 1971.

Father Nagel and Father Carey taught at Catholic University while pursuing their graduate studies. Then the Dominican Order assigned Nagel to teach at Providence College in 1934, while Carey remained at Catholic University. By 1940, both had transferred to the Saint Vincent Ferrer Priory in New York, where they joined forces to establish the New York Blackfriars Theatre. Nagel, meanwhile, had been a prominent participant in the 1937 Chicago gathering establishing the National Catholic Theatre Conference.[57]

Hartke arrived at the Dominican House of Studies across the

street from Catholic University just as Nagel was departing. He settled in to graduate studies in English, and unsurprisingly embraced the amateur Blackfriars group that had formed on the Catholic University campus.[58] Meanwhile, Nagel, Carey, and Hartke were concerned that their Dominican superiors were becoming less enamored of their theatrical avocations, and they began to seek out allies for support.

Roy J. Deferrari, the university's dean of the Graduate School of Arts and Sciences, entered the fray by providing protective bureaucratic cover for various theatrical ventures. A student of Greek and Latin literature, Deferrari completed his undergraduate education at Dartmouth College before continuing his graduate education at Princeton, where he had earned a PhD in 1915. He began his career at Catholic University upon returning from the battlefields of World War I, where he had served in the 814th Aero Squadron.

Deferrai assumed responsibility for running the Catholic University summer sessions and rose to be dean by the late 1930s. He proved himself to be a skilled administrator and a forceful personality in his own right. He reined in Nagel, Carey, and Hartke in various ways over the years, while securing their most ambitious projects. His sponsorship proved important, given the complex bureaucratic tangle within a university connected to the Vatican and the intention of Dominican superiors to chart the career paths of their pastors. Deferrai retired as dean in 1960, staying on to oversee summer programs until 1968. He died a year later, at the age of seventy-nine. His often-invisible hand made Catholic's theatrical achievements possible.[59]

Deferrai, Nagel, and Carey proposed that the National Conference launch the Blackfriars Institute of Dramatic Arts during the summer of 1936. Even though he was scheduled to be dispatched for further graduate study at Yale, Hartke convinced his superiors to allow him to participate in the National Conference gatherings, as well as in the summer institute in Washington.

The 1937 Chicago conference allowed Father Hartke to reestablish his former ties with the Loyola Community Theater, where he became acquainted with a renowned elocution instructor at Northwestern University, Josephine Callan. A recent widow, Callan agreed to teach at Catholic University for a year. She, in turn, introduced Hartke to two of her students, Gilbert Nevius and Walter Kerr. Hartke and Kerr hit it off immediately. About the same time, Hartke met teenage siblings associated with the Washington Black-friars club, Adah May and Leo Brady. Hartke brought this team together for the Blackfriars summer workshop at Catholic Univer-sity in 1937. As in 1936, the workshop included drama courses for students at local Catholic high schools as well as seven productions spread throughout the summer. [60]

Carey and Nagel rather than Hartke had created the summer "Blackfriars Institute of Dramatic Arts" for the 1936 summer ses-sion. They carried the administrative load of managing the sum-mer program from afar. Then, in 1937, Hartke—with Deferrai's support—leveraged the Blackfriars summer program to establish the new Department of Speech and Drama at Catholic University, with himself as department chair. He quickly brought Callan, Kerr, and the Bradys on board.[61]

These events left lasting strains among Hartke, Nagel, and Car-ey. Relocated to New York, Carey and Nagel pursued the creation of the Blackfriars Theatre, which opened in 1940 in a small, unused second-floor auditorium of a former YMCA on West 57th Street.[62] Their theater became one of the first Off-Broadway houses and, for some time, was a notable presence in New York's growing noncom-mercial drama scene.[63]

The company's luster began to fade in the 1960s. Blackfriars faced greater competition from a rapidly expanding Off-Broadway scene, while reforms within the Catholic Church after the Second Ecumenical Conference (Vatican II) promoted greater integration into society, including mainstream theater.[64] The building's dete-rioration imposed ever-heavier financial burdens on the company. Moreover, though Father Nagel had conceived of the company as promoting the spiritual nature of human beings and their eternal destiny, Father Carey focused more narrowly on works that pro-moted a specifically Catholic perspective on the world.[65] Father Carey's doctrinal programming choices after Father Nagel's death in 1965 attracted ever smaller audiences. The company formally disbanded in 1975, though it had been inactive since Father Carey's death in 1972.[66]

Despite their considerable achievements, Nagel and Carey remained suspicious of Hartke after the bureaucratic scrum of 1937. Underpinning the bumps and bruises of organizational infighting, Nagel and Carey held fundamentally different understandings of "Catholic theater." For them, as Matthew Donald Powell has observed, such theater should reflect the teachings and values of the Church. For Father Hartke, however, there was only one theater—a commercial, nonsectarian art form—for which a sectarian university should prepare Catholics to achieve professional proficiency. Such well-trained Catholic professionals would exert their own positive influence by bringing Catholic perspectives to the "universal" theater.[67]

A Fast Start

While attending the opening conference of the National Catholic Theatre Conference in Chicago in 1937, Father Hartke found time to visit the haunts of his youth. Already knowing of his appointment to the new drama program at Catholic University, he sought out the advice of retired Speech School dean Ralph Dennis at Northwestern University, where the younger Hartke had performed from time to time. This meeting proved fundamental for the future course of Father Hartke's vision for his new venture.[68]

Dennis advised Hartke that his biggest challenge would be to attract and to retain high-quality faculty members. He evidently encouraged Josephine Callan to apply for a faculty position. As noted above, Callan, in turn, introduced Father Hartke to Northwestern's star drama graduate student, Walter Kerr.

These conversations helped Father Hartke consolidate his own philosophy for establishing his program. Rather than offer retreads of Broadway plays, as many university drama programs were doing, his company would stage original and experimental works, as well as classics. He would attract local and national attention by bringing Broadway and Hollywood stars to lecture and perform, thereby expanding the experience of the program's student actors. He would maintain the highest professional standards, which encouraged Washington critics and audiences to consider Catholic University's productions as a worthy substitute for the troubled local professional theater scene.[69]

Father Hartke faced challenges that proved problematic before he could move ahead with his dreams. The university offered scant budgetary support, no suitable performance space, little in the way of faculty lines, few drama students, and a hopelessly amateurish drama club known as the Harlequins. Moreover, no women studied at Catholic at the time, creating vexing casting choices. Beyond such practical challenges, no one quite knew what "Catholic theater" might be. Nonetheless, he had one primary asset: himself. He was an energetic and inventive advocate for his own cause, and his inherent charm prevented nearly everyone from turning down his requests.[70]

Piecing together funds from a variety of nontraditional sources (including in-kind contributions and exchanges of services), Father Hartke assembled a stellar constellation of talent. In exchange for tuition, Leo Brady from the Washington Blackfriars Guild agreed to sign on as the program's administrative secretary. Freed of working downtown to meet her brother's tuition obligations, Leo's sister, Adah May, joined the program as its bookkeeper. Father Hartke scraped together funds to convince Josephine Callan to move to Washington for the year as the department's first full-time professor.

Hartke and Callan developed a curriculum offering playwriting, acting, directing, scenic design, makeup and costuming, ethics and aesthetics, oral interpretation of poetry, prose, and drama. They convinced a Georgetown University English professor, James Ruby, and Ruby's friend, Leon Dostert, a specialist in the history of the French theater, to volunteer as faculty members. Paul Goettlemann, a former Catholic University architecture student, similarly signed on without salary, as did the retired Metro-Goldwyn-Mayer makeup specialist Bernard McConnell.[71]

For students, Hartke enrolled seven full-time master's students and attracted eighteen nonmajors to specific courses. For productions, he enlisted actors from the Harlequins (an arrangement that proved unfortunate, given the group's focus on partying over rehearsing), and convinced nearby Trinity, Immaculata, and Dumbarton colleges to permit their women undergraduates to perform, as long as they were constantly under a chaperone's supervision. He reached out to the city's Irish and Italian parishes for audiences and donors. Finally, he secured a two-room suite of small offices, two classrooms, and a small theater in the as-yet-unfinished Music Building. By the end of first semester, the program was able to present three short plays. Other brief performances followed during the winter and spring.[72]

To ensure that his program looked more formidable than its reality might suggest, Father Hartke initiated what would become a signature pattern of celebrity speakers. He convinced Orson Welles to visit campus and lecture during the inaugural fall semester. Welles—who was in town presenting the manuscript of his fabled Mercury Theatre production of *Julius Caesar* to the Folger Shakespeare Library—already had achieved mythical status. Julie Haydon, Sara Allgood, Franc Craven, and William Gaxton—all widely known actors of the period—spent time with students later in the year. Haydon and Allgood would return to perform in department productions.[73]

Father Hartke similarly convinced the university to allow the program to retain box office receipts for the department's own use. University administrators probably did not view the arrangement as costing them much, as ticket prices ran under 50 cents. With the department's reputation growing, however, the university would force Hartke to revisit the issue of claiming all revenues for itself, in what would prove to be one among many financial conflicts between the university and the department.[74]

The department's inaugural year concluded on May 12, 1938, with the program's first major production, *Cyrano de Bergerac*. Welles had stressed the importance of classical training during his campus visit, a perspective Hartke and Callan found congenial for establishing their own approach to dramatic pedagogy. However, unsure that their charges could master Shakespeare, Callan convinced Hartke to instead stage Brian Hooker's translation of Edmond Rostand's classic play. Beset with budgetary constraints, Father Hartke reached out to the British, Cuban, Belgian, Polish, Italian, and Czechoslovak embassies for patronage. The ambassadors' presence on opening night cemented Catholic University's place in Washington's local diplomatic and cultural scenes.[75]

Earlier that spring, Father Hartke received an inquiry from Walter Kerr, the young master's student at Northwestern whom he had met the previous summer. Kerr was looking for a faculty appointment. Father Hartke immediately seized on the opportunity, proposing to his Dominican provincial that he begin to work at Catholic University for no pay, thereby freeing up his faculty budget line for Kerr. His Dominican superiors agreed to absorb the cost of supporting their young priest, and Father Hartke shifted his budget line to a new faculty position. University officials eventually discovered the subterfuge, and they agreed to pay both Hartke and Kerr.[76] Father Hartke then convinced Callan to return.

Over the course of his department's first year, Father Hartke had managed to secure national recognition with one full-time faculty member, a student secretary, and no budget. This growing reputation, in turn, immediately attracted student applications to the university and the department.

Father Hartke often credited Dean Dennis's advice to rely on good faculty and good productions as the key to his early and continuing achievements. As the curtain fell on a successful production of *Cyrano de Bergerac*, Washington had gained a major new theatrical player.[77]

Yankee Doodle Boy

Father Hartke began to rely increasingly on homegrown talent as the Catholic University theater program entered its second year. He encouraged young Leo Brady, still an undergraduate, to try his hand at writing. Brady's first work, *Brother Orchid*, became an immediate favorite that would be revived in the future. The play earned a congratulatory note from the Hollywood star Edward G. Robinson, as well as the attention of Warner Brothers (Brady, however, was not involved directly in writing the script for the 1940 film starring Robinson, Ann Sothern, Humphrey Bogart, and Ralph Bellamy). Walter Kerr wrote an original production—*Hyacinth on Wheels*—which recreated *Coriolanus* in modern dress. Kerr, in particular, proved full of fresh ideas that immediately energized the program. His classroom presence attracted new students and, perhaps more important, he and Callan formed a production team that would stage nearly three dozen plays over the next several years.

The 1938–39 season featured Brady's *Brother Orchid*; a commedia dell'arte–inspired production; Thornton Wilder's *Happy Journey*; and Kerr's *Hyacinth on Wheels*. Its success realized Father Hartke's vision of producing something new, something experimental, and something classic each year. Hartke expanded his outreach to national, Broadway, and Hollywood media, calling attention to his program's creative success. He doubled student enrollment, the number of faculty, and course offerings, while securing a solid foundation for future success.[78] The company moved Kerr's summer session production of Henri Gheon's *The Comedian*—with the popular English actor Robert Speaight in the lead—to the Sylvan Theater on the Washington Monument grounds, thereby reaping additional publicity.[79]

All these trends converged the following year with the program's first megahit: *Yankee Doodle Boy*, Kerr and Brady's musical biography of the fabled Broadway actor George M. Cohan. This production was contained within a season that included notable productions of Marlowe's *Dr. Faustus*, T. S. Eliot's *Murder in the Cathedral* (with Speaight playing Becket), and Moliere's *The Miser*.[80] Cohan's very public connection to the department firmly established Catholic University's Department of Speech and Drama as an important presence in both Washington and the nation.

Callan, who had known Cohan since childhood, introduced Hartke to the renowned actor during a trip to New York, when Cohan played Franklin Roosevelt in *I'd Rather Be Right*.[81] Callan and Hartke invited him to campus to meet with students when the touring show visited Washington. During the car ride from the university back to his hotel, Cohan confided in Hartke that Metro-Goldwyn-Mayer was about to offer him a half-million dollars for the movie rights to his story. However, Cohan was loath to do so because of his early marriage to a Jewish woman, Ethel Levey. The marriage had led to the breakup of the family vaudeville act the Four Cohans, and he did not want to sell this story to the film studios.

Hartke encouraged Brady and Kerr to try their hand at writing a biographical play, which they did while leaving out both the marriage to Levey and the actor's acrimonious confrontations with trade unions during the bitter Actors' Equity strike of 1919. The pair completed a draft script by October, with casting taking place a month later. A freshman, Gilbert Graham—later a Dominican priest—was chosen to portray Cohan. Forty-six actors played eighty-five roles, including recruits from Trinity, Immaculata, and Dumbarton as well as Leo Brady.

The expansive production proved larger than the diminutive Music Building stage, and the company struggled to adjust throughout preparations for a December rollout. Hartke plowed ahead, even though the company had no funds to support the venture, planning three shows on Saturday, Sunday, and Monday, December 16–18. Cohan attended the Monday evening performance to avoid the fans and critics who had come to the opening to see him. He correctly anticipated a frenzy of national and local press interest.

The Catholic University production team restaged the play in April 1940, when Cohan returned to Washington on his last tour, in *Return of Vagabond*. He used his appearance at the National Theatre to accept the Congressional Medal of Honor for meritorious service in World War I. And he granted Catholic University full rights to his story during the visit. Warner Brothers secured the film rights and rewrote the script for the screen, leading to its release as *Yankee Doodle Dandy* in early 1942, with James Cagney playing Cohan. The film's patriotic tone earned an enthusiastic reception during the uncertain early months of World War II. The film pleased Cohan, who died a few months later, in November.

Yankee Doodle Boy secured the place of Catholic University's Department of Speech and Drama in popular and academic theater circles. For Washington, its success underscored the program's importance as a center for innovative performance worthy of patronage. Perhaps Father Hartke's greatest achievement was his ability to form a tightly knit team that functioned as a family as much as a university faculty. Callan, Leo and Adah May Brady, Kerr, the scenic designer Ralph Brown, and others remained loyal to him and to each other. Together, they overcame uncertain finances and unstable university commitments. They shared meals and houses, and they generally devoted their lives to fulfilling Father Hartke's vision.

Remembering this period, Kerr told Hartke's biographer Santo Pietro in 1987 that "it was an astonishing group, a group of extremely workable people; and we all liked each other. Meetings were a pleasure. Rehearsals were pleasure. Friction was a minimum." Callan had expressed similar feelings in 1976, saying, "I don't think there ever was an organization that had more harmony and good feeling than we had at the beginning of the department." Hartke, for his part, proposed in 1986 that "Almighty God dropped all of them on my lap within a year."[82]

Former colleagues and students remember Father Hartke beginning every rehearsal and production with a prayer. In the summer of 1939, the university's rector, Bishop Joseph Corrigan, announced that the Graduate Department of Speech and Drama was now a full-fledged unit within the Catholic University of America. Hartke's prayers had been more than answered.[83]

A Golden Age

One summer evening in 1941, a young graduate student, home visiting his parents from Cornell University, attended a performance at Catholic University directed by Walter Kerr. Alan Schneider had been born weeks after the 1917 Russian Revolution in Khar'kiv (in today's Ukraine). His parents, both physicians, took their family to the United States in 1923, where they found jobs at the Maryland State Tuberculosis Sanatorium. Alan finished high school in Baltimore, before studying physics for a year at Johns Hopkins University. He subsequently transferred to the University of Wisconsin–Madison, where he earned a joint degree in political science and literature. After a stint back home as a radio announcer and speechwriter for Postmaster General James A. Farley, Schneider accepted a fellowship at Cornell to study drama.[84]

Schneider was so taken with Kerr's work that he went backstage and told him that he had never before seen anything of such high quality. When Kerr discovered that Schneider was finishing his master's degree, he introduced him to Hartke. Schneider was hired more or less on the spot. By December, he was directing the world premiere of recent Pulitzer Prize winner William Saroyan's *Jim Dandy*.[85] Schneider proved to be the final piece in what would become the department's golden age.

Over the next several years, Catholic University's productions included adaptations and original plays by the young superstars Walter Kerr and Leo Brady; plays directed by Father Hartke and Alan Schneider; plays with Ralph Brown, his student, Ruth Schmigelsky, and a wartime addition, Jim Waring, designing sets; Callan coaching speech; a visiting star or two joining the student casts; and Adah May Brady, somehow holding these strong and energetic personalities together behind the scenes. Their efforts provided a continuous educational experience, steeping students in every aspect of developing and creating a theatrical production, from an initial setting of fingers to typewriter to a fully developed professional or cinematic production.

Father Hartke established his own fund to aid those struggling to make financial ends meet, and he invited additions to his program more spontaneously than the university admissions office might have endorsed. Increasingly, students seeking a career onstage and behind the stage made their ways to Catholic University, allowing the department to become ever more selective. Then World War II refashioned everyone's circumstances, as some members of the department's team, including Leo Brady, served in the military.

Members of this closely knit lineup changed roles as needed, and each entering class developed its own individual character. They mounted productions of classics and experimental plays, as well as nearly two dozen original works (about a quarter of which were subsequently produced professionally).[86] As noted above, nine department productions before 1950 went on to Broadway, including six original plays (five of which were penned by Kerr).[87] Department students went on to successful careers, winning Tony Awards, Pulitzer Prizes, and other awards.[88]

Three productions capture the spirit of the period, although they in no way represent the full extent of the department's stage success.[89] In 1945, Kerr and Callan tried their hand at directing Charles and William Archer's translation of Henrik Ibsen's sprawling 1876 play *Peer Gynt*. Written in Danish verse, Ibsen populated his five-act play, based on a Norwegian fairytale, with characters drawn from his own family. After a mythical journey from the Norwegian mountains to the North African deserts, the play offered a satire of Norwegian self-absorption and, not surprisingly, attracted fulsome criticism from offended critics of the day.[90]

Kerr and Callan eliminated many of Ibsen's diversions and detours to reduce the play to the story of a man who is too obstinate and self-absorbed for his own good. The production nonetheless offered ample characters to accommodate plentiful ambitious students looking for an opportunity to appear on stage. Elizabeth Ross, who appeared in several university productions during this time, played the role of Solveig. Ralph Brown was widely praised for his masterful presentation of an expansive set confined to a limited stage.

The Washington critics raved, with the *Washington Post*'s Nelson Bell writing that the production was "a thoroughly arresting performance that immediately placed this complex and demanding work high on the roster of Catholic University's major achievements in the field of enduring drama." In response, the *Washington Star*'s Jay Carmody observed that the production kept "the audience more or less aghast with delight and surprise."[91]

In 1948, Jean Kerr's *Jenny Kissed Me* offered lighter fare. Directed by her husband Walter, the production ranked among the department's most popular plays at the time. James Waring's luminescent stage design and creative lighting, together with Leo Brady's masterful performance as Father Moynihan, enhanced the production. Built around the relationship between a crusty pastor and his beautiful niece, the plot follows the young woman as she seeks a husband. With some eighty roles, the production offered ample possibilities for student actors to demonstrate their burgeoning skills. This "charming and cozy" work later opened on Broadway, with Leo G. Carroll playing Father Moynihan.[92]

Alan Schneider's 1952 take on Thornton Wilder's *The Skin of Our Teeth* proved to be his last Catholic University production. Wilder's 1942 Pulitzer Prize–winning allegory of human folly traced humanity's presence on the planet through the Antrobus family of fictional Excelsior, New Jersey. The play's action chronicled the family's escape from an impending ice age, patriarch Antrobus's tenure as president of the Fraternal Order of Mammals, and the family's emergence from a bunker at the end of a seven-year-long war. Full of biblical references, the work largely dismissed standard narrative for a complex layering of human imperfection.[93]

In the production's program notes, Schneider wrote that the

play is "a mixture of sense and nonsense, laughter and tears, burlesque and fantasy, the Marx Brothers and Aristotle."[94] The critics
were ecstatic in their reception of the production, with the *Washington Star*'s Carmody writing, "Mr. Schneider's direction is so mer-
curial, and the technical lighting and settings of James D. Waring
so exact, that the production is as much a joy as Wilder's dashing
script. Together they have achieved not only the more zany aspects
of the play, but have conspired just as successfully on the emotional, marveling context of Wilder's appealing boost for humanity."[95]
The spectacle foreshadowed Schneider's legendary American premiere fiasco of Samuel Beckett's *Waiting for Godot* three years later
at the Coconut Grove Playhouse in Florida, when audience members stormed out after having shown up expecting vaudeville comedy, only to be confronted by Beckett's dystopia.[96]

Homegrown productions and adaptations of classic, original,
and experimental works proved emblematic of a shared theatrical
sensibility—one that began with Father Hartke and became codi-
fied through the writings of Leo Brady and Walter Kerr. From the
very beginning, Hartke envisioned theater as an all-encompass-
ing extension of Catholic faithfulness, in which every element, no
matter how minor, contributes holistically to a larger expression of
spiritual love. This stance guided him to select religiously oriented
plays each Lenten season.[97]

Taking the Show on the Road

Having secured the Catholic University Department of Speech
and Drama and its place on the Washington theater scene, the al-
ways-restless Father Hartke set his sights further afield. His labors
to connect productions on campus during the academic year to
summer and touring companies—as well as to theater, film, and
later television professionals—became distinctive hallmarks of
Catholic University's approach to drama pedagogy.

During the 1940–41 school year, Hartke made three trips to Hollywood to convince film studio executives to reach out more systematically to university drama programs—including his own—for
fresh talent, ideas, and scripts. None of his proposals linking studios and universities gained traction. Hartke nonetheless built the

beginnings of a personal network—including the famed director Alfred Hitchcock and the influential columnist Hedda Hopper— that would bring resources and publicity to Catholic University in the future. Having found California to be a barren landscape for his various plans, he turned his attention to the Midwest. [98]

Hartke and his team assessed their repertoire for an appropriate vehicle to showcase their achievements around the country. They fixed on Walter Kerr's *God's Stage* and took their show on the road.

Kerr's play—which portrays humankind's relationship with God from Aeschylus to T. S. Eliot—had received a warm reception from Washington critics when it ran from February 27 to March 4, 1941. The work, with its religious theme and minimal stage requirements, appeared ideal for touring. The company wrote to ninety-odd colleges and universities across the Midwest to propose a touring production on their campuses. They ultimately selected eight Catholic-affiliated venues in Ohio, Indiana, Illinois and West Virginia.[99]

Hartke soon went on a sabbatical to Northwestern University, leaving the Catholic drama department in Kerr's hands. Plans were shaping up for an ambitious outreach program to bring the university's theatrical achievements to a broader Catholic community. Then the Japanese attacked Pearl Harbor on December 7, 1941.

The war forced Hartke and his colleagues to revise many of their ideas—with various faculty members serving in the Armed Forces, and student recruitment shifting from gifted high school graduates to military personnel serving in the Washington area. Wartime obligations stretched faculty, staff, and students while gas rationing limited mobility. All such hardships combined to shelve plans for touring. Hartke began searching for fresh opportunities as his previous imaginings disappeared under the exigencies of war.[100]

As the war wore on, Hartke and his colleagues worked closely with the USO to provide entertainment for Washington-based troops. He reached out to wartime government workers and established his department as a touchstone for theater and film personnel stationed in town. Hartke became a habitual correspondent with soldiers and sailors on the front lines. He managed to bring star power to campus, including John Gielgud, Thornton Wilder, and William Saroyan. Hartke himself joined the cast of Catholic-oriented service films. The war enabled Dean Deferrari to integrate women once and for all into a new coeducational undergraduate program, which included degree programs in the Department of Speech and Drama. Such labors well situated Hartke, his department, and the university for expansion once the war ended.[101]

Catholic University welcomed returning soldiers onto campus at war's end, as did every US institution of higher learning. For Hartke, this meant expanding enrollments and more mature students, many of whom had some stage experience before—and during—the war. He needed a renewed opportunity for his students to earn practical as well as classroom experience. Reestablishing an ambitious touring program would help absorb the new students.[102]

Hartke's ambitions outpaced those of the university's leadership and administrators. His superiors grew concerned, for neither the first nor last time, that Hartke harbored unrealistic artistic and, most important, financial expectations. Their imaginations turned quickly to the various embarrassments that might follow perceived failure and irresponsibility. Against the advice of his closest colleagues (including Callan, Kerr, and the Bradys), Hartke decided to establish a separate organization to operate a touring schedule. The program thus would remain beyond the control of university administrators. The resulting Players, Incorporated, became an independent corporation, with Catholic University faculty members serving as trustees.[103] The Players eventually transformed into the National Players Program of the Olney Theatre Center, and it has become the longest-running classical touring theatrical company in the United States, giving nearly 7,000 performances since its founding.[104]

In September 1949, several student actors piled into two station wagons and set off with a truck containing James Waring's inventive collapsible stage set and lights. By the time they returned in February 1950, they had given 94 shows and traveled over 10,000 miles across the Midwest, performing Walter Kerr's version of *Much Ado About Nothing* as they went. Financially, the tour turned a $1,330.37 profit. The excitement generated by the tour added invaluable personal and stage experience for the players.[105]

Having succeeded in proving that touring could be an integral component of the education of stage professionals, Hartke became more expansive. The second tour included 125 bookings stretched over 18,500 miles, primarily at Catholic institutions. The tours continued, with the participants and the audiences becoming ever more successful. In 1952, the US Department of Defense invited the Players to perform near the front lines of the Korean War. To everyone's surprise, the troupe managed to make Moliere's *School for Wives* a smash hit among battle-hardened American GIs across the Pacific. The Players' connection with the US military expanded into Europe and around the world in the decades ahead.[106]

The growing links between Hartke and the US military brought other unexpected benefits. As World War II ended, Hartke used his personal networks to secure a surplus military cinema. The 550-seat theater expanded the department's existing auditorium and backstage space, enabling Hartke and his colleagues to present more ambitious productions than the diminutive Music Building had allowed. Once more, Hartke won over those university officials who needed to authorize moving the building to campus. He proved yet again that his power of persuasion liberated him from constraints that bound other faculty. The theater remained a fixture on campus until the Hartke Theater Complex opened in the early 1970s.[107]

Hartke learned, however, that having the US government as a close partner did not just reap dividends. As Senator Joseph McCarthy's boorish campaign to root out presumed communists gained speed, the Federal Bureau of Investigation visited Hartke in 1950 and asked that he fire Aline MacMachon. The actress, who had once been nominated for an Academy Award, was rehearsing for a production directed by Alan Schneider. Father Hartke did not hesitate and, though Hartke did not discuss the matter with anyone until just before his death more than three decades later, Schneider somehow discovered what had transpired. He, too, acquiesced. Josephine Callan stepped into the part on short notice. MacMachon's stage and film career did not crash to a precipitous end after the Federal Bureau of Investigation's interest in her political beliefs.[108] Hartke and Schneider were at best obtuse, and at worst too absorbed in their own pursuits to have cared.

The Players' success and other achievements offered Hartke several invaluable lessons. He learned that he could bypass his Dominican and university superiors by establishing and heading separate legal entities. He developed strong ties with the Department of Defense and other US government agencies, which consistently opened up fresh opportunities in the years ahead. He understood that potential incoming students considered the opportunity to tour to be a major attraction distinguishing Catholic University's drama program from its competitors. And he began to believe that Catholic University and Washington might be ponds too small to contain his dreams. With these lessons in mind, he set out to expand further upon the program's repertoire of stage opportunities.

Into the North Woods

After the war, Saint Michael's College in the Burlington, Vermont, suburb of Winooski similarly secured a war surplus theater building left over from a nearby airbase. The college's Humanities Department chair, Henry Fairbanks, hoped to expand the college's drama and radio school and seized on the opportunity to attract summer audiences to campus. In 1947, he established an Actor's Equity (union) summer theater on campus, drawing professional talent from Boston who were augmented by touring stars. Over time, Fairbanks and his dean, later Saint Michael's College president, the Very Reverend Gerald E. Dupont, SSE, became concerned about the superficiality of the Broadway-style fare that was being offered, as well as a drop off in box office receipts. Fairbanks had been impressed by a Players, Incorporated, performance at Notre Dame, while completing his doctoral dissertation. Noting that the Players were scheduled to perform at Saint Michael's in April 1951, Fairbanks urged Dupont to reach out to Hartke and see if it might be possible to have the company return for the summer season. After enlisting his departmental colleagues in sorting through various proposals, Hartke signed an agreement to have the Players manage the Saint Michael's Playhouse for eight weeks that summer.

The first season proved a failure. Local audiences expecting Broadway musicals did not embrace a repertoire that began with John Millington Synge's *Playboy of the Western World*. Audiences, despite solid reviews, remained small for most of the eight-week run, and revenues disappointed. The Players were overextended, as the inexperienced, primarily student managers tried to hold everything together. Saint Michael's nonetheless remained steadfast in its commitment to Hartke, and their joint venture continued.

Hartke responded by establishing a separate entity from the touring company. He invited touring members to spend the summer in Vermont under a new institutional partnership. He professionalized the theater's management, inviting recent Catholic University master's recipients Ed Warren—who would move onto a successful broadcasting career—and Bill Graham—who ultimately succeeded Hartke at Catholic University—to run the company. The arrangement proved fruitful. Though not formally connected with Catholic University, the Saint Michael's summer theater remained deeply embedded in what was an emerging family of drama programs, which included the university department mothership; the Players, Incorporated, touring company; and the University Players based at Saint Michael's. Father Hartke would be closely associated with Winooski and the theater the rest of his life (he suffered his first heart attack during a winter sojourn to the campus in 1970).

Saint Michael's casting and management remained institutionally tied to Catholic University into the 1970s. The summer theater became one of a growing number of performance opportunities the program could offer its students. Standout student performers Henry Gibson, Jon Voight, Larry Luckinbill, and Erica Slezak apprenticed at the Vermont theater. Hartke and his Catholic University colleagues worked closely with their Saint Michael's counterparts to keep the theater alive after a 1970 fire. They reconstituted the company as a cabaret theater at the Marble Island Yacht Club. The theater eventually moved into the stunning McCarthy Arts Center, which opened on campus in 1976.[109]

Summers Closer to Home

Hartke's empire continued to grow—sometimes within an expanding university department in Washington, and sometimes further afield through leveraged touring and resident companies that were formally independent yet nonetheless retained strong connections with Hartke. These arrangements empowered Hartke and his colleagues to offer incoming students a variety of onstage and backstage opportunities. It permitted them to stake a claim to a Catholic presence on the American stage.

No matter how far these prospects extended—including around the globe, on tours of military installations—they supported the growth of high-quality theater on campus. Productions originating on campus toured or went into residence at Saint Michael's, while productions perfected on distant stages returned to impress Washington audiences and critics. All these activities added vitality and creativity to a Washington theater scene that was still struggling with the malevolent impact of continuing battles over desegregation.

Another, even more advantageous opportunity arose in 1953, when the Olney Theatre requested that the Players, Incorporated, present a repertoire for its summer season.[110] Despite superficial similarities with the situation at Saint Michael's, Olney represented a different sort of opportunity altogether. The stage already was part of the local Washington theater scene, and would become steadily more so over the years, until the present time, when it is considered one of many Washington resident companies. Olney offered a year-round venue enabling the department to provide invaluable apprenticeships to students, while they could still pursue their programs of study on campus.

The Olney Theatre opened in 1938 as a summer theater venue in an abandoned roller skating rink on the former Woodlawn Lodge estate in rural Montgomery County, Maryland, about 20 miles from Washington and 30 miles from Baltimore. A vanity project of restaurateur Stephen E. Cochran, Judge Harold C. Smith, and theater manager Leonard B. McLaughlin, the theater struggled to find an audience as a "star" summer stock venue. Dairy store tycoon C. Y. Stephens purchased the property and extensively remodeled the theater in 1940. Wartime gas rationing soon forced Stephens to curtail his venture. Finally, in 1946, Stephens and Cochran reopened the facility as an Equity (union) professional theater, hosting productions featuring top-line and future stars of stage and screen, such as Tony Randall, Hume Cronyn, Jessica Tandy, Gloria Swanson, Tallulah Bankhead, and Sarah Churchill.[111]

Olney struggled to find its niche and, in 1952, Stephens offered to turn the entire enterprise over to Hartke. Given his vow of poverty, Hartke could not accept. He considered having ownership transferred to the university and the Speech and Drama Department—and even to the Dominican Order. But having been burned more than once by both, he decided that the only way to ensure the theater's continuation in perpetuity was to transfer its ownership to Players, Incorporated.[112] Players assumed the theater's artistic and administrative direction in 1953, with Hartke and his colleagues insisting that the theater be open to integrated audiences.

Managing a professional company proved a challenge for the Players, and losses followed. The Players drew ever more heavily on Catholic University faculty to take over the most important positions—including the general manager, Bill Graham; the directors, Robert Moore and Leo Brady; and the designers, James Waring and Joseph Lewis. Their collaborations steadily earned the company stronger reviews. Larger audiences followed. Ever more closely tied through the Players to Catholic University personnel, the program became artistically and financially successful by the late 1950s.[113]

The University–Players–Saint Michael's–Olney nexus proved extraordinarily creative, with each venue becoming home to high-quality, often-experimental production built around Catholic University faculty and students. The actors Roy Schneider, George Grizzard, Frances Sternhagen, John McGiver, and Olympia Dukakis, and the directors Jim Waring and Robert Moore (who later would direct *The Boys in the Band* on Broadway), gained invaluable early experience at the former roller rink.[114]

Hartke served as Olney's president for more than three decades. An unsteady period of managerial experimentation followed his retirement, with the renamed National Players eventually becoming subordinate to the nonprofit Olney Theater Corporation. Designated by the Maryland Arts Council in 1986 as a "major arts organization," Olney continues to thrive. Now surrounded by Washington's ever-expanding urban sprawl, the Olney Theatre Center for the Arts attracts over 125,000 patrons each year to performances and vibrant community-oriented arts programming.[115]

Times of Transition

All these additional enterprises augmented rather than substituted for the central role of the Department of Speech and Drama. Each venture added another pedagogical path for students to follow. The team of faculty and managers assembled throughout the 1940s provided a creative core, which ensured that the art of theater—and not the business of theatrical education and production—continued to serve as the shared objective of multiple operations.

Father Hartke continued to direct plays throughout the period. He later identified the decade between the mid-1950s and the mid-1960s as the most intense of his directorial career. Throughout his tenure at Catholic University, he directed sixty major productions, on top of which he directed another dozen for the Players. These included works by the Greek dramatists, Shakespeare, T. S. Eliot, Tennessee Williams, and Thornton Wilder. Even as he moved around the globe, he returned to his work with his students and colleagues as the touchstone of what for him remained fundamentally a spiritual journey.[116]

The core program evolved over time. Enrollments soared after the war, and the various additional enterprises launched during the 1950s naturally eroded the centrality of the degree programs and Hartke's own relationship to them. Washington's theater community evolved as well. Some of the city's most entrenched racial boundaries began to soften. The drama programs at Catholic and Howard universities tentatively reached out to one another. Some students from each institution began to move back and forth across the mile and a half that separated the two campuses.

For example, Joseph A. Walker, the much-honored playwright of *The River Niger*, completed an undergraduate degree in philosophy at Howard and was planning on pursuing a master's degree when he was called into the Air Force. After completing his military service, he earned a master's of fine arts from Catholic University, with a specialization in Elizabethan drama. He returned to teach at Howard University, and later at Springarn High School, before becoming the chair of the Theater Department at Rutgers' University's Camden, New Jersey, campus.[117]

Victories in the fight to desegregate theater venues not only empowered the Catholic drama program to reach out to African American partners. The lifting of Jim Crow–era restrictions in the city's theaters resuscitated the professional stage. The National Theatre reopened; and new companies such as Arena Stage formed. Theater lovers had options beyond what was presented at Catholic and Howard universities.

Hartke's reliance on young artists lost some of its luster as he became ever more entangled in university hiring practices. He increasingly was unable to hire the likes of the Kerrs, Schneiders, Warings, Callans, Bradys, Grahams, and Browns merely on the basis of a chance meeting.

Some of his wunderkind left. In 1951, Walter Kerr departed to accept the job as theater critic for the *New York Herald-Tribune*. Kerr became a giant among New York critics, moving to the *New York Times* once the *Trib* closed after a 1966 New York newspaper strike. Kerr garnered a Pulitzer Prize in 1978, and he was inducted into the American Theater Hall of Fame. He won perhaps the greatest honor the New York theater community can bestow when, in 1990, the Ritz Theater was renamed the Walter Kerr Theater. He died in 1996, and his wife Jean, another member of the Catholic University circle, passed away in 2003.[118]

Kerr chronicled the decline of Broadway throughout the 1970s and 1980s as crime, television, and film discouraged traditional audiences from returning to an increasingly discolored Great White Way.[119] Looking back on the 1970s, Kerr recalled one night in particular. In September 1971, he wrote, "I went to the first opening of the Broadway season. I stood outside a theater on Forty-Fifth Street, looked left toward Broadway itself and right toward Eighth Avenue, and said to myself, unoriginally but out loud, 'My God, it's a ghost town.' Here was the one-time center of the American theatrical world. And there was no one on the street."[120]

Kerr captured a stark moment when New York City, Times Square, and the Broadway theater were cascading toward their nadir. The city's fiscal crisis and the crime tsunami of the crack cocaine epidemic lay ahead. American theater was not dead, but its creative energies had transferred elsewhere, to Off Broadway as well as to regional and university theaters around the country. Kerr himself had helped initiate this movement with his work at Catholic University. New York and Broadway would rebound—with some of the city's and its theater's most vibrant glory days coming in the twenty-first century. Kerr's authoritative criticism and his earlier creative work in Washington helped prepare the ground for this resurgence.

Schneider departed two years later, building on the reputation he earned in productions at Catholic University as one of the country's most exciting and innovative directors. He eventually would gain distinction as "Samuel Beckett's favorite American director," working on several Beckett plays over three decades while engaging in a celebrated correspondence with the Irish playwright. Schneider died in 1984, after being hit by a motorcycle while posting a letter to Beckett in London.[121]

Schneider is perhaps best remembered for his direction of the disastrous American premier of Beckett's *Waiting for Godot*. Capturing the vaudevillesque character of the work, Schneider and the Broadway producer Michael Myerberg cast burlesque and film comic stars Tom Ewell and Bert Lahr as Vladimir and Estragon. Anticipating lighthearted fare in keeping with the lead actors' reputations, the opening night audience at the Coconut Grove Playhouse in Miami was stunned, confused, and then angry over Beckett's absurd tragicomedy.[122]

Lahr never forgave Schneider. Lahr's son—the renowned theater critic and historian John Lahr—records that Schneider's name in his childhood household was among a trio of words—the other two being the most classic of all Anglo-Saxon curse words—that his father banned from utterance.[123] Schneider remained no less traumatized, complaining in a letter to Beckett as late as 1973 about a supposed cabal against him led by John Lahr and his brother-in-law Martin Gottfried.[124] All machinations aside, Schneider remained in close touch with his former colleagues at Catholic University and enjoyed some of his greatest successes at Washington's Arena Stage in the 1960s and 1970s.

The historian Kenneth Campbell notes, in his dissertation about the Department of Speech and Drama at Catholic University, that the program was able to reinvigorate and replenish itself largely from within, despite the loss of such seemingly irreplaceable faculty members as Kerr and Schneider. The department frequently hired its alumni to fill new and vacated positions. Campbell argues that "as the new faculty gradually took over, and as the department expanded its sphere of operation through Players, Incorporated, changes in emphasis became noticeable. As far as play selection was concerned, there was a shift away from the dedication to the experimental in drama and a tendency to lean more heavily on the classics. This also implied a shift away from original plays.... There was a deemphasis on campus summer production."[125] The program continued to thrive with some of its most memorable productions and most successful alumni ahead.

For Washington, the Catholic University stage remained a cornerstone of the city's theatrical scene. Reviewers for the leading newspapers and audiences continued to follow every production, treating them as if they offered professional theater rather than the presentations of a university drama school. What had begun in the 1930s as a venture of Catholic "outsiders" to proclaim their presence and to bring their values to the center of American and Washington theater had, over a quarter century, moved center stage. In so doing, they expanded everyone's expectations of what theater can and should be.

A Silver Age

If the departure of Kerr and Schneider marked the end of a golden age, a silver age followed. As noted above, Father Hartke was as active as ever. His programs were expanding their breadth and depth and extending their influence around the country. Hartke became a celebrity of sorts over the course of the 1970s and 1980s—and a favorite lunch patron at such superstar watering holes as Duke Ziebert's and Mel Krupin's in Washington and Toots Shor's and the 21 Club in New York.[126] During the Kennedy administration, he became known as the "White House Priest," marching in President Kennedy's funeral cortege. He was closer still to President Johnson, becoming an intimate spiritual adviser to the Johnson family. He continued to support efforts to build an appropriate performing arts center in Washington, serving on various commissions resulting in the construction of the John F. Kennedy Center for the Performing Arts. He was a founding board member of the National

Endowment for the Arts, a prime mover in the reopening of Ford's Theatre as a performance venue, and a frequent presence on US military bases in Europe and beyond. In October 1981, *Washingtonian Magazine* named Father Hartke one of the most powerful men in Washington.[127]

At the same time, Hartke became something of a liability for his Catholic University superiors. Student unrest in 1968 had forced the university to restructure its leadership, bringing decisionmaking closer to the student body. Student and stakeholder protesters demanded a degree of transparency in previously obtuse governance structures tied to the US Council of Catholic Bishops and higher Church authorities in Rome. Lay leaders joined cardinals and bishops on the university's governing councils, expecting a more regular order in university operations. The university soon began an extended community outreach program to support the neighboring African American community in Northeast DC, an initiative that continued for decades.[128]

Hartke's freewheeling, entrepreneurial style increasingly chafed. His multiple outside obligations inhibited the hands-on management that his department required. In 1974, he eased into a special position created for him as an official liaison between Catholic University, the Catholic Church, the federal government, local government, alumni, major industries, and the media. Bill Graham eventually replaced Father Hartke as department chair, after the usual internal academic shenanigans.[129]

The department evolved as the "old guard" began to leave the scene. The timeworn team was aging, retiring, and passing away. Josephine Callan died in 1978, and Leo Brady in 1984. Father Hartke adjusted, helping the university when he could, while living in his monk's room at the Dominican House of Studies, as he had for decades. He worked closely with his biographer, Mary Jo Santo Pietro, throughout his last year of life, celebrating his fiftieth anniversary at Catholic University with a black tie gala at the Shoreham Hotel in April 1985.[130] He succumbed to cancer less than a year later, on February 21, 1986.[131]

The department charged ahead during two decades between Kerr and Schneider's departures and Hartke's retirement, attracting talent to undergraduate and graduate programs and producing memorable plays along the way. Hartke's interlocking programs enabled student theatrical professionals to gain a solid academic background on campus, tour with the Players domestically and with USO and other US government programs abroad, spend summers on stage at Saint Michael's in Vermont, and apprentice with professionals at Olney. Each of these venues demanded high professional accomplishment.

Father Hartke began petitioning university leaders for a permanent theater complex in the late 1950s. The university eventually folded his proposal into its building plans, though other needs consistently took priority. In the early 1960s, university rector Monsignor William Joseph McDonald endorsed Hartke's proposal. However, fundraising fell primarily to Hartke.[132] The always-entrepreneurial priest threw himself at the task with energy and élan.

Hartke believed that he was close to securing the required funds many times—from the education-minded owner of the *Washington Post*, Eugene Meyer; from Jerry Wolman, the owner of the Philadelphia Eagles football team; from US government programs, such as the National Endowment for the Arts; and from a massive gala extravaganza in New York organized by alumnus Ed McMahon, who was then a beloved personality appearing with Johnny Carson on *The Tonight Show*. Each effort turned into its own saga of unexpected deaths, criminal convictions, and skirmishes within the university over the allocation of funds.[133]

Construction finally began under chief architect Paul Goettelmann, chair of the university's Architecture Department, and Jim Waring, Father Hartke's trusted design guru. The blueprints included a main auditorium with a stage larger than the entire overused Music Building theater, classrooms, storage areas, smaller laboratory theaters, staff offices, a library, and seminar rooms.

The new facility opened on November 19, 1970, with a gala benefit performance of George Bernard Shaw's *The Devil's Discipline* starring the Australian actor Cyril Ritchard, who is best known for his much-loved performance as Captain Hook in *Peter Pan*. Father Hartke learned only that evening that the university and the Dominican Order had agreed to name the new performance facility in his honor. Claude Chagrin and Bill Graham's production of *Rosencrantz & Guildenstern Are Dead* followed. The Gilbert V.

Hartke Theatre's first year is best remembered for Helen Hayes's last turn on stage as Mary Tyrone in Leo Brady's production of Eugene O'Neill's classic *Long Day's Journey into Night*.[134]

Celebrities on Stage

Ever since Father Hartke's 1937 conversation with Northwestern University's dean Ralph Dennis, Hartke had remained convinced that he needed to present well-known celebrities to secure and sustain his program's reputation. Famous stars graced Catholic University's stage over the years. Helen Hayes, a native Washingtonian and the "First Lady of the American Theater," remained a loyal supporter throughout her life.

As already noted, Father Hartke and Hayes first met in the late 1920s, when the college student Hartke stormed backstage to meet the celebrity Hayes after a performance in Providence.[135] Hayes, who grew up in Washington and New York, attended Catholic schools, appeared on stage as a child, and, by the time Father Hartke met her, had already become a film and stage star. She was regarded as one of the country's most beloved thespians and leading philanthropists.

Her accomplishments won her a cupboard full of prestigious awards. Hayes remains one of a handful of performers who have won an Emmy for her work on television (1953), a Grammy for her spoken word recording (1977), and Oscars for film (1932, 1970), together with Tony Awards for Broadway performances (1947, 1958, and a 1980 Special Tony Award for Distinguished Lifetime Achievement). She received the Presidential Medal of Freedom in 1986, and the National Medal of Arts two years later.

Hartke and Hayes cooperated on numerous ventures, and promoted the arts whenever possible, including testifying together before Congress.[136] She performed several times at the Olney Theater and welcomed opportunities to step onto the campus stage with Catholic University students.

In 1963, Hayes agreed to perform in William McCleery's *Good Morning, Miss Dove* as a benefit for Catholic University, and she moved into a student dorm on campus as rehearsals began. McCleery based his play about a perfectionist schoolmarm on an earlier novel by Frances Gray Patton and a film adaptation by Eleanor Griffin.[137] Hartke began pulling on his connections. A pall fell over the project after the assassination of President Kennedy in November. Hayes moved into a university women's dormitory during rehearsals; and together, she and Hartke managed to cull through an avalanche of requests and invitations for personal appearances.

The play opened on January 22, 1964, before a beau monde audience including top members of the diplomatic corps, the press, the theater community, and New York governor Averell Harriman and Mrs. Harriman. The production ran for seventeen days, with tickets set aside at reduced prices for students and seniors. Hayes later told the *New York Times* that working with students "had forced her to realize how much there was to learn about the theater."[138]

The experience was no less memorable for the student actors. Philip Arnoult, who played the apparition of Teddy Roosevelt opposite Hayes in one of the play's dream scenes, remembered a half century later trundling off to the Library of Congress Film Collection to study news clips of the former president. He taught himself to mimic the disjointed actions of turn-of-the-century cinema. After the opening night performance, Teddy's daughter, Alice Roosevelt Longworth, approached Arnoult backstage and congratulated him by offering that his portrayal of her father was the most truthful she had seen.[139]

If Hayes's performance in *Good Morning, Miss Dove* was about sentiment, her portrayal of Mary Cavan Tyrone seven years later in Leo Brady's 1971 production of Eugene O'Neill's *Long Day's Journey into Night* was about history.[140] Now seventy, Hayes decided that the play would be her last appearance onstage, and she thus embraced this difficult role that she had longed to perform. Her dignified enactment proved masterful, and the reviews were appropriately winning. This success occurred despite Hayes having been hospitalized during the run-up to opening night. Her incapacity forced a week-long delay that created logistical challenges for Hartke, Brady, and their colleagues. The sold out three-week run nonetheless marked a highpoint in Washington theater history.

Hayes once again moved into a student dormitory during rehearsals. One spring evening, after a run-through. she settled into the dorm's television room surrounded by coeds in their bathrobes and nightgowns to watch the broadcast of the Academy Awards from Hollywood. Hayes evidently believed that her nomination for best supporting actress that year was little more than a beau geste. Completely caught off guard, she celebrated her second Oscar with Catholic University's female students.

The press loved the story of a legendary performer spending her Academy Award–winning evening drinking punch in a college dormitory rather than champagne at a swanky after-ceremony party in the Hollywood Hills. Hartke loved the resulting publicity for the celebrated drama program that he had built from little more than a dream. And the university loved a fundraising fantasy.

Peeling away the fortune of the moment, the production of *Long Day's Journey into Night* captured what Father Hartke had built. He presented an American classic by a fabled author with deep Catholic roots; produced by longtime protégé, Leo Brady; staged with a star with profound connections to Catholic faith, values, and institutions; performed by a student cast; and attracting a luminary audience. Unlike the ambitious young man who had left Chicago decades before, Father Hartke was now the epitome of an insider.

Legacies beyond a Single University

Father Hartke's commitment to the city and its cultural life ran deep. From the time of his arrival in the late 1930s, he worked assiduously to expand, cultivate, and enliven the city's theatrical enterprise. He joined with various local and national partners to integrate Washington audiences; to build a municipal performing arts center, leading eventually to the opening of the Kennedy Center; to promote companies of various sorts, ranging from Olney to the university's Brookland campus; and to reopen the historic Ford's Theatre as a performance venue.

Late in his life, Father Hartke remembered meeting a young woman who had approached him in the spring of 1949 with an idea to launch a showboat on the Potomac River.[141] Zelda Diamond Fichandler was in her early twenties at the time, and she had joined up with her husband Tom, and with her George Washington University graduate school drama professor—and former Catholic master's degree student—Ed Mangum to launch a local theater.

Zelda, a former Russian-language major, had embraced theater through her undergraduate literature courses at Cornell University. Ed, a Methodist from Texas, already had launched a small theater company at Mount Vernon Methodist Church downtown.

When the showboat idea failed to materialize, they approached Father Hartke for help in locating a building suitable for stage productions. Eventually, they landed on an abandoned movie and burlesque house, the Hippodrome. It turned out that Father Hartke knew the owners of the dilapidated building, the Lusk brothers. Out of necessity imposed by the building's condition and layout, they created a theater-in-the-round, an "arena," which was still an innovative concept at the time.

Magnum left Zelda and the "Arena Stage" in the spring of 1952. His departure opened the door to a long-running collaboration between her and Alan Schneider. At about the same time, Arena presented Dorothy Maynard, an African American singer recommended by Constitution Hall manager Patrick Hayes. Their effort quietly integrated the Washington stage. Arena allowed White and African American patrons to sit together from its very first performances. Arena would grow into a permanent fixture on the Washington scene—one that, to his everlasting pride, eventually eclipsed Father Hartke's own stage at Catholic University.

The Department of Speech and Drama at Catholic University did not outlive Father Hartke for long. Subject to campus intrigue and bouts of university-driven reorganization, the drama program evolved more simply into a high-quality undergraduate and graduate training program for theater professionals. University officials all too frequently undervalued what they had, as they looked elsewhere for prestige and recognition. In June 2018, Catholic University's Board of Trustees voted to fold the Drama Department into the Rome School of Music, Drama, and Art, in a move that many viewed as a cost-saving measure.[142] Administrators aside, Catholic University's theater artists had long since staked their claim to a place in American society and on the Washington stage.

Zelda Fichandler in front of Hippodrome Theater, 1950
(Photo, Arena Stage Records, 1950–2007 (C0017), Special Collections, Fenwick Library, George Mason University, Fairfax, Virginia. Used with permission from Arena Stage

Chapter 3

Proclaiming Regional Presence

The largest circumference of the circle is the world the theater lives in and that is a multicultural world, a world defined by the multitudinous ways in which our species expresses the universal themes. It is a story of infinite richness and variety. Arena has always been a theater of multicultural expression, and now it is even more so in the awareness that the further it can extend its reach, the richer it will become; the more it can encompass, the denser and more complex its art.
—Zelda Fichandler, 1990[1]

In early 1951, downtown Washington had hardly begun its decades-long slide into oblivion. The old Hippodrome cinema-turned-burlesque house at Ninth Street and New York Avenue NW near the Carnegie Library nonetheless stood vacant. "Winos," who sound more picturesque perhaps than the "junkies" who took their place decades later, disturbed the sensibilities of more established Washingtonians. The neighborhood was still a decade and a half away from becoming the front lines of the 1968 civil disturbances that followed the assassination of Dr. Martin Luther King Jr. in Memphis. Even so, the area felt like something of an urban edge.

One rainy night, a surreal little group of fancifully costumed characters from *Alice in Wonderland* made their way under umbrellas held by the economist Thomas Fichandler down a back alley past startled alcoholic derelicts, parading from their dressing rooms to the stage door of a new playhouse that had opened the year before. Modeled after Margo Jones's innovative theater-in-the-round in Dallas, the new auditorium appeared more like a boxing ring, with seats arranged in a square around a 16-by-20-foot rectangular playing area. For the playhouse's founder, Zelda Diamond Fichandler, this space was a magic place of the imagination.[2]

The space did not qualify as a "theater," as Zelda had discovered to her own good fortune on opening day a few months before. If it had done so, the company she and her husband Tom founded together with her former George Washington University drama professor, Edward Mangum, never would have staged its first production. As the city inspector who materialized hours before the actors were to meet their audience for the first time pointed out, "theaters" in Washington required asbestos fire curtains to receive an occupancy license. Zelda jumped into the sidecar of the inspector's motorcycle and headed off to the District Building, where she heroically secured the requisite permits. She only succeeded because the dilapidated Hippodrome, with its "arena" configuration, was no longer a "theater" but only a "stage."

Within just a few minutes, the cast of enthusiastic young actors that first evening—including future notables George Grizzard, Lester Rawlins, and Pernell Roberts—launched into a performance of Oliver Goldsmith's *She Stoops to Conquer* directed by Mangum. The now-venerated "Arena Stage" had been launched.[3]

As already noted, the Fichandlers and Mangum initially had their eyes on a 327-foot excursion boat, the SS *Potomac*, which they wanted to convert into a showboat paddling up and down its namesake river.[4] After discovering the logistical and financial challenges of operating and maintaining such a vessel, they explored various garages, warehouses, and churches.[5] When a suitable site failed to materialize, they approached Father Hartke for help in locating a building appropriate for stage productions.[6]

Eventually, they landed on an abandoned movie and burlesque house near Mount Vernon Square, the Hippodrome.[7] It turned out that Father Hartke knew the owners of the run-down building, the Lusk brothers. Out of necessity imposed by the building's condition and layout, they created a theater-in-the-round, an "arena," which was still an innovative concept at the time. They established a for-profit joint stock company—Arena Stage, Inc.—offering shares to a group of forty Washingtonians—including ambassadors, carpenters, housewives, and sports figures—and began tackling the challenges of forming a theatrical company and renovating a dilapidated building.

There is little to suggest that Zelda, her husband Tom, and their friend Ed thought much about transforming either American theater or Washington's identity when they set out to create a professional theater company. Mangum had formed an amateur theater group—the Mount Vernon Players—to try to keep theater alive in Washington's inhospitable environment.[8] Arena seemed a logical next step.

With the National Theater closed rather than integrating its audiences—and several boycotts by professional theater groups keeping touring companies away—Mangum had a difficult time finding productions for him and his students to watch.[9] Zelda, who had moved to Washington as a child when her father went to work at the National Bureau of Standards, was committed to the city and to theater.[10] Her immersion in Russian literature at Cornell University during her student days deepened her interest in the stage. Their collective response was to open a local professional theater company in Washington.

Zelda, Tom, and Ed had few models on which to base their efforts. The Little Theater Movement of the 1910s and 1920s that had inspired Thomas Montgomery Gregory and others around Howard University had run its course, battered by the economic woes of the Great Depression. As Catholic University's Father Hartke had realized when establishing his own program, the burgeoning university theater scene around the country was more conventional than creative.

Of all the models from which they could draw inspiration, Hallie Flanagan's short-lived Federal Theatre Project offered the most powerful insights into what might be possible, even though it had been unceremoniously shut down by Congress before the war.[11] Flanagan's failure in the eyes of Congress was her achievement from the perspective of the young postwar generation. Her project supported performance in communities around the country. Those artists who participated in its various efforts carried that experience with them throughout the remainder of their careers. The postwar blossoming of the American stage—of which the emergence of Arena Stage is but a single example—rested in no small measure on the creative and institutional seeds planted by Flanagan and her colleagues. Margo Jones was among those who were inspired.

Jones had served as assistant director of the Federal Theatre in Houston and, in that capacity, traveled to the Soviet Union during the late 1930s to participate in a festival organized by the Moscow Art Theatre. She returned to Texas, where she established the Houston Community Theatre and joined the faculty of the University of Texas at Austin. She subsequently gained commercial success on Broadway before moving back to the Lone Star State, where, in 1947, she opened Theatre '47 in Dallas.

Operating out of the landmark Magnolia Petroleum (Mobile Oil) Company headquarters building designed by William Lescaze, Theatre '47 was the country's first nonprofit professional resident theater and its first professional theater-in-the-round. Jones had long promoted the advantages of such physical arrangements, which brought the audience and performers closer together.

Jones died tragically in 1955, and her company closed four years later. Its success spawned a new wave of regional theaters across the country, led by her own Theatre '47 in Dallas, the Alley Theater in Houston, and Zelda's Arena Stage in Washington.[12] Theaters outside New York were staking their claims to the American stage, and Washington stood at the center of many of these efforts.

Jones's vision inspired Zelda to establish a residential company that presented a repertoire of both older and newer fare.[13] The artistic possibilities of the still-revolutionary "arena" staging concept—with its promise of connecting the audience more directly to the performers onstage—fascinated Zelda. As Zelda would later reveal, Magnum had been insistent on the arena configuration, arguing that the arrangement "took the theater back to its tribal beginnings."[14] The unusual configuration had an additional attraction, in that it helped resolve the challenges of utilizing the dumpy facilities at the Hippodrome Theatre.

The Hippodrome Years

Fitting a theater-in-the-round into the Hippodrome proved difficult. In the end, they arranged seven rows of seating along two sides and three rows on the other sides, making 247 seats available for each performance.[15] The Fichandlers and Mangum assembled a company of eight young actors drawn largely from Catholic and George Washington universities, and they somehow managed to produce seventeen plays during their first, 1950–51 season.[16]

The season began with Ed Mangum's August 16, 1950, inaugural production of Oliver Goldsmith's eighteenth-century comedy *She Stoops to Conquer*.[17] Audiences began to fill the available seats by the first weekend of the two-week run, with more than two-thirds of the available seats sold over all sixteen performances.[18]

Washington's professional community had been thirsting for live theater, and Arena managed to find an audience from the very beginning. Local drama critics—including Ernie Schier, Jay Carmody, Tom Donnelly, and Richard Coe at the city's four daily newspapers—enthusiastically promoted each new work.[19]

By 1952, a combination of health and personal reasons prompted Mangum to leave after having directed ten of Arena's early productions. The native Texan set out for Hawaii's warmer climes, where he became director of a new company in Honolulu.[20] He moved back to Austin during the 1960s to enjoy a successful career producing and teaching at Saint Edward's University.[21] Zelda called Alan Schneider at Catholic University late on the evening when Mangum shared his intention to leave. She invited him to replace the departing director. Schneider—after consulting with Father Hartke—accepted and extended his long-standing relationship with Arena Stage.[22]

The fervent audience and critical response to the sort of theater presented at Arena proved significant for reasons other than artistic ones. From the very beginning, Arena Stage sold tickets to African Americans, who were permitted to sit anywhere in the auditorium in a fully integrated audience.[23] This experience undermined old tropes that White Washingtonians would never attend a performance sitting next to Black Washingtonians.[24]

Nonetheless, as the backstage discussions among senior management and stakeholders reveal, Arena's early success rested on its embrace of the era's most innovative theater. The question of race, though always acknowledged, did not serve at first as a motiving force in decisionmaking. This would change as the company grew and the city changed. A decade-long search for a permanent home and effective management structures ultimately brought the challenge of the city's race relations to the fore. The city was shaping the stage even as the stage would reshape the city.

The Old Vat

Arena's financial stability caught up to the company's artistic success by 1953.[25] In addition to box office revenues, the Fichandlers were effective corporate fundraisers and, from the very beginning, Arena garnered robust support from individual and corporate donors.[26] A reliance on subscriptions over individual ticket purchases provided for more predictable income while mitigating against the damaging impact of bad reviews for any particular production. As the company stabilized, Zelda began to take stock of Arena's achievements and plan for a more ambitious future. Looking back, she saw that

> Arena Stage, Washington's own resident, professional repertory company, is now in its third year of operation. Over its short history it has earned a reputation for the best in theatre. It has been enthusiastically supported by Washington audiences. It has won the critical acclaim and affection of the theatrical press of Washington and New York. Patrons have admitted it from embassies and international organizations of our Capital city and by visitors from other parts of the country and from abroad. It has enjoyed solid artistic and financial success. It feels, however, that its location in Washington, DC, the Nation's Capital, gives both a special opportunity and a special responsibility to increase still further its artistic contribution. Arena Stage finds in its location in this city the possibility of becoming a theatrical landmark of national and international significance.[27]

The company had staked a claim for Washington and regional theater within a national scene dominated by New York. The company could not achieve such a vision at its present location, the Hippodrome building. She noted that "it has outgrown its badly located cramped, aesthetically inadequate headquarters and is not direct-ing its efforts toward finding a new home."[28]

The search for a new stage dominated the cozy Arena stock-holder meetings convened in the Fichandlers' Cleveland Park liv-ing room. Zelda argued that

> as we all know, the Hippodrome Building is located in one of the worst locations in Washington, in the heart of crime-rid-den Precinct One, has inadequate parking facilities avail-able to it, and is fairly inaccessible by public transportation. It is a very old building, in bad condition, impossibly heated and air conditioned, with deplorable lounge facilities, bad house lighting and a cramped seating arrangement. There are no inducements to seeing a play at Arena Stage except the play itself and the atmosphere of cordiality provided by the house and box office staff.[29]

The company's stakeholders set out to find an auditorium that could seat at least twice as many as the 247-seat Hippodrome, plus accommodate their signature arena configuration. Its stockholders voted on June 8, 1955, to cease operations at the Hippodrome at the end of the current run of *The Mousetrap*, retaining all "equipment and properties" for an-as-yet-unknown future home.[30] Over the first five years at the Hippodrome, Arena had mounted fifty-five productions, to increasing critical acclaim.[31]

This decision entailed its own perils. Caught off guard, the Lusks lashed out, prompting a prolonged and nasty legal battle. Lawsuits, countersuits, injunctions, depositions, court hearings, negations, and myriad other legal maneuvers ensued.[32] Although Arena eventually "won," the judgments in its favor were modest in relation to the energy and resources expended to achieve victory.[33]

This saga convinced Arena's leadership of an urgent need to dissolve Arena Stage, Inc., and reconstitute the theater as a non-profit organization.[34] By doing so, the company would gain ad-ditional protection from lawsuits, enhanced tax advantages, and open coffers to foundation funding. However, Arena Stage, Inc., had been incorporated in Maryland, and to reconstitute the company as a nonprofit in the District of Columbia, Arena would first need to establish itself as a DC corporation. This process dragged on into 1959, with parallel for-profit corporations—Arena Stage, Inc. (Maryland) and Arena Enterprises, Inc. (DC)—overseeing operations and searching for a new permanent home.[35]

Finally, in April 1959, the District of Columbia recognized the newly incorporated Washington Drama Society, Inc.[36] The society's sole purpose was to manage Arena Stage. The arrangement mandated an annual meeting of members, though all decisionmaking authority remained with the Board of Directors.[37]

Foggy Bottom Transitions

The Fichandlers had their eyes on the Foggy Bottom neighborhood even as they explored a number of different properties. They imagined that the theater would fit in nicely on the site of the Washington Gas Light Company's gas works (a project that eventually became the Watergate mixed-use complex).[38] They needed a place to land while they waited, and they began looking at a variety of possibilities that stood in the patch of land slated for a new bridge across the Potomac. The thought seemed to be that the contemplated highway undermined rents for property that was likely to be condemned. The Fichandlers calculated that the bridge was "at least two, perhaps three, and even five years away." Such a period would allow planning for a more permanent facility.[39] And in the end, this is precisely what happened.

Leveraging the company's strong financial standing, the directors and stockholders canceled the company's 1955–56 season as they prepared to settle into a new home.[40] Arena's stockholders stepped up and funded a new theater in the "Hospitality Hall" at the Olde Heurich Brewery in Foggy Bottom (owner Christian Heurich built a large Victorian pile of a home near Dupont Circle, which has become a neighborhood favorite).[41] The brewery had been a local signature enterprise. It brewed the city's largest-selling local beer for decades, surviving Prohibition by producing nonalcoholic beverages. Built in 1895, the facility could no longer keep up with the industry's commercial and technological changes and closed its doors in 1956. Its large reception room—"Hospitality Hall"— proved a perfect solution to Arena's dilemma.

The confluence of Rock Creek and the Potomac River supported a small industrial and working-class settlement predating the
formation of the District of Columbia. Once known as Funkstown
after an early German settler, Jacob Funk, the neighborhood took
shape around various small-scale industrial facilities. A laboring
community of Black and White—predominately Irish—workers
grew up, becoming infamous by the late nineteenth century for
teeming alleys overflowing with poor residents. Such squalid conditions prompted the formation of the Alley Dwelling Authority
during Franklin Roosevelt's New Deal, and housing conditions
began to improve. Prominent Washington institutions—most notably, the US Department of State and George Washington University—encroached on the area as downtown Washington grew. By the
1950s, a long property development process began, which would
come to be known as "gentrification."[42]

With five hundred seats and a large performance area, the intimate "Old Vat" (so nicknamed because of leftover brewing equipment) became a much-cherished theater over the course of the 43
productions there.[43] The Old Vat experience cemented long-lasting
bonds among ticket holders, actors, donors, and the company's artistic directors that lasted well into the future (with a smaller "Old
Vat Room" opening in the basement of the company's new theater
in 1976).[44] One challenge remained. The facility could never be
more than a temporary solution to Arena's search for a permanent
home, given the bridge project that already had been scheduled.

The Arena leadership was aware of the clock ticking down on
their new residence. In a letter marked "Confidential," Zelda reported to stockholders in late 1958 that the search for resolving the
company's "housing problem" was well under way. The present
building was to be torn down to make way for approaches to the
new Constitution Avenue (later Theodore Roosevelt) Bridge. Despite some hope that a troubled appropriations process might save
the day, everyone understood that Arena needed to find a permanent home. The search was taking place in a city that had embarked
on ambitious urban renewal at a time of dramatic demographic
turmoil. The theater's trajectory often tracked these social and economic transformations, forcing the company to contemplate loca-
tions once not considered suitable.

The company's management and stockholders investigated a number of options, including renting and converting existing buildings, combining with other groups, and building a new theater that it would own. As noted above, they remained interested in Foggy Bottom but knew they had to look more widely around town. They scoped out movie theaters, the Wax Museum, Hogate's Restaurant, and the Roger Smith Hotel, among many sites. Their enthusiasm for the neighboring Potomac Plaza Project on the gasworks site proved unfounded.

The Fichandlers traveled to New York to meet with the developers of the new Southwest Redevelopment Project, only to be told by its architect, I. M. Pei, that "they couldn't afford to fit us in at a rental rate [that we could afford—BR]."[45] As late as March 4, 1959, Zelda was not at all sure the company would survive, informing one job applicant that "we have not yet hit upon a solution to our housing problem; and it is so by no means definite that this organization will continue beyond next season. I would advise no one with family responsibilities to hitch their wagon to our star; it may never shoot again."[46]

From For-Profit to Not-For-Profit Theater

During this increasingly frantic search, the Fichandlers realized that, if they were to reconstitute the company as a "not-for-profit organization," it would become eligible for foundation grants. This organizational approach was unprecedented for a performing arts organization and required some quiet, behind-the-scenes legislative tweaks by Congress before Arena could proceed.[47]

When applying for nonprofit status, Arena Stage emphasized the charitable, scientific, and educational objectives of the new Washington Drama Society. Although the society's sole purpose was to support the activities of Arena Stage, "its aims were: (a) to provide instruction and practical experience for the training of the various theatrical professions; (b) to experiment with the composition and methods of presenting drama and with ways to foster the revitalization of the living theatre; and (c) to educate the public by presenting dramatic and related performances that provide a valid interpretation of life on the stage and through related community activities."[48] In this manner, the society's application aligned theatrical performance with education.

The Washington Drama Society's forty-page statement of purpose consistently amplified the organization's educational mission, in sharp contrast to American commercial theater. For-profit theatrical productions are "organized as it is on the basis of the 'one-shot production' method, providing no continuity or diversity of experience, and no continuing institutions, is absolutely and completely unequipped to provide for the training and development of theatre artists."[49] Even Arena Stage's still unusual physical configuration served an educational purpose, given that "its aim was to unite the actor and the audience in a common experience, not to separate them."[50] Several profiles of former Arena actors and artistic professionals demonstrated the success of the educational dimension of its work.[51]

The Washington Drama Society—acting through Arena Stage— would conduct "experiments" as it educated. Indeed, "the experiments Arena Stage is conducting in cooperation with the Ford Foundation represent only part of its full program of scientific exploration of problems related to the development of regional repertory theatres as a method of revitalizing the American Theatre. The importance to the future of theatre in this country of adequately testing the idea of the regional repertory theatre, of uncovering its inherent problems, and finding solutions, can hardly be overstated."[52]

This strategy underscored the place of Arena Stage and regional stage more generally in American theater. The new status closed the distance between the proposed Washington Drama Society and its action arm, Arena Stage, on one hand, and more traditional educational and scientific nonprofit organizations, on the other hand. Such creative argumentation opened the door for many others to follow.[53] Once secured, the new status provided a model for residential theater companies around the country and helped launch the swift growth of American regional theaters. From a handful of companies at the time—Alley Theatre, Houston (1947); the Mummers Theatre, Oklahoma City (1949); Arena Stage (1950); the Actor's Workshop, San Francisco (1952); the Milwaukee Repertory Company (1954); the Front Theatre, Memphis (1954); and the Charles

Playhouse, Boston (1957)—regional, nonprofit residential theatrical companies exploded, fueled by the availability of foundation grants unavailable to for-profit corporations.[54] By the mid-1960s, several regional theaters leveraged the Ford Foundation's support to form the League of Resident Theatres, so they could negotiate collectively with the Actors' Equity Association, the Stage Directors and Choreographers Society, United Scenic Artists, and other major entertainment unions. At present, there are over 70 member companies forming the League of Regional Theatres, setting the ground rules for over 1,800 theater companies outside New York.[55] Thomas Fichandler played a major role in this growth.[56]

The Ford Foundation's part in underwriting the expansion of regional theater proved pivotal. Operating through the foundation's Humanities and the Arts Division, headed by W. McNeil "Mac" Lowery, the foundation doled out $16 million to seventeen regional theaters between 1962 and 1971 (including $2.6 million to Arena).[57]

In the hypercommercialized world of American cultural production, Arena sought ways to maximize income flow within its new legal status. In reformulating their company as a nonprofit corporation, the Fichandlers expanded the range of their funding opportunities but did not eliminate their reliance on attracting audiences. The tension remained between maximizing income by filling seats and advancing innovation by producing cutting-edge works that might not attract a broad audience.

Some critics over the years have lamented Arena's concern for financial success, which they see as antithetical to advancing artistic and social agendas. As already noted, Alain Locke argued in 1922 that universities would "assure a greater continuity of effort and insure accordingly a greater permanence of result" when making the case for the Howard Players as the leader in developing African American theater.[58] Reliance on major institutional donors has its own perils, as Locke himself would discover three years later, when Howard University refused to renew his contract after he affronted a member of the Board of Trustees.[59]

The Fichandlers had no choice other than to balance their artistic creed and social vision with the demands of ticket and subscription holders, government and private foundation grant givers, and corporate and individual donors. The company's reorganization as a nonprofit expanded their opportunities for advancing their creative agenda by extending the range of possible sources of financial support. As Donatella Galella writes in her perceptive study of Arena's development, *America in the Round*, the company negotiated "different forms of capital as well as racial and US American identities, not only challenging norms but also socially reproducing them. Arena wields nonprofit status yet mobilizes for-profit thinking. It has done more than many of its peer institutions to incorporate Blackness for half a century yet still centers on Whiteness."[60]

On October 10, 1959, Arena Stage's stockholders liquidated the commercial company, turning its property and operations over to the newly formed, nonprofit Washington Drama Society.[61] The Eugene and Agnes E. Meyer Foundation, Old Dominion Fund, Twentieth Century Fund, Rockefeller Foundation, the American Security and Trust Company, and other donors provided funding for Arena to build and own a new building.[62] On March 10, 1960, the Washington Drama Society held a press conference announcing a new, purpose-built 827-seat stage-in-the-round theater for Arena designed by the Chicago architect Harry Weese (who later would design the original Washington Metrorail stations).[63] The new theater was to be located in the Southwest Redevelopment Area—off, a bit, from the new neighborhood center I. M. Pei had declared to be too expensive.

Unnoted at the time, by moving from Northwest neighborhoods adjacent to downtown to the southside, Arena Stage was relocating closer to the hometown heart of a city that was majority African American. The Southwest Redevelopment Project, of which Arena was becoming a part, already had played its own malign role in Washington's race relations. The move to Southwest meant that the city's long-standing toxic race relations could not be passed over.

Chocolate City, Vanilla Suburbs

Soon after World War II, planners and federal officials began to look for ways to improve the increasingly worn Washington urban fabric. By the mid-1950s, they had drawn up several highway and urban redevelopment projects that would destroy some of the poorest African American sections of town. Arena itself was a victim to these plans, for they forced the company to relocate from the Old Vat to make way for the approaches to a trans-Potomac crossing that blasted through Foggy Bottom.

Official Washington would achieve its lofty visions by removing African Americans and working-class Washingtonians from view. As the editorial writers at the *Washington Post* told their readers, "No doubt many residents of the area will be loath to lose their homes despite the prevailing slum conditions. They should realize, however, that the net effect of this great redevelopment effort will be to make Washington a much more pleasant place in which to live and work."[64]

These plans both fashioned, and were fashioned by, Washington's rapidly changing postwar demographic structure.[65] As noted earlier in this book, unfulfilled consumer demand after the Great Depression and World War II combined with new highways and housing to lure city dwellers to the suburbs, as was happening in other metropolitan areas across the United States.[66] Racially restrictive real estate practices eased, empowering African Americans to move to neighborhoods where they had previously been unwelcome. Washington became the first major US city with a majority African American population.[67]

During these same years, wartime and postwar booms lured rural migrants to low-wage service jobs in the city. The city became poorer. Simultaneously, city planners moved to eradicate the very neighborhoods that provided an urban foothold for impoverished migrants—the very area in the city's Southwest quadrant to which Arena Stage would relocate.[68]

Meanwhile, the region was suburbanizing. More than 1.5 million new residents moved to the Washington metropolitan region during the quarter century after the end of the war. This growth rarely found its way into the metropolitan core.[69] The overall regional population grew from 621,000 in 1930 to 1.5 million in 1950, 2.9 million in 1970, and 4.2 million in 1990. In contrast, the city's population first nearly doubled, from 486,869 in 1930 to an all-time high of 802,178 in 1950, before falling to 756,510 in 1970 and 606,900 in 1990.[70]

Consequently, the city's proportion of the metropolitan population declined from 78 percent in 1930 to 54 percent in 1950, 26 percent in 1970, and 15 percent in 1990.[71] These patterns became embedded in Arena's patron base. By the 1980s, some 40 percent of the theater's subscribers and ticket holders lived in Maryland, and another third or so drove in from Virginia. Only slightly more than a quarter of its customers came from the city.[72]

For the most part, the city was losing ground both economically and demographically to the suburbs. Private-sector employment became ever more important in the region throughout the last half of the twentieth century, with the vast preponderance of those new jobs being created in the suburbs.[73] Overall, the city lagged behind other local jurisdictions in per capita personal income, simultaneously consolidating its role as home to the largest share of families living below the poverty line.[74]

In addition to the suburbanization and metropolitanization experienced in every major American city, Washington became a magnet for poor African Americans migrating from the failed economies of the coastal South. If most African American Washingtonians found their way to the city at the beginning of the twentieth century from nearby Maryland and Virginia, migrants from declining rural economies in the Carolinas and Georgia became an increasingly large presence by the 1940s.[75] Their growing numbers accelerated the city's racial turnover, as its population changed from being two-thirds White to two-thirds African American in two decades.[76]

Newly arriving country folk had difficulty finding a secure place for themselves in the local economy. Migrants largely settled in the old, run-down, historically African American neighborhoods south of the National Mall in the city's Southwest quadrant, and also in other low-lying areas.[77] Washington's Southwest Redevelopment Project—once lauded by the prominent architectural critic Wolf Von Eckardt as bringing "suburban wholesomeness with urban stimulation" to downtown—destroyed many of the social networks that had held these neighborhoods together.[78]

As Jerome Paige and Margaret Reuss observed, "Middle- and upper-income citizens wanted the slums, which they saw as a reproach to their city, removed. They wanted a clean, sanitary and beautiful environment and they were beguiled by the promise of an increased tax base."[79] Their efforts to build highways and to remove slums echoed initiatives in nearly every major US city at the time. Washington, however, was different. Without home rule, the city was governed by Congress and its appointed commissioners, who were notoriously unconcerned about the preferences of local residents.

The Southwest slums were particularly unseemly and forlorn, a degradation made more poignant by the presence of the relatively nearby Capitol and national monuments and museums constantly in view. The 113-block project zone south of the Mall and north of the Washington Channel (an inlet of the Potomac River) was home to 22,539 residents in 1950, nearly 80 percent of whom were African Americans.[80] Hundreds of buildings had no indoor plumbing; many more were obsolete and below the current building code.[81] But even though the neighborhood was dilapidated, few residents wanted to leave. Among those of prominence, only Eleanor Roosevelt asked where these poor residents would go. No one who mattered cared to answer.

The National Capital Planning Commission's experiment destroyed 99 percent of the buildings within the project area. Consequently, almost none of the original residents remained. Only a third of the area's residents were able to secure alternative housing in public projects elsewhere in the city. Roughly 2,000 families moved into private rental units outside Southwest; while others among the displaced remained completely lost from official records. A paltry 391 residents were able to purchase homes, virtually none in Southwest.[82]

Many former residents felt disappointment, anger, helplessness, and bitterness. A quarter of the expunged residents reported five years after their relocation that they had not made a single new friend in their new neighborhoods. Only 14 percent of these former Southwest residents felt as safe in their new homes as before.[83] In contrast, in 1972, the replacement community had half as many residents, nearly 80 percent of whom were White. They inhabited 5,900 new housing units, of which only 310 were classified as being reserved for low- to moderate-income residents.[84]

The newcomers at the time—including Zelda and her colleagues at Arena Stage—were very much aware of the tensions the redevelopment plan had produced. Because the project abutted public housing projects that remained largely untouched, new arrivals found themselves going about their lives together with some of the city's poorest residents. Unlike the case in neighborhoods north of the National Mall, Southwest residents crossed racial and economic boundaries simply by walking out their front doors.

Several church and community leaders made concerted efforts to create an inclusive community. In 1961, a newcomer, the prominent White journalist Neal Pierce, became troubled by local neighborhood Black children looking longingly through a fence at his new building's swimming pool. He joined with a longtime resident, Joseph Latimore, an African American, to form the Southwest Neighborhood Assembly, which was dedicated to fostering a single community.[85] More than a half century later, the assembly remains a vital presence deeply involved in efforts to transcend boundaries that are entrenched elsewhere in the city.[86]

Arena, by relocating from the fringe of downtown in the city's Northwest quadrant to near the Southwest waterfront, had entered a vastly different urban community. On one hand, the company was nestled into a prominent corner of a completely planned neighborhood full of residents with few previous ties to one another or to their immediate surroundings. On the other hand, long-term residents in adjacent housing projects viewed with suspicion everything that Arena and the other newcomers represented.

These two faces of Southwest were visible across the street from Arena's backdoor. To the right, a few hundred yards away, stands the oldest continuously operating fish market in the country, long a cornerstone of African American DC; to the left, a similar distance away, is Washington Marina, one of the country's largest urban houseboat colonies. Arena's artists and patrons confronted the daily challenges of midcentury American urban life simply by presenting and attending a performance. The city surrounding the stage was about to shape what transpired on that stage. To stake its claim to the city from its new location, Arena needed to engage some of the deep and seemingly impermeable issues that had led Gregory, Locke, Richardson, Douglas, and others a third of a century before to develop a distinctive Black voice on the American stage.

Adjusting to a New Home

Finding a new location for Arena Stage represented a major stride forward, but only an initial step. The building had to be designed, financed, constructed, and operated. Each phase—such as the prolonged struggles to alter zoning and building codes—required Arena, Zelda, Tom, and their colleagues to change how they went about their jobs and their art.[87]

The company connected with the Chicago architect Harry Weese, who already had a thriving practice designing a variety of buildings in the stark, almost brutalist modernist style that would become admired in the 1960s and 1970s. As noted above, Weese eventually would design the original cement stations of the Washington Metrorail system a decade or so later.[88]

For all his accomplishments, Weese had never taken on the project of creating a theater.[89] The resulting 827-seat theater that debuted on Halloween 1961 with Alan Schneider's production of Bertolt Brecht's *The Caucasian Chalk Circle* was the product of intense collaboration between a mature architect who knew what he liked in building design—Weese—and an accomplished theater professional who knew what she wanted for her art—Zelda Fichandler.[90] Their partnership was powerful, as Weese and Zelda corresponded, consulted, met, and telephoned one another constantly about the smallest and largest of issues and design challenges. Together, they defined what it meant to conceive and construct a theater-in-the-round. Their mutual respect carried the project through.[91]

Arena's opening was one of Washington's signature events at the time, attracting social, political, and diplomatic notables, including a special tour for First Lady Lady Bird Johnson.[92] Architecture and theater critics joined in the celebration, fascinated by the buildings' starkly contemporary design and the as-yet-unusual configuration of its stage and seating.[93] The building's continuing durability is a sign of their successful collaboration.

Financing the new building proved to be Tom Fichandler's triumph. Tom took leave from his day job with the Twentieth Century Fund to shepherd the legal, financial, and practical process required to achieve his wife's and their architect's visions.[94] He assembled an impressive collection of grants (including $312,000 from such foundations as the Rockefeller Foundation, the Agnes E. Meyer Foundation, the Old Dominion Fund, and the Twentieth Century Fund), bonds (including $250,000 from American Security and Trust Company, and $225,000 in community-raised bonds sold in $100 units), and individual gifts (totaling $62,500). Altogether, Arena raised $1 million to cover the costs associated with the year-long construction process.

Once it was completed, the Ford Foundation awarded a grant of $863,000 to buy off the bonds and mortgages for the new building, as well as to purchase the land the theater occupied.[95] Arena achieved its goal of securing 15,000 subscribers by the 1964–65 season to ensure its future financial health.[96] Arena Stage thus entered a new era, in which for the first time its home was secure.

Operating inside the new space with the company's characteristic creativity proved more challenging. In a 1985 interview, Zelda conceded that "we did have a bad time when we moved into the new quarters. The enlarged space required a larger aesthetic, and we seemed to make all the wrong artistic choices. It wouldn't fix itself, and I lived through a number of years wondering if I knew how or could learn fast enough."[97]

Zelda did not confront the challenges alone. Performing in the larger facilities required additional staff members, with several future company stalwarts signed on board around this time, including Mel Shapiro (Zelda's assistant and later resident director), Edwin Sherin (director), Robin Wagner (designer), Marjorie Slaiman (costumiere), and, Peggy Laves (Zelda's executive assistant). The company placed an ever-greater emphasis on performing as an ensemble, blending an ever-tighter team of performers and artists into a single unit. And it tried to do so in an effort to embrace a more sophisticated aesthetic, while mastering and controlling the new space and an expanding repertoire. Looking back, Arena's leaders concluded with the advantage of hindsight that they took about a decade to adjust to the larger stage, and to their expanded role in American and Washington theater.[98]

The company's new home drove some of these modifications, but not all. Arena was no longer a lone ranger within the effort to create a vibrant regional theater. Regional, residential, and repertory theaters sprang up around the country, forcing Arena to embrace its place as a pioneer and leader (a function that often fell to Tom). Washington was changing as well, becoming ever more "Chocolate City" surrounded by "Vanilla Suburbs," forcing Arena to navigate between the two.[99]

More generally, the 1960s were a time of societal upheaval, when someone challenged and questioned every communal norm. Zelda's approach for engaging these forces consistently embraced the experimental. "For an artist, and an art institution," she noted at the time, "there is no such thing as success. There is only process. . . . Tomorrow there is another blank canvas, another empty page, and for us another play to be made into life."[100]

Who's Afraid of Alan Schneider?

Alan Schneider had no difficulty using the new building. Schneider already had established a reputation as perhaps the foremost American director of the avant-garde. As he had demonstrated with his production of Thornton Wilder's *The Skin of Our Teeth* at Catholic University in 1952, he had an unusual sensitivity for the aesthetic emerging among a new cohort of playwrights responding to the conformism of postwar life by embracing the absurd, the brittle, the humorous, the angry, and the vicious.[101] Even an infamous debacle at the premier of *Waiting for Godot* at the Coconut Grove Playhouse in Florida—when, as noted in chapter 2, audience members stormed out after having shown up expecting vaudeville comedy, only to be confronted by Samuel Beckett's dystopia—became a victory of sorts over the materialistic complacency and unthinking conformity of the 1950s version of Babbitry.[102]

As Beckett's favorite American director—and long-term correspondent—Schneider kept winning kudos for his productions of works by Beckett, Brecht, Edward Albee, Harold Pinter, and William Saroyan.[103] He did so by paying rigorous attention to technical matters, while remaining as close as possible to the words written in the script, much to the appreciation of the playwrights themselves.[104]

Just a year after the opening of the new Arena Stage, Schneider gained wide recognition with his direction of the original Broadway production of Albee's *Who's Afraid of Virginia Woolf?*—featuring Uta Hagen, Arthur Hill, Melinda Dillon, and the Arena veteran George Grizzard. In 1963, Schneider became the first director to win both the Tony Award for Broadway and the Obie Award for Off Broadway in the same year for Albee's play and the Off-Broadway production of Pinter's *The Collection*.[105]

Arena Stage could never contain Schneider. He directed across the United States and around the world, ran the theater program at the Juilliard School, and taught at the University of California in both Riverside and San Diego.[106] He eventually relocated his home base to a contemporary home surrounded by woods high above the Hudson River less than an hour from Manhattan in the artsy river town of Hastings-on-Hudson. Nonetheless, Schneider did not abandon Arena and Washington. Nearly half his productions appeared on Arena stages and, during Zelda's 1973–74 sabbatical, Schneider took over the company's artistic direction.[107] Schneider's Arena season that year included *Two by Beckett*, featuring the American theater legends Hume Cronyn and Jessica Tandy.[108]

As Zelda noted in her final tribute to Schneider after his untimely death in 1984, "We opened two theaters together, both times it was a race to get the building there ahead of the production, did 40 productions together, turned *Our Town* into Russian in a two-day, nonstop session simultaneous translation."[109] Throughout it all, she recalled, "he took such childlike delight in the magic of the theater and in the achievement of others, such joy when someone, anyone, anywhere, could make it happen."[110]

As already noted, Schneider had been born in the Ukrainian city of Khar'kiv just weeks after the Bolshevik Revolution in 1917, a connection that remained important to Zelda. Both of them were Russian speakers, she noted, and "like two good Russian souls, we had many talks over the years. But whatever the specific subject matter, and whether it was funny or sad, his encompassing theme was always that life is unpredictable."[111]

Schneider could be the very opposite of user friendly, as the Arena union representatives would learn. In response to a relatively minor bureaucratic procedure, he poured invective onto a union committee. "As I have on occasion reminded myself," he wrote, one of the ironies of the twentieth century is that the dictatorship of the proletariat took place not in the Soviet Union but in our own unions. Anyone reading your note would get the distinct impression that you have to be on the barricades daily to get decent breaks from this management or at least from me. I have no doubt whatsoever that you will strengthen your union and your ego and in the process continue to hasten the inevitable erosion of the American Theater, including this particular example. I'd wager everything I have and know that no such communication could ever have come from a group of people sincerely concerned for the larger and not the narrower aspects of their crafts.[112]

At the end of this, he signed "Sincerely in Art, Alan." Actor Bert Lahr's abovementioned urge to ban Schneider's name from his household after the Coconut Grove debacle with *Waiting for Godot* staring Lahr and Tom Ewell becomes understandable in light of such outbursts.[113]

A Secure Artistic Base

Arena provided Schneider with a reliable home base that he could not bring himself to relinquish. As he wrote to Beckett in late 1960, "Decisions piling in, continued and worsening ill health of my parents, the whole New York situation theatrically and the world situation morally and politically. Compensated for somewhat by growth of the two small ones, the efforts of my Jean, and the shelter of Hastings-on-Hudson. Having been offered permanent artistic directorship of Washington's Arena Theatre [*sic*], which opens a new building next year. Am tempted but unsure about leaving New York, freelancing, off-Broadway potentialities. Washington would offer a place and continuity of effort instead of this 'jiggling around' but not sure how much could be accomplished in situation there, how much freedom, etc. We shall see."[114]

Arena was hardly a fallback for Schneider. He frequently worked there, for example, with the now-legendary set designer Ming Cho Lee as well as with a roster of superb actors and theater professionals.[115] The son of a Yale graduate, Lee had grown up in

Shanghai before and during World War II, seizing an opportunity to study at Occidental College in Los Angeles in 1949.[116] After studying at Occidental and at the University of California, Los Angeles, he relocated to New York, where he established himself as a leading stage designer. He taught at New York University and, for four decades, at Yale University. He designed sets for regional theater, opera, and dance companies around the country as well as for the Metropolitan Opera, New York City Opera, Broadway, and Off-Broadway productions in New York. By century's end, he had won every possible award, including induction into the American Theater Hall of Fame, and he had been awarded the National Medal of Arts, had trained generations of master designers, and had gained recognition as one of the most important figures in American theater.[117]

Lee designed the sets for over twenty productions at Arena, including the renowned mountainside scenery for the company's 1982 production of Patrick Meyers's *K2*, which was directed by Jacques Levy.[118] Much of this work was in productions directed by Schneider.[119]

No one could challenge Schneider's dedication to art or his indefatigability. Dave Richards, in trying to address Schneider's contribution to American theater for readers of the *Washington Post* after Schneider's death, described Schneider as "a small, energetic man; Schneider walked with a briskness and purpose that belied his years."[120] Such purposefulness enriched Washington theater for four decades.

Schneider's premier production of Brecht's *The Caucasian Chalk Circle* at the new Arena Stage proved to be a grand success in every regard, showing off the possibilities of the new theater to their best advantage. After the play's October 1961, opening, the *New York Times* hailed the building, company, and production as a "new cultural landmark," and the editorial writers of the *Washington Post* praised the city's latest cultural asset. As fitting for Arena's edgy reputation, the choice of an "East German" playwright's work for the inauguration of a new theater in the American capital stuck some as inappropriate just ten weeks after the construction of the Berlin Wall.[121]

Zelda and Schneider underscored the company's commitment

in its new theater to innovative and restless work with Schneider's next production, of Albee's *The American Dream*, and John Mortimer's *What Shall We Tell Caroline?*—just two days after Brecht's *Chalk Circle* closed.[122] These productions carried forward their collaboration, which began with Schneider's direction of Tennessee Williams's *The Glass Menagerie* during Arena's inaugural 1950–51 season.[123]

Taking Wilder to Moscow

Schneider directed Thornton Wilder's *Our Town* four times at Arena Stage. A Depression-era play about everyday life in a fictional American town at the beginning of the twentieth century, *Our Town* has proven prone to mawkish emotionalism. But Wilder conceived of the play quite differently. He used a "metatheatrical" style to draw the potentially sentimental portrayal of a lost American utopia more clearly into the world of theater. Set in the theater in which it is being played, Wilder placed the character of the stage manager at the center of the action as a narrator, thereby removing any actual life offstage. The playwright would complain that too often the piece in the wrong hands becomes overloaded with sentimentality. Schneider's reliance on the actual text—a directorial style that served him well in his productions of Beckett—once again paid dividends in his various stagings of Wilder's American classic at Arena.[124]

Schneider first produced the play during his initial season with Arena as production director at the Hippodrome in the 1952–53 season.[125] He returned to the play two decades later with a memorable production during Arena's 1972–73 season, which was staged with Ming Cho Lee's inspired sets.[126]

The US Department of State invited Arena to take this production—together with Jerome Lawrence's and Robert E. Lee's *Inherit the Wind*—to the Soviet Union, in what became the first Russian tour by an American resident theater group. The performances in Moscow and Saint Petersburg—after trial performances at Catholic University arranged by Father Hartke—proved a triumph.[127]

By the time all the details had been negotiated and the company landed in Moscow, Arena was ready for fourteen performances in

Moscow and Leningrad, divided between both works.[128] The tour included sixty-six actors, directors, and technical staff members, plus one monkey (the hosts having refused to provide a Soviet simian to appear in *Inherit the Wind*).[129] Before departure, Wilder handwrote a touching note to the Fichandlers, in which he warned that he "had a long story with the Communists. *Our Town* was presented in the East Zone of Germany (back in 1947) and closed down by the authorities after two performances." Moreover, he noted, "no book of mine has ever been published in Russia."[130]

David Nalle, the US Embassy's exemplary Moscow-based press officer at the time, arranged to videotape the performances so that they could be shown to Soviet students who had not been able to attend in person.[131] From the embassy's perspective, *Inherit the Wind*, about the Scopes Trial over the teaching of evolution, presented the more compelling story for Moscow and Leningrad audiences.[132] They thought that the Soviets would be interested in that story's concern for the challenges of individual freedom within a context of conformism.[133]

Ming Cho Lee considered the productions to be among the most complex challenges of his career; Robert Prosky and other Arena actors recalled the experience for the rest of their lives; and the impact on the Moscow and then-Leningrad (today, Saint Petersburg) theater communities proved profound. Performing on the legendary stage of the Moscow Art Theater became a highlight for all.[134] A small number of Arena actors took the opportunity to meet with Jewish Human Rights activists in Moscow and Leningrad, causing a minor embarrassment for senior management.[135]

For the Russophile Zelda and the Ukrainian-born Schneider, the trip held special meaning. After returning to New York, Schneider excitedly wrote to Beckett, "Did you get my card from Moscow? Had a marvelous trip, hospitality most pure, and some excellent theatre. Lots of discussion about Beckett over there."[136]

Is Our Town White?

By the 1970s, Arena had staked its place in Washington and had advanced the cause of regional theater across the nation. Zelda was about to enter another fray to secure the place of African Americans on the stage.

Schneider's 1972–73 production of Wilder's classic proved noteworthy for other reasons. In 1968, the Fichandlers secured a quarter-million-dollar grant from the Ford Foundation to enlarge their company and to integrate African American onstage and offstage artists into their staffing. Mary Alice, Olivia Cole, Cynthia McPherson, Garrett Saunders, and Jay Fletcher were among the eight African Americans who joined Arena that year, and Arena consistently cast African Americans in parts long reserved for White actors.[137]

Schneider incorporated the veteran African American actor John Marriott in his 1972–73 *Our Town* production and in the Russia tour to follow.[138] Marriott, who began his career in Cleveland before moving to New York, was a veteran of stage and screen (his final film performance in 1975 was in Al Pacino's *Dog Day Afternoon*). His credits included numerous Broadway productions on stage with many of the era's leading performers. Nonetheless, his presence jarred some of Arena's White audiences.[139]

Casting Black actors in several productions of *Our Town* during the 1970s, and 1980s was no simple matter. Such actions especially bothered more than a few White Arena subscribers, producing complaints such as:

- "I found the mixed racial casting disconcerting: it did not fit the material of the plays. No mood could be established between the audience and the actors."
- "While it is noble to presume that your audience is color blind, the use of racially mixed casting, where inappropriate, interfered with the integrity of many of the plays and, in our judgment, defeated the purpose which the casting was intention."
- "We strongly resent the casting of Black actors in White roles—an occasional practice which has become routine over the years. Color-blindness simply cannot extend to the mixing of Black and White actors in 'Our Town.'"[140]

One subscriber was led to write, "My mind wandered into thinking I was attending a high school senior class play in which the teacher-director very properly exerted every effort to cast children representative of a diverse student body."[141]

Such remarks are astonishing, given both the prior and subsequent accomplishments of African American actors appearing on the Arena Stage during this period. In addition to Marriott, Mary Alice already had solid New York credentials to her name and would go on to star turns on television, film, and Broadway. She was inducted into the American Theatre Hall of Fame and won a Tony Award for best featured actress in a play for her performance in the 1987 production of August Wilson's *Fences*. Olivia Cole had graduated with honors from the Royal Academy of Dramatic Art in London before arriving at Arena, and became the first African American to win an Emmy award for outstanding supporting actress in a television movie for her performance in the 1977 miniseries *Roots*. Garrett Saunders was in the first production of *Sesame Street*. Cynthia McPherson and Jay Fletcher went on to successful television and film careers. They were accomplished artists who elevated the quality of Arena productions, as did other African American actors performing with Arena at the time, and later.

Tom Fichandler would later observe that "it was either five years too late or five years too soon, as Black artists at the time embraced a movement for self-expression and self-affirmation." This was a time, he believed, when Black theater was striking out on its own, rather than seeking integration into a large White institution. He nonetheless maintained that this effort prepared the ground for an even deeper commitment to multicultural themes, audiences, and productions later.[142]

Schneider's final 1975–76 production of *Our Town* took the stage at a moment when Schneider had three other productions playing concurrently in Washington.[143] From his chance encounter with Walter Kerr at Catholic University during the summer of 1941, Schneider had become a Washington institution of sorts, even as he continued to make his way around the world.

Jack Jefferson Takes the Ring

Zelda was coming to understand that the future of Arena Stage would lie with expanding her audience to embrace African American theatergoers in a city that was majority Black. Galella records that, by the mid-1960s, Arena began concerted efforts to reach out to Black communities in response to the flight of potential White patrons to the suburbs and the expansion of opportunities for middle-class African Americans after the era's civil rights legislation.[144] The very way in which Arena's leadership conceived of its audience and its artistic mandate changed. Arena no longer could be merely a response to highly educated, White theater lovers starved for professional productions as it had been at the outset. The question of race was becoming ever more central to who and what Arena would be.

Writing in a 1968 essay "Towards a Deepening Aesthetic," Zelda observed that "if we seek the Negro audience, we should integrate our acting companies and seek out plays that speak to Negro concerns."[145] She already had begun searching out such works.

In 1966, Zelda became familiar with the work of Howard Sackler, a White American playwright living in Britain. Sackler shared a script he had been working on for two years, an incomplete manuscript "the size of the Manhattan phonebook."[146] Zelda began applying for support to bring him to Washington. After assembling the required funding, they began working on a new play, to be staged in early 1967.[147] Their schedule would slide until late in the year, when Sackler's *The Great White Hope* burst across the Arena Stage.

Sackler's play retells the story of Black Heavyweight Boxing Champion Jack Johnson, who shocked the sporting world when he secured the title from White boxer Tommy Burns in 1908.[148] Outraged that a Black man had defeated a White fighter, the boxing world launched a search for a "great White hope" to retake the crown. James J. Jeffries reclaimed the coveted championship from Johnson in 1910, in what likely was a fixed fight, in Reno.

Johnson never cowered before Whites and proudly showed off his talents by living well and indulging in the company of White women. He later was convicted under the Mann Act, which forbade transporting women across state lines for 'immoral purposes." He headed to France via Canada to avoid jail time, before returning to the United States to serve his prison sentence. Johnson died in a North Carolina car crash in 1946. President Donald Trump posthumously pardoned Johnson in May 2018.[149]

Johnson's story seemed contemporary at a time when the

young Heavyweight champion Cassius Clay had recently changed his name to Muhammad Ali, and had become embroiled in his own headline-grabbing legal battles after his decision to refuse the military draft and serve in Vietnam. The parallels between the present and past were too powerful to ignore.[150] Nonetheless, as Galella records, Sackler maintained that the play was a universal tale of one person versus society. He even implied that he had developed the play long before Muhammad Ali's draft travails.[151]

Sackler changed "Johnson" to "Jefferson," and he consolidated some characters together to retell the story of the fight and what followed.[152] The playwright embraced the enormity of the tale, producing a rambling marathon containing three acts, twenty scenes, and 247 separate characters speaking in blank verse.[153]

Most startlingly for White theatergoers, he placed the fighter's relationships with White women at the center of his story.[154] Played by two leading actors on the verge of prominence—James Earl Jones and Jane Alexander—the production was an immediate success. After its Washington run, *The Great White Hope* ran on Broadway—where both Jones and Alexander won Tony Awards for their performances—and was made into a movie.[155]

Fichandler and the director Edwin Sherin assembled a sixty-member biracial cast for the Washington production after auditioning more than four hundred actors in New York. They included performers from the Arena resident company and Washington, with more than twenty-five actors selected from the New York auditions.[156] Local audiences had never seen anything quite like it; and the American theater had never seen a biracial couple of such depth and complexity as Jones and Alexander. The production was a triumph.[157]

A Remarkable Cast

Fichandler, Sackler, and Sherin understood that they had grabbed onto a corner of theater history. Sackler's play was long and unwieldy, filled with dozens of characters large and small. With so many acts, scenes, and characters in the final script, they worked with one of the most multiracial casts in the history of the American stage. *The Great White Hope* grew beyond anything the production team, the actors, and Arena Stage had ever attempted. Sherin arranged to have an excursion ship docked along the nearby waterfront and divided the company into two for the long rehearsals. Half worked on stage, while the other half perfected their parts on the ship, before switching off. Schedules slipped, rehearsals ran over all bounds of rectitude, and despair circled among everyone involved.[158]

Their collective triumph rested in large measure on their successful piecing together of a remarkable cast drawn from many as-yet-little-known actors. Resident company members Robert Prosky, Robert Foxworth, Ned Beatty, and Jane Alexander formed a core, around which Sherin would build outward. Two dozen cast members—including James Earl Jones—won parts at New York tryouts.[159] The performances by Alexander and Jones catapulted both to the pinnacle of the American acting profession.

Alexander had joined the Arena resident company in 1965, at the same time as Foxworth and Jon Voight. Together, they were part of an arriving cluster of new actors who expanded the company to sixteen members, the largest to that time.[160] The daughter of a New England surgeon and nurse, she tried to balance her parents' concerns for stability with her own aspiration for the stage by combining studies in mathematics and drama at Sarah Lawrence College, and by studying at the University of Edinburgh. Her commitment to acting became total after her acceptance as a member of the Edinburgh University Dramatic Society. Returning from Scotland, she began seeking out opportunities on the stage, with the opening to join the Arena resident company offering just the break she sought.[161]

Underneath her quietly controlled demeanor lurked a spirited individualist who already had been making a mark as an actor within the Arena company. Alexander was married at the time to Robert Alexander, the director of the company's children-oriented Living Stage, and she had praiseworthy performances under her belt in Arena's successful productions the previous year of Nikolai Gogol's *The Inspector General* and John Osborne's *Look Back in Anger*.[162] She was fearless in her pursuit of a character and was able to ignore the hate mail and death threats that engulfed her once *The Great White Hope* opened.[163]

Jones was born in Mississippi and was raised primarily by his maternal grandparents in rural Michigan. He developed a strong stutter as a boy and remained largely nonverbal until an English teacher, Donald Crouch, discovered his aptitude for poetry. Jones joined the University of Michigan drama club and embraced the sense of fellowship within that community of players as he toiled to make his way through a premed program. He subsequently served in the Army in Korea, and was assigned to Ranger School. In 1955, with college and military service behind him, Jones headed off to New York to try to make a go in the theater as a journeyman actor.[164]

Upon arriving in New York, Jones reconciled with his father, Robert Earl Jones, whom he had not known previously. A boxer turned actor, the elder Jones helped his son make his way through the labyrinth of a New York actor's life. The younger Jones began to thrive. He landed roles in productions of Joseph Papp's Shakespeare Festival, as well as small parts both on and off Broadway. He performed on television and in film, including an appearance in Stanley Kubrick's 1964 classic film *Dr. Strangelove*.[165] Among his early roles was a spot in the renowned 1961 Off-Broadway run of Jean Genet's *The Blacks: A Clown Show* featuring Roscoe Lee Browne, Louis Gossett Jr., Cicely Tyson, Godfrey Cambridge, Maya Angelou, Raymond St. Jacques, Abbey Lincoln, and Charles Gordone.[166]

Jones appreciated that he had secured a career-making role at Arena. He later remembered that Sackler "offered me the part. He thought that my classical training would help me take on this monumental, epic role. I knew immediately that this was a role I had to play, here was explosive drama, and poetry, and complex tragedy beautifully drawn on the page was a role of a lifetime."[167]

Jones saw himself in the play. "There were strands in my own life," he later recalled, "that I could weave into the web of this role I was about to play. My father was a boxer actor, he fought his way out of Memphis, Tennessee, during the Depression. Fighting had become a metaphor for his life."[168]

Both Alexander and Jones were primed for success as they joined with the Fichandlers, Sackler, Sherin, and a troupe of nearly five dozen actors to bring Sackler's play to life. They would go on to be among the leading American actors of their times, with Alexander winning one Tony Award and seven Tony nominations for her work on Broadway, one Academy Award and four nominations for film, and two Emmys and eight nominations for her performances on television. She was inducted into the American Theater Hall of Fame in 1994 and, between 1993 and 1997, she served as chairperson of the National Endowment for the Arts. The Arena production shaped her personal life as well. She divorced Bob Alexander in 1974, and married Sherin the following year.[169] They remained married until his death in 2017.

Jones similarly has numerous awards to his name, including two Tonys and four Tony nominations for the Broadway stage, an Academy Award and nomination for film, and two Emmys and eight nominations for his work on television, as well as a Grammy Award and nomination for the recorded spoken word. He, too, would gain induction into the American Theater Hall of Fame in 1985.

Legends Aren't Always What They First Appeared to Be

Alexander's and Jones's performances and subsequent careers secured Arena's production of *The Great White Hope* a legendary spot in American theater history. The reviews at the time, however, were less uniformly praiseworthy than memory recalls. Covered extensively by the national, New York, and Washington media, reviewers consistently appreciated that they had seen performances of extraordinary dimension.

However, reviewers simultaneously criticized Sackler's script, which they found to be meandering, unfocused, and in need of a good editorial scrubbing. Not only did the play run three and a half hours, many critics complained, the storyline tended to repeat itself unnecessarily and disintegrated into description.[170] Some perceptive reviewers—Walter Kerr of the *New York Times* among them—noted that the playwright had written a work for cinema rather than for the stage.[171] Others—such as Tom Donnelly of the *Washington Daily News*, in a review titled "There's A Play in Here Somewhere"—were more direct.[172] The script would be trimmed considerably as the work moved to Broadway and on to the Hollywood screen.[173]

Although the staging, costumes, and sets generally won praise, some patrons—most especially the distinctly ornery *New York Times* critic Clive Barnes—complained about poor acoustics.[174] Reviewers widely noted the racial significance of the production, often calling attention to the parallels with Muhammad Ali's prosecution at the time. Some, such as Barnes, found it too didactic. "The play," Barnes wrote, "is morally, if you will forgive me, too black and white."[175]

All such nits having been picked to varying degrees, the reviewers universally turned to Alexander and Jones, whose performances were declared among the most unforgettable of any recent American production. "Promethean" was applied over and over to Jones in particular, while Alexander's performance was admired for its elegance and quiet power.[176]

Audience reactions followed the trajectory of the critics' reviews. The stage manager's performance reports note concern over the acoustics and long running time. The second performance on days with two shows proved especially taxing for the performers. More telling, the manager noted that, late in the run, the performance "simply looked like a show that had been running a long time and all the company was already thinking about the next job."[177]

The Great White Hope shines when viewed through a half century of acclamatory remembrance. The production secured Arena's place at the top of the American theatrical community, making possible even more expansive national and international attention. The work's focus on race relations cemented the company's reputation as an advocate for civil rights. The company nurtured an audience that arguably has gone farther in breaking down Washington's historical racial boundaries than any other cultural institution in the city. Everything about *The Great White Hope* appears mythic when viewed with hindsight. At the time, the Fichandlers had to scramble to ensure that their success did not destroy the company they had so painstakingly built.[178]

The first challenges were financial. Many individuals and organizations would profit from the play's rousing success—but not Arena Stage. The company had spared no expense to make *The Great White Hope* a landmark of American theater, as evident in the size of the cast, the vigorous rehearsal schedule, and the length of preparation before the opening performance in December 1967. Actual costs in developing the work exceeded the funding provided by two grants from the National Endowment for the Arts and ticket sales. The company fell into deficit for the first time in years.[179]

Howard Sackler took the play to Broadway largely on his own money.[180] He was able to do so in part because Arena already had carried a substantial portion of the cost for development and initial production.[181]

Regional theater was so new—Tom Fichandler, Peter Zeisler of Minneapolis's Guthrie Theater, William Bushnell of Baltimore's Center Stage, and the attorney Morris Kaplan had established the League of Regional Theatres just a year and a half earlier—that *The Great White Hope* became among the first productions to move from a regional company to the Broadway stage. No legal and few customary frameworks existed at the time for commercial theaters and the film industry to compensate resident theaters for their contributions to new works.

Arena Stage took the issue to court, losing all financial claims to Sackler.[182] This judgment prompted rather snooty reactions from self-appointed defenders of theatrical virtue. Yale Drama School dean Robert Brustein, from his well-financed perch at one of the country's wealthiest universities, looked down at Arena's and other regional theaters' attempts to monetize their investments in new works. "We do not think of our theater as a tryout house," he told the *New York Times*'s Sam Zolotow, "but rather as a place to produce interesting plays. So we make no financial demands on the playwright, though we would be naturally grateful for any royalties voluntarily offered."[183]

Having been burned watching *The Great White Hope*'s move to New York success (the Broadway production ran for 546 performances) and on to Hollywood, Tom Fichandler mobilized the fledgling League of Regional Theatres to negotiate agreements with various stage and film associations to ensure that regional companies would be compensated for developing future works. These arrangements have shaped a thriving relationship between regional nonprofit resident companies and commercial theaters and film studios. Arena had staked regional theater's claim to legitimacy. At the time, however, the DC company was left holding the bag.[184]

Much of the cast followed the show to New York, nearly

obliterating the long-standing Arena approach of presenting works as a resident company. Actors needed to be replaced quickly for the Arena season to continue, and contracts needed to be rethought in the future. This exodus to Broadway forced Arena to scramble to keep moving ahead.[185]

The production also raised artistic expectations, which could not be matched with every new play. *The Great White Hope* was a remarkable achievement—a work of such transcendent artistic value that Sackler won the Pulitzer Prize for Drama, and Jones and Alexander won Tony and Drama Desk awards for best actor and best featured actress.

The scale of the endeavor exceeded anything Arena—and American regional theaters more generally—had attempted. The production's quality opened the national door for further works by regional companies. Martin Gottfried of *Women's Wear Daily* particularly focused his attention on the production's non–New York origins:

> This was hardly the first new American play to have its world premiere in a resident theatre. All of these theaters are eager to do new American plays and most of them have done some. But although I have hardly seen all of these premiers, it seems a safe guess that *The Great White Hope* is the best ever to have had such a birthplace. It seems safe to say because Mr. Sackler's play is also the finest that I have seen anywhere in the recent past. With the opening of such a master play, the residential movement becomes a major force—a force that New York can no longer ignore in the American theatre.[186]

The Centrality of Race

The most enduring trials revolved around the very issue that animated the work and gave it such consummate power: race. For all the very public praise that Arena accrued for presenting such a groundbreaking work about American race relations, less-public dilemmas lingered for some time. At its center, *The Great White Hope* addressed the racial turmoil of the times—all the more so because

Arena Stage had become embedded in a city deeply enmeshed in that furor. Within a matter of weeks, the city would be torn apart by communal violence after the assassination of Dr. Martin Luther King Jr. in Memphis. The play's power speaks to some of the most potent psychoses of American society. The production did not, however, challenge the systemic context of American race relations. As Galella observes, *The Great White Hope* remained "far from the radical cry of the Black Arts Movement."[187]

In discussing a new production to mark Arena's fiftieth anniversary season in 2000, then–artistic director Molly Smith acknowledged the production's legacy for the company, the city, and the nation. Writing in the production's program, Smith noted that

> because it *is* such a legend, this play is a celebration of the audacious achievements of Zelda and Tom Fichandler—and their bravery for producing the premier of this wonderful, passionate, epic play.... I think race is one of the great underlying themes of America, from long before the Civil War. We live with it in many ways here in Washington, which can feel like a very split city. But I believe that the theater is a place where we can come together. I can only imagine how it was in 1967 to see a cross-racial kiss on stage. And even today, this causes all kinds of triggers in people. Yes, there has been progress in this country, yes, there have been more open doors, but I think in some ways racism has just gone underground. I think the play really taps into that and forces us to face it.[188]

The challenge of race was hardly the sole challenge at the time. Many longtime Arena patrons expressed misgivings about the production. Not every complaint had a racial edge to it. Many patrons were put out by the production's three-and-a-half-hour running time, while some objected to indecorous language.[189]

Others simply saw the company as having lost its way. As one veteran patron wrote:

> From the beginning, the strength of Arena Stage was its vitality, its fun, its informality, even its hardships and vicis-

situdes which we shared with you when we attended performances one could identify with the players, eye to eye,
even drink coffee with them. They enjoyed it and so did
I.... That's all gone, now. This new stage is slick, the actors are slick, the productions and foyer and staff are slick.
The atmosphere is brittle and cheap, and superficial.... I
get the same "get lost, don't bother me, we're oversold" attitude that I get in New York.... Like Victoria, I am no longer
amused.... So, adios muchacha.[190]

The Fichandlers similarly had to be careful about not offending
artists in the Arena orbit who had been passed over for their break-
through production. Tom and Zelda, for instance, had become
friends with Brock and DiDi Peters. DiDi earned a PhD in political
science at Howard before launching into a career as a top African
American entertainment executive.[191] Her actor husband Brock had
checked in on the project's progress with a keen interest in securing
the lead role of Jack Jefferson.[192] His displeasure was palpable when
the role went to James Earl Jones, with the situation made even
more awkward when Zelda had to ask that the actor return the
script at the cheapest possible postal rate as the company no longer
had sufficient copies for the cast.[193]

Peters, a consummate professional, expressed his disillusionment while maintaining considerable professional dignity. "I received your letter," he wrote Zelda, "with mixed feelings of disappointment and hope. Of course, I would have loved to create this
role, and I believe I might have brought to it, the power and scope,
of that strong, isolated, and lonely man; whose destruction was inherent in himself, and preordained by society. You are really sweet
to let me know and I must reassure you, that time and experience
have grown me an outer coat of mail. It is not impervious, but it
generally works."[194]

Two years later, after Peters had won acclaim for his re-creation
of the role of Jefferson on the work's national tour, he wrote again to
the Fichandlers; this time on more solid footing. "I had planned to
write before this," he began, "but a very busy schedule has made it
impossible. You know by now that things come full circle, and Herman Levin has finally gotten me to tour with 'Great White Hope.'

Sort of ironic, isn't it? Sackler called me opening night here in Chicago to apologize for ever having doubts. In any case, I wanted to share with you the reviews I have gotten in Cleveland, and Chicago. Again, they are corroboration of your faith in my talent."[195]

To which Tom Fichandler responded on Zelda's behalf that "she asked me to write and tell you how glad she was to hear from you, and how delighted she is with your success as Jack Jefferson. I personally am delighted to hear that Sackler called you and apologized about his doubts; he has never been man enough to admit Zelda's and Arena Stage's contribution to and share some of his wealth from *The Great White Hope*, despite the part that the whole thing would never have happened without Zelda's interest, drive, and contribution."[196]

Running a "Plantation"?

Yet, in the end, race animated audiences and theater artists alike. Not all the correspondence surrounding the production was as gentle on the question of race as the just-mentioned correspondence. Numerous lost subscriptions and angry grievances revolved around the portrayal of an interracial couple and racial injustice that the play confronted directly. Such complaints would grow as the company began to engage issues of diversity more vigorously in the years ahead.[197]

Concerns arose from African Americans as well as from Whites. African Americans at times perceive as patronizing and condescending actions understood by Whites as reflecting unflinching liberality. Such interracial misinterpretation surrounded *The Great White Hope*. The eminent African American family-planning pioneer Ophelia S. Egypt scolded Zelda for failing to have "given many of our excellent resident players, especially some of the Negroes, an opportunity to play important roles. In my humble judgment, some of the people imported for such roles showed no more talent than our own players."[198] Although Zelda responded to the complaint with concern and care, the company continued to search for African American talent—as it did for all acting talent—nationally rather than locally.

The correspondence with the African American actor Bill Terry could not be passed over so readily. Marion Barry—civil rights activist and the city's future "mayor for life"—evidently introduced Terry to the Fichandlers.[199] W. Benson "Bill" Terry was a former railroad switchman, union organizer, activist, and professional boxer turned actor.[200]

Terry had trained at Columbia College and Second City in Chicago before moving to New York to study at Circle in the Square. After an initial meeting, someone at Arena had scrawled on the back of the 6-foot-2-inch, 205-pound Terry's résumé: "Ex-middleweight # Mike [sic] Terry # Will be good professional boxing help."[201] Arena brought him on to train James Earl Jones in basic boxing skills.

As Jones later recalled in his memoirs,

> Preparing for the role demanded intellectual exploration and physical exertion that I felt confident would be akin to basic training in the Army. Actually, what I had to endure was much worse than anything the Army required of me, even in Ranger training. Every morning, I got up early and ran three miles with my trainer, ex-boxer Bill Terry. He put me through my paces; the morning run, and then two hours of workouts at a gym, the whole gamut of the boxer in training—skipping rope, punching a body bag, working with weights, medicine balls, and split inner tubes for sweat bands.[202]

Terry had returned to Washington in early 1968, it seems, to work with underprivileged boys at the Westinghouse Learning Coop. The Fichandlers invited him to bring his students to Arena to see how a theater worked. The times had become tense, as the Reverend Dr. Martin Luther King Jr. was assassinated in Memphis on April 4 and much of inner-city Washington was scared by resulting civil unrest. Nonetheless, Terry sent a gracious, handwritten note to Tom on April 12, 1968, thanking him, Zelda, and Al Gibson "for signing my boys to a possible future. A future, that is, if everything goes as planned. It was people like you that replaced the gun, and my fist, with a script. Now all my social attitudes are expressed through that medium. I am sure, with half a chance, my boys will find the same avenue of expression. . . . Oh yes, in passing give my thanks to Ed, a great director. The only bad deal I got in Washington was my sinus."[203]

Within a few weeks, everything had changed. In June, Terry wrote a note on a yellow legal pad transmitting a just-published defamatory column about his treatment at Arena. The letter's last lines were underlined for emphasis, "The way I was treated in Washington has made me hate Theatre. I think I can do the Black Actor far more good from the pages of my column!"[204]

Published in his column "Hits and Near Misses on Broadway" in Chicagoland's *South Suburban News*, the article attacked everything about Arena Stage. At some point, Terry found out that his efforts training Jones had not, to his mind, been properly acknowledged in the production's original programs. More significantly, he believed that Arena had a lower pay scale for African American actors than for White performers.[205]

Among Terry's less inflammatory charges were that Zelda Fichandler was running a plantation as she broadened the Arena Stage to include African Americans in the regular Arena Company. He claimed that the same Ed Sherin whom he had praised in the private note mentioned above "got an undercover prejudice going for him, that he things [sic] is hidden, but it would hurt you at all to ball up your fist, Negro fashion, when he gives you a Joe E. Brown smile!" He cautioned Zelda not to "send Tom looking for me, for it would be better just to send the Klan that is if you know any, and I suspect you do, because I still throw a real hard left hook." All of which warmed up for the primary message: "No more separate but equal treatment, Zelda! We want the same salary and the same treatment as other actors."[206]

Terry evidently understood that he might have overstepped the bounds of propriety; or someone else concerned about possible damage to the newspaper's reputation convinced Terry that this was so. On the following Wednesday, Terry sent another hastily written note "in an attempt at an apology for the attitudes displayed by me as a reporter." "I believe," he continued, "after giving the matter thought that I have been unfair to you as a person, which is definitely not a true part of my personality."[207]

The origins of Terry's tirade are not clear from the archival record. He performed in *The Great White Hope* with the production's program offering a biographical statement equivalent to many—and longer than some—of those for the cast's other sixty-or-so performers. The program additionally lists him as "boxing instructor."[208] His complaints shared broad misgivings within Washington's African American community that the Fichandlers were trying to profit from race issues rather than engage them with an eye toward change. Whatever their cause, the correspondence reflects the tensions and misunderstandings inherent in interracial cooperation at the time—even after a liberal achievement such as *The Great White Hope*.[209]

Terry and the Fichandlers somehow remained in touch with one another. Terry returned to Arena two decades later for an impressive performance in a production of *The Cherry Orchard*. Shortly thereafter, he wrote to Zelda that he was "sitting here in Baltimore in a suite at the Tremont Hotel. They brought me here to do a couple of scenes with Tom Selleck in his new picture *Her Alibi*. So I said, since I'm off a couple of days, now is the time to get off that long awaited letter to Zelda thanking her for bringing me back in such a wonderful role. I highly appreciate you making me a part of one of the best productions of *The Cherry Orchard* done in my time in Theater. You said to me one-night backstage, 'Don't let it be twenty years again before returning to Arena,' or words to that effect. And I'm saying to you, 'pick the role and I'll play it.'"[210]

Zelda responded: "No, it won't take another twenty years (I don't think we've got another twenty!) and thank you for the heroic contribution you made to *Cherry Orchard*. You were a real trouper, and we will always be admiring and grateful."[211] Zelda had more than twenty years left, passing away in 2016. Bill had only ten, which included appearing in the movie *Forrest Gump*.

Any one of these challenges could well have undermined Arena's well-being once *The Great White Hope* moved to New York. Together, such dilemmas forced the Fichandlers and their colleagues to reinvent their company yet again. In doing so, they never faltered in their commitment to build and sustain a diverse, multiracial company and community that set a new model for what theater might be in Washington.

The Great White Hope and the various controversies swirling around it powerfully shaped Zelda's view of Arena's place in contemporary Washington. Weeks after the play's run and the civil unrest surrounding the murder of Dr. Martin Luther King Jr. thereafter, Zelda published a powerful statement in the Sunday edition of the *Washington Star* setting out her stance on theater and race relations. "There is not a day that passes," she wrote, "that each of us is not in some way caught and affected by the vibrations set in motion by the emergent human power of the Black man. And yet, we come into our theater at night as if into an unreal world and a White audience sits around a stage upon which a White company performs and we 'tell sad tales of the death of kings.' Surely, we must be in the wrong place!"[212]

Neither her passion nor her opinions faded in the months ahead. In 1970 at the dedication of the Kreeger Theater that month, she declared, "New words. New relationships. New places. New buildings. The search for new forms to express our shifting, shaking world. And no one form can capture it all."[213] Express its era, Arena tried; and would continue to do so.

The Washington Theatre Club

Arena was not alone. Washington's small but growing theater community increasingly engaged in disputes over what it meant to be an American in the 1960s and 1970s. Hazel and John Wentworth, for example, opened the Washington Theater Club during the 1950s in a cozy carriage house at 1632 O Street NW.[214] The diminutive O Street stage remained the club's signature venue for much of its existence. Located in an old carriage house halfway between Dupont Circle and Logan Circle, the theater was next to a large church along a residential block. The building had moved beyond horses, carriages, and automobiles to become a nondescript warehouse. The carriage house offered just enough room for an Elizabethan-style thrust stage surrounded on three sides by 142 seats. The neighborhood's declining fortunes combined with the building's use for storage resulted in a price the budding company could afford.

The site carried various encumbrances that would shape the theatrical venture in unexpected ways. The ever-creative couple therefore launched a theater club to own the building. The club, in turn, rented the space to the Washington Drama Center, which formally operated the company throughout its early years. The club eventually reincorporated as a standalone nonprofit organization in 1963, claiming an educational purpose as justification for tax-exempt status. Such arrangements necessitated "members," so the company charged subscribers and other patrons a $1 "membership fee" above and beyond the official ticket price. Many theatergoers initially found the space to be "sweet," "intimate," and "endearing." Audiences especially welcomed the new theater's state-of-the-art air conditioning system, which remained something of a rarity at the time. Positive reviews followed.

Like the Fichandlers, the theater mavens John and Hazel Wentworth were hungry for innovative drama of a sort absent from Washington. In 1957 they established their group to promote fresh dramatic forms, to present new ideas, and to support novice playwrights and their work. John Wentworth already directed the amateur Unitarian Players and looked to expand his presence on the city's professional stage. Hazel would assume leadership for the group after the couple's divorce during the 1960s.

The Wentworths further sought to present quality productions performed and enjoyed by diverse casts and audiences outside the noisome racial boundaries and Jim Crow customs that still marred the city. They nurtured a slightly bohemian tone, often presenting nonmainstream works, such as poetry readings accompanied by modern dance and Ionescu's *The Lesson*. In 1962, they offered a residency to Academy Award–winning actor Anne Revere, who still suffered from having been blacklisted during the McCarthy era for her earlier Communist Party affiliation. Such actions made the company an easy target for defenders of moral and political rectitude.

As with the founding days of Arena Stage, local zoning regulations and building codes were uncongenial for theater companies. The Wentworths similarly experienced petty interventions by local DC authorities. Wednesday, July 25, 1962, was rather pleasant for a Washington summer's eve, with the temperature hovering at about 70 degrees (though humidity lingered near 80 percent). Excited theatergoers were piling into the Washington Theatre Club's carriage house theater to catch a performance of Tennessee Williams's racy farce *Period of Adjustment*, then in its eighth straight week packing in theater-starved Washingtonians. Two DC detectives made their way through the crowd and stepped up to the box office to purchase tickets. Having bought the most expensive seats in the house at $3.50 each, the police officers declared the show shut down. No one had bothered to ask them for their membership cards. Chaos ensued.

Many present that night thought the play had somehow given the authorities offense. Williams' comedy portrayed what now is known as "posttraumatic stress syndrome" suffered by two returning Korean War veterans. The performance explored the men's feelings of inadequacy towards the women in their lives. The play had enjoyed a modest 132-performance run on Broadway the previous year and was finding more appreciative audiences in the nation's capital.

A beleaguered Third Precinct police Captain Raymond S. Pyles told disbelieving journalists the next day that the play's content had nothing to do with his detectives' actions. Rather, he charged, the club was violating its occupancy permit, which specified that only club members could attend performances. The play's success—combined with its posters, radio, and newspaper ads—claimed Pyles, demonstrated collusion to avoid the public hearing process required of public hall licenses in residential areas.

The city's theater-going public was not buying this explanation, especially considering otherwise lax enforcement of such permits elsewhere. Letter writers to the city's papers saw the police action as one more instance of official harassment of culture within a city lorded over by congressionally appointed commissioners intent on running the town for themselves. The club posted a $100 bond and the production continued its run until being displaced later that summer by a teen production of "Rumpelstiltskin" and chamber music concerts. The challenges posed by its unusual legal status as a "club" would plague the group for years to come.

The quirkily extravagant Midwesterner Davey Marlin-Jones came from New York to take over the company as its artistic director in 1965. Over the next seven years, the club mounted some of its most ambitious productions. In 1968, Jones and the company received the coveted Margo Jones Award honoring pioneering leaders in American regional theater for in 1968 (Subsequent

Washington honorees include Zelda Fichandler and Arena Stage, in 1971; longtime *Washington Post* critic Richard Coe, in 1990; and Howard Shalwitz, with the Woolly Mammoth Theatre Company, in 2004.) Jones remained in town as art critic for the city's CBS-TV affiliate (presently WUSA-TV) until 1987, when he moved to Las Vegas.

At its height, the club attracted 9,000 subscribers, nearly all of whom paid an extra dollar each year to retain membership. For much of its existence, the company offered actor training to children and teens as well as professional training for adults. Its chamber music ensemble—the Theater Chamber Players founded by Leon Fleisher and Dina Koston in 1968—served long-term residencies at the Smithsonian Institution and the Kennedy Center; and remains active to this day.

Before too long, however, the diminutive O Street carriage house became "cramped," "uncomfortable," and "confined"; its once-venerated air conditioning system was now simply "noisy" and "annoying." "Quaint and charming" transmuted into "old and dilapidated." Zoning regulations further impinged on the club's attempts to grow into a dramatic arts center and school. Such disquiet led the club to overextend its financial reserves for a second stage. Meanwhile, the space remained much beloved by many, and it continued to serve as a home to children's productions, poetry readings, and dance and music performances as well as puppet-theater.

The club, which proudly declared itself for years to be the smallest professional repertoire company in America, looked to expand. As 1969 became 1970, Hazel Wentworth moved their primary operations to a remodeled African American church in the city's West End. With three times the number of seats and plentiful backstage space, the new home suited the company well—at least until tax authorities and real estate developers had their way. A once-noteworthy, predominately Black, blue-collar neighborhood, the West End had fallen into disrepair after having been targeted for demolition to make way for an inner beltway circling downtown. The neighborhood came "on-line" once highway planners lost their battle to plough an interstate highway through the area. A neighborhood renewal plan released in 1972 envisioned a "new town for the West End." A Ritz Carlton hotel now stands on the site of the Washington Theater Club's final home.[215]

Between 1957 and 1974, the club staged ten world premieres, four American premieres, thirty Washington premieres, and works by sixty-four writers who had not been performed previously in the Washington region. Among its noteworthy productions were future Tony Award–winning actor Lester Rawlins's 1965 turn as Prospero in Shakespeare's *The Tempest*; Billy Dee Williams's performance later that year in William Hanley's *Slow Dance on a Killing Ground*; the 1968 world premiere of future Pulitzer Prize winner Landford Wilson's play about interracial marriage, *The Gingham Dog*; and the 1973 world premiere of Arthur Laurents's *Enclave*, featuring Peg Murray and Hal Linden. In January 1970, President Richard Nixon invited the company to the White House to perform a segment of its production *The Decline and Fall of the Entire World as Seen Through the Eyes of Cole Porter*.

The club's declaration that it offered educational opportunities eventually became the company's undoing. In the early 1970s, various courts rejected the assertion of educational status, leaving the club with an expensive property tax bill that it could not cover. Bankers foreclosed on their loans. The company folded in 1974, a victim of an emerging real estate boom that would devour poor neighborhoods across the city in its wake.

The Community Ringed Around the Theater

Arena, for its part, similarly sought to capture the changing times. The company already had moved to integrate racially when it opened in 1950.[216] Its 1968 production of *The Great White Hope* featuring James Earl Jones and Jane Alexander broke numerous racial taboos, while Arena was on its way to beginning a landmark experimentation with "nontraditional casting" that would change the complexion of the actors on stage.[217] The company similarly sought to stage works that reflected the totality of the era's social and political upheavals.

Washington theater audiences did not welcome all such ventures with open arms. For example, the company's production of Charles Gordone's Pulitzer Prize–winning "Black-black comedy" *No Place to Be Somebody* in June 1970 had unleashed a wave of angry subscription suspensions, as had a production of Peter Weiss's

The Persecution and Assassination of Jean-Paul Marat as Performed by the Inmates of the Asylum of Charenton Under the Direction of the Marquis de Sade.[218] Some subscribers viewed a spring 1971 production of Stanley R. Greenberg's docudrama *Pueblo* about North Korea's seizure of a US Naval ship and its more than eighty crewmembers as "criminal and unpatriotic," especially because it included a scene when the American flag fell to the floor.[219]

Zelda, as everyone in Washington called her, had staked her claim to the city, building an honored theatrical company that transformed the shape of American regional and residential theater by placing her company at the epicenter of the era's culture wars. Begun as a traditional company appealing to an underserved, highly educated theatrical audience, the company unfailingly sought new forms to express an ever-changing America and Washington swirling around it. Controversy did not always create friends. The company nonetheless continued to engage the leading cultural battles of the day. Seeking out new audiences, Arena's productions came to define new identities for a city that all too often was thought of as simply being about politics and little more.

The Fichandlers had been concerned with the relationship between stage and community since Arena Stage's earliest days. Their appreciation expanded and deepened as their theater took root, as they moved from location to location around the city, as they attracted diverse patrons and donors, and as they engaged students and their parents.

For a theater company predicated on the assumption that theater dwells in a multicultural world, confronting the prejudices and affirming the identities so prevalent in that world—and so powerfully apparent in the city and communities in which Arena was embedded—race necessarily became a central focus of everything the company did. This embrace of the challenges of human diversity extended well beyond sociological motives. Fundamentally and most profoundly, Arena sought to draw on the dynamisms unleashed by Washington's—and the country's—racial struggles to energize the artwork it produced out on stage.

A Second Stage

On November 29, 1970, Zelda realized another of the many dreams she would bring to life throughout her career. She had longed to have a second, experimental stage almost from the day the new theater opened ten years before. In dedicating the company's second stage, she mused that "theater buildings by themselves do not matter, because the theater event is an explosion of life and can take place anywhere. The essence of theater as an art is the storyteller looking at his audience and beginning to speak. Where the film flashes onto a screen images from the past, theater is happening only in the present, and *can* happen only in the present, in the Now, and Now can happen anyplace. Anyplace at all."[220]

Such an observation appears at first blush to be at odds with a theater leader who spent much of her professional life angsting over the vicissitudes of real estate, and at a building dedication no less. Yet she, more than many, understood the powerful impact of physical form on the theatrical experience. "Gordon Craig," she continued, "influenced Europe for half a century through a couple of performances in Hampstead in a church hall. The significance of the Brecht theater, the white half curtain, originated in a quite necessary way, in a cellar, when a wire had to be strung from wall to wall." Of course, she had to bring in the Russians. "Meyerhold," she noted, "turned to the circus and the music hall."

Theater could happen anywhere and did. Yet Arena, more than most theaters, always had been defined by a specific configuration. Just as the theater-in-the-round burst out of the proscenium box, Zelda was now in hot pursuit of something to help break down the limitations of the arena. "New words. New relationships. New Places. New Buildings," she declared. "The search for new forms to express our shifting, shaking world. And no one form can capture it all."[221]

Ever restless, Zelda had sought a new "Stage II" almost from the time the company had settled into "Stage I." As she explained at the new building's groundbreaking on August 28, 1968, "I want another physical space. Some plays work better in a one-focus backwall stage. I'm also interested in exploring the scenic challenges of the proscenium form. Also, this will give us playwright space for new works."[222]

She teamed up once more with the architect Harry Weese, with whom she worked even more closely than in the past. Together, they produced a thrust stage protruding into a fan-shaped house—not a proscenium per se, although the new hall could be easily converted into a traditional configuration when required.[223] Physically connected to the original Arena, both buildings could share a common entry when required; or they could be treated separately when preferred. The sleek addition with rounded corners gently contrasted with the earlier angular brutalism of the 1960s, offering a more soothing embrace.[224]

The Fichandlers convinced David Lloyd Kreeger to pledge a quarter-million dollars toward the new building. Several long-standing partner foundations—including the Ford Foundation, the Old Dominion Foundation, the Eugene and Agnes E. Meyer Foundation, and the Twentieth Century Fund—helped round out the more than $1.5 million required to realize Weese's and Fichandler's plans.[225]

Kreeger, the son of immigrants who opened a grocery store in New Jersey, moved to Washington as a government lawyer during the New Deal. He shifted into private practice, and he eventually became chairman and chief executive of GEICO Insurance. An avid art collector, his Philip Johnson–designed house (now a museum) showcased a superb collection of modern art. He supported awards at Catholic and Georgetown universities, sponsored the music building at American University and an auditorium at the Corcoran Gallery of Art, and became a major donor to the National Symphony Orchestra and the John F. Kennedy Center for the Performing Arts.[226] He took a personal interest in the new Arena Stage, opening the building by playing Vivaldi's *Sonata in A Minor for Two Violins and Piano* at its dedication.[227]

Zelda conceived of the 500-seat theater and basement cabaret (known as the "Old Vat Room" in a nod to the company's Foggy Bottom past) as experimental performance areas, which would enable Arena to offer more intimate works of an often explicitly untried form.[228] The Kreeger Theater became a favored space for new works, international productions—notably from Eastern Europe and Africa—and community-oriented works, often featuring African American themes.[229]

The Old Vat, for its part, featured high-end cabaret, public readings of new works, and other special projects.[230] The Chicago-based roots musician and banjo maestro Stephen Wade brought his one-person show *Banjo Dancing* to the White House in 1981 after a thirteen-month run in Chicago. He tacked on a three-week engagement at the Old Vat that lasted ten years, making his show the longest-running Off-Broadway show at the time.[231] A background report for a 1984 Arena strategic planning project praised Wade for attracting new audiences who would otherwise never have come to the theater.[232]

This additional flexibility—and income—empowered Arena to move in ever more experimental directions, even as the original theater-in-the-round provided a fresh venue for more traditional works. During the 1970s, Arena organized readings of new works by prominent actors before small groups of subscribers, who were given ample opportunity to offer their own suggestions. For example, a particularly stellar workshop in 1976 with an audience of 166 heard Lily Tomlin, Ned Beatty, Lane Smith, Conchata Ferrel, and Sadie Bond read a preliminary script by the novelist Cynthia Buchanan.[233]

Receptions tied to specific productions—such as a September 1987 gathering with Mayor Marion Barry for Lloyd Richards and August Wilson, marking the opening of Wilson's *Joe Turner's Come and Gone*, directed by Richards—attracted African American high society to Arena.[234] In the mid-1990s, to mention just one example among many, Anna Deveare Smith came as an artist in residence to work on a script about life in Washington.[235] Other notable African American women playwrights who had their works produced at Arena during the 1990s and early 2000s include Cheryl West, Pearl Cleage, Suzan-Lori Parks, and Endesha Holland.[236]

The inauguration of the Kreeger Theater expanded such possibilities for Arena's engagement with its immediate and metropolitan communities.[237] The company quickly learned how to use these opportunities for its own advantage. At the same time, challenges continued. In frustration, Zelda admitted at a 1988 Executive Committee meeting planning the next year's budget that "it's very, very difficult operating in a city with twenty other theatres with most of our customers living in the suburbs and aging along with us."[238] Various proposals arose in response over time, such as establishing a "touring" company to visit performance venues in the suburbs as a means for connecting to new audiences and communities and generating additional income.[239] As larger and larger ideas emerged, leadership remained cautious. "If we grow in other directions," senior staff members worried, "will we become IBM and spoil the nurturing and caring environment we now enjoy?"[240]

Embracing Diverse Communities

Arena's leaders began to become interested in expanding community engagement as soon as the company relocated to Southwest Washington. Such efforts always had been integrated into their marketing and fundraising strategies, to the extent that many subscribers during the Old Vat days in Foggy Bottom felt themselves to be part of one large Arena family.[241] The changing times and changing location demanded changing engagement strategies.

The Old Vat and Hippodrome had been located on the fringes of downtown, neighborhoods where residents were an afterthought. The Southwest Redevelopment Project highlighted residential construction in an effort to create a neighborhood in every sense of that word.

Ensuring success in the new location demanded securing a productive relationship with nearby residents and not just businesses and far-flung donors. Those residents, in turn, were quite diverse, even as they became compartmentalized by race and income. Large public housing projects stood within walking distance, joined together with the middle-class and luxury homes constructed during the area's renewal.

Given the rising racial tensions of the 1960s and 1970s, Arena could not ignore the realities of its neighborhood as other cultural institutions tried to do within the apartheid-like White worlds of downtown, Georgetown, Upper Northwest, and the Virginia and Maryland suburbs. Moreover, such disregard would have been an affront to the stated values of this liberal-minded, innovative theater company.

Postproduction discussions, often funded by foundation grants, became a standard feature of Arena productions. This practice has spread to numerous other Washington-based theaters over the years, even though it was unusual when first attempted in the 1960s. Such outreach endeavors date back to the company's reconfiguration as an educational nonprofit organization in the late 1950s.[242]

By the 1970s, and especially after the 1971 opening of the John F. Kennedy Center for the Performing Arts, Arena faced growing competition within the capital's entertainment community from an ever-expanding roster of large, small, and vest pocket drama companies and theaters. The most potent challenge came in the mid-1980s when Kennedy Center chair Roger Stevens invited Peter Sellars—who, at the age of twenty-seven years, was theater's enfant terrible—to revitalize the American National Theater at the Center's Eisenhower Theater.[243] The dream of establishing an American version of the Irish National Theater lived still.[244]

Stevens had hoped to establish his center as the equivalent of a European national theater based in the capital. He set Sellars up with a $6 million budget and anticipated driving away all the competition. Eighteen months later, the experiment lay in shambles as angry audiences, petulant critics, displeased funders, and unhappy actors led to Sellars's summary dismissal.[245] Having terminated Sellars, Stevens may have hoped to rebuild the American National Theater in a new guise, but this never happened. The Kennedy Center's debacle convinced some that Washington was too conservative a town to support cutting-edge theater (although debates would rage for years over whether the fault lay with audiences and critics or with Sellars's failed vision).

The Kennedy Center's inability to establish a home company left Arena Stage as the city's premier company, a position it would hold even as the community of grassroots theater companies continued to expand. As Arena's 1995 Long-Range Plan noted, the company was no longer the lone stage for high-quality theater. Arena welcomed such an expansion of theater, noting that the company "must extend the creative reach of Arena in response to our current position and a changing world."[246]

Arena frequently became a leading, and at times founding, member of various efforts to organize Washington's performing-arts organizations.[247] Such educational and community outreach programs helped secure Arena's status as this community's "mothership."[248]

Beyond theater, Arena's leaders engaged the Southwest Neighborhood Assembly and other community groups, often providing important facilities for neighborhood events.[249] For example, on December 28, 1991, Arena joined with community leaders in celebrating the opening of the Waterfront Metrorail Station nearby. The theater participated in a celebratory VIP breakfast ribbon-cutting and gave away tickets for Cheryl West's *Jar the Floor*, directed by Tazewell Thompson, to the first fifty riders to exit the new station.[250]

As early as 1978, statements of purpose fulsomely embraced cultural diversity. The fifth of twelve core artistic principles articulated at that time proclaimed that Arena embraces and embodies

> the core concept of cultural diversity in every aspect of our identity. . . . Cultural diversity is fast becoming an organic fact of life for Arena and continuing a long and historic evolution as an Arena ideal. . . . We have become a model for other theaters across America. . . . Our work as artists is of value to our community only in so far as we are able, through our work, to articulate the poetry of pluralism in a meaningful and provocative fashion.[251]

This vision was incorporated into strategic planning goals in 1984 as the plan's authors challenged the company to expand its audience "to the broadest possible spectrum of the Washington Metropolitan Community, including children and young adults, low and moderate income theater-goers, and Blacks." The resulting plan encouraged the presentation of works written and performed by African Americans and Africans, visiting performances by African drama companies, an expansion of student discount programs, and matinees for the elderly and schoolchildren.[252]

The at-times arduous—and always incomplete—search for common ground among neighbors continues. These activities have rewarded Arena with admission into the intricacy of local life that few other cultural institutions have earned—or sought. Arena, by settling south of the National Mall, faced many choices in thinking about how to engage with a subscriber base predominantly located in the suburbs and distant Northwest areas within DC. Simultaneously, they wanted to be a good neighbor to the diverse residents of varied racial, ethnic, and economic backgrounds who lived nearby.[253]

The DC Public School system initially appeared to offer robust opportunities for such engagement. Early attempts seem to have been quite successful. In October 1966, for example, 750 DC students visited Arena to see Jane Alexander, Robert Foxworth, Richard Venture, and Robert Prosky perform a play by Shakespeare and lead a discussion about him.[254]

Programs involving the city's schools fell victim to draconian budget cuts in arts education, forcing Arena to turn to the National Endowment for the Arts, the Heyman Foundation, and the Meyer Foundation to pull together a small group of actors and musicians to go out and visit various school groups and children's organizations. Foundation funding, in turn, became ever more difficult to secure as the 1960s and 1970s turned into the 1980s and 1990s.[255] With the passage of time, many educational and outreach programs fell to a company-within-the company, the Living Stage.

Joining the Jam

Robert and Jane Alexander moved to Washington when Jane joined the Arena Stage resident company in 1965. Not quite newlyweds — they married in 1962 — the couple still carried the spark of youthful enthusiasm about their love for the theater and for each other.

For Jane, who was twenty-six, joining the Arena resident company offered an unparalleled opportunity to hone her craft. For Robert, who was a decade older, being in Washington enabled him to think about how disappointed he had been acting in New York by the absence of imagination among audiences. He concluded that audiences needed to unleash their minds in order to invigorate the theater. Moreover, they needed to learn how to do so as children.

Robert remained a social activist throughout, coming to see the stage and advocacy as tightly bound together through collective enterprise. In this, he refined an improvisational vision of group theater drawn from the ideas of Konstantin Stanislavski, Federico García Lorca, Pete Seeger, and Martha Graham. His passion for community-based social action—both within a theater and at large within society—resonated deeply with Zelda.[256]

Within months of the couple's arrival, Robert launched his Children's Theater as a venture within Arena. His company's ambiguous status of being *at*—rather than *of*—Arena would complicate relations between the two throughout for the next three decades. In 1968, the venture expanded its focus, rebranding itself as the "Living Stage." Alexander would leave in 1995 to teach improvisational theater full time. The Living Stage disbanded six years later, in 2001.[257]

The charismatic visionary Alexander had a very specific notion of what he wanted to do. In a 1977 "Introduction to Living Stage" shared with members of the Arena Board of Trustees, he wrote that

> Living Stage is a small, multiracial improvisational theater company dedicated to turning on its audiences to their own creativity. The company of professional actors and actresses presents performing workshops of a ritualistic theater that depends heavily on audience participation for both its content and its dramatic shape. Living Stage can't be fully described without a demonstration—by its very nature it is participational rather than presentational—and this sketch must be considered more a blurred photograph than a detailed motion picture.

Turning to how the company performed, he added that "there is never a written script for a Living Stage performance/workshop. Everything comes to life from the emotions and thoughts of the actors and audience." Indeed, the audience "joins the jam." This happens as "scenes coalesce out of the exercises. . . . Each scene may be frozen—stopped at any point—and the audience may be asked how they would like the scene to end. The actors perform as many endings as there are suggestions." The performance/workshops end in "rap sessions" between the cast and the audience, which is limited to a maximum of two hundred, usually smaller.[258]

Alexander's concept remained fundamentally unchanged over the years, even as audiences, donors, and partner institutions evolved. Although no performance was "typical," a menu of several basic components to a performance/workshop emerged. The company consisted of a half-dozen actors—at times, more; at other times, less—with a musician who collaborated on a play around a theme relevant to a given audience.

Performances wrestled with major challenges of the day, such as drug abuse, racism, teenage suicide, teenage pregnancy, AIDS, and conflict. The goal was to draw energy from the troubled to confer dignity though self-expression.[259]

Arriving audience members—be they kindergarteners, elementary school students, teenagers, prison inmates, older adults, or the physically challenged—were presented with song, dance, and pantomime, set out on a boundary-less performance space. Performances drew from a repertoire of about eighty songs and four hundred possible stories of everyday life, as well as from excerpts derived from Shakespeare, Molière, Tennessee Williams, and Lorraine Hansberry, among many classical writers.[260] Audiences actively engaged the performers as they were asked to suggest plot twists and endings. Eventually, audiences would be invited to participate in the show, with everyone joining in a final song or rap linked to the unfolding emotional theme. The effect was to promote imaginative freedom, emotional fulfillment, and community.[261]

Initially oriented toward DC and area schools, the company expanded its reach to include inmates at the Women's Detention Center, the DC Jail, groups of economically disadvantaged children, and physically and emotionally injured men and women. With time, as Arena and Living Stage both grew, the company moved to its own home in the abandoned and once fabled Club Bali blues club at the corner of 14th and T streets NW (now long washed over by the neighborhood's rapacious gentrification, the building was home before the COVID pandemic to the millennial-friendly Matchbox Vintage Pizza Bistro).[262]

Reaching The Underserved

Living Stage became the gold standard for similar ventures drawing on the performing arts to shape discussions of tough issues and reach sequestered audiences. A favorite of national and local philanthropy, Alexander's troupe helped stake a claim to performing regularly in the city and suburbs, and toured the United States and internationally. Alexander and his colleagues formed partnerships with groups wherever he went, often leaving like-minded ensembles behind.

Visits to the District of Columbia's Lorton Correctional Campus in Virginia—which served as the city's primary penitentiary from 1910 until 2001—proved especially rewarding. According to the *Washington Post*, "No motion picture nor TV show has so excited the young prisoners at Lorton Youth Center as did the Arena Stage's Living Stage in its live and lively production of drama and music." Alexander cooperated with then–Lorton inmate Rhozier H. "Roach" Brown to establish a prison theater company, "Lorton Voices," which became a national model.[263]

Robert Alexander and Zelda Fichandler established a symbiotic relationship with one another personally as well as between the Living Stage and Arena Stage. Alexander's trend-setting vision provided successful vehicles for the community engagement Zelda valued; Zelda's institutional supports and reputation provided Alexander with crucial resources that would have been beyond the reach of his small experimental venture. Many an Arena foundation proposal inserted information about Living Stage activities when justifying community inclusion; many a Living Stage application for support included Arena's hefty organizational and political capacities. As a 1980s "Arena Stage Handbook" put it,

> Even as Arena has made its audiences an important part of the ensemble process, Living Stage Theater Company has extended the family of Arena by weaving theater into the fabric of the Washington community's daily life. Director Robert Alexander's dedicated group creates together performances involving music, acting, and movement for people who seldom have the chance to experience theater, especially children, the handicapped, the disadvantaged, and Senior Citizens. Living Stage has sought to break down the usual barrier between artists and audiences by using its performances and workshops to unlock the creativity to those audiences through their active participation. . . . Such strength has helped to forge an 'unbreakable bond' with Arena's Washington audiences.[264]

Arena took credit and embraced refracted glory when a four-teen-year-old blind girl spoke for the first time in seven years while participating in a Living Stage performance; when the Public Broadcasting System aired a television documentary about Living Stage's work; when Mayor Marion Barry declared December 13, 1982, Robert A. Alexander Day in the District; and when *Washingtonian Magazine* proclaimed Alexander "Washingtonian of the Year."[265] Living Stage similarly took pride when Arena won a Tony Award; and when Zelda later received similar honors from Mayor Barry and *Washingtonian Magazine*. Conversely, Alexander was never inclined to submit to the authority of Arena's leadership and Board of Trustees. Zelda, for her part, remained reluctant to share donors and board members with Living Stage.

From the beginning, neither Zelda nor Alexander established clear lines of authority between their companies. Living Stage provided only limited input, for example, when Arena undertook a major planning project in 1984. As the strategy document noted, "a thorough examination and discussion [of Living Stage—BR] with Board members, staff, and top leadership was not undertaken as part of the plan we are presenting."[266] A staff retreat a year later generated considerable concern over Living Stage's inattention to complying with Arena's financial controls, budgeting, and administrative procedures.[267] Uncertainties over the precise relationship between Living Stage and Arena bubbled up at Arena board meetings as Alexander courted his own board and resisted reporting to Arena's trustees. Arena's board members, quite naturally, given the attention often paid to Living Stage by the outside world, periodically requested reports and reviews.

In October 1967, the Arena Board of Trustees devoted much of its meeting to a discussion of Alexander's active participation in efforts within the DC Public Schools to prepare training materials about theater for its English teachers. Zelda endorsed these efforts, noting that, though schools were receptive to hosting actors, finding actors willing to teach was more difficult. The next meeting, in November, approved Alexander and Zelda working together to develop teacher enrichment programs and develop curricula that would bring Arena actors into the schools.[268]

Alexander's social agenda at times raised concerns among

more establishment-oriented members of the Arena board. In January 1978, a board member requested a discussion of Living Stage, asking "if the philosophy was still one of allowing children to let out their emotions with no adults present. Mr. Fichandler replied that it still is the philosophy but that Living Stage is not as strict as it once was. Adults were allowed, but must participate." After further discussion, Alexander was asked to report to the following, February, board meeting.[269]

A month later, the magnetic Alexander

held members spellbound with an eloquent and moving description of the work of Living Stage. It was in great part a repetition of a similar talk he had previously given to the Board, adding that, although the group had its difficulties in the past, it is now "hot at this time in our history." He termed Living Stage a social service arts organization, whose work is both artistic and therapeutic in that it aims to "turn people on to their own creativity."[270]

The Arena board members were so enthusiastic that there was a move to involve the board in raising funds for Living Stage, which prompted the Fichandlers to caution members to remain focused on their responsibilities to Arena. As Zelda told board members in 1976, "It is important that Arena Board not become enmeshed with Living Stage. . . . It exists for its own goals, and in the interest of its own independence, should remain separate."[271] Tom Fichandler underscored the same theme in 1978, stating matter-of-factly that "although Living Stage is a kind of adjunct to Arena and is helped in many ways—housing, administration and the like, it is financially independent."[272]

Joyfully Sing

Living Stage competed with Arena for space as well as for financial resources. By late 1980, the company moved across the street before relocating four years later to its final 14th Street home. Alexander and his backers raised the half-million dollars required to purchase and renovate their new space. Now offsite, Living Stage acted increasingly independently from Arena management and oversight.[273]

Tensions continued. A series of discussions by the Long-Range Planning Committee for Arena in the summer of 1985 provoked sharp divergences between the underlying philosophies of the two companies. There appeared to be no agreed-upon answer to the question "Who governs Living Stage?" Moreover, some Arena trustees complained about Alexander's defensiveness, arrogance, and unwillingness to engage troubled White children. Always proud of his company's diverse and multiracial composition, Alexander denied that his company was "anti-White." He maintained that, more than the main stage, Living Stage better reflected the composition of the city—to which board members replied with the suggestion that he "sell performances to private schools and other middle-class kids to raise money for the rest."[274]

Once across town, Living Stage was housed in what was still the heart of the poor African American neighborhood surrounding U Street that long had been the symbolic center of DC's "Chocolate City."[275] Senior Arena staff members mused at their meetings in the mid-1990s that they did not even know who was in charge of Living Stage.[276]

Robert Alexander stepped down from Living Stage in 1995 to spend more time teaching. The company continued operation until 2001 under a dedicated and talented creative and administrative team. Company members gradually moved on, grants became more difficult to secure, and gentrification obliterated the U Street neighborhood. A Thirtieth Anniversary Gala provided a capstone to the company's achievements, bringing together Olympia Dukakis, Angela Davis, Ossie Davis, Ruby Dee, Lena Horne, Barbara Jordan, Del Lewis, Kweisi Mfume, Ethelbert Miller, Eleanor Holmes Norton, and many more luminaries from the Washington and national African American and theater communities.[277]

Living Stage transformed how theater companies engaged with their communities, most especially with the most disadvantaged members of those communities. The company was artistically and socially innovative, and it represented the core values that Zelda and Tom Fichandler advanced through Arena Stage. Various contretemps between the Living Stage and Arena—and between Alexander and the Fichandlers—remain insignificant when viewed from their shared perspective about the social creativity of theater. The Fichandlers allowed Alexander to pursue his creative vision in the mid-1960s because it was so closely aligned with how they too saw the community, city, and nation around them. Alexander, in turn, empowered the Fichandlers to engage with hometown DC in ways that would have been impossible if Arena were merely an acting ensemble.

In a 1979 article appearing in an early issue of the *Living Stage Love Letter*, Alexander set forth a statement of purpose that captured both his own and, to a considerable extent, the Fichandlers' understanding of the role of theater in society. "All the work that we do as theater workers/educators," he wrote, "is to help people find their poetic strengths, so that they can fight their fight wherever and whatever that may be; to help people get in touch with this world through their creative imaginations, so that every person's life is important to them; to bring them to the state where they are very, very vulnerable to the human condition; and have the strength of purpose to joyfully sing the song that reveals the human condition to others."[278] Being sure that a variety of songs sung by a diverse company to varied audiences reflecting the world outside their theater's walls became a mission for the Fichandlers as well.

Breaking the Cycle of Exclusion

As devoted as the Fichandlers were to the community engagement and social activism represented by Robert Alexander's Living Stage, what happened on Arena's main stage took priority over other concerns. For the Fichandlers, there could be no contradiction. To underscore the connection between stage and community, Arena set about changing how its productions looked. By the late 1960s, Arena had become a leader in so-called nontraditional casting, without considering an actor's ethnicity, race, or gender.

The powerful emotions unleased by *The Great White Hope* combined with growing racial tensions within the city and neighborhood to convince the Fichandlers that Arena should expand African American involvement in their productions.[279] Such an effort was in keeping with the times, as many segments of American society began to search out meaningful engagement across racial lines.

In February 1968, the release of the report by the Kerner Commission (National Advisory Commission on Civil Disorders) focused attention the country's racial divide, a finding accentuated by the assassination of the Reverend Dr. Martin Luther King Jr. weeks later and the civil unrest to follow.[280] The eleven-member commission, chaired by Illinois governor Otto Kerner Jr., excoriated all levels of government for their inattention to the housing, education, social service provision, and economic opportunity for the nation's poorest.[281] "Our nation," the commission famously concluded, "is moving toward two societies, one Black, one White—separate and unequal."

Major foundations were among those to respond, devoting increased resources to support activities designed to reduce the country's racial divisions. In June 1968, Arena announced a $250,000 grant from the Ford Foundation "to integrate Black and White experiences."[282] The majority of the funds were to be used to double Arena's repertory company by recruiting African American members. Grants from the Rockefeller Foundation advanced subsequent efforts.[283]

As noted above, eight African American actors joined the Arena company—including several who enjoyed distinguished careers, such as Olivia Cole, Cynthia McPherson, and Garret Saunders—with many moving into roles previously reserved for White actors.[284] In announcing the program, Zelda was clearheaded about its purposes. "There is no sociological motive behind it," she wrote in the *Washington Sunday Star*; "the motivation is not to employ Negro actors for their own good or out of impulses of White guilt or social generosity or responsibility. These are quite worthwhile reasons, but they don't enter here. Nor do we have in mind enticing the middle-class Negro dollars into the box office till." Rather, she continued, it concerned "the emergence of the Negro Man, the Negro woman, and the Negro child into his full humanity, into the entire possibility of human power."[285]

The Fichandlers considered the three-year pilot program something of a failure. Integration of Blacks and Whites into a cohesive company proved challenging; audience members—including several longtime subscribers and donors—perceived a decline in quality; and critics became hypersensitive to the presence of interracial casts on stage.

R. H. Gardner was particularly snarky, writing in Baltimore's *Sunday Sun* that "I gather that Mrs. Fichandler is in this case using color in a symbolic sense. Negroes are alienated from society; therefore the casting of a Black actress in the part of a 'loner' makes her more lonesome."[286] Other observers immediately appreciated Zelda's wisdom in bringing new energy into Arena. Bernadette Carey, in the *Washington Post*, found that the new company "crackled, sparked, and popped simply because of their presence."[287]

As mentioned above, the Fichandlers and many others found the initial three-year experiment with interracial casting frustrating.[288] Just as the era's racial tensions had prompted Arena to reach out to the African American community, these same tensions now entered into the company as the program unfolded.

The Ford Foundation evidently reached similar conclusions, deciding not to renew the program after the initial three-year period.[289] Arena never wavered from its commitment to integrate the company onstage, backstage, and offstage. By the 1980s, Zelda continued to bring Black artists into the company. As Galella observes, this integration primarily took the form of integrating Black actors into White repertory.[290] Zelda's successor, Doug Wager, proved even more steadfast in his desire to integrate the company during the 1990s.[291]

Such determination placed Arena's leadership, at times, in confrontation with subscribers and ticketholders. Throughout the 1970s, 1980s, and into the 1990s, complaints flowed. Some found mixed racial casting "disconcerting," others "disappointing," "inappropriate," "disgusting and just plain awful." Audience grievances included those who found productions "very low class," and "extreme," to others who saw them as "gimmicky" and "unreflective" of Arena's own audiences. Some Whites claimed that Blacks did not want to see such works, while others thought having Blacks perform on stage was fine as long as they stuck to "Black" material. Criticisms began almost immediately in 1968, with the arrival of the additional cast members, and continued throughout the 1990s, after Wager had replaced Zelda as artistic director.[292]

Further grants followed—including a million-dollar award from the National Endowment for the Arts in 1989—yet they were only part of the story. Arena's leadership under the Fichandlers, during their successor Wager's tenure, and subsequently under the leadership of Molly Smith, embraced multicultural representation on its stages.[293] Artists such as Avery Brooks, Ruby Dee, Morgan Freeman, Adriane Lenox, and John Marriott—to name but a few—found a congenial home at Arena. Works by and about African American, African, and Caribbean artists and societies appeared recurrently. This presence, in turn, attracted more diverse audiences.[294]

Expanding Inclusion

The company's mission was consistent. The goal was to break what Zelda called "the cycle of exclusion and disengagement among our young people that keeps them from considering the theater as a realistic career option."[295] To achieve this end required hard work, often behind the scenes. As a 1972 staff discussion noted, the challenges were not only over who appeared on stage. "Arena Stage," the conversation concluded, "is too White an organization, we should have more Blacks in the technical area and in the company. We will have one Black in the shop, and, hopefully, three in the company next season."[296] In response, the company began reaching out to over a hundred Black drama departments at colleges throughout the country to attract job candidates.

With time, Arena's personnel became more proactive in seeking African American talent. Wager, who arrived as an intern and rose to replace Zelda as artistic director, engaged the Black community in town as well as nationally.

In pursuit of this mission, Arena appointed Tazewell Thompson as an artistic associate in the late 1980s. Thompson had acted on Broadway and Off Broadway before turning to directing. Zelda became intrigued by his direction of Aaron Copland's opera *The Second Hurricane* at New York's Henry Street Settlement and recruited him to join the Arena company. Thompson honed his directorial skills at Arena—including with productions of Ted Kociolek and James Racheff's musical *Abyssinia*, Mustafa Matura's *Playboy of the West Indies*, Tennessee Williams's *The Glass Menagerie*, August Wilson's *Fences*, and Cheryl West's *Before It Hits Home* and *Jar the Floor*—before moving on to serve as the artistic director of the Syracuse Stage and the Westport Country Playhouse, and to a notable career directing opera and dramatic theater across the country and around the world. Sustaining his relationship with Arena, by 2019 he had directed twenty productions with the company. He used his appointment at Arena during the 1990s to help the company's leaders nurture ties with African American theater artists.[297]

Jim Nicola oversaw casting during his time at Arena, hiring African American actors for the company. He was especially engaged with the Washington Nontraditional Casting Conference and was instrumental in bringing cultural diversity to the Arena stage.[298] Nicola assumed artistic leadership of the New York Theatre Workshop, where, among many works, the company produced Jonathan Larson's *Rent*, David Bowie's *Lazarus*, and Anaïs Mitchell's *Hadestown*.[299]

Wager came to Arena in 1974 as a twenty-five-year-old stage management intern and was pressed into service on stage at the last minute when an actor fell ill. By 1977, he was directing productions.[300] He had filled every possible position at Arena, and knew the entire company from the inside out by the time Zelda decided to step down after the fortieth season in 1990–91. As Zelda moved to take over the Acting Company in New York, Wager shifted into her position as artistic director.[301] The move was carefully managed to foster a sense of continuity.[302] Wager's absolute commitment to continuing cultural diversity programs was among the very first messages shared both within and outside the company. By the time of Zelda's departure, the drive to expand diversity was "an Arena Stage initiative now and forever," not "Zel-driven."[303]

Zelda remained at the Acting Company until 1994. She had been teaching at New York University since the 1980s and would continue to do so until 2009. She passed away at the age of ninety-one in Washington in July 2016.[304]

Wager continued as Arena's artistic director until 1998, when he moved on to work in New York, Philadelphia, and elsewhere. He eventually became the long-standing associate dean of Temple University's School of Theater, Film, and Media Arts. His commitment to nontraditional casting and other forms of cultural diversity at Arena remained resolute even as criticism mounted.

Recasting the Cast

Both Zelda and Wager sought outside assistance to bring about the changes they envisioned for their company. In addition to foundation support, they looked to African American groups such as the Black Theatre Alliance. The alliance, a group of New York–based African American theaters, produced important directories to Black directors, technicians, administrators, and playwrights, which became important resources for Arena when seeking new talent.[305]

Clinton Turner Davis proved to be an important partner for both Zelda and Wager in their efforts to expand the diversity of actors appearing on the Arena stage. Davis established the Non-Traditional Casting Project with the assistance of Actor's Equity Association in 1986.[306] Launched in New York, the project extended its activities to Washington, San Francisco, Cleveland, and Los Angeles, promoting nontraditional casting through symposia, lectures, scene presentations, panels, dialogues, and written documentation. Step by step, the Non-Traditional Casting Project lobbied for the inclusion of all minorities and the expansion of opportunities for minority theater professionals.[307]

As Brandi Wilkins Catanese records, Davis and his colleagues defined nontraditional casting as casting ethnic, female, or disabled actors in roles where race, ethnicity, gender, or physical capability are not necessary to the characters' development. They differentiated among casting in roles in plays in which a work is translated into a different cultural setting (cross-cultural casting); casting to give a play greater resonance (conceptual casting); casting without regard to race, ethnicity, gender or physical capacity (blind casting); and casting of actors in roles they perform in society as a whole (societal casting).

"This delineation," Catanese continues, "produces an ideologically fluid spectrum that alternately uses race to Say Something, to Reflect Truth, and at the extreme, to Say Something by Saying Nothing." Within this context, she concludes, blind casting "is in some ways the most ambitious of these approaches, particularly if audiences are expected to be blind to more than one social category at the same time."[308]

Zelda corresponded with Davis about the challenges of nontraditional casting.[309] Davis had strong Washington connections, which proved invaluable for Arena. He had been born and raised in the city, eventually graduating from Howard University's Department of Theatre Arts. Davis credits his time at Howard as crucial to his later work: "That was a rare, intense, fertile climate. Debbie Allen, Clyde Barrett, Glenda Dickerson, Harry Poe, Phylicia Rashad, Clay Gross, and the Truitts, and others all came together to combine their talents and influence each other. We were all taught by Eleanor Traylor, Vera Katz, and the great Owen Dodson, whose passion, compassion, sensitivity and mind for theatre was on the grand scale."[310]

After graduating from Howard, Davis joined the Negro Ensemble Company in New York, where he worked as an instructor, literary manager, casting director, and production supervisor. He moved to freelancing after a stint as production stage manager for Lena Horne's 1983 national and international tour. He proved to be a talented director during these years, and by the mid-1980s he was ready to tackle the challenge of racism in American theater. Working with Actors' Equity and the League of Resident Theatres, he became a key player in efforts to expand the African American presence onstage. He later promoted African performing arts, and was involved in the Cultural Olympia at the 1994 Atlanta Olympic Games.[311]

There were limits. After a half century of promoting nontraditional casting, the sight of African American actors playing "White" roles still startles some. In February 2019, Arena staged a production of *The Heiress*, Ruth and Augustus Goetz's adaptation of Henry James's novel *Washington Square*. Set in the New York high society of the 1850s, the story revolves around an heiress—Catherine Sloper—confronting a nefarious suitor. The striking African American actor Lorene Chesley played one of Catherine's cousins. Immediately upon her entrance, the audience members seated directly behind me chirruped and clucked about how a servant would have been the only African American woman who would have been permitted into such a house at such a time and place. Even at Arena Stage, it seems, not every patron has embraced nontraditional casting more than a half century after it became a norm.[312]

For all of Arena's connection with—and concern for—the city

and its diverse communities, the company has remained focused nationally when seeking talent and ideas. Like many other theaters in town, Arena largely ignored the vibrant explosion of new music forms—go-go for Blacks, and punk for Whites—that swept across Washington in the late 1980s. Another difficult time for the city, the era experienced a wave of intense violence accompanying the arrival of crack cocaine in poor neighborhoods. Few theaters wrestled directly with what was happening.

Reviewing a 1988 performance by the No-Neck Monsters Theatre Company, the *Washington Post*'s Joe Brown questioned why so few Washington theaters had incorporated the indigenous music of the city—go-go, hip-hop, and rap—into their productions. Having just seen a performance of Ralph Brown's *Sanctuary DC*, based on the playwright's forays into homeless shelters and runaway encampments, Brown chastised the mainstream theater community. "Scott Richards' jittery synthesized rhythms," he noted, "throb[bed] with a harsh but musical urban edge." These sounds, Brown offered, gave the production "an added authenticity from the sounds of the streets."[313]

"Authenticity" was never the goal of Arena's efforts at nontraditional casting. For Zelda, such a search was misguided. As she argued in 1988,

> theater belongs to the world of the imagination. It is no one place, it is every place and anyplace, it is merely an empty space to be filled in any way we wish. We have always had it, it is as old as our curiosities, our fears, our hungers, our need to understand and control our lives. The theater is a game we organize quite deliberately and play out with a proper sense of seriousness and ceremony so that we may discover what our dreams are telling us, why we have done what we have done, where our feelings could take us, and how we can overcome our enemies from within and without. . . .
>
> Suppose the premise of this theatre company, its founding principle, was that the human spirit could be embodied in unpredictable and newly imagined ways, thereby astonishing the spectator and revealing meanings never before

anticipated, sloughing off old ways of looking at things, and opening them up to the heart... . Casting a role is giving a specific living and breathing persona to an imaginary (imagined) figure who exists in a specific social, political and philosophic imagined world.[314]

From this perspective, "nontraditional" was not nontraditional at all.

The Gospel According to Sophocles

Arena began staging Black musicals in 1973 with an unforgettable production of a musical adaptation of Lorraine Hansberry's *A Raisin in the Sun*. A favorite of local critics, *Raisin* enjoyed a long run and moved on to Broadway, where it won a number of Tony Awards.[315] The production opened the way for several important musical productions, including Duke Ellington's *Sophisticated Ladies* in 2010, which was staged in the historic Lincoln Theater. Ellington frequently performed before and after he had moved to New York in the theater's downstairs Lincoln Colonnade nightclub.[316]

Many of these productions were staged to draw in African American audiences, and nearly all conformed to long-standing forms emerging from the previously discussed musical theater formulas developed at the end of the nineteenth century and beginning of the twentieth century. But one production stood out as outside well-worn models.

During the early years of the Howard Players, Thomas Montgomery Gregory had argued that African American talent and perspectives could invigorate Western classical traditions in at least two ways. One was through the performance of Western theatrical characters by African American actors. The second was the presentation of European classical material through the lens of African American traditions. In 1984, Arena presented Washington audiences with a astonishing example of such a wholesale reconfiguration of Western tradition through translation into African American convention: Lee Breuer and Bob Telson's *The Gospel at Colonus*.

Breuer founded the experimental Mabou Mines theater company in 1970 as a resident company at La MaMa Experimental

Theatre Club in New York's East Village. He envisioned the group as an artist-driven experimental collective that would generate original work and reimagine adaptations of the classics. Named after mines in Nova Scotia, the company became a major conduit bringing trends from Europe's avant-garde scene to New York and North America.[317]

During the early 1980s, he teamed up with the Brooklyn-reared musician Telson. Telson had studied with Nadia Boulanger in France and graduated with a music degree from Harvard University before moving into the world of rock. Among his early ventures was the underground Revolutionary Music Collective, featuring the young Bonnie Raitt on vocals. His eclectic tastes led to work with the Philip Glass Ensemble, the salsa kings Tito Puente and Machito, and a turn as organist for the Gospel group Five Blind Boys of Alabama.[318] Together, Breuer and Telson hit on the idea of presenting the Sophocles tragedy *Oedipus at Colonus* as a Gospel sermon at an African American church service.[319]

The resulting *The Gospel at Colonus* premiered at the Brooklyn Academy of Music's Next Wave Festival in late 1983 and was nominated as a finalist for a Pulitzer Prize in 1985. It traveled to Philadelphia, to Washington, and on to such cities as Minneapolis, Houston, and Los Angeles before a brief Broadway run in 1988.[320] Arena, for its part, was careful to present itself as a coproducer rather than as a stop on a national tour.[321] The production hit Washington like a lightning bolt when it played in December 1984.[322]

The fifty-seven-member cast reenacted the story of the blinded Oedipus in exile, as narrated by a Pentecostal preacher (Morgan Freeman), and performed by a brilliantly white-suited, six-person Oedipus (Clarence Fountain and the Five Blind Boys of Alabama), Antigone (Isabell Monk), Cleon (Robert Earl Jones), and Theseus, King (Carl Lumbly), to the accompaniment of a Chorus (J. J. Farley and the Original Soul Stirrers, J. D. Steele Singers, a nine-piece orchestra, and Wesley Boyd's Washington-based Gospel Working Choir).[323] As David Richards noted in the *Washington Post*, seldom has the Arena Stage been so full. And rarely has an Arena production been so spirited.[324]

The experience of witnessing the production in the intimate arena setting proved awe-inspiring. Many recall the music above all else, with the cast album proving a major event in itself.[325] Others were struck by how utterly appropriate the opening proclamation of a biblical reading from "the Book of Sophocles" seemed. Even the stage manager could not contain a sense of excitement in the normally matter-of-fact performance reports for each show: "The Joint's Jumping!" (November 28, 1984); "Lots of Energy for the End of a Long Week" (December 2, 1984); "Great Show!!! Truly Outstanding!!" (December 22, 1984); "Spirited and Fine Closing Performance" (December 30, 1984).[326]

The Gospel at Colonus destroyed racial lines and divisions, at least for one evening among those in its audience. The African American *Washington Post* columnist Courtland Milloy observed that, unlike those in other cities, Washington's theatergoers were a "mostly White, conservative audience," which "has been a restrained group that sits and ponders, occasionally clapping to the sounds of gospel songs. But that's okay. The play still affects the spirit in a manner that gives credence to the meaning of the word 'gospel': good news." Milloy added, "What we have here is a spiritual happening, a bold and daring theatrical production in a city accustomed to events like President Reagan joining Black students in the Ellipse to light a Christmas tree." [327]

A quarter of a century later, a Russian colleague confided to me that he understood for the first time that the Soviet Union would not survive the evening I took him to see Arena's *Gospel at Colonus*. He kept trying to imagine Clarence Fountain and the Five Blind Boys entering down the stairs of a Moscow theater in their bright white suits singing the words of Sophocles in Gospel time. He could not. The Soviet Union had become too stultified to produce such a joyous and intelligent celebration of humanity across the ages.

Community Matters

On a pleasant Sunday evening in April of the bicentennial year 1976, Zelda stood next to the actor Christopher Plummer on stage in New York and, before a national television audience, accepted the first Tony Award from the American Theatre Critics Association to honor a resident theater company outside New York. The award recognized Arena Stage's artistic and institutional leadership in advancing the cause of regional theater. Zelda's claims to legitimacy long had been staked on the Washington company, and on other regional companies. She graciously acknowledged the contributions of her Arena colleagues in remarks that praised the growth of living theater across the country. [328]

The Critics Association has presented a Tony to regional theaters annually ever since, recognizing that the art form is no longer the property of New York or any other single location. Then as now, Arena has remained a trendsetter within the regional theater movement. Arena's ability to evolve and to adjust to epochal transformations in the world around it remains astonishing in light of what has occurred in the theater, the city, the country, and the world since the company sprang to life in 1950.

Leadership has remained a critical factor in Arena's continuing success. Established by true visionaries in the Fichandlers, Arena has constantly found new ways to thrive, both artistically and institutionally. The seamless transition from Zelda to Doug Wager's leadership after the successful fortieth-anniversary season perhaps should not be a surprise. Wager, after all, had grown up professionally within the company—moving from intern to artistic director. As Wager told Galella, "When Zelda left, it wasn't so much a changing of the guard as a passing of the torch. Or, as she said, maybe I'm not passing the torch. I'm just passing the fire."[329]

Wager was deeply committed to an inclusive vision of American society and art. He extended Zelda's efforts at multiracial casting and, in winding down the company's commitment to international theater, created space for works that presented a complex, multicultural American landscape. As Galella recounts, this commitment brought him into direct confrontation with an era of rising opposition to and contestation with multiculturalism as the American right stood in stronger hostility to what they saw as attacks on Whites, males, middle-class values, and Western traditions.[330] This evolving environment created numerous financial obstacles for the company.

Budget challenges forced Wager to furlough staff to be able to realign the payroll with the available funds. Such efforts, in turn, brought him into conflict with board members, who expected more immediate financial returns. Viewing the theater's physical location outside the bounds of official Washington, some on the board began lobbying for the company to move to a rising entertainment district across the National Mall around a new sports arena at Gallery Place. Together with the professional sports complex, the Shakespeare Theater and Woolly Mammoth secured the neighborhood as a place to be. Many on the board—wanting to lock in a traditional audience base by relocating to an area considered safe by wealthy White patrons—demanded that the company move.

Wager dug in, citing the opening of a new Metro station a block away as well as Arena's long-standing presence in Southwest DC. Galella argues that Wager was the key player in resisting board demands that the company move. The contretemps, along with related budget troubles, led Wager to leave.[331] City officials, meanwhile, envisioned an expansive waterfront project across the street from Arena. Once the possibility of a relocation surfaced, the District government responded by working in partnership with Arena management to keep the stage at its location.

A Fresh Start

The transition from Wager to Molly Smith in 1998 could have proven fraught because, for the first time, Arena reached beyond its own professional family for direction. The company was larger, more complex, and more tested than ever before. A new leader from outside the organization could have faced a difficult time.

Smith's appointment has proven brilliant.[332] She redesigned the company's image, slowly dismantled the resident company in favor of more flexible casting and productions, and abandoned the Fichandlers' interest in international theater in favor of a concentration on American works. She refined the company's reputation and artistic trajectory in light of her own preferences and tastes. Simultaneously, she continued the company's engagement with the city around it as well as its leadership in the American theater community.

A native of Washington State, Smith attended Catholic University before going on to receive a master's degree in theater from American University. Early-1970s Washington proved to be formative for her. She regularly attended shows around town—most notably at Arena—and met others who would become leaders within her generation in American theater. Her family had moved to Alaska during her teenage years, and, after graduation, she headed back to Juneau, where she founded Perseverance Theatre. Like Arena, Perseverance would become widely known for cross-cultural programming. She learned along the way—both in Alaska and in other directorial assignments around North America—to surround herself with people who dream large.[333] Nineteen years later, she returned to DC as Arena's director.[334]

Smith's big dream was to build Arena into a national center for American artists—her own updated and more realistic version of T. Montgomery Gregory's dream of a "National Negro Theater" and of Father Gilbert V. Hartke's notion of a "National Catholic Theater." She launched a variety of programs—including residencies for playwrights; gatherings both large and small to discuss the future of American theater; and research and training facilities to commission, incubate, develop, and perform new American works. Her imagined unbroken path from idea to stage succeeded most famously with Benj Pasek, Justin Paul, and Steven Levenson's 2015 musical *Dear Evan Hansen*. This work, which was developed at Arena, was first performed there, before moving to Off Broadway, and Broadway, where it won a Tony Award in 2017.[335]

Arena has launched workshops for more than a hundred productions, produced some forty world premieres, and staged numerous early productions since Smith arrived, including nine projects that made their way to Broadway.[336] Many of these works—as well as dramatic, new productions of such classics as Rodgers and Hammerstein's *Oklahoma!* (2011)—have explored multicultural intricacies not brought to the fore in previous productions.[337]

Smith reimagined Arena Stage physically as well as artistically. Between 2008 and 2010, the company moved to temporary quarters across the Potomac in Arlington's Crystal City; and it performed in other venues in the city, such as the historic Lincoln Theater, along what was once Black Washington's "high street," U Street NW. She teamed with the Vancouver architect Bing Thom to renovate the original Weese Arena Stage—now renamed the Fichandler Stage—and the Kreeger—and she brought them under the same roof with additional performance and research spaces as the Mead Center for American Theater.[338]

Thom brought a slice of the Pacific Northwest's architectural elegance to Washington by creating a new megastructure that encapsulates Zelda's two theaters under a sweeping cantilevered roof, floating over open glass walls, and complex concrete forms creating new spaces. The building included a small, flexible experimental theater with basket-weaved walls—the Kogod Cradle—and provided space for support services, offices, research, and education centers.[339] Among Washington's most distinctive buildings, the new Arena complex makes a powerful commitment to the city. Once completed, Arena's arresting new building, in turn, anchors a neighborhood that has added a major new residential, commercial, and entertainment hub—known as the Wharf—along the Potomac River shore.

By the late 2010s, the Wharf had grown into one of the nation's largest redevelopment projects. When Phase One of the development opened in October 2017, the area added two office buildings, two apartment buildings, two condominium buildings, thirty-one restaurants, three concert venues, three hotels, four piers, three parks, and an upgraded fish market. Of the 870 residential units—649 were rentals and 220 were for purchase townhomes and condominiums—150 units were designated "affordable" for those making 30 percent and 60 percent of area median income. A similarly scaled Phase Two is scheduled to open in 2022.[340] Meanwhile, many among the area's longer-term residents fell below the city's median income.[341] Consequently, the stark social, economic, and racial contrasts that were apparent when Arena came to the area in 1961 have hardly diminished. Arena, for its part, has continued to engage both older and newer residents of the neighborhood.

Intertwined with the Neighborhood

As Arena reaches its seventh decade, the company ranks among the most racially integrated cultural spaces in Washington. This achievement is the result of sustained commitment and hard work dating back to Arena's first production, when Ed Mangum and the Fichandlers opened their new company's doors to integrated audiences. Arena has been a leader in bringing African American themes and performers to White Washingtonians, and it has reaped financial and artistic rewards for doing so.

Proof of this achievement becomes ever more striking in comparison with the records of other major Washington cultural institutions in a city that has been bedeviled by the question of race. Approaching the third decade of the twenty-first century, Washington is still a city where newcomers routinely try to shut down manifestations of African American street culture as "nuisances;[342] swank Georgetown stores find it acceptable to post advertisements at bikeshare stands about how "We're cleaning up DC" above the photo of a young Black woman with an Afro, thereby exclaiming without words who has to be cleansed;[343] and, club managers deny gigs to world-class performers because their skin is too dark.[344]

Southwest DC—once the site of one of the nation's largest slave markets and, later, home to the city's poorest Black rural migrants—has stood at the center of this racial maelstrom. In 1846, in response to intense lobbying by Alexandria merchants to stave off federal interference in that city's lucrative slave trade, Congress retroceded the District's lands across the Potomac to Virginia. This move reduced Southwest to a remnant of its original territory, leaving it as the geographically smallest of Washington's four quadrants.[345]

In the 1950s and 1960s, the huge Southwest redevelopment effort—which attracted Arena in the first place—simultaneously displaced thousands of African American residents. The neighborhood nonetheless was never completely "cleansed." Southwest remains the most racially balanced of all the city's quadrants, with approximately even numbers of Black and White residents. The new neighborhood attracted middle-class residents of all races. Their apartments and homes have stood cheek-by-jowl with public housing projects, which are predominantly home to poor African Americans. As a result of this compactness, Black and White, and middle-class and working-class residents, have cohabited the area, even as they have not integrated with one another. Community leaders, such as the above-mentioned Neal Pierce and Joseph Latimore, fought to bridge racial and economic divides. The Fichandlers, Wager, and Smith joined in such efforts with passion and distinction, both onstage and offstage.

The typical White Arena subscriber of decades past would drive in from the suburbs and park as closely as possible to the theater. Perhaps they would venture as far as the tourist-oriented restaurants along the nearby waterfront. The typical African American patron similarly would drive to the theater, perhaps from uptown or the close-in suburbs. They, too, would park as close to the theater as possible, perhaps heading off to the historic fish market to pick up fresh crabs along the way.

Once inside the theater, both entered the most unusual of Washington spaces, a bigotry-free place. Given the toxicity of Washington race relations, the creation of such a space is a remarkable achievement. In return, Arena has been awarded financially by an expanded patron and donor base—and artistically, by bringing African American talent into its company at every level.

Most redeveloping neighborhoods in Washington experience a more complete racial turnover. Long-gentrified areas—such as Georgetown, Foggy Bottom, and the West End—have dropped off the mental maps of Washington's African Americans, even as they were added to those of Washington Whites. Once home to a thriving blue-collar African American community, the zip code for the West End and Foggy Bottom now has the highest rents in the entire city. The area around U Street and 14th Street NW, once the hub of one of the most prominent African American communities in the country, comes in a close second, and is now well beyond having a majority of Whites.[346]

The importance of a site's presence on the mental maps of residents from diverse backgrounds is important. When planning the Shakespeare Theatre Company's Harman Center for the Arts, Sidney Harman advocated that the facility be in a neighborhood frequented by both Black and White Washingtonians. He insisted that the Harman Center open downtown near the Gallery Place Metrorail Station and the city's main sports arena, which are frequented by all the city's various groups. Harman understood better than most that integrated audiences depend on integrated neighborhoods. Sidney Harman Hall, which opened in 2007, continuously attracts both Blacks and Whites to performances, in part because both feel at home in the area.[347]

The site for a new Arena Stage favored by some board members in their battles with Doug Wager similarly would have moved the company to a high-income downtown neighborhood.

Unlike many neighborhoods across Washington, however, Southwest has remained on the mental maps of daily life among both Blacks and Whites. On any pre-COVID Friday or Monday evening at the outset of the twenty-first century, perhaps the city's most integrated crowds walk into Westminster Presbyterian Church to hear jazz and blues. For more than two decades, the Reverend Brian Hamilton and the church's congregation—together with former Redskin football player and singer Dick Smith—have welcomed all city and area residents for inexpensive concerts featuring the best musicians in town.[348] Whites, Blacks, young, old, wealthy, and poor of all genders, professions, and backgrounds mix easily, united by a love for music. The church is less than two blocks from Arena, just across the Duck Pond that itself at times brings neighbors closer together.

Many paths have led Arena to become one of the most successful demonstrations of the creative power of multicultural integration in the face of prejudice. Artistic, sociological, and moral explanations all have their place. So does Arena's physical location and its embrace of its immediate neighborhood and community. The chance opportunity to relocate across town from the centers of White Washington transformed what Arena could—and has—become.

The inclusion of African Americans in all aspects of Arena's operations is noteworthy and marks an important chapter in the struggle to confront prejudice from the Washington stage. In challenging prejudice, however, it could never affirm identity. As Galella writes, "The theatre, its leadership, and its supporters did not have deliberately racist intentions, and they did not personally exclude Black people, but instead they contributed to racially unequal outcomes."[349]

Bringing African Americans into the Arena company and audience did not challenge existing hierarchies. Arena Stage as a White institution has not—and cannot—represent a response to another driving force behind the engagement of African Americans with theater: the desire to present stories written by Blacks, performed by Black theater companies, for the enjoyment of Black audiences. That search leads elsewhere.

Robert Hooks at the Last Colony Theater, 1974
(Source: DC Black Repertory Company Alumni Association)

Chapter 4

Proclaiming Community Presence

If you're a Black artist, your work is cut out for you.
—Robert Hooks, 2018[1]

Much had changed in the half century since T. Montgomery Gregory and his colleagues at Howard University founded the Howard Players. Washington theaters had been desegregated; African American performers had gone mainstream. Howard's drama program garnered national and international accomplishments. Arena Stage formed and was well on its way to becoming one of the nation's leading advocates for nontraditional casting and regional theater. The new Federal City College established the city's first music programs dedicated to Gospel, jazz, and other genres of Black American music. An English professor at the college, Gil Scott-Heron, was perfecting a distinctive African-based poetic style that would earn him the signature "Grandfather of Rap."[2] Numerous African-oriented dance companies flourished around town, spinning off from Howard's own distinguished dance program. A new Hispanic immigrant community began to take shape that would generate a theater scene of its own.

The founders of the Howard Players would have found astonishing changes in Washington race relations as they surveyed stages across the city. However, their initial dream of presenting powerful Black stories told by Black performers and writers to Black audiences for the advancement and entertainment of the Black community remained stillborn. Neither Washington nor the country was quite ready for the fiery content of what Gregory, Willis Richardson, and others would have seen so many decades before as "Black theater." By the late 1960s, change even on this front was in the air.

As the Christmas season settled over the city in 1972, Robert Hooks was on a mission. "I'm stone broke," he told *Washington Post* theater critic Richard L. Coe, "and I turn down jobs because I know what's more important. We've got to have Black theater in this country and especially in this city."[3] Nearly a half century later, Hooks returned to Washington to be honored by Mayor Muriel E. Bowser, who had declared October 18, 2018, to be "Robert Hooks Day." Hooks used the occasion to underscore yet again the importance of having Black stories to tell.[4] Despite all that had transpired on the Washington and the American stages, the quest for Black stories told by Blacks for Black audiences all too often remains illusory.[5]

Avoiding Boundaries

Securing a permanent audience for African American dramatic performances has proven difficult for several reasons. Beginning with financial trials, African American companies of heightened professional ambition need to attract White audiences and funders to make ends meet. Although this requirement is perhaps not as imperative as a half century ago, African Americans have only recently begun to generate sustainable levels of interest and financing for Black theater.

Content similarly presents difficult challenges. The long-standing debates evident when Thomas Montgomery Gregory and Alain LeRoy Locke tangled with Edward Christopher Williams, Carrie Clifford, and Anna Julia Cooper in the Drama Committee of the NAACP's Washington chapter a century ago over the purpose of African American theater remain unresolved. Is the utility of Black theater to serve as propaganda for the cause? Or should it reflect Black sensibilities within the context of exploring the universal human condition? What constitutes "Black" theater? Is the goal to present Black themes within the context of a theater culture that the United States inherited from Europe? Is it to draw extensively on African performance traditions? If so, does the action on stage constitute "theater" as it generally is understood by Americans, including African Americans?

Over time, many Black theorists and theater practitioners have come to embrace a vision of Black theater as a communal, ritual drama capable of healing and restoring.[6] Ritualist pageantry and recurrent symbols become more important within this context than linear storytelling and character development as understood in the Euro-Atlantic canon.[7] This perspective is deeply rooted in African traditions and sensibilities that traveled to the New World in the holds of slave ships. Such an African aesthetic necessarily recalibrates standards of evaluation from those used for judging European-inspired theater.[8]

Tensions among African American theater practitioners and audiences remain at times as sharply divisive as a century ago.[9] The judgment of their White counterparts carry proportionately less weight in such discussions than before. The retention of White patrons and donors so necessary for financial sustainability nonetheless remains essential.

African performance traditions tend to present holistically a variety of genres—such as musical, dance, and spoken words—working in harmony with one another.[10] Boundaries so clearly delineated in European traditions blur in the African performance customs brought to the Americas by African slaves.[11] Many Black theater enterprises in Washington and elsewhere have melded theater and performance dance into a singular presentation. Sustained effort over several decades has sought out Africanisms within African American theater, rather than imposing African models onto an American stage that has itself evolved for three centuries.[12] The imposition of White theatrical concepts onto the Black stage obscures as much as it clarifies the meaning and import of Black theater.

Imamu Amiri Baraka (LeRoi Jones) forced a radical repositioning of Black theater within the African American community. As a poet, dramatist, fiction writer, and music critic, Baraka became a lightning rod for critics of a Black Nationalism that had been coalescing throughout the 1960s. For many Whites—and not a few African Americans—Baraka was too full of rage, a proponent of racism against Whites, anti-Semitism, and being antipolice.[13] Long associated with his hometown of Newark (where his son was elected mayor), Baraka began his intellectual engagement with the New York "Beat Poets" of the early 1960s, moving to ever more radical—at times revolutionary—stances later in life. Eventually, he would teach at such major universities as the State University of New York at Buffalo, the State University of New York at Stony Brook, and San Francisco State University.[14]

Jazz deeply informed Baraka's understanding of the world, as he often looked to Miles Davis as a role model. His 1963 history of Black music in America from slavery to contemporary music— *Blues People: Negro Music in White America*—remains a seminal work of jazz criticism. Baraka demonstrated the continuity inherent in several Black musical genres, including the role music played in establishing citizenship in the New World.[15]

Baraka's impact in redefining Black theater proved no less noteworthy. As Abiodun Jeyifous writes,

> No one man or single institution can personalize the course of history, but it seems that in periods of extreme radical awareness and revolutionary confrontation, some individuals may seem to embody the complex forces of historical becoming. Thus, every critic and enthusiast of contemporary Black theater, even observers calculatedly cool to its stated goals and aspirations, all agree on one point: The central role of Imamu Amiri Baraka and the two theater groups he founded, the Black Arts Repertory School and Theatre in Harlem and, later, the Spirit House of Newark. . . . It seems that within a general context of an intense radicalization and politicization of the arts in the country there emerged a distinct movement toward Black cultural and political nationalism. Baraka dominated the cultural aspect and, in his own peculiar style, emphasized its political nature.[16]

Baraka's views were formed in part by his engagement with Washington intellectuals during his time studying philosophy and drama at Howard University during the 1950s.[17] The question of the meaning of Blackness that so animated his work had been front and center at the university during his time on campus. A decade later, he penned the work that radically altered Black theater: *The Dutchman*.[18]

Titled to evoke the Dutch slave ships that brought Africans to the New World, the work tells the story of a White woman—

Lula—and a Black man—Clay—meeting on a New York City subway train. Full of racial and sexual symbolism, the play revolves around Lula's attempt to control Clay (perhaps as a stand-in for a White integrationist project) and his deep resistance to her manipulation. The play ends with Lula stabbing Clay through the heart as he attempts to leave the train.[19] The original New York production opened in March 1964 at the Cherry Lane Theatre in Greenwich Village, winning the Obie Award for best Off-Broadway play of the season. Jennifer West played Lulu and, importantly for this story, Robert Hooks played Clay.[20]

As Larry Neal recalls, "It was LeRoi Jones' *Dutchman* that radically reordered the internal structure of Black theater, first of all by opening up its linguistic range and breaking with the social realism which dominated the forties and fifties, and second (more important and in spite of vague allusions to the theater of [Antonin] Artaud and the absurdists) through the decidedly utilitarian strategy which informs the play—it is implicitly but very clearly addressed to the radical sector of Black socio-political consciousness."[21]

Baraka's work resonated in a Washington African American creative community that was becoming radicalized around a vision of resistance by a disenfranchised, now-majority-Black city. His personal connections with this community dating back to his student days at Howard heightened his influence.

Nonetheless, questions persisted. Blacks have long won acceptance in musical theater, even as they have written, composed, and performed works of parody and humiliation. How can Blacks forge ahead beyond this legacy? Are Blacks performing European and Euro-American classics expanding the base for Black theater? Where is the space for Black stories told by Black playwrights and performed by Black artists before Black audiences? Why should African American actors eschew the professional and financial opportunities offered by White theaters?

August Wilson's ten-play *Pittsburgh Cycle* (1982–2005)—chronicling the life of that city's African American Hill District decade by decade throughout the twentieth century—easily ranks among the greatest contributions to American letters. Wilson told the stories of ordinary Black Americans with force, empathy, and passion. Generally respectful of the classical traditions of the American stage,

Wilson displayed the lasting influence of earlier African forms in his work. In particular, his collage approach to storytelling elevates characters over linear plot development. Theater critics were at times less than fulsome in their praise of his scripts, especially in the beginning, as they did not completely appreciate or accept what to them were meandering storylines. But his achievement—and that of African American storytelling—could no longer be ignored as one play followed another, and Wilson garnered six nominations and two Pulitzer Prizes for Drama, an achievement rarely matched in American letters.[22]

The search for answers to such questions nonetheless continues. They are no less important than during the New Negro Movement after World War I, and during the civil rights era following World War II. They were similarly unresolved during the Black Arts Movement of the 1960s and 1970s, and largely remain so today in the era of Black Lives Matter activism.

If, as recorded earlier in this book, Washington was a major center for the New Negro Movement before African American culture's primary attention shifted to New York, DC remained a significant hub for the Black Arts Movement a half century later.[23] As the story heads into the 1960s and 1970s, the animating energy of the Black American stage indisputably shifted to New York. However, the distance between Washington theatrical life and New York life has never been large, and we see the arrival in Washington of African American cultural leaders from New York and elsewhere. DC's contribution to the explosive vitality of Black arts during the 1960s, 1970s, and 1980s—the era between Baraka and Wilson—simultaneously remained intensely local, even as activists helped shape national trends. It was a moment when Black Washington powerfully and forcefully proclaimed its presence.

Chocolate City

The city's racial mix reveals a great deal about a period when many in DC proudly proclaimed the District to be "Chocolate City."[24] According to Census data, the city moved from 35.0 percent Black in 1950 to 53.9 percent Black in 1960, on to a high of 71.1 percent Black in 1970. Since that time, the proportion of the city's population classified as Black has declined—to 70.3 percent in 1980, 65.8 percent in 1990, 60.0 percent in 2000, 50.7 percent in 2010, and an estimated 47.1 percent in 2017.[25]

The question of home rule remained perhaps the tenderest wound throughout this period, given that it connected directly with Black political disenfranchisement and physical displacement; concerns that have continued for more than a half century.[26] As already noted, city residents had been allowed to vote in presidential elections since the early 1960s. They gained an elected school board in 1968. In 1971, local residents were extended the right to elect a nonvoting delegate to the US House of Representatives. Such measures mattered little, in light of the absence of local electoral control over the District government. The passage of the DC Home Rule Bill in late 1973 was a partial step forward, as it was approved by residents the next spring. Congress nonetheless retained the right to overrule DC's municipal actions.[27]

There could be no doubt that congressional opposition to local governance was racially motivated. Proposals to expand local prerogatives routinely fell to a quiet death in the House of Representatives' District Committee, which was chaired for two dozen years by a segregationist South Carolina congressman, John McMillan, who had no pretense of being anything but racist. One day, in an especially abhorrent insult, he dispatched a truckload of watermelons to be delivered to city administrators at the District Building.[28]

The strength of connections between identity and cultural expression that took shape during these years—especially in music— helps to explain the powerful backlash against gentrification and displacement today. During the late 1960s, the local musician Chuck Brown created an infectious musical style combining a distinctive Latin-tinged beat with a call-and-response vocal track that came to be known as go-go.[29] The music emerged on Washington's streets and in its rough-and-tumble nightclubs. Go-go quickly became the anthem of DC's African American working class, pounded out on plastic pails by kids at subway stations, performed by homegrown bands such as the Junk Yard Band coming out of the Barry Farms projects, and promoted by popular groups such as Rare Essence, How Cold Sweat, and Shug-Go.[30]

Alarmed at the disorder and crime sometimes associated with

go-go venues, the city's police carefully tracked performances, working with various licensing authorities to shut down clubs after violent incidences. The construction of a new baseball stadium for the Washington Nationals led to the demolition of several popular venues. In the spring of 2019, noise complaints by White newcomers in historically African American neighborhoods led to a powerful backlash against trying to control the music. A petition signed by over 80,000 signatories demanded that the music be played on the streets, with several demonstrations involving thousands of enthusiasts stopping traffic to the beat of live go-go bands along U Street.[31] The DC Council—with the approval of Mayor Muriel E. Bowser—named go-go as the city's official music in 2020.[32]

The powerful economic transformation that has swept across Washington in recent decades has not only driven longtime residents out of town; it has become a form of cultural urbicide.[33] The fate of the DC Black Repertory Company (DCBRC) becomes a story of community identity within this context, one linking the city's early-twentieth-century artistic debates to those of the early twenty-first century.

Robert Hooks was the son of a blue-collar family living in the city's Foggy Bottom neighborhood. His father died working on the railroad when he was two; his mom kept the family going as a seamstress, sewing at every available moment.[34] At the turn of the 1970s, Hooks established the DCBRC.[35] A Kennedy Center program from June 16, 1973, described the DCBRC as "developing a Black theater company that is a powerful and vital statement to the Black community; an outlet capable of imparting meaningful ideas."[36] Hooks's company was part of a broader artistic movement in the city promoting African American perspectives on the arts.[37] Around this time, Topper Carew formed the New Thing Art and Architecture Center in Adams Morgan, seeking to integrate the arts with inclusive urban planning.[38]

New York's Negro Ensemble Company

Hooks previously had joined with Douglas Turner Ward and Gerald S. Krone to found the Negro Ensemble Company (NEC) in New York in 1967.[39] The opening was made possible in part by support from the Ford Foundation.[40] Hooks, Ward, Krone, and the Ford Foundation identified programs of free instruction to hone theatrical skills for aspiring young performers as an essential task for the new company.[41]

Krone concentrated on backstage functions, growing over time into a noteworthy producer. Hooks, for his part, already had enjoyed considerable stage success. He made his Broadway debut in 1960, in *Tiger, Tiger Burning Bright*; had replaced Louis Gossett Jr. in the Broadway production of *A Raisin in the Sun*; had replaced Billy Dee Williams in *A Taste of Honey*; and had filled in after James Earl Jones left Jean Genet's *The Blacks*. He eventually would go on to a highly successful film and television career. In 1964, as already noted, he originated the role of Clay in Amiri Baraka's *The Dutchman*.[42]

Hooks had crossed paths with Ward along the way. Douglas Turner Ward was well along on becoming a highly acclaimed playwright, actor, and director in his own right.[43] The son of Louisiana sharecroppers, Ward came to New York after injuries ended a scholarship-supported football career at Wilberforce College and then the University of Michigan. Reaching Manhattan, he found work as a journalist with the *Daily Worker* and began writing plays and acting through the Communist Party's youth league. He moved on to publishing at the *New York Times* and began to appear on Broadway.[44]

Ward, who died in early 2021, always viewed NEC as being in a dynamic relationship with Whites. "Our particular theater," he told the *Los Angeles Times*, "is consciously aimed at Black people, not to the exclusion of Whites."[45] Ward would remain closely associated with NEC, where he served as artistic director for nearly four decades. His success continued well into the future with productions of *A Soldier's Play* (1982) and *The River Niger* (1972), together with performances in *Ceremonies in Dark Old Men* (1969), among many achievements that included a prestigious Drama Desk Award.

The company initially was controversial within the African American community because of its inaugural location downtown in White Greenwich Village, its reliance on support from major mainstream foundations, and its use of "Negro" in its title. As Joseph Papp pointed out, the company was intentionally somewhat conventional in its outlook. It always attempted to attract both Black and White audiences to its productions, and it succeeded.[46] NEC has become the "National Negro Theater" dreamed of by Thomas Montgomery Gregory.[47]

Ward brushed aside criticisms as "to be expected."[48] And once it opened at the start of 1968, NEC established its bone fides.[49] The student workshop proved such an immediate hit that the company faced challenges selecting students from an applicant pool too large to accommodate.[50]

NEC's combination of controversy and success prompted another discussion at the time about the meaning of Black theater. Cecil Smith, in the *Los Angeles Times*, wrote: "In these days of Black power and Black militancy and Harlem's Black Arts Council which was found to be training guerrilla warriors, 'Black theater' has the connotation of a dramatic organization storming the ramparts of Whitey. The only thing the NEC is militant about . . . is the art of the theater itself."[51]

Walter Kerr, perhaps drawing on his experiences in Jim Crow Washington while teaching at Catholic University, proved more outspoken in a major article in the *New York Times*. "We are here talking about a kind of opportunism," he proclaimed, "and opportunism has never been particularly repugnant to the White man in the course of his own self-advancement. A White man would readily forgive a Black man for taking advantage of anything going, even if seizing the salary means crawling a bit; White men are used to crawling to White men and think little of it." One challenge for American theater is that "Whites do not see many Negroes in their homes, nor do Negroes see Whites in theirs, not socially, not as young brides, not as real-life ladies. Whites do not see many Negroes in their offices, at least not after they have passed the reception desks." For Kerr, "very little in the way of rationalization is needed to defend Robert Hooks's determination to found the Negro Ensemble Company. Quite apart from developing actors and directors, Mr. Hooks may discover playwrights. . . . If there is anything the American theater needs, it is playwrights, and, not even the most commercial of Broadway producers is going to ask the color of the hands that typed a good new script."[52]

Over the years, NEC has gathered numerous awards, supported the premier of major works by African American authors (including Paul Carter Harrison, who had been teaching at Howard for some while before developing *The Great Macdaddy* for NEC[53]), and promoted the acting careers of a who's who of American actors (including, to name but a few, Debbie Allen, Avery Brooks, Roscoe Lee Browne, Godfrey Cambridge, Laurence Fishburne, Danny Glover, Louis Gossett Jr., Samuel L. Jackson, Cleavon Little, Phylicia Rashad, Roxie Roker, Esther Rolle, and Denzel Washington).[54] These efforts have led Ward to be called "the Godfather of Black Theatre."[55]

As Hooks recalled the story, he "was doing *Dutchman* at the Cherry Lane Theatre downtown and I was living in Chelsea at the time. And one Monday night, which is the actor's night off, I was asked to come and speak at the Hudson Guild in Chelsea about Blacks in the Theater and the various problems they were having to face. The talk was well received and afterwards the kids came up to ask all sorts of questions. Now I lived right across the street and knew most of these young people. So I said, 'If you're really and truly interested in theatre, come over to my house. I'm off on Monday nights.'"[56]

These Monday night mentoring sessions grew to sixty or more people, causing alarm among his neighbors who did not understand why so many young Black men and women were showing up in their building. Hooks started the "Group Theatre Workshop" in his living room, even knocking out a wall to build a theater.[57]

For Hooks, the group functioned as family. "The kids relate to each other in the most basic ways," he told Nat Nentoff in the *New York Times*. "That is not only the essence of theatre but also, by my criteria, it makes for the essential foundation of a real repertory company. Here they get to know themselves and each other, and that knowledge has to grow freely, through improvisation. They don't achieve that quality of relationship in settlement houses or recreation centers, nor would they get it in the usual acting schools."[58]

Hooks was able to arrange for the young company to perform at the Cherry Lane Theatre when the theater did not have performances scheduled. These recitals caught the attention of critics and funders.[59] His efforts to support student actors nonetheless led to his eviction, so he moved to a loft and expanded the workshop.[60] Along the way, he joined forces with Ward, hired Krone, and, before long, launched NEC.[61] Hooks told reporters as his career simultaneously took off that his success only advanced from his helping others.[62] "The kids have taught me so much," he told the *New York Amsterdam News* on his twenty-ninth birthday. "They've given me insights into myself as a person, as an actor, and as a Negro Actor."[63]

From New York to Washington

Even as he was working with Ward, Krone, and others in New York, Hooks had his sights set on returning to Washington to launch an African American company there.[64] After the assassination of the Reverend Dr. Martin Luther King Jr., Washington's presidentially appointed mayor-commissioner, Walter Washington—who later would become the city's first elected home rule chief executive—reached out to Hooks to see if he might come back to help the city find ways to connect with homegrown artistic talent. The fabled community activist and media personality Petey Green called as well and helped to convince Hooks to make the move.[65] Hooks was taken immediately with the idea, especially when he began to consider the extraordinary talent the city had to offer.[66]

During the autumn of 1970, Hooks contacted Zelda and Tom Fichandler at Arena Stage to discuss his plans for establishing a company equivalent to NEC in Washington. As the Arena staff meeting minutes record, Hooks inquired about using Arena as a base for the new company. "He has talked with Zel and Tom," the minutes note, "about the possibility of using some of our facilities and producing in one of the theatres during dark periods (pardon the pun). He would like to have a 20-week session during the summer in the Kreeger. This DC Black Repertory Co. would use the former administrative offices not needed by us."[67]

For whatever reason—perhaps the attitude evinced by the line "pardon the pun"—Hooks did not follow-up with the Fichandlers. By early spring, the staff minutes record that "Bobby Hooks is not coming to Arena. He probably will be located in the Old Arthur's nightclub on 13 and E Street NW [in the basement of the Warner Theatre—BR]. Zel and Tom think this is really better this way because we really don't have the facilities available that Bobby would have wanted."[68]

Hooks explored further. Roger L. Stevens, chairman of the Kennedy Center, proved more forthcoming, offering to open up center theaters—especially smaller venues—to Hooks's new company.[69] Eventually, with the city's help, the DCBRC secured "the Colony Theater" when it stopped showing movies.[70] Changing the name to "the Last Colony" (a name for the city used by home rule advocates), the DCBRC settled into its new home at Georgia Avenue and Farragut Street NW, at the northern edge of Petworth, a predominantly Black, blue-collar neighborhood at the time.[71] Hooks formally launched the company in February 1971 with a $30,000 grant from the Meyer Foundation.[72]

As noted earlier, in founding the DCBRC, Hooks brought together a senior artistic staff, including Artistic Director Motojicho (Vantile Whitfield), Vocal Director Bernice Reagon, and Choreographers Louis Johnson and Mike Malone. All had deep DC roots. Motojicho graduated from Dunbar High and Howard University before heading to Hollywood. Reagon moved to the city after graduating from Spelman College in Atlanta to pursue a PhD at Howard. She would become a fixture at the Smithsonian Institution. Malone, who had come to Washington to earn a degree in French at Georgetown University, had tap-danced with Josephine Baker while studying at the Sorbonne. Johnson captured the attention of his teachers in the DC Public Schools while growing up in the U Street neighborhood. Encouraged by his early mentors, he headed off to the School of American Ballet in New York City, where he studied with Jerome Robbins and George Balanchine. Charles Augins joined Johnson and Malone as the company's ballet master. A child of Arlington, Virginia, across the Potomac, Augins would move on to New York and London acclaim before returned to Washington's Ellington School.

A Vibrant Center of Black Arts

Washington in the late 1960s and throughout the 1970s into the 1980s was an effervescent center of Black arts. Animated by the local struggle for home rule and national conflicts over civil rights and the Vietnam War, African American Washington mobilized through churches, schools, civic associations, and arts groups.

Boundaries among groups within the Black community became less important than in the past—although they never completely disappeared—as African Americans of varied ages, educational levels, types of professional achievement, skin hues, economic resources, and faith engaged with one another in a city that had become almost three-quarters Black.

Denied suffrage rights until the mid-1970s, Washington's African Americans looked to their churches, community organizations, and the performing arts to find voice.[73] Dozens of activists flowed into the city from around the country, with a core centering on the Student Nonviolent Organizing Committee (SNCC) coming to form a ruling elite for the new home rule local government after 1973.[74] Marion Barry, the Reverend Douglas Moore, Ivanhoe Donaldson, John A. Wilson, and Frank Smith—among many from SNCC—joined with local activists such as Walter Fauntroy, Julius Hobson, and David A. Clarke to create a tight network of community organizers and rivals. Together, they would move easily into the District Building and the new District Council, much to the chagrin of the agents from the Federal Bureau of Investigation who maintained constant surveillance over their activities.[75]

Beyond political agendas, African American artists, performers, and musicians embraced an artistic vision that tore down long-standing European-defined boundaries among artistic genre. Two organizations among many, both founded as 1967 turned into 1968—one by an act of Congress, and the other by community will—exemplify these efforts: Federal City College (FCC), and the New Thing Art and Architecture Center.

The city's system of public higher educational institutions depended, like all public institutions in the city, on congressional action. Until the mid-1950s, public schools at all levels existed in racial pairs. By the 1960s, the District of Columbia Teachers College grew out of a merger of the city's Black and White pedagogical colleges that traced their origins to the Normal School for Colored Girls founded by Myrtilla Miner in 1851. In 1966, Congress moved to consolidate and simplify this system, establishing Washington Technical Institute and Federal City College. The new home rule District Council merged these institutions in 1977 to form the University of the District of Columbia.[76]

During its brief existence as an autonomous institution between 1968 and 1976, FCC played a formative role in the city's expanding African American arts community. The young college's second president, Harland Randolph, had arrived at its founding as vice president for planning and development. He would serve as president for three tumultuous years, during which he was constantly buffeted by students for being too pro-establishment, and by Congress as being too radical.[77]

Randolph had been the first African American senior class president at Ohio State in the early 1950s, and he continued on at the school to earn his doctoral degree in social psychology.[78] Though FCC had been initially conceived as a small, selective liberal arts institution with about 700 students, Harland oversaw the introduction of an open admissions policy at FCC, which rapidly expanded the student body to over 6,000.

The school named the noted pianist and music historian Hildred Roach to head its Music Department. Roach would become the author of important syncretic works stressing the significance of African heritage for African American music. While recognizing the impact of European traditions through White masters on enslaved Black music makers, the Fisk University–trained Roach persistently returned in her academic writing to the African origin of Black American music in all its multiplicity of categories.[79] Unsurprisingly, she built the department around Black American musical genre and styles, recruiting the Fisk graduates Robert "Bobby" Felder to lead a jazz program and William H. Moore to establish a gospel choir. The jazz historian Ernest Dyson rounded out the department. African American cultural expression dominated the school's arts programs at a time when other schools still denied the legitimacy of Black cultural expression.[80] Gil Scott-Heron arrived to teach in the English Department in 1972.

Howard University's Music Department finally accepted jazz as a worthy genre for study at the same time, in 1968.[81] As the university's Music Department evolved, its drama and dance programs continued their decades-long engagement with African American cultural forms and communities.

Topper Carew's New Thing

Simultaneously, Topper Carew's New Thing Art and Architecture Center responded to and reshaped perceptions of Black culture. Carew grew up in Boston and became a civil rights worker in Mississippi and Maryland. He attended Howard University to study architecture, and subsequently earned undergraduate and graduate degrees from Yale. Carew later secured a PhD in communications from Union Graduate School and the DC Institute for Policy Studies.[82]

Carew established the New Thing in 1966 in the still-edgy Adams Morgan neighborhood. The organization's name came to mind when local kids repeatedly asked, "What's that new thing up the street?"[83] Six years later, he won a community fellowship at the Massachusetts Institute of Technology, which encouraged his exploration of film as a media of social change. He subsequently became a producer at Boston's public television station, WGBH, and has been a force behind numerous efforts in increase an African American presence in film and television.[84] One of his early film ventures—*DC Cab* (1983)—drew on his experiences working around the city while heading up the New Thing.[85]

The New Thing offered courses in photography, art, music, and the martial arts. As Philip D. Carter wrote in 1970,

> in a city of sharp contrasts between rich and poor, renaissance and decay, the neighborhood around 18th Street and Columbia Road NW seems perplexingly headed several ways at once. Known in recent times as Adams Morgan, this 237-acre hillside in the center of the city seems forever on the verge of some dramatic self-renewal or disintegration, continually wrenched toward polar extremes. At the once-proud intersection of 18th and Columbia, the venerable Ambassador Theater now is a muddy vacant lot; the Peoples Drug store across the street is closed and empty; Gartenhaus Furs, Inc., once the jewel in the neighborhood crown, has packed its minks and sables off to Bethesda.[86]

This was the perfect setting for Carew, who told Carter in a statement that resonates ever more presciently in rapidly gentrifying Washington, "What makes this community interesting is also its problem. If you're living good and I'm a junky, we're never really talking about the same thing. What about the poor people who are down scuffling at the bottom of the barrel? They don't think the neighborhood's 'interesting'."[87]

Carew's New Thing indeed was making the neighborhood more "interesting," thereby launching some of the first tentative steps toward what eventually would become a tidal wave of gentrification.[88] The group sponsored weekly jazz performances at Saint Margaret's Episcopal Church, which featured stand-out artists such as Grammy winner Shirley Horn; the French Society of Arts, Sciences, and Letters Gold Medal Honoree Andrew White; the post-bop saxophonist Byron Morris; and a local DC public school music teacher on her way to stardom, Roberta Flack—as well as many top-flight local and visiting artists. The New Thing added a radio station, which gave the legendary DC jazz disc jockey Rusty Hassan his start, and sponsored an acclaimed African dance program for children.[89] The New Thing embraced a fluid, unstructured approach to its students.[90] Within a couple of years, 55 staff members were working with 350 students in a variety of artistic endeavors intended to provide a background in Black creativity missing in more formal school curricula at the time.[91]

Over the course of the summer 1968, when the city was still reeling from the civil unrest that had followed the assassination of the Reverend Dr. Martin Luther King Jr. only months before, Carew created a stir with an Africa-centric street mural near the corner of 18th Street and Florida Avenue NW. He and a team of New Thing artists had started painting a mural portraying African gods as a demonstration of Black self-respect. City inspectors moved to have it painted over and turned down a permit request on technical grounds. Carew eventually carried the day when the sign was deemed noncommercial. The unveiling turned into a community celebration, accompanied by the New Thing's African Heritage Dancers and Drummers led by Melvin Deal.[92]

Drummers and Dancers

Melvin Deal is a DC original. He grew up in the city during the 1950s and matriculated at Howard University during the early 1960s. While a student at Howard, he discovered Caribbean dance at the Casbah nightclub on U Street. Thinking the dances African, he developed a teaching program and dance group through Howard University community outreach programs. He founded his African Dancers and Drummers while still a freshman in 1959.[93] He soon discovered that he had learned forms of African dance that had passed through a Caribbean filter, which led him back to the African roots of the dance form he had embraced. He later studied in Ghana and Nigeria.[94]

As Tamara Lizette Brown has noted,

> African dance is that dance characterized by bent knees, use of the entire foot, the isolation of body parts, polyrhythm, repetition of movement, music and dance as interrelated, individualism within a group cohesiveness, and functionalism in its relation to real life. In its traditional forms it is performed to celebrate and, or pacify nature to remedy disease, for success in war and hunting, for initiation, to relate a tale or historic event, and to praise deities. Dance on the African continent as practiced by various cultural groups is not meant to simply portray life, it is a part of the life of the people.[95]

Modern African dance entered the United States with immigrants from the continent and moved to the concert stage during the 1930s. Charles Williams founded the Hampton Institute's Creative Dance Group in 1934, while Maryrose Reeves Allen long demonstrated interest in African dance forms at Howard University. Other groups followed, such as Arthur Hall's Afro American Dance Ensemble in Philadelphia.[96] Interest grew as former colonies on the continent gained independence and established embassies at the United Nations in New York and in Washington. Deal's African Heritage Dancers and Drummers proved a perfect complement to Topper Carew's programs at the New Thing. Deal launched his troupe within the New Thing during the late 1960s, while maintaining close ties to Howard University as he expanded his vision.[97]

Deal's African Heritage company offered public performances around town, including an April 1973 appearance at the as-yet-fledgling Kennedy Center, which would lead to repeated Kennedy Center performances over the decades ahead.[98] The company became a favored entertainment at embassy and official functions around town, which enabled Deal to expand his teaching and youth programs.[99] Deal himself won every conceivable honor a Washington arts professional might receive, including being named by *Washingtonian Magazine* in 1981—together with Father Hartke—a Washingtonian of the Year.[100]

As the company developed—and as its various educational and community outreach programs garnered strength—Deal's company spawned other African-oriented dance companies and programs. Washington became a must stop for dance ensembles touring from the African continent and elsewhere. Over time, the city became a major center for African performance dance, both in the size and scale of the offerings available in the city and in the diversity of dance styles performed.[101]

During the early 1990s, a Howard University business student, Brian Williams, traveled to South Africa to teach small business skills. He was caught off guard by South African gumboot dancing, which reminded him of the dances he had performed while "stepping" with his fraternity brothers at Howard. Together with South African partners, Williams organized the first Step Afrika! International Cultural Festival in 1994. His new group took root in Washington and has grown into a major international company performing locally, on Broadway, and in several dozen countries across Europe, the Americas, Asia, Africa, the Middle East, and the Caribbean. In 2011, he joined forces with the Phillips Collection and mounted a full-length performance work celebrating Jacob Lawrence's iconic Migration Series paintings. Williams's story is but one of many illustrating the depth of commitment to African dance throughout the Washington community, including Melvin Deal and his pioneering African Heritage Dancers and Drummers.[102]

Designing a Community

Carew remained deeply engaged in design and planning projects while in Washington. He and Tunney Lee, for example, mobilized neighborhood residents to design what is now the Marie H. Reed Recreation Center at a time when local school authorities rarely engaged communities in their projects.[103] The new Morgan School was among the first to be planned as a racially integrated school from the beginning.

All these activities were part of a larger mission, as Carew told the *Washington Post* in 1969, to raise the city's awareness of Black culture. "There is a cultural void in the city because Washington is 65 percent Black and most of the cultural organizations, which are White, are programmed to control culture in the Black community."[104] Months later, Carew was an animating force in the establishment of a Blues Festival at Howard University.[105] He began to be invited to national meetings and groups to share his experiences.[106] Before long, he was being mentioned as a Black "power broker."[107]

The *Washington Post* eventually dubbed Carew "Washington's street dude-social butterfly of the '60s," capturing his ability to reach out to the streets as well as to boardrooms.[108] Noting that he was successful at securing grants from White groups, the *Post* noted in 1975, with a twinge of nostalgia, that "he has a new image. No longer does he sport the towering Afro, which brought him his nom de guerre, Topper. His hair is nearly trimmed. So Topper Carew is the same galvanizing—and controversial—force he was here several years ago when he courted white liberals and mingled with street dudes, pried grants loose from foundations and bumped heads with Black opponents who charged him with selling out the race to advance his personal interests."[109]

Carew's more integrationist approach was countered by institutions such as Gaston Neal's New School of Afro-American Thought, which similarly reached out to the African American community from its location near the intersection of 14th and U streets NW. Neal's goal was to "stress discipline and training," while being "brutally honest and truthful about the situation of the Black man in America." Stokely Carmichael worked through Neal's New School early on, and Neal constantly faced challenges from ever more radical activists. The movements swirling around Federal City College, the New Thing, the New School, and Howard University mutually reinforced one another to cultivate a pulsating Black arts scene throughout the city. They did so with an eye toward educating youth. As Dick Gregory wrote at the time, "To teach Black kids theater, Black arts, or show business is like lighting a light, and that light will cast out darkness uptown or downtown, depending on where you sit in relationship to the lamp."[111] Hooks himself spoke of a desire to provide opportunities so that "kids who want to become something else besides cab drivers and construction workers" can do so.[112]

Meanwhile, a new force was beginning to make herself felt. Peggy Cooper had just graduated from George Washington University and moved on to law school to prepare for a career in arts administration. She teamed up with close friend, Mike Malone, to draw on her summer experience running street camps for the city's Recreation Department to start dance workshops for teenagers. In 1969, at the age of twenty-two, Cooper joined the luminaries George Stevens Jr. and J. Carter Brown and other civic leaders on an expanded Mayor's Arts Commission Advisory Board, where she began her lifelong push for a DC high school of the arts.[113]

Robert Hooks and his new DC Black Repertory Company arrived at this movement's apogee.[114] At the same time, this effervescent cultural ecosystem of university, public, and community nonprofit organizations and activists rested on less ambitious business models than Hook's Actors' Equity (unionized) company. Major foundations and federal agencies began to shift their attention away from the arts during the parsimonious years of the Carter administration, a trend that would accelerate during Ronald Reagan's presidency. Hooks soon found himself constantly running up a descending financial escalator he could not reverse.

The DC Black Repertory Company

As already noted, Hooks pulled together a remarkable team to guide the DCBRC. Its board included many of Washington's leading African American business leaders, including James O. Gibson (who served on several major government and foundation projects), Clifford Alexander (who would be appointed secretary of the Army during the Carter administration), M. Carl Holman (president of the National Urban Coalition), Flaxie Pinkett (a real estate executive), and Peggy Cooper. The company's senior creative staff included Artistic Director Motojicho (Vantile Whitfield), Vocal Director Bernice Reagon, and Choreographers Louis Johnson and Mike Malone. The company embraced professional actors—including Debbie Allen, Glenda Dickerson, Sati Jamal, and Lynn Whitfield—together with apprentice performers connected to ambitious outreach and education programs.[115] Young theater artists in training at the University of Maryland and Bowie State—including future director Jaye Stewart; future Hollywood actors Kene Holliday and Belina Logan; future Broadway choreographer David Cameron; future Screen Actors Guild, New York Chapter, president and film and television actor Mike Hodge; and New Federal Theater originator Woodie King Jr.—enthusiastically signed on. The company became so tight that, a half century later, its alumni association sustains a profound energy and joyous spirit.[116] Those who remained in theater, and those who did not, recall their experiences as a training ground of the first order.[117]

From the beginning, Hooks acknowledged that discovering and presenting works that would speak to African American audiences posed a prime challenge.[118] Hooks believed that Blacks had not embraced theatergoing as a primary leisure activity because the American repertoire did not speak to them. He felt that a vigorous program of workshops for youth would attract new audiences for his main stage productions. At the age of thirty-four, when the DCBRC opened, Hooks evinced a mixture of youthful energy and mature realism.[119] Hopes ran high.[120]

The DCBRC's initial productions were modest affairs and, throughout its history, it relied on an investment from the artists that transcended whatever compensation they received.[121] Hooks began with an amateur production of *Imamu*—an evening of short works by Imamu Amiri Baraka directed by Motojicho—over a mid–October 1972 weekend.[122] The professional company followed in December, with the world premiere of Evan Walker's *Coda*, while the dance unit offered a workshop production featuring the choreography of Louis Johnson and Mike Malone in late November.[123]

Johnson and Malone followed with a more ambitious program at the newly opened Last Colony Theater in January.[124]

Imamu set the tone for the DCBRC's artistic aims, consisting of a major one-act play—*A Black Mass*—followed by several smaller works. The choice of *A Black Mass* was not lost on reviewers. The story revolves around a scientist in a Black society creating the first White beast in pursuit of pure scientific knowledge without thinking of the consequences of unleashing White people on the planet.[125] Sympathetic reviewers welcomed the opportunity to see what they considered to be an important work, though they were less taken with Motojicho's direction and the amateurs' self-conscious acting.[126] Spectator reaction was less cautious. "The audience responded the other evening with applause and crises of 'That's right,' and 'Tell the truth' when references were made to 'the beast' in *A Black Mass*."[127]

That Motojicho—known as a larger-than-life character with a sharp sense of humor who could be gruff or forgiving as the situation required—knew his audience should be no surprise. Born Vantile Whitfield, he grew up in the U Street community, and was a football star at Dunbar High and Howard University, combining athletic and artistic achievement.[128] After studying drama at Howard, he enrolled as one of the first African Americans to study at the Film School of the University of California, Los Angeles.[129] In 1963, he joined with the distinguished African American actor Frank Silvera to found the American Theatre of Being in Los Angeles and established the Performing Arts Society of Los Angeles to train inner-city Angelino youth in the performing arts.[130] That same year, he and Silvera teamed up to take a production of James Baldwin's *The Amen Corner* in New York, making Motojicho the first Black production designer to work on Broadway.[131]

Motojicho moved back east in 1971 to head up a multi-million-dollar program to expand the reach of the National Endowment for the Arts into African American communities.[132] During his seven-year tenure at the endowment, he oversaw nearly $50 million in grants to arts in Appalachian, Native American, Latino, and African American communities.[133] He continued his work in film and television as well as teaching youth in Los Angeles and Chicago after his departure from Washington, winning dozens of awards along the way.[134]

The company's first full professional production in its new home—Evan Walker's *Coda*—tackled an explosive issue of the day as it traced the return of Lonnie Duncan from service in Vietnam. The son of a successful middle-class family in Harlem, Duncan had been slated to enter law school before his military service and was to have joined his father's legal practice. Instead, the enraged Lonnie joins the Black Liberation Movement.[135] Finding the play "absorbing and powerful," the *Washington Post* critic Richard Coe wrote that "there are drawbacks to the tightly knit story that both sharper playing and more decisive writing can resolve." Coe thought that Motojicho's direction was helpful in bringing clarity and motivation to the performances of some of the younger members of the cast.[136]

Opening night was a social event, "with a first-night crowd dressed in everything from Black ties to dashkikis."[137] Among the 10 percent of the audience who were White were the Kennedy Center Board chair, Roger L. Stevens; Mrs. Polk Guest, the head of the Friends of the Kennedy Center; and Norman Feigan, of the National Council of Arts. African American notables included Congressman Ron Dellums, the actor Yaphet Kotto, and former Miss Black America Stephanie Clark. The architect James Hook's makeover of the old movie house won universal praise.[138]

Seeing the company's initial success, the Washington Theater Club and Arena Stage began to produce Black-oriented works.[139] Within a year, a half-dozen Black theater companies had formed around DC.[140] For the moment, Hooks's success was catalytic.

Upon This Rock

The company's second full-length production at the Last Colony featured Bernice Reagon's musical pageant *Upon This Rock*, presenting the company's acting and dance wings. Divided into two sections, the first featured songs, and the second included the local premiere of Louis Johnson's *No Outlet* and a performance of Mike Malone's earlier work, *Spirit*. The show was held together loosely by a shared narrative in a "folk-mythic mode."[141] The image of the rock carried through in the set design. As the *Washington Post* critic Alan Kriegsman noted, "The concept of a rock—a material formed under intense pressure, hard, resistant, enduring—is identified with the theme itself, the strength and solidity of Black people in the teeth of oppression."[142]

Audiences reacted more enthusiastically than the critics, who were a bit churlish about some of the performance's ragged edges. Kriegsman found the production long on authenticity and effervescence yet short on organization. He would have preferred a leaner show, which, he suggested, would not have undermined the evening's essential message.[143]

Charles Farrow of the *Baltimore Afro-American* suggested that the "fabulous dance company might be easing up off of its technical command of the art form," so that "some warning bells should sound and send the dance masters in to pull the company back up to previous levels of excellence." Farrow offered that "Bernice Reagon's program cantata was a precious collection of traditional Black songs, . . . a tightly and beautifully structure program."[144] Everyone agreed that Reagon, Johnson, and Malone represented a unique resource for Hooks.

Bernice Reagon moved to Washington upon graduation from Spelman College in her native Georgia on a Ford Foundation fellowship to work on her PhD at Howard University.[145] She already had been deeply involved in the Freedom Singers, organized by the Student Nonviolent Coordinating Committee, and easily linked to the lively community of SNCC activists that had landed in Washington during the civil rights movement. Reagon joined the Smithsonian Institution shortly before completing her PhD, and, in 1976, she directed its program on Black American culture. She later became a curator of music history at the National Museum of American History.

Reagon has continued her association with the Smithsonian as curator emeritus and holds a long-term appointment as a Distinguished Professor of History at American University. Her many honors include a MacArthur Foundation Genius Award, the presidential medal for contributions to the humanities, and a Grammy nomination.[146] In 1973, while teaching a vocal workshop at the DCBRC, she established a four-person ensemble (which grew into six members), modeled in part on the Five Blind Boys of Alabama, whom Reagon knew from her youth. The group's name derived from Psalm 81:16: "Sweet Honey in the Rock."[147]

Louis Johnson arrived in the heart of Washington's U Street neighborhood as a young boy during the 1930s, and he quickly benefited from the area's dense network of church and civic organizations. Teachers in the local school and gymnastic instructors at the Anthony Bowen YMCA spotted his talents and enrolled him in the Jones Haywood School of Dance. This school opened a pathway to the School of American Ballet in New York City, where he caught the eyes of Jerome Robbins and George Balanchine. By the 1950s, Johnson had performed for the New York City Ballet and in several Broadway productions.[148]

Frustrated by the limited opportunities open to him as a Black dancer, Johnson turned to choreography.[149] He proved his talents and, after productions at the New York City Ballet Club, he won kudos for his choreography of Langston Hughes's *Black Nativity* in 1961. Johnson started his own company for a while, and worked closely with Hooks and Ward at NEC.[150] He continued choreographing for the Washington Ballet, the Metropolitan Opera, the Alvin Ailey Dance Company, and the Dance Theater of Harlem, as well as such notable Broadway shows as *Treemonisha, Purlie, Cotton Comes to Harlem, The Wiz*, and numerous other works.[151]

Johnson remained dedicated to advancing performance dance in DC, as evidenced by his work with the DCBRC. He taught for many years at Howard, where he elevated dance to a full-fledged major.[152] He simultaneously directed the dance division of the Henry Street Settlement in New York.[153] As already noted, he would be a victim of the 2020 COVID-19 pandemic.[154]

Mike Malone grew up in Pittsburgh before entering Georgetown University to earn a degree in French. A tap dancer in his teens, Malone won notoriety as the first African American drum major of the suburban Penn Hills High School's 120-member marching band in 1959.[155] He was a regular star on the local teenage dance scene.[156]

Following graduation from Georgetown University, Malone pursued his early ambition to teach languages to Paris. He returned to Washington to earn a graduate degree in French literature from Howard, and he later entered the graduate degree program in theater at Catholic University.[157] After a stint on Broadway, he established the Everyman Street Theatre in the late 1960s, and joined the DCBRC from its beginning. He would teach at Howard until his death in 2006.[158] His Kennedy Center productions of Hughes's *Black Nativity* remained a holiday favorite for many Washingtonians until the end of the twentieth century. In 1974, as discussed below, he teamed up with Peggy Cooper to initiate efforts that led to the creation of the DC Public School System's Duke Ellington School for the Arts.[159]

Johnson and Malone brought on Charles Augins as their ballet master. Augins had grown up in Arlington, Virginia, and trained at the Jones Hayward School. After his time with the DCBRC, he would move to New York and London, where he worked on Broadway and West End productions, in opera, and with rock performers including the Rolling Stones, Stevie Wonder, David Bowie, and Sting. He later returned to Washington, where he headed up the Dance Department at the Duke Ellington School for the Arts.[160]

The DCBRC continued to evolve, participating in community-oriented events, expanding its training programs, and offering a variety of smaller new works.[161] Washington progressively gained a reputation as a center for Black theater as other companies and funding agencies responded to the company's initial success.[162] Hooks, Motojicho, Reagon, Johnson, Malone, and Augins represented a gathering of talent rarely brought together in Washington for a sustained period. The April 1973 opening production of Jean Genet's fabled 1958 play *The Blacks* for a three-week run at the Kennedy Center's Eisenhower Theater would prove to be an "event."

The Blacks

The Kennedy Center's chairman, Roger L. Stevens, was good on his earlier promise to Robert Hooks to bring his new company to the center.[163] In the spring of 1973, Kennedy Center Productions, Inc., fully funded a production of Jean Genet's *The Blacks*. This was the first time a Black theater group had produced a work on the Kennedy stage since its opening a year and a half before.[164] Both Stevens and Hooks denied the show's purpose as attracting more Blacks to what already had become a predominantly White institution. Rather, it was to "see more Black relevance here," as, to quote Hooks, there was "not that much Black representation right now."[165]

Genet's work was well known from the previously mentioned

1961 Off Broadway show that gave a push to the careers of several Black actors—including, as already noted, James Earl Jones, Roscoe Lee Browne, Louis Gossett Jr., Cicely Tyson, Godfrey Cambridge, Maya Angelou, Raymond St. Jacques, Abbey Lincoln, Brock Peters, and Charles Gordone.[166] It no longer felt quite as edgy after a decade of growing Black Power activism and the radicalization of the Black stage.

As Hooks acknowledged, some Black literary figures criticized the work as "too European." Hooks denied the possibility of shock value. "Just to clarify," he told reporters, "I still believe the first purpose of theater is to entertain. You can't bludgeon people with a message. You have to entertain them. This play is theater to the nth degree. It is a masterpiece—ultimate theater."[167]

No one seems to have notified either Genet, or his agents in the United States, who claimed not to have known about the production until the day before it was to open. Instead, the Kennedy Center had contacted another agent, Ninow Karlweis of New York. During legal proceedings initiated by Genet's attorney, Alexander Boskoff, to halt the production, attorneys for the Kennedy Center and the DCBRC "claimed they had contacted a Greek who said he had the rights to American presentation of the play." Boskoff argued that the center's behavior was an example of "cavalier, blatant disregard for the author's rights."[168] US District Court judge William B. Jones refused to close the show, though litigation continued for some time.[169]

Hooks had been drawn to the original 1961 production of *The Blacks*, which he had seen in New York: "I left the theater completely hypnotized by the powerful statement I had just witnessed. But how, I wondered, could Jean Genet, a White writer, capture so vividly the unique feelings of an oppressed non-White people? My search for the answer began immediately." Hooks discovered that Genet was an outcast, whose mental, physical, and artistic shocks gave him "the sensitive and profound insight into our—the Black man's—bitter struggle against worldwide oppression." Hooks saw the play as a highly theatrical vehicle for universalizing the Black ghetto: "The people are enraged by years of oppression, abuse, and deception. They see the destructive changes brought about in them, both individually and as a community, and realize that they have to form a strong unified force if they are to survive. They band together as a cohesive, positive, and powerful force."[170] Genet's play became a metaphor for Hooks's own goals for his company.

Critics were uncertain in their assessment of *The Blacks*. Hooks's direction and performance as Deodatus Village generally received praise. However, Clive Barnes complained in the *New York Times* that "the large cast is unequal." And Richard Coe told *Washington Post* readers that "in the higher realms of criticism, Hooks' production could easily be scorned."[171] Don Sanders was more positive in his review for the Associated Press. Sanders found the production "fast-paced, with the cast running up and down a series of broad steps to a platform where the 'Whites'—played by Blacks wearing masks—watch proceedings and comment on them."[172] Barnes, Coe, and Sanders agreed that the original play had been overtaken by the emergence of Black Power over the course of the decade after its opening (though Barnes suggested perhaps Genet foresaw what was coming).

The production's ambition and its Kennedy Center venue weighed in with most reviewers.[173] Barnes, noting the center's status as a national performing arts center, hoped "some of our legislators see it." Coe recorded criticism for the choice of a White Frenchman's work for a Black company on an American government-supported stage. "Hooks, as leader," Coe wrote, "deserves his choices and his case rests in having that tyranny is not a matter of color but of the heart."

When the curtain came down on the production of *The Blacks* for the last time on the Eisenhower Theater's stage, Hooks and the DCBRC could count many remarkable accomplishments in a short time. They had attracted top-flight artists, found a home, connected with their community, and held their own on the larger national stage. But now the DCBRC's challenge was shifting from building a beginning to sustaining a continuous presence.

Dazzling Hopes

The DCBRC began its second season with enthusiasm and hope. The troupe's first season had proven more successful than not. Robert Hooks was becoming a regular on the local social, artistic, and media scenes (including numerous television appearances).[174] Yet, the decades-long debates over what constituted "Black" theater remained compelling. Hooks held firm to his convictions that DC needed "a theater of permanence, continuity and consistency, providing the necessary home base for the Black artist to launch a campaign to win his ignored brothers and sisters as constant witness. Not a segregated theater or a separatist one." [175] In this vain, the company scored a hit with its audiences with *Changes*, a musical written and directed by Motojicho with music and lyrics by Valerian E. Smith.[176]

A musical "collage of Black lifestyles," *Changes* was a work of unusual provenance.[177] Smith was a Howard University–educated south Louisiana dentist who happened to be Motojicho's father-in-law.[178] He fancied himself something of a playwright and composer working primarily in children's and community theater.[179]

Critics were not much taken with the work's artistic value. Richard Coe wrote that "Motojicho probably would admit 'Changes' isn't yet where he wants it, but he's working in the right direction for a formless, loosely linked yarn that's more of a revue than a closely knit book." No matter, as Coe told his *Washington Post* readers, "When 'Changes' is good, it's very, very good and when it isn't—wait a bit." [180] Whatever his limitations as a playwright, dentist Smith had an ear for Black vernacular music, which opened the door on Johnson and Malone's choreographic musicianship. Moments of "deliciously imaginative comedy" combined with "highly listenable songs" and "energetic, skilled performances from its zestful company" to make for a thoroughly enjoyable evening.[181] And this was especially true for African American audiences familiar with the characters and situations playing out before them.

Baltimore Afro-American critic Charles Farrow's review communicates why the play proved so successful: "Something great still happens when you attend a performance at the DC Black Repertory Theatre for the very first time. People come away positively unglued at the intensity of the Blackness of the production and the sight and sounds of so many Black people grooving to the same vibrations." Farrow continued: "It is not that 'Changes' offers much new in ideas, but rather how they handled often told incidents, familiar to the Black community.... 'Changes' communicates! It manages to deal with issues and images clearly and there ain't no way that you cannot understand and nod a meaningful 'Right On.'"[182] Its closing ended in celebration.[183]

But within a few weeks, despair replaced euphoria. Grant renewals failed to materialize, and revenue fell short of expenses. "We can no longer depend on foundations to support us," Hooks told the *Washington Post*. "The support is there but it's very minimal. We can only appeal to our friends and responsible citizens of this community to help us."[184] Hooks postponed the remainder of the season.[185]

Financial fortunes improved, and the season continued. A destructive spiral toward financial catastrophe nonetheless began.[186] As Tom Shales put it in the *Washington Post*, "Washington's DC Black Repertory Company has had its share of downs but not quite its share of ups—as far as economic health is concerned, anyway. Since its founding in 1972, the company has faced more financial crises than it should have."[187]

The DCBRC was hardly alone among local and national arts organizations in needing money. Hooks launched his company just as arts funding everywhere began to tighten. Locally, the Washington Theater Club and the National Ballet folded, while the Opera Society of Washington struggled to keep the lights on. Federal largess after the end of the booming Lyndon Johnson years began a long, torturous contraction, while foundations similarly started to lose interest in the arts.[188]

Artistic praise also became more difficult to gain. Joel Dreyfus complained in his review of the company's next production—*Don't Leave Go My Hand*—that "the material of this play and the last, 'Changes,' have done little to develop with any depth the characters they expose to us. We never know the reasons for their behavior, other than the most superficial ones."[189]

Black audiences and critics seldom shared similar reactions with establishment White critics. In July 1974, for example, the company enjoyed a highly successful five-day tour of the Caribbean, where audiences better appreciated its African-influenced aesthetic.[190]

A short time later, audiences enthusiastically embraced the company at the National Park Services' Carter Barron Amphitheater on the Black side of Rock Creek Park.[191] The company similarly joined with the National Park Service in offering performances at Fort Dupont Park east of the Anacostia River.[192] Various artists associated with the DCBRC participated in the rapidly expanding Smithsonian Folklife Festival that took root throughout the 1970s, and would take their work to Nigeria in 1977 at the time of the pathbreaking Second Black and African Festival of Arts and Culture (known as FESTAC).[193]

Owen's Last Song

Hooks managed one more significant production during the 1974–75 theatrical season, an adaptation of *Owen's Song* celebrating the writing of Howard University's Owen Dodson.[194] As noted earlier in the book, Owen Dodson joined the Howard University faculty in 1940 and remained a prominent fixture on the Washington African American cultural scene for the next three decades. The Brooklyn-raised, Yale-educated poet and theater director served as chair of Howard's Drama Department while simultaneously writing and directing plays around the country. In doing so, he animated a department that trained some of late-twentieth-century African America's brightest theater, dance, and movie talents.

Mike Malone, who had worked with Dodson at Howard, joined with the renowned Howard choreographer Glenda Dickerson to produce a work bringing Dodson's poetry and writings to life on the stage. Again and again, they discovered a common theme running through Dodson's work, that of "climbing a powerful long ladder to catch the bird of freedom." They drew on this image to suggest "a young man's fleeting vision of freedom as a lovely swan, who will disappear and reappear through life's turmoils and temptations." Malone and Dickerson conceived of the production as a "richly visual" embroidery of twenty-two performers moving through a series of images to a score composed by Clyde-Jacques Barrett and Dennis Wiley.[195]

Hooks, Malone, and Dickerson regarded the work as a "pure form of ritual theater," which they believed to be essential to the African and African American performance aesthetic.[196] *Washington Post* critic Coe was enchanted: "There is a blending of theatrical sophistication with Black legends which, in Dodson's subtle rhythmical words, themselves have been winnowed and refined."[197] So too were the sold-out audiences that lined up on Georgia Avenue trying to catch performances during the final week of the production's six-week run at the Last Colony Theater.[198]

The DCBRC achieved box office and artistic success rarely within the grasp of any company; and it did so with a work deeply rooted in the Washington community. Hooks achieved everything that T. Montgomery Gregory had hoped would be possible for Black theater in Washington. Unfortunately, this achievement proved to be too late.

Owen's Dream enjoyed a two-week run at the Kennedy Center's Eisenhower Theater in early 1975 with the same cast and creative team as at the Last Colony, but without the DCBRC affiliation. Hooks bet instead on mustering the company's resources on other works at the Last Colony. The Kennedy Center negotiated special dispensation from the League of Resident Theatres—the regional association launched in part by Tom Fichandler and Arena Stage a decade before—for the thirteen non-Equity performers from the original cast to appear in the remounted production.[199]

Coe's review of the new production was even more glowing than his earlier critique. "Devised for the DC Black Repertory Company by Glenda Dickerson and Mike Malone from the writings of poet Owen Dodson and set to music by Clyde-Jacques Barrett and Dennis Wiley," he wrote,

> this is a Black ritual work of uncommon sensitivity. It could only have been created by contemporary Black artists, having at its roots that wonder called "oral history," quickened by the prescience to embody it. This sense of ritual, sometimes solemn, sometimes passionate, sometimes mystical, sometimes baffling, is magnificently expressed through the movements staged by Dickerson and Malone.[200] What a creative team they make, and how exhilarating it is to have watched the work of both over these several recent years.[201]

Owen's Song was a triumph—the accomplishment of a half century and more of striving to create, nurture, and sustain a vibrant African American performing arts community in Washington. It marked the apotheosis of an unending struggle between pride and prejudice on the Washington stage.

Telling the Black American Saga through Song

The connections between song, dance, and drama within African and African American culture continuously ran through the DC-BRC's productions. For Black History Week in February 1975, the company staged a Saturday afternoon performance featuring Black song that told the story of the race in America. The hour-long matinee featured Sweet Honey in the Rock, the company's voice unit led by Bernice Reagon. Though initially intended for children, word spread and adults came to the performance, paying the $1 admission charge to get into the Last Colony. The subsequent performances eventually reached over 2,000 students during matinee specials throughout the week.[202] The show was the hit of that year's Black History Week events.[203]

The program began with an African chant and moved ahead with work songs, emancipation songs, and freedom songs sung by a tightly disciplined quintet. *Washington Post* reviewer Angela Brown-Terrell described what would become the group's signature performance style. The group, she wrote, "performs original and traditional songs of the Black experience. The five women members, all in their twenties, sing a cappella (but with occasional piano accompaniment), blending in tones from the bird-like soprano of Tia Juana Starks to the low, almost guttural notes of Carol Mallard and Reagon. Along with other members Pat Johnson and Diana Wharton, Sweet Honey produces, said Reagon, 'the Black vocal techniques as taught in the Black church.'"[204]

Later that year, the DCBRC and Sweet Honey in the Rock performed an original work based on "the full range of Black music" to tell the story of a day in the lives of ordinary Washington Blacks, from the bus ride to work at a government job, through a day at the office, and the ride home. The performance—*A Day, a Life, a People*—"distilled, focused, and fully exploited" the company's talents and became a hit for the holiday season.[205] The company's song performances became successful on their own terms, with Sweet Honey in the Rock beginning to tour nationally.[206]

Praise continued as the ensemble started to record and move onto the concert stage. "I shouted for joy," wrote the *New Pittsburgh Courier* critic Earl Calloway, "when I heard the singing of Sweet Honey in the Rock on their recent Redwood Records release, because they are bringing to contemporary audiences the precious incomparable music that our forefathers had been performing for decades."[207] Similar reviews became regular fare no matter how far away from Washington the company performed.[208] With time, the group's political and social activism moved front and center.[209]

By the group's tenth anniversary, Sweet Honey was enjoying global success, as Patrice Gaines-Carter noted in the *Washington Post*: "By word of mouth, people around the world have come to know Sweet Honey in the Rock, a durable, ever-changing Washington-based quintet of Black women who sing of protest and love—without musical accompaniment. They have toured England, Germany, and 11 cities in Japan, recorded four praised albums without benefit of slick advertising, and have survived constant turnover in the size and membership of the group."[210]

Endless rave reviews and awards would follow, with equally marvelous articles for the group's twentieth, twenty-fifth, and thirtieth anniversaries.[211] The Public Broadcasting System aired the award-winning filmmaker Stanley Nelson's 2005 television documentary about the group in its *American Masters* series honoring the country's top performing artists.[212] Nearly a half century—and over twenty singers and a couple of Grammy Awards—later, the group's exceptional style, political message, and repertoire remain intact.[213]

"Black Folks Sure Can Dance"

In 1976, Mike Malone teamed with Peggy Cooper and WTOP-TV, the city's CBS affiliate, to produce a documentary tracing the history of Black dance in the United States. Drawing on the language of W. E. B. DuBois's 1903 work *Souls of Black Folk*, Malone told an interviewer from the *Washington Post Magazine* that "Black folks sure can dance, as we all know (despite the many exceptions I know). And for many years dance was our best—our safest—medium of expression. But I don't think it was an escape as much as a means of dealing with a situation. It was also a way of holding onto our past... . We have an entertainment here, certainly, but that can be a vehicle for information people need to have."[214]

The resulting broadcast—*Genesis: Juba and Other Jewels, a Song-Step of Black America*—won critical acclaim, and was especially noteworthy in that it was the production of a local station. The show—which appeared during the country's bicentennial year—traced dance from Africa to the plantations, to minstrel shows, up to the disco music of the 1970s.[215] Malone and Cooper joined with documentary filmmaker Gardner Compton as well as with many dancers and designers from the DCBRC in producing what by all accounts was a landmark show. The production drew added sustenance from the new School of the Arts that Malone and Cooper were working to create at Washington's Western High School.[216]

Malone had worked closely with Hooks and Louis Johnson in creating the DCBRC's dance company. However, various artistic and financial strains eroded their shared sense of enterprise and, in July 1975, Johnson and Malone dissolved their three-year joint leadership of the DCBRC's Dance Company "over managerial difficulties."[217] The company's twelve dancers joined with Johnson in forming the new "Louis Johnson Dance Theater." Malone remained with Hooks, retaining the title "DC Repertory Dance Company," and held on to existing grants to the company. Augins, for his part, continued on to international success before, as already mentioned, heading up the Ellington School's Dance Department.

Those involved in the breakup wove together differing stories to explain what had happened. Johnson supporters pointed to frustration among the dancers over not having been paid on time and claimed that the performers had asked that Johnson join them. Malone's followers suggested that Johnson was failing to keep up with the times artistically.[218] Dance had remained central to Hooks's vision for the company and instrumental in successful productions such as *Owen's Song* just months before. Either way, the break was a blow to the company.

Johnson lined up a number of engagements, including having the company appear in the Broadway production of Scott Joplin's *Treemonisha*.[219] He devoted ever more time and energy to building Howard University's performance dance program into a full-fledged, degree-giving department. His company performed regularly at Howard's Ira Aldridge Theater, where it explored Black musical and dance themes.[220]

Johnson similarly remained loyal to Doris Jones and Claire Haywood, who had given him his start.[221] As noted above, Jones and Haywood were struggling to keep their Capitol Ballet company afloat despite artistic recognition and accomplishment.[222] An April 1987 contretemps over competing Kennedy Center benefit galas between Jones and Haywood's Capitol Ballet and Mary Day's Washington Ballet left ill will and insufficient revenues.[223] Lois England, the Washington Ballet's board president, presumed that the Black Capitol Ballet would stand down and cancel its event to make room for the White company to benefit. The resulting battered feelings turned a scheduling conflict into a racial incident.[224] The assumption that the Black company should immediately give way to the interests of the White company raised many concerns that supporters of the Washington Ballet considered ballet to be a White art form.[225] Day and England simply bullied their way through. The Capitol Ballet, which had been struggling to regain its balance after a hiatus of four years, began performances at the University of District of Columbia a year later.[226] But the Capitol Ballet never recovered, and it closed in 1989; the Jones Heywood Dance School continues to thrive.[227]

Johnson's ties to New York—and especially to the Alvin Ailey Company and Arthur Mitchell's Dance Theater of Harlem—remained strong, keeping the door open to numerous fruitful collaborations in the future.[228] The company enjoyed strong reviews in New York, as did his choreography for New York–based companies.[229] His Broadway credits include such successful productions as *The Wiz*, *Purlie*, and *Lost in the Stars*.[230] Johnson worked at the Metropolitan Opera on various productions, including *Aida*.[231] He staged acts for Aretha Franklin and the Temptations, and he worked in Hollywood.[232] He became a leading choreographer, and was regarded as American dance royalty.[233] All the while, he continued his effort to nurture young dancers, both in Washington and at New York's Henry Street Settlement.[234]

Malone followed a different trajectory, though both Johnson and Malone sustained long-standing affiliations with Howard

University. Malone became a leader in the growing street-theater movement of the 1970s, and worked continuously to promote dance among Washington's largely Black youth.[235] He worked on various television projects, including a version of *Black Orpheus* for public television with Debbie Allen.[236] He simultaneously enjoyed success on larger stages, such as when he choreographed Cleveland's Karamu House tribute to Langston Hughes at Lincoln Center in New York.[237] His productions of Hughes's *Black Nativity* at the Kennedy Center and elsewhere became popular holiday favorites.[238] Meanwhile, he found steady work choreographing for Washington productions of musicals such as *Dreamgirls* and *Mr. Holiday's Blues*.[239]

Malone was deeply engaged in public service, be it choreographing a 1986 performance of *Fame* for twelve American and ten Soviet "Peace Child" groups or planning the 1989 grand reopening of the historic Lincoln Theatre on U Street.[240] His most impressive legacy, as discussed below, was the instrumental role he played in establishing Washington's Duke Ellington School of the Arts.

Johnson, Malone, and Augins were remarkable artists and civic leaders who came together with Robert Hooks during the 1970s. Their contributions embedded dance within the DCBRC's artistic vision of bringing African predispositions to blend various performance forms together on the stage. Their achievements constitute a fundamental component of the company's legacy.

Winding Down

The DCBRC soldiered on for two years after *Owen's Song*, constantly mired in a financial quagmire that began to fray tempers and loyalties. Some efforts gained critical acclaim. *Washington Post* critic Richard L. Gee told readers that the company's January 1975 production of Douglas Turner Ward's *Day of Absence* was not to be missed.[241] The company's fall 1976 salute to the poet Gwendolyn Books provided a final success.[242]

The trend line, however, was bending downward. In June 1976, the company relocated a mile closer to downtown on Georgia Avenue in a cost-saving effort.[243] However, in December 1976, the DCBRC shut its doors.[244] Hooks expressed disappointment, blaming "meager government support, the failure of fund-raising campaigns, and 'complacency' in Washington" for the company's demise. The Kennedy Center's Roger Stevens called the closing a shame, noting that the company "couldn't get financial support."[245]

Hooks was forthright in setting out deeper concerns. The DC-BRC folded at a time when there was a boom on Broadway and elsewhere in Black musicals. This was, for Hooks, "a theatre of diversion." The challenge for Black—and for American—theater has been to engage with the disturbing presence of Black existence within the comfort zone of potential White audience members and donors.

"Just as in real life," Hooks told readers of the *Washington Post*, "a Black playwright—sight unseen, play unheard—is soothsaid as too bothersome a prod to the sleeping conscience. Even sympathetic advisers constantly bug the craftsman to shun racial themes and aspire to that temple of Olympian universality which all White playwrights ironically enough can enter merely by getting themselves born." Hooks concluded with a call that echoed those who had so enthusiastically launched the efforts of the Howard Players to create the National Negro Theater a half century before:

> A theater of permanence, continuity and consistency, providing the necessary home base for the Black artist to launch a campaign to win his ignored brothers and sisters as constant witness. Not a segregated theater or a separatist one. Blacks constitute a numerical minority in America, but the Black experience from slavery to now has always been of critical importance to this country's existence. There's no reason why Whites could not participate in a theater dedicated to exploring and illuminating that experience if they found inspiration in the purpose. It won't be me, but hopefully somebody can really, finally, pull it off for good old DC.[246]

Assessing an Interrupted Experiment

Because they were beset by organizational and financial challenges from the beginning, Hooks and his partners never enjoyed sufficient creative space to find a consistent point of view and identity.

Tamara Lizette Brown argues that the DCBRC failed to establish an optimal balance between two masters: the Black community and the White funding establishment.[247] The company further tried to focus on the city's Black cultural life within larger, universal artistic goals. As T. Montgomery Gregory, Willis Richardson, and others had discovered decades earlier, achieving such a balance is fraught with trials within an African American community, which itself is divided over the most appropriate balance between protest and propriety. Brown argues that Hooks sought a middle ground between revolutionary theater and establishment money by drawing on African traditions of ritual theater to break free of the Western canon.[248]

Donatella Galella approaches the story from a different perspective, noting that Hooks's "mission was to develop and produce Black artists, administrators, and audiences in the nation's capital, where he was born."[249] In the process, Hooks saw the opportunity to bring Black people together across their own internal divisions.[250] The White Washington theater community generally stepped aside. Motojicho was the single artistic director among major Washington commercial, noncommercial, and university theaters not attending a June 3, 1973, Smithsonian symposium on Washington theater.[251]

A focus on the company's relationship with the Black community highlights the DCBRC's considerable achievements as various legacy companies and initiatives achieved success. In particular, the company's music and dance programs spawned powerfully successful performers who have enlivened the city's—and America's—artistic life. The DCBRC's failure was first and foremost one of the Washington and American cultural marketplace rather than due to internal creative or organizational shortcomings.[252]

Few African American theater companies have been able to succeed without attracting somewhere about a fifth to a quarter of their audience and donor base from the White community.[253] Even the most prestigious and long-lived ones, such as NEC, have confronted periodic funding crises.[254] Although African American Washington welcomed Hooks's company and identified with its artistic achievements, donations remained anemic.[255] Foundation funding was difficult to sustain after an initial flurry of support in an era when philanthropic attention was beginning to shift elsewhere.[256]

Box office receipts rarely made up the difference. Many African American patrons complained about poor parking arrangements at the Last Colony; while many Whites considered Petworth a dangerous, crime-ridden, "no-go" zone. The old cinema required considerable and, at times, expensive maintenance to meet company and audience expectations. The last-minute effort to stave off the inevitable by moving the company a mile down Georgia Avenue toward downtown failed to alter the company's fate.

Commentators, beginning with the company's short life span between 1972 and 1976, frequently imply a failed experiment. Their conclusion ignores the high artistic quality of the DCBRC's productions and its powerful creative legacy for the city and the nation. The company succeeded in providing an all-important professional space where Black authors could tell Black stories through Black actors supported by Black theater professionals to Black audiences. As Hooks later noted, every American city needs a cornerstone Black cultural institution to promote artistic achievement within communities, both in terms of reaching out to youth and in terms of showcasing professional achievement. DCBRC, for a while, provided such a touchstone.[257]

Olive Barnes caught the tenor of the company in a November 1974 review of *Owen's Song* for the *New York Times*.[258] Barnes lavished praise on the production, which she described as "beautiful" and "a "kind of pictogram for freedom." She continued:

> There is an infectious joyousness to the piece; a visual beauty adds a swiftly poetic message. . . . This is a seamless masque and it is quite impossible to see where choreography starts or drama ends. It has the essence of poetry to it, with a grandeur of concept and a simplicity of effort. It has a style of its own, and trades in images. It is an unusually pregnant piece of theater, subtly suggestive of future possibilities, perhaps of some concept of the dance/music/poem staged with theatrical grace.

Earlier in her review, Barnes observed, "As the Black theater finds itself, it is moving farther and farther from the White theatre. The Black Repertory has opened its season with a striking musical and dramatic collage called *Owen's Song*, and its content, style, manner, impact and intention have virtually nothing to do with White theater. There are similarities—both Frederic Chopin and Jelly Roll Morton played much the same piano—but it is the differences that count."

Barnes felt compelled to comment on the audience. "I first saw the company last year when it went to the Kennedy Center to give Jean Genet's *The Blacks*," she wrote, "but last weekend I saw the company for the first time in its own context, in its own home at the Last Colony Theater on Georgia Avenue. The theater itself is an old transformed movie house (significantly, it used to be called just the Colony), and it makes a very nice home for the Black Repertory, more opulent but perhaps not so challenging as the NEC theater on St. Mark's Place."

"One difference I did notice," she continued, "was that the proportion between Black and White spectators was markedly up on Black in Washington. Whether this is a plus or a minus, I wouldn't know. Somehow, my liberal bleeding heart tells me that it is good, and my common sense suggests that the reason for it is simply that in Washington the theater is solidly within the Black district. It is as if the NEC were in Harlem."

The Rep, Inc.

The closing of the DCBRC touched off a round of recrimination over the absence of a Black theater company in a majority Black city. Various theories were trotted out—competition for Black works from White theaters, the habits of Black audiences and donors, limited local funding opportunities, leadership qualities—some, no doubt, with considerable explanatory power. Such a discussion has been repeated periodically over subsequent decades.[259]

Meanwhile, a nonunion legacy company—The Rep, Inc.—continued without missing a beat. Reviewing the new company's first production, Langston Hughes's *Simply Heavenly*, the *Washington Post* critic Louise Reid noted that the new company operated as a workshop with many of the original company members remaining on board. Reid praised the production as "an example of how good acting can transform a cliché-ridden story into a production that rivets the interest."[260]

Other companies tried to enter into the space left by the collapse of the DCBRC. Paul Allen of the now-defunct Washington Theater Club presented Black-themed works with some success at the Paul Robeson Center on O Street NW.[261] Out-of-town companies similarly had their sights set on Washington audiences.[262]

The Rep, Inc.—under the artistic direction of Jaye Stewart and executive director Lyn Dyson for much of its existence—continuously produced African American repertoire until Stewart's death in 1996.[263] Stewart had grown up in Washington, was committed to advancing local theater, and became immediately attracted to Hooks's project. He graduated from the University of Maryland and Morgan State University before working with the Howard University communications school. He acted on stage and screen—including a turn in *All the President's Men*—and wrote plays. In the mid-1980s, he moved to Chicago, where he enjoyed success until his untimely death in 1996.[264] All the while, Stewart kept his connection with the Rep in Washington. Dyson had acted and worked behind stage at the DCBRC, and similarly brought continuity to the new company.[265]

The Rep moved around, performing initially at the DCBRC's last stage on Georgia Avenue as well as in smaller venues across the city, before settling after two decades in a diminutive performance space in Brookland in Northeast DC.[266] Stewart performed elsewhere, while Dyson went into business, heading up the Multi-Media Training Institute in the 1990s. The company's youth audience base did not seem to mind its peripatetic existence and, from time to time, the Rep, Inc., was able to lure established talent. In 1992, for example, the singer, songwriter, poet, and activist Oscar Brown Jr. spent several months in residence developing new works.[267]

The Rep managed to forge ahead with more modest ambition than the original DCBRC, leading many to overlook or downplay its continued existence. Commenting on the company's tenth anniversary, Dyson explained, "I think we had to go through a period of four or five years for the public to forget about the failure of the DC Black Rep and allow us to move forward on our own merits. But it is happening now."[268] Indeed, the company was becoming part of a theatrical ecosystem filling up with smaller, nonunion companies pushing artistic boundaries to reinvent the Washington theater scene.[269]

Some critics praised the smaller company as a step forward. In 1978 *Washington Post* critic Richard L. Coe noted that "since its name was reduced from the DC Black Repertory Company, the Rep., Inc., has become a far tighter, infinitely more professional group, in its smaller auditorium."[270] Stewart and Dyson hit bigger stages from time to time, as in the spring of 1979, when they took a production to New York's Lincoln Center.[271] Ongoing workshops and training courses proved to be a key to this success by preparing community artists for stage careers beginning in the Rep, Inc.'s own productions.[272]

Like the original DCBRC, the Rep, Inc., retained its focus on holistic theater that melded various performance genre into a unified whole. Music, dance, and mime had their place on the Rep, Inc.'s stage. Miles White observed in the *Baltimore Afro-American* that "what infuses this production with an exciting uniqueness as the concept of dance and movement as dominating elements in the story, rather than language, to impart the plot."[273]

Although numerous other Black theater companies came and went, the Rep, Inc., kept the legacy of the DC Black Repertory Company alive for two decades.[274] The smaller company trained dozens of theater professionals, cultivated a loyal audience, and presented plays by Blacks about Blacks for Blacks. Stewart, Dyson, and their colleagues revived the core questions that animated T. Montgomery Gregory, Willis Richardson, and so many others nearly a century before: What is Black theater? What do Blacks bring to larger theatrical forms? How does pride confront prejudice from a theatrical stage? So when the Rep, Inc., also disappeared, one fundamental question remained: How can the nation's capital—with its large, animated, well-off African American community—not support a Black theater company?

Others Respond

Many in Washington and elsewhere have periodically honored Hooks and the DCBRC's achievements and legacies. Columnists retell the story of the heroic company that failed.[275] A half century later, the District of Columbia formally honored Hooks with a day set aside in his name. The company has sustained a lively alumni association, which has provided fellowship and support to former company members as they have moved through their successful careers.[276] Hooks himself has enjoyed no scarcity of success in his long film, television, and stage career to follow.[277]

The story of the company's demise, in fact, is more complex than one of rise, success, and fall. In December 1976, the DC Black Repertory Company closed as a professional "Equity" (union) house. The voice and dance units already had attained autonomous lives of their own. In shutting down, the Board was careful to transfer the workshops and training divisions to a "nonprofessional assembly of 50–75 people under the direction of Vantile Whitfield, who uses the name Motojicho in theater circles, [and] is expected to do some productions."[278] This unit—which would evolve into the Rep, Inc. Whitfield—meanwhile enjoyed success in Hollywood, Chicago, and elsewhere.[279]

The DCBRC did not evaporate in a single instance. The company spawned a number of astounding progenies across its sparkling yet brief lifetime. Its demise nonetheless left one of the nation's most lively centers of African American culture without a fully professional Black theater company.

Many tried to eliminate this deficit in the Washington theater scene. In 1989, several area community theaters led by John L. Moore III banded together to establish the African Continuum Theater Company (ACTCo) to assist African American community theaters and to improve the quality and visibility of their work.[280] The consortium recruited Jennifer Nelson to manage the consortium shortly thereafter and, in 1995, Nelson transformed the loose alliance of community theaters into a unified and vivacious company.[281]

As a playwright, actor, director, producer, and teacher, Nelson has been a mainstay of the Washington theater scene for years (as acknowledged by the 2019 Helen Hayes Tribute for lifetime achievement and contributions to Washington theater).[282] A one-time president of the League of Washington Theatres, she has worked in various capacities for virtually every major company in town, including long stints with Ford's Theatre and Mosaic Theater.[283]

Nelson arrived in Washington in 1972 and made the city her home after professional sojourns to New York, Texas, and elsewhere.

The daughter of an actor-turned-Army employee, she was drawn to theater watching her father perform in community performances in Sacramento. After earning an undergraduate degree and working towards an MFA at the University of California, Davis, Nelson headed to San Francisco for a professional break from school (she eventually would complete her graduate training at the University of Texas at Austin). A phone call from Living Stage founder Robert Alexander changed her life.[284]

Nelson took a chance on Alexander's invitation to audition for his Living Stage Company, the community outreach troupe associated with Arena Stage discussed earlier in the book. Alexander would come to be Nelson's mentor. She crossed the continent and ended up staying with Living Stage for twenty-six years.[285]

Nelson acted, directed, and wrote for companies around town as she rose through the Living Stage company, eventually holding nearly every possible position except the most senior one. Told that senior leadership was the domain of males, Nelson left and joined the fledgling African Continuum Theatre consortium, where she remained eleven years before moving to Ford's Theatre for another seven years, and on to a productive freelance career.[286] Among her many successful works was *The Hip Hop Nightmares of Jujube Brown*, which went from Arena Stage's Old Vat Room to the New York Hip Hop Theatre Festival and the National Black Theater Festival in North Carolina in 1998.[287]

Nelson transformed ACTCo from a consortium of community groups into a single company with four full-time employees supported by foundation grants, performing at the Source Theater on 14th Street NW and other venues around town.[288] The journey was not an easy one. Often plagued by insufficient space for rehearsals and productions as well as funding concerns, Nelson learned "the importance of networking and leveraging connections to acquire and share resources."[289]

In 2007, Melvin D. Gerald Jr. arrived at ACTCo as managing director from Arlington's Signature Theatre.[290] The company enjoyed great success under Nelson—and later under Gerald's leadership—producing several dozen fully staged productions and many more staged readings of new works by playwrights of color, including more than two dozen women.[291]

ACTCo shut down in 2015 due to insufficient funds. The closing occurred despite generous foundation support over the years, a surfeit of worthy new works, stellar performances, and robust ticket sales. This success prompted the region's theater companies to bring plays by African Americans to their stages. Yet, as with Hooks's DCRBC, ACTCo failed to activate and maintain a group of African American donors sufficiently drawn to theater to sustain a DC-based Black theater company.[292]

Others have tried to launch African American theater companies in the Washington area. Initially, when renowned Tony Award–winning Broadway director and Producer Kenny Leon joined with Jane Bishop in 2002 to establish the True Colors Theater Company, the group was based in Washington as well as Atlanta. Leon had worked—and would later work—on Washington stages with considerable distinction. True Colors enjoyed success when the company performed Langston Hughes's *Tambourines of Glory* at the recently renovated and reopened Lincoln Theatre on U Street in 2004; and continued to work in the region through 2007. By the end of the 2000s, however, the company had consolidated its operations in Atlanta, where it has emerged as a major regional and national force promoting African American theater classics, community outreach, and theatrical education.[293]

More recently, the highly regarded playwright, dramaturg, producer and advocate Jacqueline E. Lawton has worked assiduously to expand the presence of African American theater in Washington and around the nation from a variety of institutions.[294] The unrest after the murder of George Floyd in the summer 2020 similarly prompted numerous efforts throughout the DC theater community to bring Black perspectives to the Washington stage. The struggle begun a century ago to bring a permanent and prominent presence to DC theater continues.

School's In

As noted above, Peggy Cooper was a fast starter. She grew up in a prominent Mobile, Alabama, African American family during the 1950s and 1960s and became a civil rights activist after run-ins with local Whites over segregation as a high school student. She graduated from Saint Mary's College in Indiana and moved on to earn a second degree at George Washington University, where she founded the university's Black Student Union.[295] She developed a passion for the arts as an expression of community during her first years in Washington, where she secured appointment on the Mayor's Arts Commission Advisory Board.[296] She continued her education, earning a law degree from George Washington University to better position herself to promote the arts.[297]

By the late 1960s, Cooper had sponsored Black arts and transported inner-city students to festivals she had organized. She joined with Mike Malone to create summer arts workshops for high school students, a program that piqued her interest in the possibility of launching a public high school for the arts in DC.[298] She and Malone would make this effort their lives' work.[299]

Cooper became a leading civic figure on the Washington scene. She married into the Cafritz family (a match that would end in divorce). The Cafritz clan successfully built a local real estate empire, which supported their well-known commitment to funding the local arts scene. She served as president of the DC School Board between 2000 and 2006, and she held any number of other positions throughout her life, bringing together social activism, the arts, and education. She amassed one of the largest private collections of African American and African art, much of which was lost in a catastrophic 2009 house fire.[300] She began rebuilding the collection, which she left at her 2018 death to the Ellington School and the Studio Museum in Harlem.[301] None of these accomplishments, however, outshone her deep commitment to establish and nurture a high school for the arts.

Cooper Cafritz and Malone had begun their efforts to create a school of the arts before they joined Hooks at the DC Black Repertory Company. They continued to work on the project while she served on the company's board and he worked as a choreographer for company productions. She once proclaimed that she had given herself five years to start the school while still an undergraduate, and she continued her efforts through law school.[302]

Cooper Cafritz established a pilot Workshop for Careers in the Arts, offering DC public school students training in dance, drama, art, and filmmaking. During this period, she gained the support of the system's assistant superintendent, George R. Rhodes, and secured various grants to launch the new school. At one point, the school system considered purchasing the original headquarters of the National Geographic Society downtown for the new school. When this effort failed, Cooper Cafritz, Malone, and Rhodes—with major assistance from Mayor Walter Washington—shifted their focus to the formerly White Western High School just north of the Georgetown University campus.[303] In 1974, the public school system launched a new school for the arts at Western High, which eventually was named after local cultural icon Edward "Duke" Ellington.[304]

These efforts overlapped with Cooper Cafritz's and Malone's work at the DCBRC. The Ellington School would grow into one of the city's brightest success stories. With roughly five hundred students in each class, Ellington regularly ranks among the city's best-performing schools. Dozens of Ellington alumni—such as the comedian Dave Chappelle, the opera singer Denyce Graves, the rapper-bassist Meshell Ndegeocello, the jazz trumpeter Wallace Roney, the sculptor Marja Vallila, and the actor Rosalyn Coleman Williams—have gained international recognition in dance, theater, opera, jazz, and the other arts; scores have enjoyed successful careers as arts professionals; and hundreds more have lived lives well lived.

The Ellington School frequently has courted controversy. Early on, the appearance of an African nude sculpture nearly shut the school down before it had gained initial momentum.[305] The additional financial resources required to elevate the arts curriculum above the public school norm frequently have proven difficult to secure.[306] Proposals have surfaced periodically to relocate the school out of Georgetown so that it could be "closer to where its students live."[307] During the 2010s, a lavish three-year renovation project ran $100 million over budget.[308] Shortly thereafter, an investigation by DC Public Schools erroneously claimed that many nonresident students were attending the school without paying out-of-city tuition.[309]

Through it all, the students' achievements and successes have ensured the school's lasting triumph.[310] The Duke Ellington School of the Arts remains perhaps the proudest legacy from an era when

Chocolate City generated creative energy fueled by pride while confronting prejudice to proclaim presence from the Washington stage.

Bringing Disparate Traditions Together

The 1970s marked the beginnings of a profound social makeover. The Washington metropolitan region ranked among the fastest-growing in the country, and was about to become a major immigrant gateway city.[311] The footprint of theater evolved as the city and its suburbs grew and changed. The Montgomery County Recreation Department, for example, established its "Street '70" Program in 1970. That outreach initiative grew into the Silver Spring–based Round House Theater. By 1993, the company had severed its ties with the county to become a free-standing professional and educational center with theaters in Silver Spring and Bethesda. Its full seasons of new works and classics draw over 50,000 patrons each year.[312]

The region's foreign-born population would increase fivefold over the next half century, with immigrants arriving from 193 countries to form a highly diverse community that no single immigrant group dominates (immigrants from El Salvador form the largest foreign-born community, but constitute only one-tenth of all newcomers). The city simultaneously became a preferred destination for a fresh generation of university graduates. This growth spread throughout the metropolitan region. In town, immigrant communities—especially from Central and South America—grew up around the very same transitioning Adams Morgan neighborhood that had served as the New Thing's base just a few years earlier. Newcomers used theater to establish their presence in the city, region, and nation. As in the past, the city's large international community provided a ready audience for productions drawing on imported artistic traditions and performed in foreign languages.

The Argentine actor and director Hugo Medrano came to town just as these demographic changes were becoming incontestable.[313] He initially worked in the city's only Spanish-language theater at the time, a bilingual children's theater company, Teatro Doble.

Washington rarely has been considered a major outpost of

Spanish-language culture—though perhaps it should be. The city's long-established Latin diplomatic community draws heavily on well-educated intellectuals steeped in traditional Spanish-language letters. As the political, ideological, and philosophical conflicts unleashed by the geopolitics of the Cold War ebbed and flowed, cultural creators—including several future giants from across South America—came to and left Washington, depending on the ascendancy of left- or right-wing political regimes back home.

Less visible, though no less significant for the development of Spanish-language culture in the city, when Medrano arrived the Washington metropolitan region was becoming a home to immigrants. At first, the migrants arrived came from countries torn by civil strife, and they were followed soon thereafter by economic emigrants.

This was a moment when English translations of Latin American literature were moving to the top of best-seller lists. Growing interest in Latin American magical realism lured more than a few non-Spanish-reading intellectuals further and further into Spanish literary traditions. This was especially true in Washington, a city that was home to a well-educated and worldly professional middle class.

By the 1970s, demand in Washington exploded for both highbrow and lowbrow Spanish-language-based culture. Medrano appeared just at this seminal moment. Making his way around the city's Spanish-speaking communities, he encountered Rebecca Read, a former dancer who was working at the Organization of American States. Medrano and Read settled into the as-yet-ungentrified, multicultural bohemian Adams Morgan neighborhood that was home to Topper Carew's New Thing.

In 1976, operating out of a typical Victorian-era brick DC townhouse not far from Carew's New Thing, Medrano and Read—who married one another—joined with their friends to establish the Grupo de Artistas Latinoamericanos, or GALA. This consortium embraced visual artists, writers, dancers, singers, musicians, and actors who wanted to nurture Latinx culture in Washington. GALA's productions presented Latin American works performed in Spanish as well as in English. From the very beginning, the Medranos and their colleagues sought to integrate their Latin American artistic traditions and sensibilities into the larger Washington cultural community.

Early GALA productions showcased the political themes of the era. Many immigrants in Washington at the time had fled their homelands for political reasons, including intellectuals who were escaping dictatorships. These migrants were joined by large numbers of Central American migrants escaping civil war, so politics naturally stood at the top of everyone's mind. GALA quickly developed an additional educational mission, presenting children's plays and working with community leaders to transfer Latinx cultures to the next generation. Such outreach and children's theater efforts have remained central to GALA's operations.

By the turn of the twenty-first century, GALA had become a widely respected and much-praised presence on the DC cultural scene. During its first three decades, the company produced nearly 150 plays in Spanish and English while supporting poetry, music, and dance programming. The company established a network of actors who came from across the Americas to perform in Washington, and it thus became a leading institutional touchstone for the city's growing Hispanic community. Nonetheless, GALA still did not have a permanent home.

As the twentieth century came to a close, the DC government requested proposals for the redevelopment of the historic Tivoli Theater in the increasingly multicultural Columbia Heights community to support the area's revitalization. The Tivoli, which was designed by the noteworthy theater architect Thomas W. Lamb, was a city landmark when it opened in 1924. The theater survived as a cinema until the April 1968 civil disturbances after the assassination of the Reverend Dr. Martin Luther King Jr., when the neighborhood suffered severe damage and was slow to recover. The building was boarded up in 1976, and it sat vacant for the next quarter century.

The Medranos had long been interested in the building, and they joined in a proposal submitted by the Horning Brothers developers to convert the building into a mix of offices and retail with a theater. City officials were taken with the idea of returning the Tivoli to its original theatrical purpose as well as recognizing GALA's contributions to the neighborhood over the previous decades.

In 2005, the Medranos moved their company into its now-permanent home.

Over the course of the company's residence at the Tivoli, GALA has consolidated its presence in the ever-growing Washington theater scene. Recognition has followed with the company winning several Helen Hayes Awards and the Medranos being named 2010 Washingtonians of the Year by *Washingtonian Magazine*.[314] The company's outreach programs have become a mainstay of child-oriented cultural programming in the city; and its highly professional and innovative productions regularly attract wide and diverse audiences—all just two miles uphill from the White House.

In 2017, GALA premiered the first Spanish-language production of Lin-Manuel Miranda's *In the Heights* to glowing reviews. The show was a triumph for the values expressed by GALA's founders four decades earlier—and all the more so because it appeared in one of the nation's most lively multicultural urban neighborhoods, Columbia Heights, in a treasure of a theater originally designed by one of the country's most distinguished theater architects.

The at-times-difficult-to-please *Washington Post* critic Peter Marks could hardly contain his enthusiasm. "So there is a sense of linguistic homecoming for this kaleidoscopic story of contemporary life among the Americans of Puerto Rican, Dominican, Cuban, and Mexican descent in Manhattan's Washington Heights to be sung," he wrote in April 2017, "in the language of its rollicking, struggling characters. And how grand for GALA Hispanic Theatre, the tenacious company tackling Spanish and Latin American plays in Columbia Heights, to be the one to produce it."[315]

The search for affirmation of a distinct community identity and presence echoed previous efforts by Black Washingtonians to define themselves and their communities through theater. While seeking to advance the cause of Black theater, Gregory looked to the experience of the Irish National Theater in Dublin. When Lady Gregory, Edward Martyn, and William Butler Yeats founded Dublin's Abbey Theatre in 1904, they were not intent on advancing universal values. Instead, they wanted to promote Irish stories told by Irish writers to Irish audiences for Irish culture. In the process, their company came to have a profound influence on English theater, and on European and global drama more generally. None were separatists (although they were nationalists challenging British domination). Rather, they promoted a distinctive dramatic style, which spoke to the pride of the Irish people as they confronted prejudice.[316]

Arena Stage at the Mead Center for American Theater, November 2020
(*Photo by Blair A. Ruble*)

Curtain Call

The Stage Is Set

There were tanks on our city street and because we are not a state, the mayor had only certain avenues that she could respond to this threat.
—*Molly Smith, 2020*[1]

Arena Stage, like theater companies around the world, spent the summer of 2020 struggling to find new ways to reach and to sustain its audience in light of the several-months-long shutdown resulting from the COVID-19 pandemic. Molly Smith and her colleagues began to produce documentary films about current events based on scripts written by playwrights who would base their segments on their own experiences combined with interviews featuring everyday people. Actors performed the resulting monologues in documentary films made available on the company's website.

Initially, these brief productions told stories of the pandemic, ranging from individual reflections on quarantine-imposed isolation to the grief of having lost a love one. The third such production—*The 51st State*—responded to a summer of unrest and protest unleashed in the city by the murder of George Floyd at the hands of the Minneapolis police.[2] Long-standing grievances over inequality, representation, and presence exploded onto DC's streets. Without full statehood, city leaders were limited in their response to the drama unfolding across their community and the nation. Theater, once again, provided a voice that the US Constitution did not. Arena Stage—and many other theater companies across the Washington region—became vehicles whereby citizens could stake their claims to justice.

The summer of 2020 was, in some ways, distressingly similar to the summer of 1919 that had prompted the city's African Americans to action from stages and streets alike. Yet much had changed. DC now had a limited but elected city government; its economy and population were larger, more diverse, and in many instances were better off than had been the case a century before. Washington had grown from a provincial town into a metropolitan megaregion; Washington theater had transformed into a community of national—and even international—significance.

Metropolitan Eruption

Father Hartke found himself at the center of the world's attention on November 25, 1963, when he joined the procession behind the caisson carrying President Kennedy's casket to Arlington National Cemetery. Hartke, who would become a spiritual adviser to President Johnson and his family in the months ahead, was soon known as the "White House Priest." Like the city that had become his home, he previously only had caught the nation's attention at moments of official solemnity. Now he seemed to be everywhere.

The Kennedy administration marked something of a turning point for the city and its cultural community. DC's population stood at about 300,000 in 1910 when the Howard Drama Club began; and it had doubled by 1990 (after declining since a high point of 800,000 in 1950). Its metropolitan region, which hardly existed at the beginning of the twentieth century, approached 4 million at that time; and would grow to six million by 2020.[3] Washington would become a place to watch continuously.

Population statistics alone suggest that the patron base for theater passed a tipping point toward sustainability at some point during the 1960s. Raw numbers are only part of the story. The Washington of Thomas Montgomery Gregory, Alain LeRoy Locke, Willis Richardson, and Georgia Douglas Johnson was indeed the small, southern town of lore. That city began to change once Franklin D. Roosevelt took office. Roosevelt's New Deal greatly expanded the reach of the federal government, attracting hundreds of social reformers (including Zelda Fichandler's parents) from cities such as Chicago and New York, where they expected to find theater.

World War II greatly extended all aspects of government operations, while the postwar period transformed Washington into a major international center. Hundreds more international affairs and finance specialists—together with foreign diplomats and international civil servants—filled an ever-increasing number of buildings around town and the suburbs beyond with highly educated officials, administrators, and bureaucrats who demanded high-minded entertainment.

The Kennedy administration consolidated this new cultural scene and made the city into a magnet for young, idealistic college students and youth. DC became a major college town, a new status, which was ever more apparent throughout the 1960s as youthful social activism grew and protesters took to the streets.

As the Cold War competition with the Soviet Union evolved into ever-higher levels of technological achievement, hundreds of engineers and scientists arrived, inventing, among many accomplishments, the Internet. After the Cold War, the Washington area became the focal point for biogenetic science as local researchers mapped the human genome.

A robust audience for live theater and performance was sure to be found somewhere among these new Washingtonians. The challenge became how to supply the compelling theater demanded by such audiences while simultaneously reaching out to the hometown DC that predated it.

Expanding Supply

Conventional wisdom suggests that the opening of the John F. Kennedy Center for the Performing Arts on September 8, 1971, marks Washington's coming of age as a cultural center. Without question, the Kennedy Center proved to be a catalytic institution for the city's performing arts. If nothing else, the center provided a consolidating focal point easily accessible to suburbanites and car-driving city dwellers alike. The center, however, remained cut off from the city by a spider web of interstate highway ramps. The architects and planners designing the complex never thought of it as an enhancement to an urban streetscape or neighborhood (which is among the reasons why Father Hartke preferred other sites).

The idea of the Kennedy Center began long before, when Father Hartke and numerous public-minded Washingtonians began to lobby the federal government for a center city municipal auditorium free from the encumbrances of Jim Crow. Functioning as they do, Congress, the federal government, and the various political players produced a worthy outcome a bit at odds from any single initial vision. For all its locational and design flaws, however, the Kennedy Center has provided important performance spaces and institutional support for the ever-more-vibrant performing arts scene.

However, cultural Washington demanded more—more performance spaces, more performing artists—more closely tied to communities and the city itself. Touring companies presenting pre-and-post Broadway runs would no longer satisfy Washingtonians.

Setting the Stage

The central protagonists of this book—those who were part of Howard University, Catholic University, Arena Stage, and the Black Arts Movement—created the artistic and bureaucratic conditions that made the late-twentieth-century upsurge in Washington arts possible. Over the course of several decades, they established community bone fides, cleared away bureaucratic and regulatory underbrush, beat back meddlesome regulations and law enforcement practices, garnered political support, created connections and organizations, fashioned the requisite infrastructure, and cultivated the audiences and donors required to support the Washington theater community. They did so while upholding artistic achievement of the first order.

Their story is about the art—and about more. It offers a social history of twentieth-century Washington theater that reveals the foundations upon which artistry becomes possible. These more pragmatic achievements led the way for scores to follow. By late in the century, newcomers to the Washington arts scene found a comprehensive support system for their visions.

And arrive they did. To name but a very few of the theater professionals who have enriched the Washington scene in recent years: Howard Shalwitz, Roger Brady, and Linda Reinisch opened

Woolly Mammoth Theater in 1980; Michael Kahn established the Washington Shakespeare Theater Company from within the Folger Theater Company during the mid-1980s; Joy Zinoman and Russell Metheny founded Studio Theater in 1988; Eric Schaeffer and Donna Migliaccio began Signature Theater in 1990; Round House Theatre left the clutches of the Montgomery County government to become a free-standing professional company in 1993.

By the turn of the century, a wave of theater construction expanded Arena Stage's facilities, extended performance possibilities at the Kennedy Center, and provided state-of-the-art homes for the Shakespeare Theater Company, Studio Theater, Woolly Mammoth, Signature, and Round House, among many. These facilities empowered their companies and, simultaneously, fostered a vibrant cityscape. The city and region thus developed a viable theater ecosystem that could support high-quality professional theater in ways not possible when T. Montgomery Gregory, Father Gilbert V. Hartke, the Fichandlers, and Robert Hooks set out to establish their companies.

The twentieth-century city encountered here is unrecognizable to those who have come to Washington only recently. Today's Washington is, in the words of American University's Derek Hyra and Sabiyha Prince, "a 21st-century urban powerhouse." While other municipalities contended with decline or economic stagnation during the Great Recession of 2008, the nation's capital and its metropolitan region boomed. Its recent rise in global stature and increased population have thrust DC into discussions as one of America's most appealing and prosperous cities.[4]

It is also the case that long-standing inequalities remain stark. Fissures of class, race, and other variables foster uneven development and influence social relations in assorted ways. In 2018, the largest single group of income tax filers in the District (about a third) earned over $100,000 a year, followed by the second-largest group (about a quarter) earning less than $25,000 a year. In 2010, the average net worth of White families in the city was eighty-one times higher than the average family net worth of African American families.[5] These pressures bring both energy and tension to local theater.

Theater Matters

Karen Zacarías in many ways was a typical twenty-first-century "New Washingtonian."[6] She moved to the city in 1991 at the age of twenty-two years to work on Latin American policy issues at a think tank, having just graduated from Stanford University a few weeks before. A year later, she took a course in playwriting at Georgetown University, while her day job helped her pay off student loans. Having gone as far as a young university graduate might in Washington's policy world without additional education, she set her sights on graduate school. Her life path, however, began to veer from the Washington norm. In 1995, she entered a graduate creative writing program at Boston University, where she focused on writing for the stage.

Zacarías was familiar with the secretive, contentious, and ego-driven world of the arts. Born into a prominent Mexico City artistic family—her grandfather, Miguel Zacarías, had been a successful writer and director in Mexican cinema—she shunned the self-indulgence, self-importance, and destructive behavior she saw in the art world.[7] Public policy seemed more comfortable. Her family had moved to Massachusetts when she was a child so that her father could study at Harvard University. Later, he headed the Pan American Health Organization's AIDS program in Washington.

Washington continued to tug on Zacarías in ways the city would not have a century earlier. The city now offered bountiful opportunity for writers and professional couples. So she returned to the city to launch the Young Playwrights' Theater. This nonprofit group follows in the distant footsteps of Thomas Montgomery Gregory decades before, when he similarly taught playwriting to DC high school students from a faculty perch at Howard University.[8] Zacarías married a lawyer, Rett Snotherly, started a family in Adams Morgan, and found time to write and to teach as an adjunct professor at Georgetown University.

Zacarías has written several well-received plays that have been performed at some of the nation's leading theaters, including the Kennedy Center, Arena Stage, GALA Hispanic Theater in Washington; the La Jolla Playhouse; the Cleveland Play House; and the Goodman Theatre in Chicago. Her works include dramas and comedies, children's works, and social commentaries. She was among the first five playwrights selected for Arena Stage's play-wright-in-residence program, which provided three years of support.[9] Her comedy *The Book Club Play* about what happens to people devoted to books when a film crew arrives proved to be the first work produced under the new program.[10]

As her career and reputation has flowered, Zacarías has drawn more heavily on her Washington experiences.[11] Her fourth main-stage production at Arena Stage in 2017, *Native Gardens*, captured the tenor of early-twenty-first-century Washington as the city experienced unrelenting demographic change. Though she has claimed that the story is not about her and her family, it tracks the experiences of many Washingtonians—especially from the Latinx community—as the immigrant presence has grown. Similarly, as with the plays produced by local African American writers a century before, she used the stage to capture a moment when outsiders were establishing their claim to the city, affirming their identity as Washingtonians, and forging their pathway to becoming insiders.[12]

As retold by Lori McCue of the *Washington Post*,

> The comedy takes place entirely in the Northwest Washington backyards of two neighboring families: Tania and Pablo, a Latinx couple who are new to the city and have a baby on the way; and Frank and Virginia, white empty nesters with a prize-winning garden. . . . When the young couple discovers that their property line actually extends right over the neighbors' pristine flowerbed, an initially mild squabble ends with the grown adults lobbing acorns—and racially tinged insults—across the fence.[13]

The property dispute becomes a metaphor for the theft of land from people of color by White people; and Frank's invasive peonies and hydrangeas (or "immigrant plants") threaten Tania's garden of environmentally friendly indigenous plants (her "native garden").[14]

Such neighborhood tiffs reveal a Washington that simultaneously profoundly differed from the city that was home to Thomas Montgomery Gregory, Alain LeRoy Locke, Willis Richardson, and Georgia Douglas Johnson; yet it appears similarly perplexed by boundaries of race, class, confession, and ethnicity. Theater has prospered as never before within this new—yet not so new—Washington. With the nation's second-largest pre-COVID theatrical audience, five dozen or more theater companies, and plentiful opportunities for theater artists and their audiences to enjoy live performances of numerous genres, Washington's theater world has evolved well beyond the story told here.[15]

Nonetheless, some earlier characteristics remain. Theater and the performing arts generally are still about more than aesthetic accomplishment. The arts pull back the curtain on the city's distinctive urban face. A century removed from the outset of this story, Molly Smith, for example, has been driven to new creative ends by the spectacle of National Guard troops on and military helicopters over the city's streets beyond the control of local officials. Theater—even in a pandemic online form—still speaks of the need for Washingtonians to stake their claim to the city and nation. For many of the city's artistic practitioners, Willis Richardson's appeal a century ago for a theater that reveals the soul of a people rings more loudly than ever before.[16] The need to proclaim presence from the Washington stage remains compelling.

Notes

Abbreviations in Notes

AS Alan Schneider, "Schneider (Alan) Papers," Online Archives of California Collection Guide

ASR Arena Stage Records, 1950 - 2007 (C0017), Special Collections, Fenwick Library, George Mason University, Fairfax, Virginia.

FWTCR Washington Theater Club Records, Production Files, 1960-1979, Special Collections Research Center, George Washington University, Washington.

HUFLVT Howard University Founders' Library, Library Division, Vertical Files.

LSR Living Stage Records (C0277TFP), Special Collections, Fenwick Library, George Mason University, Fairfax, Virginia.

MAP Maryrose Allen Papers (Collection 160), Moorland-Spingarn Research Center, Howard University, Washington.

OVDP Owen Vincent Dodson Papers (Collection 27), Moorland-Spingarn Research Center, Howard University, Washington.

TFP Thomas C. Fichandler Papers, 1950 - 1997 (C0197), Special Collections, Fenwick Library, George Mason University, Fairfax, Virginia.

TMGP T. Montgomery Gregory Papers, (Collection 37), Moorland-Spingarn Research Center, Howard University, Washington.

UA University Archive, Moorland-Spingarn Research Center, Howard University, Washington.

ZFP Zelda Fichandler Papers, 1950 - 2000 (C0010), Special Collections, Fenwick Library, George Mason University, Fairfax, Virginia.

Introduction

1 Refrain from "Washington, DC," This originally was recorded in Gil Scott-Heron's 1982 album, Moving Target, released under the Arista

Label. Subsequently, it was published by White Metal Music, Ltd., in 1994, and is available on Gil Scott-Heron's album Minister of Information, released in compact disc format by Peak Top Records in 1994.

2   Tamara Lizette Brown, "Lingering Lights from America's Black Broadway: Negro Renaissance to the Black Arts Movement, African-American Concert-Theatrical Dance in Washington, D.C.," PhD diss., Howard University, Washington, 2004, 53.

3   Program for *Rachel*, Washington, March 3–4, 1916, TMGP, box 4, folder 131.

4   Errol Hill, "Introduction," in *The Theater of Black Americans: A Collection of Critical Essays*, ed. Errol Hill (New York: Applause Theatre and Cinema Books, 1980), 1–11, at 2–3.

5   Jacqueline Moore, *Leading the Race: The Transformation of the Black Elite in the Nation's Capital, 1880–1920* (Charlottesville: University of Virginia Press, 1999).

6   Hazen D. Turner, "A History of the District of Columbia Branch of the National Association for the Advancement of Colored People, 1913–1950," PhD diss., University of Maryland, College Park, 1954; Lewis Newton Walker Jr., "The Struggle and Attempts to Establish Branch Autonomy and Hegemony: A History of the District of Columbia Branch National Association for the Advancement of Colored People, 1912–1942," PhD diss., University of Delaware, Newark, 1979.

7   Angelina W. Grimké, *Rachel: A Play of Protest* (Boston: Cornhill Company, 1916).

8   Program for Rachel.

9   Koritha Mitchell, *Living with Lynching: African American Lynching Plays, Performance, and Citizenship, 1890–1930* (Urbana: University of Illinois Press, 2011).

10   Henry D. Miller, *Theorizing Black Theatre. Art Versus Protest in Critical Writings, 1898–1965* (Jefferson, NC: McFarland & Company, 2011), 51–85.

11   Miller, 224.

12   Miller, 75.

13   Miller, 7–20.

14   Jeffrey C. Stewart, *The New Negro: The Life of Alain Locke* (New York: Oxford University Press, 2018), 276–78.

15   T. Montgomery Gregory, "Director's Report for 1921," unpublished manuscript, 1922, TMGP, box 37, folder 80, 1.

16   Stewart, *New Negro*, 276–78.

17   Mary Jo Santo Pietro, *Father Hartke: His Life and Legacy to the American Theater* (Washington: Catholic University of America Press,

2002); Kenneth Campbell, "A Descriptive History of the Origins, Development and Theoretical Bases of Theatrical Production at the Speech and Drama Department of the Catholic University of America, 1937–1957," PhD diss., University of Denver, Denver, 1965, University Microfilms 66-11, 769.

18 Matthew Donald Powell, "The Blackfriars Guild of New York, 1940–1972: An Experiment in Catholic Theatre," PhD diss., University of Wisconsin–Madison, 1984, University Microfilms 84-19959, 19.

19 Campbell, "Descriptive History," 40–143.

20 Santo Pietro, *Father Hartke*, 144–45.

21 Santo Pietro, 144–45, 150–54.

22 Campbell, "Descriptive History," 87–201.

23 Santo Pietro, *Father Hartke*, 159–63.

24 Santo Pietro, 163–68.

25 Campbell, "Descriptive History," 87–201.

26 Arthur Miller, "The American Theater (1955)," reprinted in *The American Stage: Writing on Theater from Washington Irving to Tony Kushner*, ed. Laurence Senelick (New York: Library of America, 2010), 548.

27 Laurence Maslon, "Essay: In the Beginning," in *The Arena Adventure: The First Forty Years*, ed. Laurence Maslon (Washington, DC: Arena Stage, 1990), 9–10; Maslon, "The 1950s," in *Arena Adventure*, ed. Maslon, 10–11; Maslon, "The 1950–51 Season," in *Arena Adventure*, ed. Maslon, 12.

28 Helen Sheehy, *Margo: The Life and Theatre of Margo Jones* (Dallas: Southern Methodist University Press, 1989).

29 This is a story told by Donatella Galella, *America in the Round: Capital, Race, and Nation at Washington, DC's, Arena Stage* (Iowa City: University of Iowa Press, 2019).

30 For further discussion of these trends and the relationship of the Southwest Redevelopment Project to them, see Chris Myers Asch and George Derek Musgrove, *Chocolate City: A History of Race and Democracy in the Nation's Capital* (Chapel Hill: University of North Carolina Press, 2017), 320–54; and Howard Gillette, *Between Justice and Beauty: Race, Planning, and the Failure of Urban Policy in Washington, DC* (Philadelphia: University of Pennsylvania Press, 1995), 163–64.

31 Ronald M. Johnson, "LeDroit Park: Premier Black Community," in *Washington at Home: An Illustrated History of Neighborhoods in the Nation's Capital*, ed. Kathryn Schneider Smith (Washington: Columbia Historical Society and Windsor Publications, 1988), 139–47.

32 Ben W. Gilbert and the Staff of the *Washington Post, Ten Blocks from the White House: Anatomy of the Washington Riots of 1968* (New York: Frederick A. Praeger, 1968), 3.

33 FWTCR, 1960–79.

34 "Meeting of the Board of Trustees, Washington Drama Society, Inc., October 21, 1972," ASR, box 104, folder 4; "Staff Meeting Minutes, May 31, 1974," in ASR, box 104, folder 11.

35 This story is told by Blair A. Ruble, *Washington's U Street: A Biography* (Washington and Baltimore: Woodrow Wilson Center Press and Johns Hopkins University Press, 2010), 219–22; and Asch and Musgrove, *Chocolate City*, 355–89.

36 Gilbert, *Ten Blocks*; and J. Samuel Walker, *Most of 14th Street Is Gone: The Washington, DC, Riots of 1968* (New York: Oxford University Press, 2018).

37 Michael Fauntroy, *Home Rule or House Rule: Congress and the Erosion of Local Governance in the District of Columbia* (Lanham, MD: University Press of America, 2003); Laura Pearlman, *Democracy's Capital: Black Political Power in Washington, DC, 1960s–1970s* (Chapel Hill: University of North Carolina Press, 2019).

38 Natalie Hopkinson, *Go-Go Live: The Musical Life and Death of Chocolate City* (Durham, NC: Duke University Press, 2012).

39 "Topper Carew's New Thing," *Washington Post*, January 10, 1969.

40 "The History Makers: Topper Carew," www.thehistorymakers.org/biography/topper-carew.

41 Roxanne Roberts, "Longtime African American Actor Robert Hooks on the State of Black Theater, Then and Now," *Washington Post,* October 26, 2018.

42 This story is told with references by Ruble, *Washington's U Street*, 249–51.

43 See the Sweet Honey in the Rock website, www.Sweethoney.com.

44 Gia Kourlas, "Louis Johnson, Dancer Who Leapt From Genre to Genre, Is Dead at 90," *New York Times*, April 15, 2020.

45 "Mission and History," Duke Ellington High School for the Performing Arts website, www.ellingtonschool.org/about/history-mission/.

46 See, e.g., Sid Smith, "Dream Time," *Chicago Tribune*, May 26, 1994; and Lawrence Bommer, "Classic 'Journey' Follows Monk to Enlightenment," *Chicago Tribune*, May 5, 1995.

47 Jeffrey R. Henig, *The George Washington University Center for Washington Areas Studies Washington Studies Series No. 9: Gentrification in Adams Morgan. Political and Commercial Consequences of Neighborhood Change* (Washington, D.C.: George Washington University, 1982), 2–3.

48 Henig, 4–6, 64–65.

49 Henig, 64–65.

50 Asch and Musgrove, *Chocolate City*, 320–54; Derek S. Hyra, *Race, Class, and Politics in the Cappuccino City* (Chicago: University of Chicago

Press, 2017); Sabiyha Prince, *African Americans and Gentrification in Washington, DC: Race, Class and Social Justice in the Nation's Capital* (New York: Routledge, 2016).

Chapter 1

1   T. Montgomery Gregory, "Director's Report for 1921," unpublished manuscript, 1922, TMGP, box 37, folder 80, 1.
2   Lester A. Walton, "The Future of the Negro on the Stage," *The Colored American Magazine*, 1903, 439–42.
3   Constance McLaughlin Green, *The Secret City. A History of Race Relations in the Nation's Capital* (Princeton, NJ: Princeton University Press, 1967), 172–75.
4   Marcia McAdoo Greenlee, "A Methodology for the Identification, Study and Evaluation of Afro-American Places," PhD diss., George Washington University, Washington, 1982.
5   Abhay Aneja and Guo Xu, "The Costs of Employment Segregation: Evidence from the Federal Government under Wilson," unpublished paper, University of California, Berkeley, School of Law and Haas School of Business (August 23, 2020).
6   Errol Hill, "Introduction," in *The Theater of Black Americans: A Collection of Critical Essays*, ed. Errol Hill (New York: Applause Theatre and Cinema Books, 1980), 1–11, at 2–3.
7   Koritha Mitchell, *Living with Lynching: African American Lynching Plays, Performance, and Citizenship, 1890–1930* (Urbana: University of Illinois Press, 2011), 9–10.
8   Mitchell, 84.
9   Mitchell, 31.
10   Mitchell, 121.
11   Mitchell.
12   Jeffrey C. Stewart, *The New Negro: The Life of Alain Locke* (New York: Oxford University Press, 2018), 276–78.
13   Miller, *Theorizing*, 21–40.
14   "T. M. Gregory Dies at 84, Former Howard Professor," *Washington Post*, November 26, 1971.
15   Conversations with Sheila Gregory Thomas, Washington, April 25, 2018, and February 15, 2019.
16   John Kelly, "In World War I, a DC Professor Fought for Black Officers' Participation," *Washington Post*, February 6, 2019.
17   Marvin McAllister, "Shakespeare Visits the Hilltop: Classical Drama and the Howard College Dramatic Club," in *Shakespearean Educations: Power, Citizenship, and Performance*, ed. Coppélia Kahn, Heather S.

Nathans, and Mimi Godfrey (Dover: University of Delaware Press, 2011), 219–46, at 239–41.

18 T. Montgomery Gregory, "Director's Report for 1921," unpublished manuscript, 1922, TMGP, box 37, folder 80, 1.

19 Rayford W. Logan, *Howard University. The First Hundred Years, 1867–1967* (New York: New York University Press, 1969).

20 David L. Lewis, *District of Columbia: A Bicentennial History* (New York and Nashville: W. W. Norton and American Association for State and Local History, 1976), 105–10.

21 Lillian G. Dabney, "History of Schools for Negroes in the District of Columbia, 1807–1946," PhD diss., Catholic University, Washington, 1949.

22 Edward Christopher Williams, *When Washington Was in Vogue: A Love Story*, with commentary by Adam McKible and Emily Bernard (New York: Amistad/HarperCollins, 2003).

23 Paul Laurence Dunbar, "Negro Society in Washington," *Saturday Evening Post*, December 1901, 9.

24 Langston Hughes, *The Big Sea,* republished in *The Collected Works of Langston Hughes, Volume 13: The Big Sea*, edited by Joseph McLared (Columbia: University of Missouri Press, 2002), 165.

25 Lead Belly (Huddie William Ledbetter), "The Bourgeois Blues," recording (New York: Musicraft Records, 1939).

26 Charles Frederick Weller, *Neglected Neighbors: Stories of Life in the Alleys, Tenements and Shanties of the National Capital* (Philadelphia: John C. Winston, 1909), 9.

27 James Borchert, *Alley Life in Washington: Family, Community, Religion, and Folklife in the City, 1850–1970* (Urbana: University of Illinois Press, 1980), 223.

28 For further discussion of this history, see Blair A. Ruble, *Washington's U Street. A Biography* (Washington and Baltimore: Woodrow Wilson Center Press and Johns Hopkins University Press, 2010), 19–41.

29 This definition of a "zone of contact" comes from Mary Louise Pratt, "Arts in the Contact Zone," *Profession 91*, 33–40, as republished by David Bartholomae and Anthony Petrosky, eds., *Reading the Lives of Others* (Boston: Bedford Books of St. Martin's Press, 1995), 180–95.

30 Thomas L. Riis, editor, *The Music and Scripts of* In Dahomey (Middleton, WI: A-R Editions, 1996); Langston Hughes, *Fine Clothes to the Jew* (New York: Alfred A. Knopf, 1927); Jean Toomer, *Cane* (New York: Liveright, 1993; orig. pub. Boni & Liveright, 1923); Edward Kennedy "Duke" Ellington, *Music Is My Mistress* (Garden City, NY: Doubleday 1973), 14–17.

31 Logan, *Howard University*, 218.

32 William Gilbert, "The Howard College Dramatic Club," *Howard University Journal* 8, no. 7 (November 11, 1910): 1.

33 "Howard Players," *Howard University Bulletin*, March 15, 1957, 16–17; Clifford L. Muse Jr., "The Howard University Players," unpublished manuscript, July 15, 2003, UA, box 7.

34 McAllister, "Shakespeare Visits," 219–25.

35 McAllister; Kenneth R. Manning, *Black Apollo of Science: The Life of Ernest Everett Just* (New York: Oxford University Press, 1983).

36 Tamara Lizette Brown, "Lingering Lights," 44–147.

37 McAllister, "Shakespeare Visits," 219–27; Denise J. Hart, "Unsung Women: How Forrest and Cook Helped Create the Howard Players Drama Club at Howard," paper presented at 60th Anniversary Conference for the Department of Theatre Arts at Howard University, Washington, 1979.

38 Muse, "Howard University Players."

39 "She Stoops to Conquer," *Howard University Journal* 6, no. 26 (April 23, 1909): 1, 4.

40 William Gilbert, "The Rivals," *Howard University Journal* 7, no. 24 (April 8, 1910): 2–3.

41 Bettye Gardner and Bettye Thomas, "The Cultural Impact of the Howard Theatre on the Black Community," *Journal of Negro History* 55, no. 4 (October 1970): 253–65.

42 Ruble, *Washington's U Street*, 136–44; Blair A. Ruble, "Seventh Street: Black DC's Musical Mecca," in *DC Jazz: Stories of Jazz Music in Washington, DC*, ed. Maurice Jackson and Blair A. Ruble (Washington, DC: Georgetown University Press, 2018), 35–36.

43 Brown, "Lingering Lights," 73.

44 Washington Dramatic Club Programs for May 31, 1912, and May 30–31, 1913, TMGP, box 4, folders 133–34.

45 Mary C. Henderson, *Theater in America: 200 Years of Plays, Players and Productions* (New York: Harry N. Abrams, 1986).

46 Mitchell Loften, *Black Drama: The Story of the American Negro in the Theatre* (New York: Hawthorn Books, 1967), 16–17.

47 Henderson, *Theater in America*, 11.

48 Eileen Southern, *The Music of Black Americans: A History* (New York: W. W. Norton, 1997), 89.

49 James V. Hatch, "Introduction: Two Hundred Years of Black and White Drama," in *The Roots of African American Drama. An Anthology of Early Plays, 1858–1938*, ed. Leo Hamalian and James V. Hatch (Detroit: Wayne State University Press, 1991, 15–37, at 18.

50 Loften, *Black Drama*, 18.

51 Jim Haskins and Hugh F. Butts, "America's Debt to the Language

of Black Americans," in *The Theater of Black Americans: A Collection of Critical Essays*, ed. Errol Hill (New York: Applause Theatre and Cinema Books, 1980), 79–88.

52   Ken Emerson, *Doo-dah! Steven Foster and the Rise of American Popular Culture* (New York: Simon & Schuster, 1997).

53   David Carlyon, *Dan Rice: The Most Famous Man You've Never Heard Of* (New York: Perseus, 2001).

54   Eleanor W. Traylor, "Two Afro-American Contributions to Dramatic Form," in *The Theater of Black Americans: A Collection of Critical Essays*, ed. Errol Hill (New York: Applause Theatre and Cinema Books, 1980), 45–60.

55   Loften, *Black Drama*, 16.

56   Carlyle Brown, *The African Company Presents Richard III* (New York: Dramatists Play Service, 1994).

57   Loften, *Black Drama*, 24–26.

58   Bernth Linfdors, *Ira Aldridge* (Rochester: University of Rochester Press, 2011).

59   Sterling A. Brown, "Negro Character as Seen by White Authors," *Journal of Negro Education* 2, no. 2 (April 1933): 179–203.

60   Joanne Gabbin, *Sterling A. Brown: Building the Black Aesthetic Tradition* (Westport, CT: Greenwood Press, 1985).

61   Maurice Peress, *Dvorak to Duke Ellington: A Conductor Explores America's Music and Its African American Roots* (New York: Oxford University Press, 2004), 31–33.

62   Peress.

63   Camille F. Forbes, *Introducing Bert Williams: Burnt Cork, Broadway, and the Story of America's First Black Star* (New York: Basic Civitas Book, 2008), 73–76.

64   Maurice Jackson, "Jazz, 'Great Black Music,' and the Struggle for Racial and Social Equality in Washington, DC," in *DC Jazz: Stories of Jazz Music in Washington, DC*, ed. Jackson and Ruble, 1–34.

65   Peress, *Dvorak to Duke Ellington*, 32–38.

66   David Gilbert, *The Product of Our Souls: Ragtime, Race, and the Birth of the Manhattan Musical Marketplace* (Chapel Hill: University of North Carolina Press, 216), 43.

67   Helen Armstead Johnson, "*Shuffle Along*: Keynote of the Harlem Renaissance," in *The Theater of Black Americans: A Collection of Critical Essays*, ed. Errol Hill (New York: Applause Theatre and Cinema Books, 1980), 79–88.

68   Johnson.

69   Forbes, *Introducing Bert Williams*, 78–85.

70   Loften, *Black Drama*, 47–53.

71 Gerald Bordman, *Musical Theatre: A Chronicle* (New York: Oxford University Press, 1978), 190.
72 Forbes, *Introducing Bert Williams*, 119–29.
73 Jackson, "Jazz."
74 Johnson, "*Shuffle Along*," 84–100.
75 Walton, "Future of the Negro."
76 Leonard Hall, "A Racial Drama Born at Howard," *Washington Daily News*, Spring 1922. Harold Bledsoe, the student lead in a play about the life of Toussant L'Overture, eventually became a lawyer and political figure in Detroit and gained notoriety as the first African American to cast a ballot in the Electoral College when he was one of the Michigan electors supporting Franklin Delano Roosevelt in 1936.
77 Kenneth MacGowan, "Negro University Has Dramatic Department on the Lines of Harvard's," *New York Globe and Commercial Advertiser*, March 26, 1921, TMGP, box 3, folder 95.
78 Stewart, *New Negro*, 1–252.
79 "Harlem Renaissance 9: Washington, DC," in *Encyclopedia of the Harlem Renaissance*, ed. Cary D. Wintz and Paul Finkelman (New York: Routledge, 2004), vol. 1, 525–28, at 526
80 Conversations with Sheila Gregory Thomas, Washington, February 15, 2019.
81 George Pierce Baker, *Dramatic Technique* (Rockville, MD: Wildside Press, 2011).
82 Baker, 252–53.
83 Stewart, *New Negro*, 303–5.
84 Hart, "Unsung Women."
85 Montgomery Gregory, "Race in Art," *The Citizen* 1, nos. 1 and 2 (1915).
86 Montgomery Gregory, "Director's Report for 1921," TMGP, box 3, folder 80.
87 Gregory, "Director's Report," TMGP, box 3, folder 77, 1.
88 "Advisory Council of the Negro Theatre," TMGP, box 2, folders 46–54.
89 "Howard Players Correspondence A–Z," TMGP, box 2, folders 47–54.
90 Letter quoted in *Playbill* for Howard Players' performance of Ridgely Torrence's *Simon, The Cyrenian* for delegates to the World Disarmament Conference on December 12, 1921, TMGP, box 2, folder 52.
91 Alain Locke, "Steps Toward a Negro Theatre," *Crisis* 24 (1922): 66–68.
92 Dorothy Chansky, *Composing Ourselves: The Little Theatre Movement and the American Audience* (Carbondale: Southern Illinois University Press, 2005).
93 Christine Rauchfuss Gray, *Willis Richardson: Forgotten Pioneer of African-American Drama* (Westport, CT: Greenwood Press, 1999), 45.
94 Edna Kenton, *The Provincetown Players and the Playwrights' Theatre, 1915–1922* (Jefferson, NC: McFarland, 2004).

95 Cecelia Moore, *The Federal Theatre Project in the American South: The Carolina Playmakers and the Quest for American Drama* (New York: Lexington Books, 2017).

96 Robert C. Benchley, "Drama," *Life*, November 3, 1921, 18.

97 ohn W. Dean, *Warren Harding* (New York: Henry Holt, 2004).

98 "World Disarmament Conference 1921 Materials," TGMP, box 2, folders 55–70.

99 "News Release: Distinguished Foreigners Witness Play by Howard University Players," December 13, 1921, TMGP, box 2, folder 70.

100 Hart, "Unsung Women."

101 The *Chicago Defender* emphasized the Players' future work in its coverage of the event; "Howard Players Stage New Race Drama," *Chicago Defender*, December 24, 1921.

102 Programs, TMGP, box 5, folders 71-105; box 4, folders 135–39; and HUFLVF.

103 Robert M. Dowling, *Eugene O'Neill: A Life in Four Acts* (New Haven, CT: Yale University Press, 2014).

104 Eugene O'Neill, *The Emperor Jones* (Mineola, NY: Dover, 2011).

105 "Reviews of Emperor Jones," TMGP, box 4, folder 131.

106 "Reviews of Emperor Jones."

107 "Reviews of Emperor Jones."

108 Poster for *Emperor Jones*, March 28–April 2, 1921, TMGP, box 15.

109 "Players Repeat *Emperor Jones*; Howard University Amateurs Present O'Neill's Play at Belasco Again," *Washington Herald*, April 22, 1921.

110 "Howard Students in Stirring Play Led by C. S. Gilpin, Noted Actor, They Delight Big Audience at Belasco," *Washington Evening Star*, March 29, 1921.

111 Earle Dorsey, "Mr. Gilpin Enters," *Washington Herald*, March 27, 1921.

112 "Howard Players Give Weird Play," *Washington Evening Star*, April 2, 1921.

113 "Players Repeat *Emperor Jones*."

114 Stewart, *New Negro*, 304.

115 Personal communication, the Rev. Dr. Sandra Butler-Truesdale, Washington, September 22, 2020.

116 Personal communication, the Rev. Dr. Sandra Butler-Truesdale, Washington, October 12, 2020.

117 Undated "Director's Report" by Montgomery Gregory, probably from 1922, TMGP, box 3, folder 77.

118 Programs Posters, and manuscripts, TMGP, box 4, folders 107–13; collection 37, box 5, folders 71–105; Muse, "Howard University Players."

119 Stewart, *New Negro*, 303–6.
120 Zachary R. Williams, *In Search of the Talented Tenth: Howard University Public Intellectuals and the Dilemmas of Race, 1926–1970* (Columbia: University of Missouri Press, 2009), 20–34.
121 Ruble, *Washington's U Street*, 83–88.
122 Jacqueline Goggin, *Carter G. Woodson: A Life in Black History* (Baton Rouge: Louisiana State University Press, 1997), 50–57.
123 Gray, *Willis Richardson*, 17–18.
124 Clifford L. Muse Jr., "The Howard University Players," unpublished manuscript, July 15, 2003, UA, box 7.
125 Resignation letter of Cleon Throckmorton, June 7, 1922, TMGP, box 2, folder 53.
126 T. M. Gregory Dies at 84, Former Howard Professor," *Washington Post*, November 26, 1971.
127 Montgomery Gregory, "Our Book Shelf: '*Cane*,'" *Opportunity. A Journal of Negro Life* 1, no. 12 (December 1923): 374–75.
128 "Negro's Opportunity in Drama Here, Says Gregory in Lyceum Lecture," *Trenton Evening Times*, April 22, 1925.
129 T. Montgomery Gregory, "The Negro in Drama," in *Encyclopedia Britannica*, 14th edition, vol. 17 (New York: Encyclopedia Britannica Corporation, 1929).
130 "T. M. Gregory Dies."
131 Conversation with Sheila Gregory Thomas, Washington, February 15, 2019.
132 Alain LeRoy Locke and Thomas Montgomery Gregory, *Plays of Negro Life: A Source-Book of Native American Drama* (New York: Harper & Brothers, 1927).
133 Conversation with Sheila Gregory Thomas, Washington, February 15, 2019.
134 Conversation with Sheila Gregory Thomas, Washington, April 25, 2018.
135 *So You Think You Know Who You Are*, season 7, episode 1, April 3, 2016.
136 "T. M. Gregory Dies."
137 Stewart, *New Negro*, 477.
138 Stewart, 301.
139 Eugene C. Homes, "Alain LeRoy Locke: A Sketch," *Phylon: The Atlanta University Review of Race and Culture* 20, no. 1 (1959): 82–89.
140 Stewart, *New Negro*, 354–403.
141 Stewart, 403–7, 420–29.
142 Stewart, 407–19.
143 Stewart, 453–76.

144 James A. Miller, "Black Washington and the New Negro Renaissance," in *Composing Urban History and the Constitution of Civic Identities*, ed. John J. Czaplicka, Blair A. Ruble, and Lauren Crabtree (Baltimore: Johns Hopkins University Press, 2003), 219–41, at 222.

145 Stewart, *New Negro*, 477–78.

146 Stewart, 477.

147 Stewart, 492–536.

148 Richard Kluger, *Simple Justice: The History of* Brown v. Board of Education *and Black America's Struggle for Equality* (New York: Alfred A. Knopf, 1976), 124.

149 Jonathan Scott Holloway, *Confronting the Veil: Abram Harris, Jr., E. Franklin Frazier, and Ralph Bunche, 1919–1941* (Chapel Hill: University of North Carolina Press, 2002), 48–49.

150 Alain Locke, "The Negro and the American Theatre" (1927), as quoted by Larry Neal in "Into Nationalism, Out of Parochialism," in *The Theater of Black Americans: A Collection of Critical Essays*, ed. Errol Hill (New York: Applause Theatre and Cinema Books, 1980), 293–300, at 294.

151 Alain Locke, "The Message of the Negro Poets," *Carolina Magazine* 58, no. 7 (May 1928): 5–15.

152 Stewart, *New Negro*, 539–43.

153 As quoted by Stewart, 539.

154 Alain Locke, "Steps Toward a Negro Theatre," *Crisis* 24 (1922): 66–68.

155 Nellie McKay, "Black Theater and Drama in the 1920s: Years of Growing Pains," *Massachusetts Review* 28, no. 4 (1987): 615–26.

156 Loften, *Black Drama*, 64-72.

157 Sister M. Francesca Thompson, OSF, "The Lafayette Players, 1917–1932, in *The Theater of Black Americans: A Collection of Critical Essays*, ed. Errol Hill (New York: Applause Theatre and Cinema Books, 1980), 211–30.

158 Bernard L. Peterson, *The African American Theatre Directory, 1816–1960* (Westport, CT: Greenwood Press, 1997).

159 Loften, *Black Drama*, 91–110.

160 H. L. Mencken, "Contribution to 'The Negro in Art. A Symposium,'" *The Crisis* 31 (1926): 220.

161 Susan Quinn, *Furious Improvisation: How the WPA and a Cast of Thousands Made High Art Out of Desperate Times* (New York: Walker & Company, 2008); Elizabeth A. Osborne, *Staging the People: Community and Identity in the Federal Theatre Project* (New York: Palgrave, 2011).

162 Miller, *Theorizing*, 103.

163 Ronald Ross, "The Role of Blacks in the Federal Theatre, 1935–1939," in *The Theater of Black Americans: A Collection of Critical Essays*, ed.

Errol Hill (New York: Applause Theatre and Cinema Books, 1980), 231–46.

164 C. W. E. Bigsby, "Three Black Playwrights: Loften Mitchell, Ossie Davis, Douglas Turner Ward," in *The Theater of Black Americans: A Collection of Critical Essays*, ed. Errol Hill (New York: Applause Theatre and Cinema Books, 1980), 148–67.

165 Richard France, *Orson Wells on Shakespeare: The WPA and Mercury Theatre Playscripts* (New York: Routledge, 2002).

166 *A Study Guide for Clifford Odets's "Waiting for Lefty"* (Farmingham Hills, MI: Gale Study Guides, 2019).

167 Hallie Flanagan, *Arena: The History of the Federal Theatre* (reprint edition) (New York: Benjamin Blom, 1965; orig. pub. 1940).

168 Loften, *Black Drama*, 103.

169 Ross, "Role of Blacks."

170 Ross, 100–110; Miller, *Theorizing*, 116-122; Edith J. R. Isaacs, "The Negro in American Theatre," *Theatre Arts* 25, no. 8 (1942): 539.

171 Miller, *Theorizing*, 128-131.

172 Miller, 126-128.

173 Ethel Pitts Walker, "The American Negro Theatre (ANT)," in *The Theater of Black Americans: A Collection of Critical Essays*, ed. Errol Hill (New York: Applause Theatre and Cinema Books, 1980), 247–60.

174 Joanne Gabbin, *Sterling A. Brown: Building the Black Aesthetic Tradition* (Westport, CT: Greenwood Press, 1985).

175 "Obituary: Ossie Davis—Actor and Activist Against Racial Stereotyping," *The Guardian* (London), February 7, 2005.

176 Bernard L Peterson Jr., "Willis Richardson: Pioneer Playwright," *Black World* 26, no. 6 (April 1975): 40–48, 86–88.

177 Gray, *Willis Richardson*.

178 North Carolina Department of Cultural Resources, *1898 Wilmington Race Riot Commission* Report, May 31, 2006, www. history. ncdcr. gov/1898-wrrc/report. Also see David Zucchino, *Wilmington's Lie: The Murderous Coup of 1898 and the Rise of White Supremacy* (New York: Atlantic Monthly Press, 2020).

179 Gray, *Willis Richardson*, 7–31.

180 Miller, *Theorizing*, 69.

181 George-McKliney Martin, "Willis Richardson," in *The Black Renaissance in Washington* (Washington: DC Public Library Lab, 2018).

182 Martin.

183 Willis Richardson, "The Hope of a Negro Drama," *Crisis* 21 (1919): 338–39, at 338.

184 Gray, *Willis Richardson*, 113–14.

185 Martin, "Willis Richardson."

186 Willis Richardson, "Hope."

187 Gray, *Willis Richardson*, 58–59.

188 Leo Hamalian and James V. Hatch, eds., *The Roots of African American Drama: An Anthology of Early Plays, 1858–1938*, 159–85.

189 Robertson Davies, *Happy Alchemy. On the Pleasures of Music and the Theatre* (New York: Viking, 1997), p. 351.

190 These themes are explored by Ruble, *Washington's U Street.*

191 Willis Richardson, ed., *Plays and Pageants from Life of the Negro* (republished edition) (Jackson: University Press of Mississippi, 1993).

192 Willis Richardson and May Miller, eds., *Negro History in Thirteen Plays* (Washington: Associated Publishers, 1935).

193 Miller, *Theorizing*, 92-93.

194 Hamalian and Hatch, *Roots of African American Drama*, 161.

195 Gray, *Willis Richardson*, 17–18.

196 Program for *The Chip Woman's Fortune and Salomé*, Howard Theatre, Washington, April 1, 1923, TMGP, box 4, folder 132.

197 Gray, *Willis Richardson*, 17–18.

198 Percy Hammond, "The Theaters: The Ethiopian Art theater," *New York Tribune*, undated, TMGP, box 3, folder 97.

199 Peterson, "Willis Richardson."

200 Gray, *Willis Richardson*, 17–18.

201 Gray, xvii.

202 Gray, 82–84; Peterson, "Willis Richardson."

203 Peterson.

204 Willis Richardson, "The Broken Banjo," *The Crisis* 31 (1926): 225–27.

205 Gray, *Willis Richardson*, 84–85.

206 Peterson, "Willis Richardson."

207 Gray, *Willis Richardson*, 21.

208 Gray, xix.

209 Gray, 23–29.

210 Peterson, "Foreword," in "Willis Richardson," vii–xiv.

211 Mitchell, p. 150.

212 Gloria T. Hull, *Color, Sex, and Poetry: Three Women Writers of the Harlem Renaissance* (Bloomington: Indiana University Press, 1987); Judith Stephens, *The Plays of Georgia Douglass Johnson from The New Negro Renaissance to the Civil Rights Movement* (Urbana: University of Illinois Press, 2006).

213 James A. Miller, "Black Washington and the New Negro Renaissance," at 228-229.

214 Gray, *Willis Richardson*, 19.

215 Darwin T. Turner, "Langston Hughes as Playwright," in *The Theater of Black Americans: A Collection of Critical Essays*, ed. Errol Hill (New

York: Applause Theatre and Cinema Books, 1980), 136–47; and, Miller, *Theorizing*, 106-109.

216 Michael S. Harper, ed., *The Collected Poems of Sterling A. Brown* (Evanston, IL: Northwestern University Press, 1996); Mark A. Sanders, ed., *A Son's Return: Selected Essays of Sterling A. Brown* (Boston: Northeastern University Press, 1996).

217 Sterling A. Brown, "Negro Character as Seen by White Authors."

218 "James Butcher Dies," *Washington Post*, July 28, 1994.

219 Clifford L. Muse Jr., "The Howard University Players"; Rayford W. Logan, *Howard University*, 281–82.

220 Errol G. Hill and James V. Hatch, *A History of African American Theatre* (New York: Cambridge University Press, 2003), 258–61.

221 "Owen Vincent Dodson (1914–1983)," in *The Roots of African American Drama: An Anthology of Early Plays, 1858–1938*, ed. Leo Hamalian and James V. Hatch, 328–29.

222 C. Gerald Fraser, "Owen Dodson Is Dead at 68; Major Figure in Black Drama," *New York Times*, June 22, 1983; James V. Hatch, *Sorrow Is the Only Faithful One: The Life of Owen Dodson* (Urbana: University of Illinois Press, 1995), 249–50.

223 Hatch, *Sorrow*, 47–60.

224 Hatch, 60–89.

225 Hatch, 120–30.

226 Hatch, 194–97.

227 Hatch, 218–20.

228 Conversation with Sheila Gregory Thomas, February 15, 2019.

229 Hatch, *Sorrow*, 246.

230 John F. Kennedy Center for the Performing Arts, program for *Owen's Song: A Joyous Musical Celebration*, Washington, 1975.

231 Hatch, *Sorrow*, 131–43.

232 Fraser, "Owen Dodson."

233 Clifford L. Muse Jr., "The Howard University Players;" *Howard University Bulletin*.

234 Tamara Lizette Brown, "Lingering Lights," 325.

235 Brown, 156–67.

236 Brown, 167–69.

237 Brown, 169.

238 Brown, 169–71.

239 Joe Holley, "Lifelong Love of Modern Dance Took Her from Germany to DC," *Washington Post*, November 5, 2006.

240 Holley.

241 "Constitution of Howard University Modern Dance Group Within Department of Physical Education for Women," MAP, box 8, folder 11.

242 "Danced in a Dance Symposium with Sarah Lawrence College, Adelphi College, and Bennett College at Henry Street Playhouse in New York City," MAP, box 8, folder 11.
243 "Performances," MAP, box 8, folder 11.
244 "Reviews," MAP, box 8, folder 11.
245 "Teaching Materials," MAP, box 8, folder 11.
246 Brown, "Lingering Lights," 177–80.
247 Brown, 197–99.
248 Brown, 198–209.
249 "Washington-Area Obituaries of Note: Bernice Hammond Jackson, Dance Studio Founder," *Washington Post*, May 7, 2016.
250 Brown, "Lingering Lights," 200–209.
251 Brown, 221–32.
252 Patricia Sullivan, "Doris Jones, 92; Founded Integrated Ballet School in DC," *Washington Post*, March 23, 2006.
253 Ruble, *Washington's U Street*, 173–222.
254 Bettye Gardner and Bettye Thomas, "The Cultural Impact of the Howard Theatre on the Black Community," *Journal of Negro History* 55, no. 4 (October 1970): 253–65.
255 Loften, *Black Drama*, 199; Miller, *Theorizing*, 184-189; Kimberly W. Bentson, "The Aesthetic of Modern Black Drama: From MIMESIS to METHEXIX," in *The Theater of Black Americans: A Collection of Critical Essays*, ed. Errol Hill (New York: Applause Theatre and Cinema Books, 1980), 61–78.
256 Hatch, *Sorrow*, 195–204.
257 Grace C. Cooper, "Joseph A. Walker: Evolution of a Playwright," *New Directions* 2, no 4 (1975), //dh.Howard.edu/newdirections/vol2/iss4/4.
258 Miller, *Theorizing*, 143–46.
259 Geoffrey A. Wolff, "Howard University Accents the Negative in Baldwin Play," *Washington Post*, November 1965; program for *Blues for Mister Charlie*, UA, box 43.
260 Hatch, *Sorrow*, 168–72.
261 "*Hamlet* Papers," OVDP, box 4, folder 120.
262 Hatch, *Sorrow*, 170.
263 Hatch.
264 Richard L. Coe, "Negroes in 'Hamlet," *New York Times*, July 20, 1951.
265 Jay Carmody, "Howard U. 'Hamlet' Best of Its Drama Offerings," *Washington Evening Star*, July 21, 1951.
266 Lois Taylor, "Hamlet," *Washington Afro-American*, July 24, 1951.
267 Rayford W. Logan, *Howard University*, 394–95.
268 James V. Hatch, *Sorrow*, 151–64.

269 Hatch, 154–55.

270 Reviews from Scandinavian Tour, collected by US Embassy in Copenhagen, Christen Fribert, "A Dark Evening," *Københaven* [Copenhagen], September 21, 1949; Paul Gjesdahl, "The American Negro Students Received a Heart Welcome," *Arbeiderbladet* (Oslo), September 14, 1949; Henrik Neiiendam, "Negro Guest-Performance at Alle-Scenen," *Ekstrabladet* (Copenhagen), September 21, 1949]), OVDP, box 5, folder 123.

271 Hatch, *Sorrow*, 151–64.

272 Hatch, 162.

273 Hatch, 163.

274 "*Pastures'* Benefit for Colored Denied," *Washington Post*, February 11, 1933.

275 "Letter to the Editor: True Friend of the Colored Race, Washington," *Washington Post*, March 29, 1936.

276 Constance McLaughlin Green, *The Secret City: A History of Race Relations in the Nation's Capital* (Princeton, NJ: Princeton University Press, 1967).

Chapter 2

1   Reverend Gilbert V. Hartke, OP, Aside, November 1950, as quoted by Kenneth Campbell, "A Descriptive History of the Origins, Development and Theoretical Bases of Theatrical Production at the Speech and Drama Department of the Catholic University of America, 1937–1957," PhD diss., University of Denver, Denver, 1965, University Microfilms 66-11,769, 301–2.

2   Personal Communication, Richard Mennen, Baltimore, MD, December 14, 2020.

3   Mary Jo Santo Pietro, *Father Hartke: His Life and Legacy to the American Theater* (Washington: Catholic University of America Press, 2002), 157–58. For an overview of the July 1919 race riots, see Blair A. Ruble, *Washington's U Street: A Biography* (Washington and Baltimore: Woodrow Wilson Center Press and Johns Hopkins University Press, 2010), 83–88.

4   Santo Pietro, *Father Hartke*, 158–59.

5   Santo Pietro, 157–72.

6   Santo Pietro, 158–59.

7   Ruble, *Washington's U Street*, 128.

8   Ruble.

9   Santo Pietro, *Father Hartke*, 159–63.

10   Santo Pietro, 163–68.

11 Santo Pietro.

12 Santo Pietro, 159.

13 *Sing Our, Sweet Land, The Playbill*, International Theatre, New York, 1944.

14 Campbell, "Descriptive History," 145; Santo Pietro, *Father Hartke*, 163.

15 Margaret M. McGuinness and James T. Fisher, eds., *Roman Catholicism in the United States: A Thematic History* (New York: Fordham University Press, 2019).

16 Pew Research Center Religion & Public Life Study, www.Pewforum.org/religious-landscape-study/.

17 US Conference of Catholic Bishops, "Catholic Colleges and Universities in the United States," www. usccb.org/beliefs-and-teachings/how-we-teach/catholic-education/higher-education/catholic-colleges-and-universities-in-the-united-states.cfm.

18 Campbell, "Descriptive History," 1–3.

19 Sharon Samber, "After a Century, the Largest Catholic Church in North America Is Finally Complete," *USA Today*, December 9, 2017.

20 "A Catholic University: The Zeal of a Few Prelates Rewarded," *New York Times*, June 15, 1885.

21 "A Brief History of Catholic University," www.cua.edu/about-cua/history-of-CUA.cfm.

22 Chris Myers Asch and George Derek Musgrove, *Chocolate City: A History of Race and Democracy in the Nation's Capital* (Chapel Hill: University of North Carolina Press, 2017), 26–30, 65–68.

23 Margaret H. McAller, "'The Green Streets of Washington': The Experience of Irish Mechanics in Antebellum Washington," in *Urban Odyssey: A Multicultural History of Washington, DC*, ed. Francine Curro Cary (Washington: Smithsonian Institution Press, 1996), 42–62.

24 McAller, 47–50; Asch and Musgrove, *Chocolate City*, 24–26.

25 Asch and Musgrove, *Chocolate City*, 31–34.

26 Asch and Musgrove, 47–50; McAller, "Green Streets," 24–26.

27 McAller, "Green Streets," 51.

28 "Our History—Since 1858," in *St. Augustine Catholic Church* (Washington: St. Augustine Church, 2009).

29 Mona E. Dingle, "*Gemeinshcaft* and *Gemütlichkeit*: German American Community and Culture, 1850–1920," in *Urban Odyssey*, ed. Cary, 113–34.

30 McAller, "Green Streets," 53.

31 Howard Gillette Jr. and Alan M. Kraut, "The Evolution of Washington's Italian American Community," in *Urban Odyssey*, ed. Cary, 154–72.

32 Gillette and Kraut, "Evolution," 161–65.

33 Santo Pietro, *Father Hartke*, 5–17.

34 Santo Pietro, 9–13.
35 Santo Pietro, 13–22.
36 William A. Hinnebusch, *The Dominicans: A Short History* (New York: Society of St. Paul, 1975).
37 Santo Pietro, *Father Hartke*, 23–26.
38 Santo Pietro, 27–42.
39 Campbell, "Descriptive History," 1–44.
40 Maureen Murphy, "From Scapegrace to Grásta: Popular Attitudes and Stereotypes to Irish American Drama," in *Irish Theater in America: Essays on Irish Theatrical Diaspora*, ed. John P. Harrington (Syracuse: Syracuse University Press, 2009), 19–37.
41 Benjamin A. Baker, *A Glance at New York in 1848: A Musical Farce— Complete Libretto* (New York: Theatre Arts Press, 2015).
42 David A. Wilson, *Thomas D'Arcy McGee: The Extreme Moderate, 1857– 1868* (Montreal: McGill–Queen's University Press, 2011).
43 Murphy, "From Scapegrace to Grásta."
44 John P. Harrington, "Introduction," in *Irish Theater in America: Essays on Irish Theatrical Diaspora*, ed. John P. Harrington (Syracuse: Syracuse University Press, 2009), xi–xv.
45 Christopher L. Berchild, "Ireland Rearranged: Contemporary Irish Drama and the Irish American Stage," in *Irish Theater in America*, ed. Harrington, 38–53.
46 James Leverett, "An Octoroon: The Octoroon," SohoRep website, April 1, 2014, sohorep.org/an-octoroon-an-essay-by-james-leverett.
47 Mick Moloney, "Harrigan, Hart, and Braham. Irish America and the Birth of the American Musical," in *Irish Theater in America*, ed. Harrington, 1–18.
48 As quoted by Moloney, "Harrigan," 18.
49 Matthew Donald Powell, "The Blackfriars Guild of New York, 1940– 1972: An Experiment in Catholic Theatre," Ph.D. diss., University of Wisconsin–Madison, 1984, University Microfilms 84-19959, 19.
50 Powell, 24–28.
51 Powell, 28–32.
52 Powell, 32–33.
53 Powell, 33–35.
54 Emmett Lavery, "The Catholic Theatre: New Thought on Old Form," *America*, December 5, 1936, 197.
55 Powell, "Blackfriars Guild," 36–38.
56 At the beginning of the twenty-first century, the American Shakespeare Theater in Staunton, Virginia, opened a recreation of the original indoor seventeenth-century London Blackfriars and has performed there since. Eric P. Nash, "A Virginia Theater True to Shakespeare," *New York Times*, October 21, 2001.

57 Powell, "Blackfriars Guild," 39–45.
58 Santo Pietro, *Father Hartke*, 39–45.
59 "Roy J. Deferrari: An Inventory of the Roy J. Deferrari Papers at the American Catholic History Research Center and University Archives — Biographical Note," archives.lib.cua.edu/findingaid/deferrai.cfm.60
60 Santo Pietro, *Father Hartke*, 45–49.
61 Campbell, "Descriptive History," 1–26.
62 Powell, "Blackfriars Guild," 52–60.
63 Powell, 300–318.
64 Powell, 307–11.
65 Powell, 308–18.
66 Powell.
67 Powell, 316–18.
68 Santo Pietro, *Father Hartke*, 53–55; Campbell, "Descriptive History," 24–25.
69 Campbell, "Descriptive History," 37–38.
70 Santo Pietro, *Father Hartke*, 53–63.
71 Santo Pietro.
72 Santo Pietro; Campbell, "Descriptive History," 14–15.
73 Santo Pietro, *Father Hartke*, 59–60.
74 Santo Pietro, 60–62.
75 Santo Pietro, 62–63.
76 Santo Pietro, 66–67.
77 Santo Pietro.
78 Santo Pietro, 67–68.
79 Campbell, "Descriptive History," 33–43.
80 Campbell, 43–55.
81 This account taken from Campbell, 77–86; and Santo Pietro, *Father Hartke*, 69–74.
82 Santo Pietro, *Father Hartke*, 74.
83 Santo Pietro, 76.
84 AS, Background, oac.cdlib.org/findaid/ark/13030/t2489n8v3/.
85 Campbell, "Descriptive History," 73.
86 Campbell, 40–143.
87 Santo Pietro, *Father Hartke*, 144–45.
88 Santo Pietro, 144–45, 150–54.
89 A complete list of Catholic University Theater Productions between 1937 and 1957 is given by Campbell, "Descriptive History," 359–68.
90 Toril Moi, *Henrik Ibsen and the Birth of Modernism: Art, Theater, Philosophy* (New York: Oxford University Press, 2006), 34–36.
91 This account is based on that of Campbell, "Descriptive History," 103–5. Nelson Bell's review appeared in the *Washington Post*, and

Jay Carmody's review appeared in *Washington Star*, both on April 2, 1945.

92   Campbell, "Descriptive History," 133.

93   Kyle Gillette, *Thornton Wilder's "The Skin of Our Teeth"* (New York: Routledge, 2016).

94   As quoted by Campbell, "Descriptive History," 179.

95   Campbell.

96   James Lardner, "Alan Schneider's 25 Years of Staging Beckett and 'Waiting for Godot,'" *Washington Post*, March 15, 1981.

97   Campbell, "Descriptive History," 296–315.

98   Santo Pietro, *Father Hartke*, 103–9.

99   Santo Pietro, 109–15.

100   Santo Pietro, 116–18.

101   Santo Pietro, 117–30.

102   Campbell, "Descriptive History," 202–16.

103   Campbell.

104   National Players Website, www. nationalplayers.org.

105   Campbell, "Descriptive History," 226.

106   Campbell, 227–45; Santo Pietro, *Father Hartke*, 216–30.

107   Santo Pietro, 146–49.

108   Santo Pietro, 155–56.

109   Santo Pietro, 203–15.

110   Campbell, "Descriptive History," 270–95.

111   Campbell, 270–80; Santo Pietro, *Father Hartke*, 234–37.

112   Santo Pietro, 234–37.

113   Campbell, "Descriptive History," 281–95.

114   Santo Pietro, *Father Hartke*, 241.

115   Santo Pietro, 242–44.

116   Santo Pietro, 197.

117   "Obituary: Joseph A. Walker, Jr., 67, Tony-Winning Playwright," *Washington Times*, February 3, 2003.

118   Frank Rich, "The Drama Critic Who Made the Pulse Race," *New York Times*, October 20, 1996.

119   For further discussion of this decline, see Hillary Miller, *Drop Dead. Performance in Crisis, 1970s New York* (Evanston, IL: Northwestern University Press, 2016), 55–76.

120   Walter Kerr, *Journey to the Center of the Theater* (New York: Alfred A. Knopf, 1979), xi.

121   Maurice Harmon, "Introduction," in *No Author Better Served: The Correspondence of Samuel Beckett & Alan Schneider*, ed. Maurice Harmon (Cambridge, MA: Harvard University Press, 1998), vii–xvi.

122   John P. Harrington, "Beckett and America," in *Irish Theater in America*, ed. Harrington, 114–23.

123 John Lahr, *Joy Ride: Show People and Their Shows* (New York: W. W. Norton, 2015), 399.

124 Letter from Alan Schneider to Samuel Beckett, February 13, 1973, in *No Author Better Served*, 301–4.

125 Campbell, "Descriptive History," 171–73.

126 Santo Pietro, *Father Hartke*, xiii.

127 Santo Pietro, 245–332.

128 Sabiyha Prince, *African Americans and Gentrification in Washington, DC: Race, Class and Social Justice in the Nation's Capital* (New York: Routledge, 2016), 22–23.

129 Santo Pietro, *Father Hartke*, 345.

130 Program for Gala Evening Honoring Father Gilbert V. Hartke's 50 Years at Catholic University, Shoreham Hotel, Washington, April 12, 1985, in Zelda Fichandler Papers (C0010), Special Collections, Fenwick Library, George Mason University, Fairfax, VA, box 70, folder 19 ("Father Hartke").

131 Santo Pietro, *Father Hartke*, 357–63.

132 Santo Pietro, 255–69.

133 Santo Pietro, 295–307.

134 Santo Pietro, 307–13.

135 Santo Pietro, 23–26.

136 Santo Pietro, 172, 231.

137 William McCleery, *Good Morning, Miss Dove: A Play in Three Acts* (New York: Samuel French, 1963; reprinted 1991).

138 McCleery, 264–65.

139 Private communication, Philip Arnoult, Baltimore, October 12, 2018.

140 Santo Pietro, *Father Hartke*, 311–13.

141 Santo Pietro, 170–72; "Timeline for S.S. *Potomac*," in Zelda Fichandler Papers (C0010), Special Collections, Fenwick Library, George Mason University, Fairfax, VA, box 65, folder 3 ("S.S. *Potomac*").

142 "Drama Department Becomes Part of New School," June 5, 2018, Catholic University website; this article is no longer available on the website; but see "Welcome to Catholic University's Newest School" at https://arts.catholic.edu/.

Chapter 3

1 Zelda Fichandler, "Introduction," in The Arena Adventure: The First Forty Years, ed. Laurence Maslon (Washington: Arena Stage, 1990), 6–8, at 8.

2 Zelda Fichandler, "Introduction," 7.

3 Laurence Maslon, "Essay: In the Beginning," in *Arena Adventure*, ed.

Maslon, 9–10; Maslon, "The 1950s," in *Arena Adventure*, ed. Maslon, 10–11; Maslon, "The 1950–51 Season," in *Arena Adventure*, ed. Maslon, 12.

4   "Timeline for S.S. Potomac," in Zelda Fichandler Papers (C0010), Special Collections, Fenwick Library, George Mason University, Fairfax, VA, box 65, folder 3 ("S.S. Potomac").

5   Laurence Maslon, "Essay," in *Arena Adventure*, ed. Maslon, 9–10.

6   Mary Jo Santo Pietro, *Father Hartke: His Life and Legacy to the American Theater* (Washington: Catholic University of America Press, 2002), 170–72; "Timeline for *S.S. Potomac*."

7   The area near the Carnegie Library on the edge of downtown had once served as an important and stable neighborhood before entering a prolonged period of decline beginning before Arena arrived. See Sabiyha Prince, *African Americans and Gentrification in Social Justice in Washington, D.C.: Race, Class and Social Justice in the Nation's Capital* (New York: Routledge, Taylor & Francis Group, 2016), 66–68.

8   Santo Pietro, *Father Hartke*, 170–72.

9   Maslon, "Essay," 9–10.

10   Dennis Kennedy, *The Oxford Encyclopedia of Theatre and Performance* (New York: Oxford University Press, 2003), 456–66.

11   Elizabeth A. Osborne, *Staging the People: Community and Identity in the Federal Theatre Project* (New York: Palgrave, 2011).

12   Helen Sheehy, *Margo: The Life and Theatre of Margo Jones* (Dallas: Southern Methodist University Press, 1989).

13   Maslon, "Essay."

14   "Edward Mangum Dies at 87," *Washington Post*, January 13, 2001.

15   Maslon.

16   Laurence Maslon, "1950–51 Season," in Maslon, *Arena Adventure*, ed. Maslon, 12.

17   Laurence Maslon, "1950s," in *Arena Adventure*, ed. Maslon, 10–11.

18   "Box Office Report for 1950," ASR, box 25, folder 34.

19   Maslon, "1950s."

20   "April 18, 1952, Resignation Letter from Edward Mangum," ASR, box 103, folder 1.

21   Paul Harris, "Obituary: Edward Mangum," *Washington Post*, January 18, 2001.

22   Santo Pietro, *Father Hartke*, 171–72.

23   "In the Process Series, 1978," ASR, box 17, folder 7, 9.

24   Santo Pietro, *Father Hartke*, 171–72.

25   "Arena Stage, Inc., 1950–56, Quarterly Financial Statements," ASR, box 24, folder 42.

26   "Corporate Donors, ASR, boxes 24 and 25.

27   Zelda Fichandler, "Arena Stage: Future Plans, 1953," ASR, box 17, folder 4.

28   Fichandler, "Arena Stage: Future Plans."
29   Zelda Fichandler, "Report to the Stockholders of Arena Stage, Inc., by Zelda Fichandler, Managing Director, on the Necessary Expansion of Arena Stage, June 8, 1955," ASR, box 103, folder 1, 2–3.
30   Fichandler, "Report to the Stockholders."
31   "Arena Stage Handbook, circa 1980," ASR, box 15, folder 7.
32   "Minutes of a Special Telephone Meeting of the Board of Directors, Arena Stage, Inc., July 29, 1955," ASR, box 103, folder 3.
33   "Minutes of a Regular Meeting of the Board of Directors, Arena Stage, Inc., March 9, 1956" and "Minutes of a Regular Meeting of the Board of Directors, Arena Stage, Inc., April 17, 1956," ASR, box 103, folder 3.
34   "November 19, 1957, Letter from Albert M. Berkowitz, Secretary, to All Stockholders," ASR, box 103, folder 3.
35   "Minutes of a Special Meeting of Stockholders, Arena Stage, Inc., December 2, 1957"; "Incorporation of Arena Enterprises, Inc., in Washington, D.C., August 8, 1956"; "Report of the Managing Director, Arena Stage, Meeting of Board of Directors, January 15, 1957"; "Board of Directors Memorandum to Stockholders of Arena Enterprises / Arena Stage, June 19, 1958"; and "Minutes of Board Meeting, The Washington Drama Society, Inc., May 7, 1959" — all ASR, box 103, folder 3.
36   "Book I: The Washington Drama Society Meeting Minutes, Part 1 of 5, 1959–1961," ASR, box 103, folder 7.
37   "Minutes of the Sixth General Membership Meeting of the Washington Drama Society, June 14, 1965," ASR, box 103, folder 8.
38   "Managing Director's Report, January 4, 1956" and "Minutes of Regular Meeting of the Board of Directors, Arena Stage, Inc., May 28, 1956," ASR, box 103, folder 1.
39   "Minutes of Regular Meeting of the Board of Directors, Arena Stage, Inc., August 7, 1956," ASR, box 103, folder 1.
40   "Arena Stage Corp. Info, 1960," ASR, box 24, folder 40.
41   Laurence Maslon, "The 1956–57 Season," in Arena Adventure, ed. Maslon, 20.
42   Chris Myers Asch and George Derek Musgrove, "Not Gone, Not Forgotten: Struggling over History in a Gentrifying DC," Washington Post, October 19, 2012.
43   "Arena Stage Handbook, circa 1980."
44   "Arena Stage Handbook, circa 1980."
45   "Letter from Zelda Fichandler to Stockholders, October 15, 1958," ASR, box 14, folder 5.
46   "Letter from Zelda Fichandler to F. Cowles "Stirck" Strickland, March 4, 1959," ASR, box 4, folder 7.

47   "Arena Stage Corp., Inc., 1960," ASR, box 24, folder 40.

48   "Exhibit B: Statement and Purposes of Washington Drama Society, Inc. (Undated c. 1950s)," ASR, box 60, folder 9, 1.

49   "Exhibit B," 3.

50   "Exhibit B," 6.

51   "Exhibit B," 17–19.

52   "Exhibit B," 26.

53   "Exhibit B," 27.

54   Joseph Wesley Zeigler, *Regional Theatre: The Revolutionary Stage* (New York: Da Capo Press, 1977).

55   League of Regional Theatres website (http://lort.org/); Richard Zoglin, "Bigger Than Broadway," *Time,* May 27, 2003.

56   Zeigler, *Regional Theatre.*

57   As reported by Donatella Galella, *America in the Round: Capital, Race, and Nation at Washington, DC's, Arena Stage* (Iowa City: University of Iowa Press, 2019), 36.

58   Alain Locke, "Steps Toward a Negro Theatre," *Crisis* 24 (1922): 66–68.

59   Jeffrey C. Stewart, *The New Negro: The Life of Alain Locke* (New York: Oxford University Press, 2018), 477.

60   Galella, *America in the Round,* 4–5.

61   "Arena Enterprises, Inc., Dissolution, 1960," ASR, box 24, folder 33.

62   Laurence Maslon, "The New Building," in *Arena Adventure,* ed. Maslon, 26–27.

63   "Press Conference with Harry Weese for the Washington Drama Society to Present the Building Model and Plans," March 10, 1960, ASR, box 14, folder 6.

64   This is from a 1957 editorial, as quoted by Howard Gillette Jr., *Between Justice and Beauty: Race, Planning, and the Failure of Urban Policy in Washington, DC* (Baltimore: Johns Hopkins University Press, 1995), 163.

65   For further discussion of these trends and the relationship of the Southwest Redevelopment Project to them, see Chris Myers Asch and George Derek Musgrove, *Chocolate City: A History of Race and Democracy in the Nation's Capital* (Chapel Hill: University of North Carolina Press, 2017), 320–54. Concerning the more general process of Gentrification and its interrelationship with home rule, see Sabiyha Prince, *African Americans and Gentrification*; and Lauren Pearlman, *Democracy's Capital. Black Political Power in Washington, 1960s–1970s* (Chapel Hill: University of North Carolina Press, 2019).

66   Ronald M. Johnson, "LeDroit Park: Premier Black Community," in *Washington at Home: An Illustrated History of Neighborhoods in the Nation's Capital,* ed. Kathryn Schneider Smith (Washington, DC: Columbia Historical Society and Windsor Publications, 1988), 139–47.

67   Ben W. Gilbert and the Staff of the *Washington Post, Ten Blocks from the White House: Anatomy of the Washington Riots of 1968* (New York: Frederick A. Praeger, 1968), 3.

68   Zachery M. Shrag, "The Freeway Fight in Washington, DC: The Three Sisters Bridge in Three Administrations," *Journal of Urban History* 30, no. 5 (2004): 648–73.

69   DC History Curriculum Project, *City of Magnificent Intentions: A History of the District of Columbia* (Washington, DC: Intac, 1983), 438.

70   Carl Abbott, "Dimensions of Regional Change in Washington, DC," *American Historical Review* 95, no. 5 (1990): 1367–93; Dennis E. Gale, *Washington, DC: Inner-City Revitalization and Minority Suburbanization* (Philadelphia: Temple University Press, 1987), 12.

71   Robert Manning, "Multicultural Washington, DC: The Changing Social and Economic Landscape of a Post-Industrial Metropolis," *Ethnic and Racial Studies* 21, no. 2 (1998): 328–54, at 338.

72   "In the Process," ASR, box 17, folder 7, 27.

73   Abbott, "Dimensions," 1376–77. For further discussion of these trends, see Blair A. Ruble, *Creating Diversity Capital: Transnational Migrants in Montreal, Washington, and Kyiv* (Washington and Baltimore: Woodrow Wilson Center Press and Johns Hopkins University Press, 2005), 68–76.

74   Duane R. Taylor, *Home Rule in the District of Columbia: The First 500 Days* (Washington: University Press of America, 1977).

75   Elliot Liebow, *Tally's Corner: A Study of Negro Streetcorner Men* (Boston: Little, Brown, 1967), 17–18.

76   Sam Smith, *Captive Capital: Colonial Life in Modern Washington* (Bloomington: Indiana University Press, 1974), 16–17.

77   Paul K. Williams and Gregory J. Alexander with the Southwest Neighborhood Assembly, *Images of Modern America: Southwest, DC* (Charleston: Arcadia Publishing, 2017); George W. Carey, Leonore Macomber, and Michael Greenberg, "Educational and Demographic Factors in the Urban Geography of Washington, DC," *Geographical Review* 58, no. 4 (1968): 515–37.

78   Gillette, *Between Justice and Beauty*, 163.

79   Jerome S. Paige and Margaret M. Reuss, *Safe, Decent, and Affordable: Citizen Struggles to Improve Housing in the District of Columbia, 1890–1982*, Studies in D.C. History and Public Policy 6 (Washington: Center for Applied Research and Urban Policy, University of the District of Columbia, 1983), 20.

80   Paige and Reuss.

81   DC History Curriculum Project, *City of Magnificent Intentions*, 460–61.

82   Gillette, *Between Justice and Beauty*, 163–64.

83   Gillette.

84   Gillette, 163; DC History Curriculum Project, *City of Magnificent Intentions*, 463.

85   Neal Pierce, private communication, February 12, 2019.

86   Williams and Alexander, *Images*. This is also evident on the organization's website, www.swdc.org.
87   "Building and Show Research Publicity," ASR, box 120, folder 9.
88   Robert Sharoff, "On the Life and Work of Chicago Architect Harry Weese," *Chicago Magazine*, July 7, 2010.
89   Sharoff.
90   "Program. Arena Stage 1961–1962: First Season in the New Theater. The Caucasian Chalk Circle, October 30–November 26, 1961)," ASR, box 147.
91   The voluminous correspondence between Weese and Zelda Fichandler concerning the building of the new Arena Stage is found in several files in ASR boxes 192, 193, 194, and 195. Weese's undated memo to file, titled "Notes on the Arena Stage Building," is particularly insightful; box 192, file 6.
92   Maslon, "New Building," 26–27; "The New Building," ASR, box 117, folders 1–8.
93   Richard L. Coe, "Washington's Arena Stage," *Gentlemen's Quarterly* 32, no. 1 (March 1962); Jay Carmody, "A Dream Comes Vividly True," *Sunday Star*, November 3, 1961. Also see the additional coverage in newspapers ranging from the *Dallas Morning News* to the *New York Times* and *Washington Post*, as contained in "SW Arena History (Building), 1960–61," ASR, box 192, folder 6.
94   Maslon, "New Building,"
95   Maslon.
96   Laurence Maslon, "Essay: The 1960s," in *Arena Adventure*, ed. Maslon, 24–25.
97   Maslon, 24.
98   "New Building," 26.
99   Maslon, "Essay: The 1960s," 25.
100 Maslon, 24.
101 Kenneth Campbell, "A Descriptive History of the Origins, Development and Theoretical Bases of Theatrical Production at the Speech and Drama Department of the Catholic University of America, 1937–1957," PhD diss., University of Denver, Denver, 1965, University Microfilms 66-11,769, 103–5.
102 See the discussion in chapter 3 above; and see Rocio Paola Yaffar, "Godot Is Back at Coconut Grove," *Southern Playbill*, April 26, 1996; and John Lahr, *Joy Ride: Show People and Their Shows* (New York: W. W. Norton, 2015), 399.
103 "Program: Arena Stage 1961–1962: First Season in the New Theater, 'The Time of Your Life,' May 14–June 10," ASR, box 147, folders 1–14; Alan Schneider, "The Arena Stage in London, Paris, Milan, and Washington," *Theatre Arts*, April 1957, ASR, box 170, folder 18; and, James Lardner, "Alan Schneider's 25 Years of Staging Beckett and 'Waiting for Godot,'" *Washington Post*, March 15, 1981.

104 Maurice Harmon, "Introduction," in *No Author Better Served: The Correspondence of Samuel Beckett & Alan Schneider*, ed. Maurice Harmon (Cambridge, MA: Harvard University Press, 1998), vii–xvi, at ix; Walter Kerr, "Whose Play Is It?" *New York Times Magazine*, October 12, 1969, 66–72; Mel Gussow, "Alan Schneider, 66, Director of Beckett, Dies," *New York Times*, May 4, 1984.

105 "Alan Schneider," *News from Arena Stage*, March 1973, ASR, box 89, folder 36.

106 Mell Gussow, "Alan Schneider Resigns as Head of the Julliard Theater Center, *New York Times*, March 3, 1979.

107 Laurence Maslon, "Essays: The 1970s," in *Arena Adventure*, ed. Maslon, 44–45.

108 "Arena Stage Stagebill: Two by Samuel Beckett (September 18–October 7)," ASR, box 149, folder 9.

109 Zelda Fichandler, "A Tribute to Alan Schneider," typescript dated May 22, 1984, ASR, box 89, folder 27, 4.

110 Fichandler, 3.

111 Fichandler, 8.

112 "April 20, 1974, Memo from Alan Schneider to the Deputy Committee (Halo Wines, Stanley Anderson, Howard Witt)," ASR, box 89, folder 35.

113 As mentioned in chapter 4 above. John Lahr, *Joy Ride: Show People and Their Shows* (New York: W. W. Norton, 2015), 399.

114 Alan Schneider, "Letter to Samuel Beckett, November 26, 1960," cited in *Correspondence*, ed. Harmon, 75–76.

115 Arnold Aronson, *Ming Cho Lee: A Life in Design* (New York: Theatre Communications Group, 2014).

116 Aronson, 20–33.

117 Aronson, 274–79.

118 Aronson, 208–12; Laurence Maslon, "Essay: The Making of *K2*," in *Arena Adventure*, ed. Maslon, 78–79; "Ming Cho Lee," ZFP, box 76, folder 10.

119 Aronson, *Ming Cho Lee*, 140–47.

120 David Richards, "Staging the Inner Life: Director Alan Schneider & His Theater of Humanity," *Washington Post*, May 4, 1984.

121 Laurence Maslon, "The 1961–62 Season," in *Arena Adventure*, ed. Maslon, 29.

122 "Programs, Arena Stage 1961–1962: First Season in the New Theater— 'The American Dream' and 'What Shall We Tell Caroline' (November 28–December 25)," ASR, box 147, folder 11.

123 "Programs. Arena Stage, 1950–51," ASR, box 147, folder 1; Maslon, "1950–51 Season."

124 J. D. McClatchy, "Preface," in *Thornton Wilder: Collected Plays and Writings on Theater*, ed. J. D. McClatchy (New York: Library of America, 2007).

125 Laurence Maslon, "The 1952–53 Season," in *Arena Adventure*, ed. Maslon, 14.

126 Laurence Maslon, "The 1972–73 Season," in *Arena Adventure* ed. Maslon; Aronson, *Ming Cho Lee*, 145.

127 *Arena Stage Stagebill: Our Town*, Catholic University's Hartke Theatre, Washington, September 26–27, 1973, ASR, box 149, folder 9.

128 "USSR Tour: US Department of State, 1972–1973, Contractual Documents," TFP, box 7, folder 12.

129 "September 4, 1973, letter from Mark B. Lewis, Director of Cultural Presentations, US Department of State, to John Chancellor, NBC News," TFP, box 7, folder 12; "Personnel Manifest for Tour of Russia," TFP, box 7, folder 14.

130 "April 13, 1973, Letter from Thornton Wilder to Mr. & Mrs. Fichandler," TFP, box 7, folder 14.

131 "USSR Tour, US Department of State, 1972–73, Contractual Documents," TFP, box 7, folder 12.

132 "USSR Tour, US Department of State, 1972–73."

133 "September 4, 1973, Letter from Mark B. Lewis, Director of Cultural Presentations."

134 "Essay: The Tour of Russia," in *Arena Adventure*, ed. Maslon, 52–53.

135 "Communication: Arena and Russia, 1973," ASR, box 120, folder 11.

136 "Alan Schneider Letter to Samuel Becket of July 11, 1973," in *No Author Better Served: The Correspondence of Samuel Beckett & Alan Schneider, Correspondence*, ed. Harmon, 305.

137 Laurence Maslon, "Essay: The 1968 Repertory," in *Arena Adventure*, ed. Maslon, 42.

138 Arena Stage, *Program: Our Town*, December 15, 1972–January 21, 1973; Moscow/Leningrad Program, "Vashingtonskii dramaticheskii teatr 'Arena Steidzh'" (Washington: US Department of State, 1973), ASR, box 116, folder 15.

139 "John Marriott Papers," New York Public Library Archives and Documents, http://archives.nypl.org' scm/20731.

140 "Subscription Non-Renewals," ASR, box 14, folder 9.

141 "Subscription Non-Renewals."

142 Maslon, "Essay: The 1968 Repertory."

143 Laurence Maslon, "1975–76 Season," in *Arena Adventure*, ed. Maslon, 59.

144 Galella, *America in the Round*, 46.

145 As quoted by Laurence Maslon, "Essay: The Great White Hope," in *Arena Adventure*, ed. Maslon, 38–39.

146 Maslon.

147 Maslon.

148 Geoffrey C. Ward, *Unforgivable Blackness: The Rise and Fall of Jack Johnson* (New York: Alfred A. Knopf, 2006).

149 John Eligon and Michael D.Shear, "Trump Pardons Jack Johnson, Heavyweight Boxing Champion," *New York Times*, May 24, 2018.

150 William C. Rhoden, "In Ali's Voice from the Past, a Stand for the Ages," *New York Times*, June 30, 2013. Also see the voluminous historical materials contained in *"The Great White Hope*: Dramaturgical Files," ASR, boxes 231n35.

151 Galella, *America in the Round*, 75–77.

152 *"The Great White Hope*, 1967–68, Scripts," ASR, box 404, folders 1, 3, 4, and 5.

153 Maslon, "Essay: The 1960s," 24–25; *"The Great White Hope*," ASR, box 234, folders 2, 3, and 4.

154 *"The Great White Hope*: Dramaturgy," ASR, box 231, folders 5, 7; box 232, folders 4, 5, 6, and 7; box 234, folders 1, 2, and 3; box 235, folders 1, 2, and 3; Howard Sackler, *The Great White Hope: A Drama in Three Acts* (New York: Samuel French, 1968).

155 Howard Sackler, *The Great White Hope: A Play* (New York: Dial Press, 1968); Vincent Canby, "Great White Hope Brought to Screen," *New York Times*, October 12, 1970.

156 Laurence Maslon, "Essay: The Great White Hope."

157 Maslon.

158 *Program: The Great White Hope, December 7, 1967–January 14, 1968* (Washington: Arena Stage, 1967).

159 Maslon, "Essay: The Great White Hope."

160 Laurence Maslon, "The 1965–66 Season," in *Arena Adventure*, ed. Maslon, 36.

161 Jane Alexander, *Command Performance: An Actress in the Theater of Politics* (New York: Public Affairs, 2000).

162 Laurence Maslon, "The 1966–67 Season," in *Arena Adventure*, ed. Maslon, 37.

163 Kate Stout, "Shooting Star," *United Airlines Magazine*, May 1985, 48–52.

164 James Earl Jones and Penelope Niven, *James Earl Jones: Voices and Silences* (New York: Charles Scribner's Sons, 1993), 1–89.

165 Jones and Niven, 111–15.

166 Jones and Niven, 115–23.

167 Jones and Niven, 188.

168 Jones and Niven, 189.

169 "Jane Alexander, 1970–1990: Wedding Invitation," ZFP, box 1 folder 09.

170 This account is based on reviews from the *Saturday Review, Playboy, Variety, St. Louis Review, Boston Herald Traveler, Boston Sunday Globe, Chicago Daily News, Baltimore Sun, Washington Evening Star, Washington Daily News, New Haven Register, Washington Post,* and *New York Times,* among many collected in the Arena Stage Archives. *"The Great White Hope* reviews, press, 1967–68," ASP, box 176, folder 1.

171 Walter Kerr, "You Can't Just Watch," *New York Times,* December 24, 1967.

172 Tom Donnelly, "There's a Play in Here Somewhere," *Washington Daily News,* December 14, 1967.

173 Sackler, *Great White Hope;* Galella, *America in the Round,* 62–63.

174 Clive Barnes, "Theater: 'The Great White Hope,' a Chronicle of a Modern Othello, Opens in Washington," *New York Times,* December 14, 1967.

175 Barnes.

176 *"The Great White Hope,* Reviews, Press, 1967–68," ASP, box 176, folder 1.

177 *"The Great White Hope,* 1967–1968: Performance Reports," ASR, box 535, folder 10.

178 Laurence Maslon, "Essay: The Great White Hope," in *Arena Adventure,* ed. Maslon, 38–39.

179 "Minutes of a Meeting of the Board of Trustees, Washington Drama Society, Inc., September 30, 1968," ASR, box 104, folder 3.

180 Carol Lawson, "Howard Sackler, 52, Playwright Who Won Pulitzer Prize, Dead," *New York Times,* October 15, 1982.

181 Galella, *America in the Round,* 63–64.

182 "Author of 'Great White Hope' Wins Purse, Crown," *New York Times,* May 6, 1969.

183 Sam Zolotow, "Arena Stage Fails in 'White Hope' Bid," *New York Times,* October 11, 1968.

184 Galella, *America in the Round,* 63–64.

185 "Meeting of the Board of Trustees, Washington Drama Society, Inc., May 21, 1969," ASR, box 104, folder 2.

186 Martin Gottfried, "Theater," *Women's Wear Daily* 16, no. 1 (January 1969).

187 Galella, *America in the Round,* 61.

188 Molly Smith, "Director's Notes," *Program: The Great White Hope, August 25–October 15, 2000* (Washington: Arena Stage, 2000), 16–17.

189 "Audience Response, ASR, box 1, folder 10.

190 Letter dated February 16, 1968, ASR, box 1, folder 10.

191 Cathy Connors, "Mrs. Brock Peters Memorialized Here," *New York Amsterdam News,* March 25, 1989.

192 "Letter from Zelda Fichandler to Brock Peters, February 16, 1967," ASR, box 66, folder 4.

193 "Letters from Zelda Fichandler to Brock Peters, April 13, 1967, and May 5, 1967," ASR, box 66, folder 4.

194 "Letter from Brock Peters to Zelda Fichandler, May 24, 1967," ASR, box 66, folder 4.

195 "Letter from Brock Peters to Zelda Fichandler, October 4, 1969," ASR, box 66, folder 4.

196 "Letter from Thomas C. Fichandler to Brock Peters, October 9, 1969," ASR, box 66, folder 4.

197 "Directors' Correspondence with Zelda Fichandler. 1958–1998, ASR, box 5, folders 5, 6, and 7.

198 "Letter from Ophelia S. Egypt, June 9, 1969," ASR, box 1, folder 10.

199 "Letter from W. Benson 'Bill' Terry to Tomas C. Finchandler, June 29(?), 1968," ASR, box 67, folder 1.

200 "Obituary: Chicago-Trained Actor W. Benson Terry," *Chicago Tribune*, April 3, 1968; "Obituary: W. Benson Terry; Stage, Screen, TV Character Actor," *Los Angeles Times*, April 2, 1998.

201 Handwritten résumé for W. Benson "Bill" Terry, ASR, box 67, folder 1.

202 James Earl Jones and Penelope Niven, *James Earl Jones: Voices and Silences* (New York: Charles Scribner's Sons, 1993), 189–90.

203 "Letter from W. Benson 'Bill' Terry to Tomas C. Finchandler, April 12, 1968," ASR, box 67, folder 1.

204 "Letter from W. Benson 'Bill' Terry to Tomas C. Finchandler, June 29(?), 1968," ASR, box 67, folder 1.

205 Bill Terry, "Hits and Near Misses on Broadway," *South Suburban News* (Harvey, IL), June 29, 1968.

206 Terry.

207 "Letter from W. Benson 'Bill' Terry to Tomas C. Finchandler, June 29 (?), 1968," ASR, box 67, folder 1.

208 "Program: Arena Stage 67/68 World Premiere, *The Great White Hope* by Howard Sackler (December 7, 1967–January 14, 1968)," ASR, box 148, folder 5.

209 For further discussion of these issues, see Galella, *America in the Round*, 56–86.

210 "Letter from W. Benson "Bill" Terry to Zelda Fichandler, October ?, 1988," ASR, box 148, folder 5.

211 "Letter from Zelda Fichandler to W. Benson 'Bill' Terry, October 15, 1988," ASR, box 148, folder 5.

212 Zelda Fichandler, "Arena to Create a New Inter-Racial Stage Force," *Washington Sunday Star*, June 30, 1968.

213 "Remarks by Zelda Fichandler at the Dedication of the Kreeger Theater, November 29, 1970," ASR box 25, folder 22.

214 FWTCR, 1960–79.

215 "Meeting of the Board of Trustees, Washington Drama Society, Inc.,

October 21, 1972," ASR, box 104, folder 4; "Staff Meeting Minutes, May 31, 1974," in ASR, box 104, folder 11.

216 Materials released by Arena Stage frequently claim to be "the first." However, White Washingtonians always were permitted to attend performances in "Black venues," even as African Americans could not sit among White patrons on the "other side of town." Moreover, Catholic University, as discussed above, had permitted African American patrons into a limited number of performances in the mid-1940s, which involved performances by students from Howard University.

217 Vera J. Katz, "Art and Advocacy: The Pulse of Clinton Turner Davis," *Black Masks* 11, no. 4 (November–December 1995): 5–6, 19.

218 "Audience Response," ASR, box 1, folder 10. Also see "Program: Arena Stage 1969–70, Charles Gordone's *No Place to Be Somebody* (May 28–July 5)," ASR, box 148, box 8.

219 "Audience Response," ASR, folder 1, box 11; "Directors' Correspondence with Zelda Fichandler, B-F, 1962/98" ASR, box 4, folder 5; and "Program: Arena Stage, 1970–71, Pueblo (February 26–April 4)," in ASR, box 195, folder 3.

220 "Remarks by Zelda Fichandler at the Dedication of the Kreeger Theater, November 29, 1970," ASR, box 25, folder 22.

221 "Remarks by Zelda Fichandler."

222 Laurence Maslon, "Essay: The 1970s," in *Arena Adventure*, ed. Maslon, 44.

223 Maslon, "Essay: The 1970s."

224 "Background Information, Architectural Drawings, Publicity circa 1968–70," ASR, box 194, folder 10; "Stage II: Press Kit, Kreeger Information, 1968–1970," ASR, box 194, folder 11; "Arena II Correspondence, 1969–70," ASR, box 194, folder 15.

225 Maslon, "Essay: The 1970s," 44.

226 Glenn Flowler, "David Lloyd Kreeger Dead at 81, Insurance Official and Arts Patron," *New York Times*, November 20, 1990.

227 Maslon, "Essay: The 1970s," 44; "Kreeger Dedication, 1970," ASR, box 116, folders 2 and 10.

228 Maslon, "Essay: The 1970s," 44.

229 Maslon, "Essay: The 1970s," 44; Laurence Maslon, "The Eastern European Connection," in *Arena Adventure*, ed. Maslon, 66–67. Also see the discussion by Galella, *America in the Round*, 89–122.

230 Laurence Maslon, "Essay: Special Productions," in *Arena Adventure*, ed. Maslon, 84–85.

231 "Banjo Dancing Production File," ZFP, box 10, part 1, folder 3.17.

232 "What Is the Reputation of Arena Stage with Our Audience? Undated Supporting Work for the Strategic Planning Process in 1984," ASR, box 104, folder 4.

233 Barbara Gamarekian, "Plays in Progress Sell Out to Audiences in the Capital," *New York Times*, January 21, 1976; Don Shirley, "Getting In on the Act, with Pros and Cons," *Washington Post*, January 13, 1976.

234 "Reception for Lloyd Richards and August Wilson on September 23, 1987," ZFP, box 142, folder 5.

235 "Anna Deveare Smith," ASR, box 14, folders 4.

236 Galella, *America in the Round*, 165.

237 "Arena Stage Arts in Education Group Minutes," ASR, box 105, folder 3.

238 "Remarks to Executive Committee Meeting of July 19, 1988, on 88/89 Budget," ZFP, box 142, folder 5.

239 "Senior Staff Meeting Minutes, November 1, 1988," TFP, box 39, folder 23, 1.

240 "Senior Staff Meeting Minutes," 2.

241 "Audience Response," ASR, box 1, folders 10, 11, and 14.

242 "The Washington Drama Society Meeting Minutes," ASR, box 103, folders 7 (1959–61), 8 (1962–65); box 114, folder 1 (1965–68).

243 Dolly Langdon, "A Weird Debut in Washington, DC Preserves Peter Sellars' Rep as the Theater's Turbulent Boy Wonder," *People Magazine*, June 3, 1985.

244 Aaron Grunfeld, "Why American Needs a National Theatre: But It Might Look Different Than You Think," *Playbill.*, December 21, 2015.

245 Robert D. McFadden, "Peter Sellars, Director of Theater in Kennedy Center, Takes a Leave," *New York Times*, August 10, 1986; Louise Sweeney, "For embattled Peter Sellars, an Intermission: Avant-Garde Director Plans a Busy Sabbatical," *Christian Science Monitor*, September 26, 1986.

246 "Long Range Plan, 1995," ASR, Virginia, box 17, folder 17, 1.

247 See, e.g., "Minutes of a Meeting of the Board of Trustees, Washington Drama Society, Inc., February 11, 1966," concerning the formation of United Performing Arts of Washington, bringing together the Institute of Contemporary Arts, National Ballet Company, Opera Society of Washington, Washington Performing Arts, Washington Theatre Club, and Arena Stage with Thomas Fichandler serving as Treasurer, ASR, box 104, folder 1, 1.

248 This was a turn of phrase used by Molly Smith, artistic director of Arena Stage, during a conversation, Washington, January 15, 2019.

249 Neal Pierce, private communication, February 12, 2019.

250 "Waterfront Metro Station Opening, 1988–1992," ASR, box 199, folder 11.

251 "In the Process Series, 1978," ASR, box 17, folder 7.

252 See "'Gang of Five' Meeting Minutes and Related Materials, 1984," ASR, box 104, folder 4; as well as "The 1974–75 Season," in *Arena*

Adventure, ed. 56–57; and "The 1987–88 Season," in *Arena Adventure,*
ed. 94–95.

253 Only about a quarter of Arena subscribers have consistently come
from the District of Columbia. In 1991, for example, city residents
accounted for just 24 percent of 188,200 subscription tickets and 19
percent of 86,270 single full-price tickets. The remainder of sales
were more or less evenly divided between residents of Virginia and
Maryland. This pattern is repeated throughout the late twentieth and
early twenty-first centuries. "Proposal to Philip Morris," ASR, box
17, folder 18, 27.

254 "Letter from Edward G. Winner, Supervising Director, Special
Programs, Public Schools of the District of Columbia, October 27,
1966," ASR, box 104, folder 1.

255 "Meeting of the Board of Trustees, Washington Drama Society, Inc.,
November 11, 1969," ASR, box 104, folder 2, 2.

256 Laurence Maslon, "Living Stage," in *Arena Adventure,* ed. Maslon,
34–35.

257 "Guide to the Living Stage Records, 1965–2001," in LSR.

258 "Introduction to Living Stage, 1977," ASR, box 25, folder 22.

259 Maslon, "Living Stage," 34.

260 "Meeting of the Board of Trustees, Washington Drama Society, Inc.,
January 28, 1976," ASR, box 104, folder 3, 1.

261 Maslon, "Living Stage," 34.

262 Maslon.

263 Maslon.

264 "Arena Stage Handbook circa 1980," ASR, box 15, folder 7, 16.

265 Maslon, "Living Stage," 65–81.

266 "Arena Stage Future Plan, 1984," ASR, box 15, folder 6, 12.

267 "Minutes of Retreat, April 5 and 6, 1985 (Rough Draft)," TFP, box 39,
folder 24, 11.

268 "Minutes of a Meeting of the Board of Trustees, Washington Drama
Society, Inc., October 16, 1967," and "Minutes of a Meeting of the
Board of Trustees, Washington Drama Society, Inc., November 6,
1967," ASR, box 104, folder 1.

269 "Minutes of an Informal Meeting of the Board of Trustees, Washington
Drama Society, Inc., January 19, 1978," ASR, box 104, folder 3, 2.

270 "Minutes of a Meeting of the Board of Trustees, Washington Drama
Society, Inc., February 22, 1978," ASR, box 104, folder 3, 3–4.

271 "Meeting of the Board of Trustees, Washington Drama Society, Inc.,
June 10, 1976," ASR, box 104, folder 3, 3.

272 "Meeting of the Board of Trustees, Washington Drama Society, Inc.,
October 15, 1978," ASR, box 104, folder 3, 3.

273 "Untitled Announcement, *Living Stage Love Letter,* vol. 2, no. 2
(November 1980)," 1; "Letter for Kathy Kissman, Assistant Managing

Director of the Living Stage Company to Mr. Lee Rubenstein, LGR, Inc, about Rent and Cost of Moving"; "Memorandum to the Executive Committee of the Washington Drama Society from the Living Stage Committee, February 6, 1984"—all in ZFP, box 1, folder 10.

274 "Notes from Long-Range Planning Committee, July 16, July 31, and September 11, 1985," ZFP, box 1, folder 10.

275 Blair A. Ruble, *Washington's U Street: A Biography* (Washington and Baltimore: Woodrow Wilson Center Press and Johns Hopkins University Press, 2010), 227–60.

276 "Minutes of Senior Staff Meeting on September 12, 1995," and "Minutes of Senior Staff Meeting on December 5, 1995," ASR, box 104, folder 6.

277 Minutes of Senior Staff Meeting on December 5, 1995," ASR, box 104, folder 6.

278 "A Statement of Purpose by Robert Alexander," *Living Stage Love Letter*, vol. 1, no. 4 (December 1979)," ZFP, box 1, folder 10, 8.

279 Laurence Maslon, "Cultural Diversity," in *Arena Adventure*, ed. Maslon, 102.

280 US National Advisory Commission on Civil Disorders, *The Kerner Report: The 1968 Report of the National Advisory Commission on Civil Disorders* (New York: Pantheon Books, 1968).

281 Appointed by President Lyndon B. Johnson during the summer of 1967, commission members included Otto Kerner, governor of Illinois and chair; John V. Lindsay, mayor of New York and vice chair; Edward Brooke, senator from Massachusetts; Fred R. Harris, senator from Oklahoma; James Corman, congressman from California; William McCulloch, congressman from Ohio; Charles Thornton, Litton Industries; Roy Wilkins, NAACP; I. W. Abel, United Steelworkers of America; Herbert Turner Jenkins, police chief, Atlanta, Georgia; Katherine Graham Peden, commissioner of commerce, Kentucky; and David Ginsburg, lawyer.

282 Zelda Fichandler, "Arena to Create a New Inter-Racial Stage Force," *Washington Sunday Star*, June 30, 1968.

283 "Rockefeller Foundation," ZFP, box 52, folder 11.

284 Maslon, "Essay: The 1968 Repertory," 42.

285 Fichandler, "Arena to Create a New Inter-Racial Stage Force."

286 R. H. Gardner, "New Role for Negro Actors: Arena Stage Has Ford Grant to Let Them Take White Parts," *Baltimore Sunday Sun*, September 27, 1968.

287 Bernadette Carey, "New Integrated Troupe Bows at Arena Stage," *Washington Post*, September 22, 1968.

288 Maslon, "Essay: The 1968 Repertory."

289 Galella, *America in the Round*, 50–51.

290 Galella, 50.

291 Galella, 159–67.

292 See, e.g., the correspondence found in "Subscription Non-Renewal, 1991–1992," ASR, box 14, folder 9.

293 Maslon, "Cultural Diversity."

294 Maslon.

295 Maslon.

296 "Mini-Staff Meeting Minutes, August 25, 1972," ASR, box 104, folder 11.

297 Maslon, "Cultural Diversity."

298 "Letter from Doug Wager to Clinton Turner Davis, July 6, 1997," ASR, box 4, folder 4.

299 Olivia Clement, "What It Takes to Ruin the Tony-Winning Off-Broadway New York Theatre Workshop," *Playbill*, January 8, 2018.

300 Laurence Maslon, "The 1973–74 Season," in *Arena Adventure*, ed. Maslon, 55; Laurence Maslon, "The 1976–77 Season," in *Arena Adventure*, ed. Maslon, 62.

301 Laurence Maslon, "Arena At a Glance: Artistic," in *Arena Adventure*, ed. Maslon, 104.

302 "Doug Wager and Zelda Fichandler Outgoing Correspondence, 1987," ASR, box 14, folder 15.

303 "Notes on Transition of Leadership, from Reagan Byrne, Submitted to Stephen Richard," ASR, box 14, folder 15.

304 Bruce Weber, "Zelda Fichandler, a Matriarch of Regional Theater, Dies at 91," *New York Times*, July 29, 2016.

305 "Mark Primus, ed., *Black Theatre: A Resource Guide, 1974*," ZFP, box 53, folder 17.

306 Bandi Wilkins Catanese, *Racial Transgression and the Politics of Black Performance* (Ann Arbor: University of Michigan Press, 2011), 11.

307 Vera J. Katz, "Art and Advocacy," 19.

308 Catanese, *Racial Transgression*, 12–13.

309 "Clinton Turner Davis Correspondence," ASR, box 4, folder 5.

310 Katz, "Art and Advocacy," 5.

311 Katz.

312 *The Heiress*, Arena Stage Production, Washington, February 22, 2019.

313 Joe Brown, "'Sanctuary': Worthy but Unresolved," *Washington Post*, December 6, 1988.

314 Zelda Fichandler, "Casting for a Different Truth," *American Theatre* 5, no. 2 (May 1988): 18–23, at 18.

315 Galella, *America in the Round*, 124–51.

316 Galella, 151.

317 "About The Company," Mabou Mines Website (www. maboumines. org).

318 Dan Sullivan, "Stage Review: Greek Tragedy, Gospel Singing Mix in 'Colonus,'" *Los Angeles Times*, December 6, 1985.

319 "'Script: The Gospel at Colonus,' Text by Lee Breuer, Music by Bob Telson, Lyrics by Lee Breuer and Bob Telson, Revised Performance Version, Draft 5, November 30, 1983, Brooklyn Academy of Music," ASR, box 404, folder 4.

320 See Mel Gussow, "The Gospel at Colonus," in *The New York Times Guide to the Arts of the 20th Century* (New York: Taylor & Francis, 2002), 2765–86; and see the materials contained in *"The Gospel at Colonus,"* ASR, box 404, folder 3.

321 *"The Gospel at Colonus* Wrap Files," ASR, box 535, folders 5–8; and box 560, folders 1 and 2.

322 *"The Gospel at Colonus,* Reviews and Articles, November 23–December 21, 1984," ASR, box 175, folder 17.

323 Laurence Maslon, "The 1984–85 Season: The Gospel at Colonus," in *Arena Adventure*, ed. Maslon, 86–87.

324 David Richards, "The Greeks as Gospel, 'Colonus' at Arena: Past and Present in an Exultant Musical, *Washington Post* (date unclear)," ASR, box 404, folder 3.

325 Joe Brown, "An Oedipal Conflict: Sophocles Meets a Different Kind of Chorus," *Washington Post*, November 30, 1984.

326 *"Gospel at Colonus,* 1984 Performance Reports," ASR, box 535, folder 9.

327 Courtland Milloy, "'Gospel': It's Good News," *Washington Post*, December 16, 1984.

328 "The Tony Award," in *Arena Adventure*, ed. Maslon, 60.

329 October 2014 conversation, Doug Wager with Donatella Galella, as recorded by Galella, *America in the Round*, 122–23.

330 Galella, 159–61.

331 Galella, 172–77.

332 "Laura Connors Hull, Director of Communications, 'Arena Stage Identity Redesign: Create Brief (August 1, 1997)," ASR, box 104, folder 8.

333 "Special Report: Why Nothing Can Stop Arena Stage with Molly Smith at the Helm," Theatermania.com, September 23, 2017.

334 Rebecca Paller, "From Alaska to DC with Arena Stage's New Director, Molly D. Smith," *Playbill*, February 5, 1998.

335 Caroline Jones, "Why So Many DC Plays End Up on Broadway. A History of DC's Dominant Role in the National Theater Scene," *Washington City Paper*, October 19, 2017.

336 "Leadership: Molly Smith," Arena Stage website, www.arenastage.org/about-uswhos-who/leadership.

337 Peter Marks, "'Oklahoma!' Makes a Joyful Return to Arena Stage,"

Washington Post, July 17, 2011. Also see the discerning discussion of this production by Galella, *America in the Round*, 192–217.

338 "Project Fact Sheet: The Mead Center for American Theater," Arena Stage website, www.arenastage.org.

339 Terry Ponick, "Inside Arena Stage's New Mead Center," dctheatrescene website, dctheatrescene.com/author/terry-ponick/.

340 Arielle Levin and Derek Hyra, "The Wharf: A Monumental Urban Regeneration Waterfront Development in Washington, DC," conference paper, Woodrow Wilson Center Urban Sustainability Laboratory (Washington) and the Korea Housing & Urban Guarantee Corporation (Seoul), On-Line Symposium on Urban Regeneration in Comparative Perspective, September 9, 2020, 44–45.

341 Levin and Hyra, 20–21.

342 Rachel Kurzius, "Shaw's Metro PCS Store Has Been Forced to Turn Off Its Go-Go Music, Owner Says," DCist website, dcist.com/story/19/04/08/shaws-metro-pcs-store-has-been-forced….

343 Advertisement for "Reformation, The Go-to Clothing Brand for California Cool Girls," Georgetown, 3030 M Street NW, posted on the 14th and U Streets NW Capital Bikeshare stand, April 8, 2019.

344 Sharón Clark and Yoshiko M. Herrera, "The Sunny Side of Essentialism: Race and Jazz in Contemporary Russia," paper presented at Midwest Political Science Association Conference, Chicago, April 2, 2019, 29.

345 Steven J. Diner, *Democracy, Federalism, and the Governance of the Nation's Capital, 1790–1974*, Studies in DC History and Public Policy 10 (Washington: Center for Applied Research and Urban Policy, University of the District of Columbia, 1987), 7–8, 13–14.

346 "Rent Trend Data for Washington, District of Columbia," www.rentjungle/average-rent-in-washington-rent-trends/.

347 Jane Harman, private communication, May 2, 2019.

348 Blair A. Ruble, 'Making Community Work: The Importance of the Performing Arts," in *Performing Community: Short Essays on Community, Diversity, Inclusion, and the Performing Arts* (Washington: Woodrow Wilson Center, 2014), 4–7.

349 Galella, *America in the Round*, 12.

Chapter 4

1   Roxanne Roberts, "Longtime African American Actor Robert Hooks on the State of Black Theater, Then and Now," *Washington Post*, October 26, 2018.

2   Judith A. Korey, "From Federal City College to UDC: A Retrospective

on Washington's Jazz University," in *DC Jazz: Stories of Jazz Music in Washington, DC*, ed. Maurice Jackson and Blair A. Ruble (Washington, DC: Georgetown University Press, 2018), 145–70.

3   Richard L. Coe, "Hooks: Starting a Theater Is Nothing New," *Washington Post*, December 8, 1972.

4   Sam P. K. Collins, "Theater Giants Look Back on DC Black Repertory Company," *Washington Informer*, August 8, 2018.

5   Michael Paulson and Nicole Herrington, "How These Black Playwrights Are Challenging American Theater," *New York Times*, April 25, 2019.

6   Errol Hill, "Introduction," in *The Theater of Black Americans: A Collection of Critical Essays*, ed. Errol Hill (New York: Applause Theatre and Cinema Books, 1980), 1–11.

7   Shelby Steele, "Notes on Ritual in the New Black Theater," in *Theater of Black Americans*, ed. Hill, 30–44.

8   Kimberly W. Bentson, "The Aesthetic of Modern Black Drama: from *Mimesis* to *Methexix*," in *Theater of Black Americans*, ed. Hill, 61–78.

9   Margaret B. Wilkerson, "Critics, Standards and Black Theatre," in *Theater of Black Americans*, ed. Hill, 318–25; Eric Bentley and Stanley Kauffman, "Two Views by White Critics: (1) Must I Side with Blacks or Whites?; (2) Enroute to the Future," in *Theater of Black Americans*, ed. Hill, 336–40.

10   James Hatch, "Some African Influences on the Afro-American Theatre," in *Theater of Black Americans*, ed. Hill, 13–29.

11   Robert Farris Thompson, "An Aesthetic of the Cool: West African Dance in *Theater of Black Americans*, ed. Hill, 99–111.

12   Hatch, "Some African Influences."

13   Jerry Gafio Watts, *Amiri Baraka: The Politics and Art of a Black Intellectual* (New York: New York University Press, 2001).

14   Daniel Slotnik, "Amiri Baraka, Polarizing Poet and Playwright, Dies at 79," *New York Times*, January 10, 2014.

15   LeRoi Jones, *Blues People: Negro Music in White America* (New York: Harper Perennial, 1999).

16   Abiodun Jeyifous, "Black Critics on Black Theatre in America," in *Theater of Black Americans*, ed. Hill, 327–37, at 327–28.

17   Loften Mitchell, *Black Drama: The Story of the American Negro in the Theatre* (New York: Hawthorn Books, 1967), 199.

18   Imamu Amiri Baraka, *Dutchman* (New York: Faber & Faber, 1967).

19   Christopher Baker, "A Trip with the Strange Woman: Amiri Baraka's 'Dutchman' and the Book of Proverbs," *South Atlantic Review* 78 (2013): 110–28.

20   Mitchell, *Black Drama*, 199–200.

21   Larry Neal, "Into Nationalism, Out of Parochialism," in *Theater of Black Americans*, ed. Hill, 293–300, at 296.

22   No author has been nominated more than Wilson, and only Eugene O'Neill, Edward Albee, and Robert E. Sherwood have won the award more than twice. Other playwrights to win the prize two times are George S. Kaufman, Lynn Nottage, Thornton Wilder, and Tennessee Williams; see archive.nytimes.com/www.nytimes.com/ref/theater/theaterspecial/pulitzers.html.

23   Mitchell, *Black Drama*, 183–225.

24   Chris Myers Asch and George Derek Musgrove, *Chocolate City: A History of Race and Democracy in the Nation's Capital* (Chapel Hill: University of North Carolina Press, 2017).

25   These data from various censuses are summarized in "Demographics of Washington, DC," *Wikipedia*.

26   For further discussion of these connections see Asch and Musgrove, *Chocolate City*; Sabiyha Prince, *African Americans and Gentrification in Washington, DC: Race, Class and Social Justice in the Nation's Capital* (New York: Routledge, 2016); Derek S. Hyra, *Race, Class and Politics in the Cappuccino City* (Chicago: University of Chicago Press, 2017); and Lauren Pearlman, *Democracy's Capital: Black Political Power in Washington, DC, 1960s–1970s* (Chapel Hill: University of North Carolina Press, 2019).

27   Pearlman, *Democracy's Capital*; Asch and Musgrove, *Chocolate City*.

28   Harry S. Jaffe and Tom Sherwood, *Dream City: Race, Power and the Decline of Washington, DC* (New York: Simon & Schuster, 1994), 44–66.

29   Kip Lornell and Charles C. Stephenson Jr., *The Beat: Go-Go Music from Washington, DC* (Oxford: University Press of Mississippi, 2009).

30   Natalie Hopkinson, *Go-Go Live: The Musical Life and Death of Chocolate City* (Durham, NC: Duke University Press, 2012).

31   See, e.g., Elliot Williams, "Why Last Night's #MOECHELLA Protest Was a Big Deal for DC," *Washingtonian Magazine*, May 2019.

32   Marissa J. Lang, "Go-go Is Signed into Law as the Official Music of DC," *Washington Post*, February 19, 2020.

33   "Urbicide" is the destruction (or homicide) of an urban neighborhood or city supporting a socioeconomic, ethnic, racial, or religious group. For further discussion of this concept, see Martin Shaw, "New Ways of the City: 'Urbicide' and 'Genocide,'" in *Cities, War, and Terrorism: Towards an Urban Geopolitics*, ed. Stephen Graham (London: Blackwell, 2004), 141–53.

34   Lloyd Grove, "The Happy Hookses," *Washington Post*, May 24, 2000.

35   "The History Makers: Robert Hooks," www.thehistorymakers.org/biography/Robert-hooks-41.

36   John F. Kennedy Center for the Performing Arts, *Playbill*, June 16, 1973.

37   Tamara Lizette Brown, "Lingering Lights from America's Black Broadway: Negro Renaissance to the Black Arts Movement, African-American Concert-Theatrical Dance in Washington, DC," PhD diss., Howard University, Washington, 2004, University Microfilm 31-47525, 242–75.

38   "The History Makers: Topper Carew," www.thehistorymakers.org/biography/topper-carew.

39   Michaela Williams, "Professional Negro Ensemble Formed," *Los Angeles Times*, May 12, 1967.

40   "$434,000 Grant Will Set Up Theatre Company, Workshop," *New York Amsterdam News*, May 13, 1967.

41   William Glover, "A Break for the Negro Performer," *Los Angeles Times*, June 25, 1967.

42   "History Makers: Robert Hooks"; John Carmody, "Multi-Talented Robert Hooks Tries TV," *Washington Post*, August 23, 2967; Steve Reice, "Hooks Proves Dropping Out of Temple U. Wins Fame," *Atlanta Constitution*, May 18, 1968; Cynthia Lowry, "Robert Hooks Wants to Be a Producer," *Chicago Tribune*, February 18, 1968; "Robert Hooks Will Star in 'Crosscurrent,'" *New York Amsterdam News*, December 5, 1970.

43   Brown, "Lingering Lights," 279–80.

44   Brown, 279–80.

45   Dan Sullivan, "Insider's View of Black Theater, Its Goals, Future," *Los Angeles Times*, August 10, 1969.

46   John J. O'Connor, "Profile of Negro Ensemble Company," *New York Times*, September 14, 1987.

47   Brown, "Lingering Lights," 282–84; Howard Taubman, "Negro Theater Project: A Drama Expert Assails Ford Grant as Furthering Artistic Segregation," *New York Times*, July 18, 1967; Sam Zolotow, "Negro Ensemble Leases Theater," *New York Times*, July 27, 1967.

48   Douglas Turner Ward, "Being Criticized Was to Be Expected," *New York Times*, September 1, 1968.

49   "4-Play Season Set by Ensemble Co.," *New York Amsterdam News*, November 25, 1967; Sara Davidson, "Negro Ensemble Co. Ready for Jan. 2 Debut," *Boston Globe*, December 26, 1967; Clive Barnes, "Theater: 'Lusitanian Bogey' Opens, *New York Times*, January 3, 1968; Dan Sullivan, "The Theater: Confrontation in a Tribe," *New York Times*, April 15, 1968; Melvin Tapley, "NEC's Second Production Has Sensitive Portrayals," *New York Amsterdam News*, May 2, 1968; Lewis Funke, "The First Year Was Just Fine," *New York Times*, June 16, 1968;

"All-Black Stage Company Fulfills Actor's Dream," *Chicago Daily Defender*, July 31, 1968.

50   Frank Langley, "It's Black Eye for Black Man," *Atlanta Constitution*, November 2, 1968.

51   Cecil Smith, "Spotlight of the Resurgent Negro Theater," *Los Angeles Times*, February 4, 1968.

52   Walter Kerr, "The Negro Actor Asks Himself: 'Am I A Negro or Am I an Actor,'" *New York Times*, October 15, 1967.

53   Martin Gottfried, "The Great Macdaddy," *Women's Wear Daily*, February 14, 1974; Richard L. Coe, "Over and Over, Say It Black," *Washington Post*, March 8, 1969.

54   "About the Negro Ensemble Co.," *American Masters*, Public Broadcasting Service, television broadcast, August 18, 2004; "Douglas Turner Ward Chronology," *Douglas Turner Ward Quarterly*, issue 3 (March 14, 2011).

55   "Welcome to Our First Issue," *Douglas Turner Ward Quarterly*, issue 1 (September 16, 2010).

56   "Welcome."

57   Nat Hentoff, "You're Hot, You're Poor, You're Nothing,'" *New York Times*, November 14, 1965.

58   Hentoff.

59   Robert Hooks, Remarks, DC Black Repertory Alumni Zoom Conference on Why Black Theater Matters, Forty-Ninth Anniversary of DCBRC, October 18, 2020.

60   Richard Kilberg, "Interview: Robert Hooks on the NEC, Its Beginnings, Its Legacy," *Douglas Turner Ward Quarterly*, issue 5 (September 24, 2011).

61   Hentoff, "You're Hot."

62   Marjory Adams, "Robert Hooks Enthuses Over Negro Repertory," *Boston Globe*, March 26, 1967.

63   "Thinking of Others Paved Bobby Hooks Way to Success," *New York Amsterdam News*, April 30, 1966.

64   Robert Hooks, Remarks.

65   For more on DC legend Ralph "Petey" Greene, see Lurma Rackley, *Laugh If You Like, Ain't a Damn Thing Funny: The Life Story of Ralph "Petey" Greene as told to Lurma Rackley* (Tinicum, Penn.: Xlibris, 2007). Also see Blair A. Ruble, *Washington's U Street: A Biography* (Washington and Baltimore: Woodrow Wilson Center Press and Johns Hopkins University Press, 2010), 173–222.

66   Roberts, "Longtime African American Actor Robert Hooks."

67   "Staff Meeting Minutes, Friday, October 2, 1970," ASR, box 104, folder 10.

68 "Staff Meeting Minutes, Wednesday, March 10, 1971," ASR, box 104, folder 10.

69 "Kennedy Center Opens Doors for New Repertory Company," *Baltimore Afro-American*, June 5, 1971.

70   Roberts, "Longtime African American Actor Robert Hooks."

71 This story is told with references by Ruble, *Washington's U Street*, 173–222.

72 Gus Constantine, "Black Theater Is Launched," *Washington Evening Star*, February 26, 1971.

73 This story is told with references by Ruble, *Washington's U Street*, 173–260.

74 For further discuss on the role of SNCC in Washington at the time see Lauren Pearlman, *Democracy's Capital*; and Anne M. Valk, *Radical Sisters. Second-Wave Feminism and Black Liberation in Washington, DC* (Urbana: University of Illinois Press, 2010).

75 This story is told with references by Ruble, *Washington's U Street*, 200–222.

76 University of the District of Columbia website, https://www.udc.edu/about/history-mission/.

77 University of the District of Columbia website.

78 "Negro Elected Senior Class Head at Ohio State," *Jet Magazine*, May 21, 1953.

79 See, e.g., Hildred Roach, *Black American Music: Past and Present* (Boston: Crescendo, 1973); and Hildred Roach, *Black American Music: Past and Present*, 2nd revised edition (Malabar, FL: Krieger, 1992).

80 Korey, "From Federal City College to UDC, 145–48.

81 Lauren Sinclair, "No Church Without a Choir: Howard University and Jazz in Washington, DC," in *DC Jazz*, ed. Jackson and Ruble, 129–43.

82 "History Makers: Topper Carew."

83 Angela Terrell, "'What's That New Thing up the Street?' It's a Black Cultural Center," *Washington Post*, August 13, 1972.

84 "'Say, Brother' Makes Debut," *Chicago Defender*, October 8, 1975;"Black Producer Named to New Top-Level Post," *Baltimore Afro-American*, October 9, 1976; "Black Firm Co-sponsors PBS Program," *New Pittsburgh Courier*, October 24, 1981; Dorothy Gilliam, "Human Rights," *Washington Post*, February 16, 1983; Michael Kernan, "That Summer Thing," *Washington Post*, August 19, 1984; David J. Fox and Nina J. Easton, "Can Hollywood Do the Right Thing?" *Los Angeles Times*, July 16, 1991; Christopher Vaughn, "'Unforgettable' Night for Cole at Image Awards," *Chicago Tribune*, January 16, 1992.

85 See, e.g., Gary Arnold, "Rollicking 'DC Cab': Top-Notch Fare,"

Washington Post, December 15, 1983; "Mr. T Softens in His Role in DC Cab," *Atlanta Daily World*, December 15, 1983; "DC Cab: Topper Carew's Brainchild," *Baltimore Afro-American*, January 2, 1984; and, "'DC Cab' Puts Comedian in Fast Lane," *Boston Globe*, January 5, 1984.

86   Philip D. Carter, "DC Neighborhood in State of Flux," *Washington Post*, February 12, 1970.

87   Carter.

88   For further discussion of the origins of gentrification in Washington, See Asch and Musgrove, *Chocolate City*.

89   Rusty Hassan, "Jazz Radio in Washington, DC," in *DC Jazz*, ed. Jackson and Ruble, 91–106.

90   Leon Dash, "Center Seeks to Give Girls More Than Games," *Washington Post*, October 26, 1967.

91   Hollie I. West, "The New Thing: An Innovative Cultural Center," *Washington Post*, August 9, 1969.

92   Jim Hoagland, "African Mural: A Sign or Symbol?" *Washington Post*, August 2, 1968; Martin Weil, "Drums Mark Completion of Mural," *Washington Post*, August 4, 1968.

93   Jenice Armstrong, "For 30 Years, Teaching a Dance of Self-Esteem," *Washington Post*, November 16, 1989.

94   Brown, "Lingering Lights," 242–75.

95   Brown, 243.

96   Brown, 244–55.

97   "The New Thing: Heritage Dancers," *Baltimore Afro-American*, June 21, 1969.

98   Brown, "Lingering Lights," 264–65; Michael Kernan, "Melvin Deal's Community Art," *Washington Post*, November 11, 1970.

99   See, e.g., Karen Bates-Logan, "Taking Steps to Teach the African Heritage," *Washington Post*, December 17, 1981; Hamil Harris, "African Drummers Keep Rhythms to Heal Generations," *Washington Informer*, January 2, 2019.

100   Hamil Harris, "African Drummers Keep Rhythms to Heal Generations."

101   Pamela Sommers, "Africa's Varied Riches," *Washington Post*, January 1988.

102   For further discussion, see Blair A. Ruble, "C. Brian Williams and Stepping," *in Performing Community 3: Short Essays on Community, Diversity, Inclusion, and the Performing Art* (Washington, DC: Woodrow Wilson Center, 2018), 63–65.

103   "School Eyed for All Morgan Residents," *Washington Post*, December 7, 1968.

104 "Topper Carew's New Thing," *Washington Post*, January 10, 1969.

105 Hollie I. West, "Blues Festival: Top Stars in 3-Day Event," *Washington Post*, October 9, 1970.

106 Grace Glueck, "The Future Is Not What It Used to Be," *New York Times*, November 30, 1969.

107 Michael Kerman, "Topper Carew Is a Busy Man: When a Power Broker Is Black, He Is a Busy, Busy Man," *Washington Post*, March 27, 1971.

108 Jacqueline Trescott, "Toasting Topper," *Washington Post*, September 25, 1975.

109 Hollie I. West, "Carew's New (Thing) Image," *Washington Post*, September 25, 1975.

110 James O. Gibson, "Black Arts: The Creative Spirit," *Washington Post*, January 26, 1969.

111 Dick Gregory, "Can Black and White Artists Still Work Together?" *New York Times*, February 2, 1969.

112 Louis Salta, "Capital Will Get Theater for Blacks," *New York Times*, March 17, 1971.

113 Judith Martin, "'Biggest Nobody' on Arts Unit," *Washington Post*, June 29, 1969.

114 Sally Quinn, "Meet Robert Hooks," *Washington Post*, February 26, 1971.

115 Roberts, "Longtime African American Actor Robert Hooks."

116 "Celebrating the Birthdays of Vantile Whitfield and Jaye Stewart," DCRBC Alumni Association Webcast (September 8, 2020).

117 As recalled on the company's forty-ninth anniversary zoom conference DC Black Repertory Alumni Zoom Conference on Why Black Theater Matters, October 18, 2020.

118 Judy Harkison, "Black, but Not Bleak, Theater Future," *Washington Post*, August 13, 1971.

119 Arleen Jocobson, "Robert Hooks Comes Home and Brings Black Theater with Him," *Washington Post*, January 10, 1972.

120 See, e.g., "Editorial: Black Culture," *Washington Post*, November 23, 1971; Richard L. Coe, "Grants for the Theater," *Washington Post*, November 29, 1972; and Richard L. Coe, "Hooks Starting a Theater Is Nothing New," *Washington Post*, December 8, 1972.

121 DC Black Repertory Alumni Zoom Conference on Why Black Theater Matters, October 18, 2020.

122 Hollie I. West, "Legitimate Black Images," *Washington Post*, October 13, 1972.

123 Alan M. Kriegsman, "Black Dance: Lively Debut," *Washington Post*, November 11, 1972; Samuel A. Hay, "Black Repertory," *Baltimore Afro-American*, December 2, 1972.

124 Jean Battey Lewis, "Alvin Ailey Dance Theater," *Washington Post*, January 12, 1973.

125 Samuel A. Hay, "Imamu," *Washington Post*, October 21, 1972.

126 Hay.

127 West, "Legitimate Black Images."

128 See, e.g., "Howard Offering "Summer and Smoke,'" *Washington Post*, December 5, 1954; "Education Notes: Howard University Honorees," *Atlanta Daily World*, March 24, 1955; "Art Directors Cite Winning Posters Here," *Washington Post*, April 17, 1957; "Bison Grid Star Cops Art Awards," *Baltimore Afro-American*, May 11, 1957; and "Howard Football Players Annex," *Chicago Defender*, May 18, 1957.

129 Yvonne Shinhoster Lamb, "Arts Administrator, Playwright Vantile Whitfield Dies," *Washington Post*, January 23, 2005.

130 Sylvie Drake, "Curtain Calls Unlikely as '71 Ends Run," *Los Angeles Times*, December 29, 1971.

131 Lamb, "Arts Administrator."

132 "Whitfield Heads Art Grants Project," *Los Angeles Times*, December 16, 1971; Phil Casey, "Matching Funds for Arts Program," *Washington Post*, December 16, 1971; "Grassroots in Arts," *Baltimore Afro-American*, February 17, 1973.

133 Lamb, "Arts Administrator."

134 Lamb.

135 Richard L. Coe, "The Holiday Theater Bills," *Washington Post*, December 17, 1972.

136 Richard L. Coe, "Absorbing and Powerful 'Coda,'" *Washington Post*, December 11, 1972.

137 Janette Smyth, "Black Premier," *Washington Post*, December 9, 1972.

138 Richard L. Coe, "Absorbing and Powerful 'Coda.'"

139 Annie R. Crittenden, "Black Theater," *Washington Post*, January 14, 1973.

140 Angela Terrell, "Black Troupes in DC," *Washington Post*, January 14, 1973; Angela Terrell, "The 'Sage' of Black Stage," *Washington Post*, January 14, 1973; Richard L. Coe, "Drama of Character," *Washington Post*, January 18, 1973.

141 Alan M. Kriegsman, "Effervescent 'Rock,'" *Washington Post*, January 25, 1973.

142 Kriegsman.

143 Kriegsman.

144 Charles Farrow, "Upon This Rock," *Baltimore Afro-American*, February 3, 1973.

145 See the Bernice Johnson Reagon website, www.bernicejohnsonreagon.com/about/.

146 "Spelman Grad Is MacArthur Fellow," *Atlanta Daily World*, August 8, 1989.

147 See the Sweet Honey in the Rock website, www.Sweethoney.com.

148 "The History Makers: Louis Johnson," www.Thehistorymakers.org/biography/louis-johnson-40.

149 Jennifer Dunning, "Louis Johnson: 'I Love Dance—Any Kind of Dance,'" *New York Times*, September 28, 1975.

150 "Louis Johnson Dance Company Presentation Here March 1," *Atlanta Daily World*, February 14, 1961; Arthur Todd, "The Art of the American Negro Is One of Our Foremost National Treasurers," *New York Times*, July 2, 1961; Anna Kisselgoff, "Louis Johnson Dance Theater Makes Its Debut at St. Marks," *New York Times*, February 18, 1969.

151 See, e.g., Jean Battey, "Gospel Drama Staged by Choreographer," *Washington Post*, July 2, 1964; Jean Battey, "Dance Repertory Holds Promise," *Washington Post*, February 23, 1964; Clive Barnes, "A Paris Festival," *New York Times*, June 16, 1966; Charles Crowder, "Cathedral Festival Is Impressive," *Washington Post*, July 18, 1967; "Dance Series Starts Friday," *Washington Post*, October 24, 1967; Don McDonagh, "Dance Bill Offers Works of 3 Blacks," *New York Times*, May 2, 1969; Margo Miller, "Alvin Ailey Says: Let's Dance All We Know," *Boston Globe*, May 18, 1969; Richard L. Coe, "'Music' Man," *Washington Post*, February 26, 1970; Vivian Robinson, "A Stageful of Talent Makes 'Purlie' a Hit," *New York Times*, March 21, 1970; and Ronal Henahan, "'Treemonisha,' the Legend Arrives," *New York Times*, October 22, 1975.

152 "History Makers: Louis Johnson"; Barbara Lewis, "Profile of a Professional," *New York Amsterdam News*, December 3, 1975.

153 Lewis, "Profile."

154 Gia Kourlas, "Louis Johnson, Dancer Who Leapt From Genre to Genre, Is Dead at 90," *New York Times*, April 15, 2020.

155 "'Mike' Malone Is Drum Major at Penn Hills," *Pittsburgh Courier*, August 1, 1959.

156 "Teen Age Dance Races, Picnic Fill Mid-Week," *Pittsburgh Courier*, August 11, 1962.

157 "Local Artist Looms on DC Horizon," *Pittsburgh Courier*, June 7, 1975.

158 Richard L. Coe, "Street Theater's 'Esteban,'" *Washington Post*, July 23, 1971.

159 Robert Simonson, "Mike Malone, Director and Choreographer, Died at 63," *Playbill*, December 11, 2006.

160 "Honoring Charles Augins," DC Black Repertory Alumni Zoom Conference on Why Black Theater Matters, Forty-Ninth Anniversary of DCBRC (October 18, 2020).

161 Annie R. Crittenden, "A Time for Nostalgia and Vitality," *Washington Post*, March 2, 1973; "Folksy Fun-Filled Fair," *Washington Post*, May 30, 1973; "Three 'Lifestyles,'" *Washington Post*, July 13, 1973; "Snapshot of Ghetto Survival," *Washington Post*, July 19, 1973.

162 Richard L. Coe, "Theatre," *Washington Post*, September 9, 1973; "Arts Unit Gets Grant for Interns," *Hartford Courant*, November 16, 1971; Richard L. Coe, "Six Provocative Weeks," *Washington Post*, November 11, 1973; "Washington: An Upsurge of the Arts," *New York Times*, November 28, 1973.

163 "Kennedy Center Opens Doors."

164 Tom Shales, "Black Play for Center," *Washington Post*, April 12, 1973.

165 Shales.

166 James Earl Jones and Penelope Niven, *James Earl Jones: Voices and Silences* (New York: Charles Scribner's Sons, 1993), 115–23.

167 Jones and Niven.

168 Timothy S. Robinson, "Genet Files Suit," *Washington Post*, June 13, 1973.

169 "Judge Rejects Dramatist's Claim," *Hartford Courant*, June 14, 1973.

170 Robert Hooks, "Genet's 'The Blacks': Finding the Truths," *Washington Post*, May 27, 1973.

171 Clive Barnes, "DC Black Repertory Stages Jean Genet's 'Blacks,'" *New York Times*, May 30, 1973; Richard L. Coe, "'The Blacks': Justified," *Washington Post*, May 38, 1971.

172 Don Sanders, "New Faster-Paced 'Blacks,'" *Los Angeles Times*, May 31, 1973.

173 Alan M. Kriegsman, "Humanity Series," *Washington Post*, April 12, 1973.

174 Alan M. Kriegsman, "'Heron Test': The Drug Problem Without Hysteria," *Washington Post*, January 23, 1974; Richard L. Coe, "A Closing, a Celebration," *Washington Post*, January 25, 1974; "'Black Journal' Celebrates 'National Communications for Freedom Week,'" *New Pittsburgh Courier*, May 9, 1974.

175 Robert Hooks, "Theater: The Boom That Zaps," *Washington Post*, December 19, 1976.

176 Richard L. Coe, "Finding American Theater," *Washington Post*, December 6, 1973.

177 Coe.

178 Richard Coe, "The '30s Goes on Stage," *Washington Post*, November 29, 1973.

179 "Dr. Valerian E. Smith," Find a Grave website, www.findagrave.com/memorial/29261328/valerian-e_-smith.

180 Richard L. Coe, "Original Musical 'Changes,'" *Washington Post*, December 7, 1973.

181 Coe, "Original."

182 Charles Farrow, "Black Theatre: DC Rep New Musical 'Changes,'" *Baltimore Afro-American*, December 22, 1973.

183 Richard L. Coe, "A Closing, a Celebration," *Washington Post*, January 25, 1974.

184 Joel Dreyfuss, "A Season Postponed," *Washington Post*, March 29, 1974.

185 Richard L. Coe, "Red, Yellow, Black, White . . . ," *Washington Post*, March 28, 1974; "Charlie Cherokee Says," *Chicago Defender*, March 19, 1974.

186 Richard Prince, "A Benefit With a Twofold Message," *Washington Post*, June 24, 1974; Joel Dreyfuss, "Working Behind the Scenes, Appealing for Theatrical Aid," *Washington Post*, September 9, 1975.

187 Tom Shales, "'Happy Ending' for Black Repertory Company?" *Washington Post*, June 24, 1974.

188 Tom Shales, "In the Shadow of Big Brother: City Cultural Crisis?" *Washington Post*, July 7, 1974.

189 Joel Dreyfus, "Don't Leave Go My Hand," *Washington Post*, June 15, 1974.

190 Alan M. Kriegsman, "DC Repertory Abroad," *Washington Post*, July 3, 1974.

191 Angela Terrell, "Two Years, No Fears," *Washington Post*, September 5, 1974; John Carmody, "Three Hosts for 'AM America,'" *Washington Post*, September 5, 1974; Jacqueline Trescott and Tom Zito, "Carter Barron's New Look," *Washington Post*, September 18, 1975.

192 Joel Dreyfuss, "Black Rep's 'Daybreak Dreams,'" *Washington Post*, July 18, 1975; Lynn Darling, "'Dreams' from DC Black Repertory," *Washington Post*, July 31, 1975.

193 Pam Lambert, "Nothin' but a Hound Dog," *Washington Post*, July 30, 1975; DC Black Repertory Alumni Zoom Conference on Why Black Theater Matters, Forty-Ninth Anniversary of DCBRC, October 18, 2020.

194 Richard L. Coe, "Theater," *Washington Post*, September 8, 1974.

195 Richard L. Coe, "'Owen's Song': Musical Movement Set to Poetry," *Washington Post*, October 25, 1974.

196 Joel Dreyfus, "Success, Survival and the Black Repertory," *Washington Post*, December 1, 1974.

197 Coe, "'Owen's Song.'"

198 Dreyfus, "Success."

199 Coe, "'Owen's Song.'"

200 Jacqueline Trescott, "Dramatic Expression a 'Gentlized' Vantage," *Washington Post*, April 11, 1976.

201 Richard L. Coe, "With a Sense of Ritual," *Washington Post*, January 1, 1975.
202 Angela Brown-Terrell, "Singing the Black Saga," *Washington Post*, February 12, 1975.
203 Anegla Brown-Terrell, "Celebrating Black History Week," *Washington Post*, February 8, 1975.
204 Brown-Terrell, "Singing."
205 Joel Dreyfuss, "About a Day in a Few DC Lives," *Washington Post*, December 19, 1975.
206 Hollie I. West, "Black American Folksongs," *Washington Post*, May 10, 1975.
207 Earl Calloway, "Black Tradition Flows Through 'Sweet Honey In the Rock,'" *New Pittsburgh Courier*, December 22, 1978.
208 Paul Grein, "Sweet Honey: Right Taste, Right Time," *Los Angeles Times*, December 2, 1980.
209 Connie Johnson, "Sweet Honey in Rock: Commitment to Change," *Los Angeles Times*, April 2, 1982.
210 Patrice Gaines-Carter, "'Sweet Honey' Tastes Flavor of Success on Its Anniversary," *Washington Post*, November 17, 1983.
211 See, e.g., Geoffrey Himes, "After 20 Years, Honey Still Sweet," *Washington Post*, November 19, 1993; Geoffrey Himes, "Sweet Honey at 25; Solid as a Rock," *Washington Post*, November 20, 1998; Felicia R. Lee, "Translating Flaubert, In the Gospel Tradition," *New York Times*, October 20, 2004.
212 Stanley Nelson, director, *Sweet Honey in the Rock: Raise Your Voice* (New York: Firelight Media, 2005).
213 Roger Catlin, "Sweet Honey in the Rock Has Been Making Music, and Taking a Stand for 43 Years," *Washington Post*, May 13, 2016.
214 Tack Mann, "Dances of Black Folk," *Washington Post*, March 28, 1976.
215 Joel Dreyfuss, "And, Black Life on 'Genesis,'" *Washington Post*, April 3, 1976.
216 Mann, "Dances."
217 Jacqueline Trescott, "Still Dancing, But Differently," *Washington Post*, July 24, 1975.
218 Trescott.
219 Trescott; Daniel Cariaga, "'Treemonisha': A Long, Hard Road," *Los Angeles Times*, November 13, 1978.
220 Alan M. Kriegsman, "A Rich Ballet Weekend," *Washington Post*, May 7, 1977.
221 Angela Terrell, "Black Ballet Landmark," *Washington Post*, January 17, 1972.
222 Mary Ann French, "Making Her Pointe, Doris Jones Still Bringing

Blacks to the Barre," *Washington Post*, May 15, 1993; Jennifer Dunning, "Doris W. Jones, 92, Ballet Dancer Who Founded School for Blacks," *New York Times*, April 4, 2006.

223 Alan M. Kriegsman, "Washington's Ballet Bonanza," *Washington Post*, April 19, 1987.

224 Jacqueline Trescott, "The Benefit Pas De Deux," *Washington Post*, April 4, 1987.

225 This is a story compellingly told in Tamara Lizette Brown, "Lingering Lights from America's Black Broadway: Negro Renaissance to the Black Arts Movement, African-American Concert-Theatrical Dance in Washington, DC," PhD diss., Howard University, Washington, 2004, University Microfilm 31-47525, 189–241.

226 Alan M. Kriegsman, "Capitol Ballet, Capital Night," *Washington Post*, May 14, 1988.

227 Brown, "Lingering Lights," 231–32.

228 Jennifer Dunning, "A Dancer Who had a Dream," *New York Times*, April 14, 1974; Lewis Segal, "Harlem Troupe at Ambassador," *Los Angeles Times*, November 14, 1978.

229 See, e.g., Don McDonagh, "Dance: Louis Johnson," *New York Times*, August 15, 1976; Jennifer Dunning, "Dance: Ballet Hispanico," *New York Times*, October 19, 1979; Anna Kisselgoff, "The Joffrey Ballet's Eclectic Flair," *New York Times*, November 1, 1981; and Jennifer Funning, "A Dance Troupe Rebounds: Dance Theater," *New York Times*, January 23, 1983.

230 Alan M. Kreigsman, "Louis Johnson: High Stepping in the Land of Oz," *Washington Post*, October 21, 1978; Billy Rowe, "Odd Couple Funny Choice for Blacks," *New York Amsterdam News*, September 4, 1982.

231 Mel Tapley, "Dance Architect Louis Johnson Choreographs Met's 'Aida,'" *New York Amsterdam News*, June 5, 1985.

232 Pamela Sommers, "Dance Whiz," *Washington Post*, March 11, 1983.

233 Clive Barnes, "The Ailey Is Becoming Establishment," *New York Times*, April 27, 1975.

234 George Jackson, "Dance: The Force of Fusion," *Washington Post*, July 28, 1993; Jennifer Dunning, "A Blending of the Unlike," *New York Times*, May 22, 1997.

235 "Mike Malone: Local Artist Looms on DC Horizon," *New Pittsburgh Courier*, June 7, 1975; Emily Isberg, "DC Dance Ensemble Gets Ready to 'Turn It Out' for 'City Dance '78,'" *Washington Post*, May 4, 1978; Sonsyrea Tate, "Arts DC Develops Discipline," *Washington Post*, August 13, 1987.

236 Jacqueline Trescott, "How One of the 'Girls' Got Her Name in Lights:

Auditions, Anxiety, and Then . . . Hollywood," *Washington Post*, June 15, 1977.

237 Mel Gussow, "Theater: Tribute to Langston Hughes," *New York Times*, May 8, 1979.

238 See, e.g., Alvin Klein, "Rousing, Foot-Stomping 'Black Nativity,'" *New York Times*, December 18, 1983; Sarah Kaufman, "Malone Restages 'Black Nativity,'" *Washington Post*, December 16, 1994; Pamela Sommers, "'Black Nativity': Glory in the Highest Spirit," *Washington Post*, December 15, 1995; William Triplett, "'Black Nativity': A Bright Star," *Washington Post*, December 19, 1997; and Nelson Pressley, "'Black Nativity's' Subdued Rebirth," *Washington Post*, December 22, 1999.

239 See, e.g., Leonard Hughes, "This 'Dreamgirls' Is a Dream of a Show," *Washington Post*, July 16, 1992; Lloyd Rose, "Studio's Spirited 'Spink,'" *Washington Post*, May 19, 1993; Jacqueline Trescott, "Making It in Choreography Takes Fancy Footwork," *Washington Post*, July 3, 1994; Lloyd Rose, "'Love! Valour!' Playing to a Full House," *Washington Post*, March 6, 1997; and Jane Horwitz, "'Wicked' This Way Comes," *Washington Post*, November 18, 1997.

240 "22 Soviet, US Young People Perform Musical for Peace," *Boston Globe*, September 2, 1986; Linda Wheeler, "The Lincoln Preps for an Encore," *Washington Post*, May 23, 1989.

241 Richard L. Gee, "Black Repertory Company's 'Evening of Comedy,'" *Washington Post*, January 9, 1975.

242 Richard L. Coe, "DC Black Rep's Salute to Gwendolyn Brooks," *Washington Post*, October 22, 1976; Dorothy Gilliam, "A Passage in Eras, Mind and Manner," *Washington Post*, November 13, 1976.

243 William Gilden, "Repertory Relocation," *Washington Post*, June 9, 1976.

244 Jacqueline Trescott, "DC Rep Closing Out," *Washington Post*, December 9, 1976.

245 Jacqueline Trescott, "Hooks: 'Disappointed,'" *Washington Post*, December 11, 1976.

246 Hooks, "Theater."

247 Brown, "Lingering Lights," 285–98.

248 Brown.

249 Donatella Galella, *America in the Round: Capital, Race, and Nation at Washington, DC's, Arena Stage* (Iowa City: University of Iowa Press, 2019), 98.

250 Muriel Morisey, "Founding a Black Rep Theater," *Washington Post*, September 19, 1970.

251 Richard L. Coe, "Cooperation among the Theaters," *Washington Post*, June 3, 1973.

252   For discussion of various structural issues inhibiting the development of independent black theater at the time, see Paul Delaney, "From Coast to Coast, the Black Audience Grows," *New York Times*, October 10, 1976.

253   See, e.g., Billy Row, "Negro Actor's Guild in Trouble," *New York Amsterdam News*, February 24, 1979; and Mel Tapley, "Woodie King Jr.: Black Theatre's Miracle Man," *New York Amsterdam News*, October 13, 1979.

254   See, e.g., Barbara Lewis, "Has Ward Retreated from NEC's Goals?" *New York Amsterdam News*, December 10, 1977; Hilary De Vries, "A Black Theater Group Faces New Hurdles," *New York Times*, January 7, 1990; and Glenn Collins, "While Broadway Is Feasting, Small Troupes Are Starving," *New York Times*, June 23, 1992.

255   Jacqueline Trescott, "Fade-Out: It Has Talent, Money, a Stable Middle Class; So Why Hasn't DC Had a Black Repertory Company for the Past Decade?" *Washington Post*, November 7, 1993.

256   For a selection of articles tracking the arc of public and private funding for the arts in Washington and the nation, see Myra MacPherson, "Congress, Funds and the Arts," *Washington Post*, March 15, 1973; Mel Gussow, "National Endowment Puts Government into Role of Major Patron of the Arts," *New York Times*, August 12, 1973; Carla Hall, "Funding Debate," *Washington Post*, October 22, 1980; Carla Hall, "DC Council Debates Arts Budget," *Washington Post*, January 22, 1981; Joseph McLellan, "The Arts Budget," *Washington Post*, February 20, 1982; Jacquline Trescott, "After Bautista: Money and the Arts," *Washington Post*, March 25, 1984; Mary Battista, "24 Arts Groups to Share $200,000 NEA Grant," *Washington Post*, November 13, 1985; and Dorothy Gilliam, "Time to Bolster Black Culture," *Washington Post,* October 12, 1987.

257   Hooks, Remarks, October 18, 2020.

258   Olive Barnes, "'Owen's Song' at the D.C. Black Repertory Company," *New York Times*, November 1, 1974.

259   Nelson Pressley, "DC Theater's Uncast Role," *Washington Post*, October 3, 1999.

260   Louise Reid, "Simply Heavenly," *Washington Post*, March 18, 1977.

261   Richard L. Coe, "Rousing 'Inner City,'" *Washington Post*, August 2, 1977.

262   Jacqueline Trescott, "Director Steps Toward a National Black Theater," *Washington Post*, September 18, 2002.

263   "Jaye Stewart, Director-Playwright," *Washington Post*, October 30, 1996; Kenan Heise, "Actor, Playwright Jaye Stewart," *Chicago Tribune*, October 19, 1996.

264 Kenan Heise, "Actor, Playwright Jaye Stewart," *Chicago Tribune*, October 19, 1996.

265 Trescott, "Fade-Out."

266 Jeanne Cooper, "The Rep's Celebrity in Residence," *Washington Post*, April 25, 1992.

267 Cooper.

268 David Richards, "Survival of the Fittest: The Rep Inc.," *Washington Post*, June 28, 1982.

269 James Lardner, "The Young Producers," *Washington Post*, September 28, 1980.

270 Richard L. Coe, "'Trilogy' by Any Other Name," *Washington Post*, January 18, 1978.

271 Don Shirley, "Black Theater in Washington," *Washington Post*, May 20, 1979.

272 Patricia Jones, "Stamina Key to Survival With New Rep, Inc., Theater," *Washington Post*, September 28, 1978.

273 Miles White, "The Love Story in Prime Mime," *Baltimore Afro-American*, March 8, 1980.

274 Edward Engel, "Curtain Rising for Local Black Theater Troupes," *Washington Post*, January 31, 1991.

275 See, e.g., Lyn Tuck, "Paying Homage to Robert Hooks," *Washington Post*, November 22, 1977; and Barbara Lewis, "The Rep: A Dream Deferred," *New York Amsterdam News*, March 26, 1983.

276 See, e.g., Sam P. K. Collins, "Theater Giants Look Back on DC Black Repertory Company," *Washington Informer*, August 8, 2018.

277 "The History Makers: Robert Hooks," www.thehistorymakers.org/biography/Robert-hooks-41.

278 Trescott, "DC Rep."

279 See, e.g., Sid Smith, "Dream Time," *Chicago Tribune*, May 26, 1994; and Lawrence Bommer, "Classic 'Journey' Follows Monk to Enlightenment," *Chicago Tribune*, May 5, 1995.

280 Collection Guide, African Continuum Theater Company archives (Collection 0088-SCPA), Michelle Smith Performing Arts Library, University of Maryland, College Park, https://archives/lib/umd/edu/repositories/4/resources/287.

281 Jordan Ealey, "Black Theatre: Jennifer L. Nelson reflects on African Continuum Theatre Company," DC Theatre Scene website (December 9, 2020).

282 Ravelle Brockman, "Helen Hayes Tribute Recognizes Jennifer L. Nelson as DC Theater Trailblazer," *DC Metro Theater Arts*, May 6, 2019, https://dcmetroarts.com/2019/05/06/helen-hayes-tribute-jennifer-nelson.

283 "An Interview with Director Jennifer L. Nelson," Black Theatre Matters, February 9, 2017, https://blacktheatrematers.org/2-17/02/28/an-interview-with-director-jennifer-l-nelson/.

284 Nelson interview.

285 Nelson.

286 Nelson.

287 Lloyd Rose, "Hip Hop's Familiar Beat," *Washington Post*, March 10, 1998.

288 Nelson interview.

289 Jordan Ealey, "Black Theatre: Jennifer L.Nelson."

290 Nelson Pressley, "Melvin D. Gerald, Jr.: Bridging an Important Gap," *American Theatre*, January 1, 2007.

291 "Women Directors of DC: Jennifer L. Nelson," Jacqueline Lawton Blog, November 20, 2012, https://www. Jacquelinelawton.com/blog/women-directors-of-dc-jenifer-l-nelson.

292 DeNeen Brown, "What Is the State of Black Theater in DC?" *Washington Post*, January 6, 2012.

293 True Colors Theatre Company website, http://www. Truecolorstheatre.org.

294 See Jacqueline E. Lawton's website, https://www.Jazquelinelawton. com.

295 Adam Bernstein, "Peggy Cooper Cafritz, Grande Dame of the Washington Arts and Education Scene, Dies at 70," *Washington Post*, February 18, 2018.

296 Judith Martin, "'Biggest Nobody' on Arts Unit," *Washington Post*, June 29, 1969.

297 Angela Terrell, "Two Roads to Community Involvement," *Washington Post*, February 28, 1971.

298 Jack Mann, "Peggy Cooper and the Art of the Grant," *Washington Post*, October 27, 1974.

299 Justin Blum, "A Is for Activist: DC Schools President Peggy Cooper Cafritz Raises Her Hand," *Washington Post*, May 21, 2002.

300 Penelope Green, "Everything in a Big Way: The Washington Saloniste Has Had Epic Triumphs and Losses, Including a Fire That Destroyed Her Art Collection; Now She's Built It All Back," *New York Times*, January 15, 2015.

301 David Montgomery and DeNeen L Brown, "Fire at Home of Peggy Cooper Cafritz Scorches Washington's Cultural Landscape," *Washington Post*, July 31, 2009.

302 Jean Battey Lewis, "Peggy Cooper's Single-Handed Dream Factory," *Washington Post*, September 6, 1970.

303 Lewis.

304 Adrienne Manns, "A High School for the Arts," *Washington Post*, May 9, 1974.
305 Bart Barnes, "Nude Art Flap at Western," *Washington Post*, January 9, 1976; "Compromise Ends Dispute at Western," *Washington Post*, January 21, 1976; "Settling Differences at Western High," *Washington Post*, January 26, 1976.
306 Hollie I. West, "Hard Times at Ellington High," *Washington Post*, May 11, 1980.
307 Bill Turque, "Ellington Arts School Might Be Moved Out of DC's Ward 2," *Washington Post*, January 17, 2010.
308 Michelle Goldchain, "Duke Ellington School of Arts Finishes Modernization $100M over Budget," *Curbed*, August 18, 2017.
309 Peter Jamison, "Renowned DC High School Plagued by Enrollment Fraud, Investigation Finds," *Washington Post*, May 11, 2018.
310 See, e.g., Barbara Gamarekian, "It's an Artistic Life at Duke Ellington High School," *New York Times*, August 7, 1985; Kara Swisher, "DC's Arts Achievers," *Washington Post*, September 27, 1988; and Jacqueline Trescott, "The Ellington Experience: The Proof Is in the Pupils," *Washington Post*, June 5, 1994.
311 Audrey Singer, Samantha Friedman, Ivan Cheung, and Marie Price, *The World in a Zip Code: Greater Washington, DC, as a New Region of Immigration* (Washington: Brookings Institution Press, 2001).
312 Lloyd Rose, "In Round House's Corner: The Director with an Actor's Instincts," *Washington Post*, May 3, 1998.
313 GALA Theatre website, //en.galatheatre.org/.
314 *Washingtonian Magazine* website, www.washingtonian.com/2011/01/21/2010-washingtonians-of-the-year/.
315 Peter Marks, "GALA's 'In the Heights': Party Like It's 2017," *Washington Post*, April 24, 2017.
316 Mary Trotter, *Ireland's National Theater: Political Performance and the Origins of the Irish Dramatic Movement* (Syracuse: Syracuse University Press, 2001).

Curtain Call

1   Molly Smith, as quoted by Jason Fraley, "Arena Stage Tackles DC Statehood, Racism in Streaming Film '51st State,'" WTOP News, September 30, 2020.
2   See the Arena Stage website, www.arenastage.org/tickets/51st-state/.
3   Carl Abbott, "Dimensions of Regional Change in Washington, DC," *American Historical Review* 95, no. 5 (1990): 1367–93; Dennis E. Gale, *Washington, DC: Inner-City Revitalization and Minority Suburbanization* (Philadelphia: Temple University Press, 1987), 12.

4   Derek Hyra and Sabiyha Prince, editors, *Capital Dilemma: Growth and Inequality in Washington, DC* (New York: Routledge 2016), xiii.

5   Marissa J. Lang, "The District's Economy Is Booming, but Many Black Washingtonians Have Been Left Out, Study Finds," *Washington Post*, February 11, 2020; Commission on African American Affairs District of Columbia Government, *An Analysis: African American Employment, Population & Housing Trends in Washington, DC* (Washington: Georgetown University, 2017).

6   DeNeen Brown, "Playwright Karen Zacarías Finds Inspiration in Arena Stage's Residency Program," *Washington Post*, October 14, 2011.

7   Svich Caridad, "Main Content Areas Karen Zacarias: An Interview," *TheatreForuum–International Theater Journal*, Winter–Spring 2006, 9–11.

8   Young Playwrights' Theater website, www.youngplaywrightstheater. org/.

9   Brown, "Playwright Karen Zacarías."

10   Karen Zacarías, *The Book Club Play* (Chicago: Dramatic Publishing Company, 2009), product BM 1000.

11   Roger Catlin, "Bringing an Empowered Cinderella to the Stage," *Washington Post*, February 23, 2017.

12   Keith Loria, "A DC Dinner Party Inspired Karen Zacarías' New Comedy 'Native Gardens,'" DCTheatreScene website, dctheaterscene. com/2017/09/13/dc-dinner-party-inspired-karen-zacarías-new-comedy-native-gardens/; Lori McCue, "In Arena Stage's 'Native Gardens,' New Neighbors Cross the Line of Civility," *Washington Post*, September 27, 2017.

13   McCue, "In Arena Stage's 'Native Gardens.'"

14   McCue.

15   Theatrewashington website, theatrewashington.org.

16   Willis Richardson, "The Hope of a Negro Drama," *Crisis* 21 (1919): 338–39.

About the Author

Blair A. Ruble is a Distinguished Scholar at the Woodrow Wilson International Center for Scholars in Washington. Previously, he held several positions at the center, including vice president for programs, director of the Kennan Institute, and director of the Urban Sustainability Laboratory. He received his undergraduate degree with Highest Honors from the University of North Carolina at Chapel Hill (AB, 1971) and his graduate degrees from the University of Toronto (MA, 1973; PhD, 1977). He is the author of seven monographs and the coeditor of more than twenty volumes.

Index

Abbey Theatre (Dublin, Ireland), 89, 263

Abyssinia (Kociolek & Racheff), 194

Actors Church Alliance (ACA), 98

Actors' Equity Association, 7, 87, 106, 115, 142, 196, 231

Actor's Workshop (San Francisco), 141

Adams Morgan (DC): gentrification in, 13–14, 227; Latin American community in, 260, 261, 272; New Thing Art and Architecture Center, 11–12, 218, 224, 226–29, 231, 261

Adelphi College, 74

African Continuum Theater Company (ACTCo), 255–57

African Grove Theatre (New York), 30–31

African Heritage Dancers and Drummers, 228–29

Albee, Edward, 6, 150, 317n22; *The American Dream,* 154; *Who's Afraid of Virginia Woolf?,* 150–51

Aldridge, Ira, 30–31, 43, 71

Alexander, Clifford, 232

Alexander, Jane, 159–63, 165, 176, 184

Alexander, Robert, 160, 162, 184–94, 256

Alice, Mary, 156, 157

Allen, Debbie, 71, 74, 76, 197, 221, 232, 248

Allen, Maryrose Reeves, 72–74, 77, 228

Allen, Paul, 253

Alley Theater (Houston), 134, 141

Allgood, Sara, 104

All My Sons (Miller), 71

Alvin Ailey Company, 247

The Amen Corner (Baldwin), 76, 233

America in the Round (Galella), 143

The American Dream (Albee), 154

American National Theater, 182

American Negro Theatre (New York), 59

American Security and Trust Company, 143, 149

American Shakespeare Theater (Staunton, Virginia), 295n56

American Theatre of Being (Los Angeles), 233

Amram, David, 77

Anderson, Anthony, 76

Anderson, Marian, 86

Anderson, Mrs. Sherman, 65

Aneja, Abhay, 18–19

Angelou, Maya, 161, 238

Anna Lucasta (Yordan), 59

Apollinaire, Guillaume, 52

Archer, Charles and William, 109

The Arena Adventure: The First Forty Years (Fichandler), 10

Arena Stage, 9–10; African Americans and, 155–59, 165–72, 191–99, 309n216; Children's Theater

and, 185; diversity of community surrounding, 176–77, 181–84; expansion of, 178–81, 271; Foggy Bottom redevelopment and, 143–47; founding of, 131–34; *The Great White Hope* production, 158–72; Kreeger Theater added, 178–81; leaving Hippodrome, 136–38; Living Stage and, 184–94; relocation of, 136–40, 148–50; Schneider and, 150–54; subscriber demographics, 311n253; transition to not-for-profit theater, 140–43
Arnoult, Philip, 126
Arrah-na-Pogue (Boucicault), 96
Association for the Study of Negro Life and History, 63–64
Association Publishers, 63
Augins, Charles, 12, 75, 223, 237
authenticity, 198, 235

Baker, Benjamin: *A Glance at New York,* 95
Baker, George Pierce, 36, 37, 38
Baker, Josephine, 12, 35, 223
Baker, R. M.: *For One Night Only,* 27
Balanchine, George, 12, 75, 223, 236
Baldwin, James: *The Amen Corner,* 76, 233; *Blues for Mr. Charlie,* 76
Bandana Land (play), 34
Bankhead, Tallulah, 117
Baraka, Imamu Amiri (LeRoi Jones), 71, 213–14; *Blues People: Negro Music in White America,* 214; *The Dutchman,* 76, 214–15, 219; *Imamu,* 232, 233
Barnes, Albert, 52
Barnes, Clive, 163, 239
Barnes, Olive, 251
Barrett, Clyde-Jacques, 197, 242, 243

Barry, Marion, 14, 169, 180, 188, 224
Basilica of Saint Mary (Alexandria), 91
Battle, Hinton, 75
Baxter, Dorothy, 88
Bay, Charles Ulrick, 81
Bayou Legend (Dodson), 71
Beatty, Ned, 160, 180
Beckett, Samuel, 6; *Waiting for Godot,* 111, 121, 150
Beery, Wallace, 93
Before It Hits Home (West), 194
Belafonte, Harry, 59
Belasco Theatre (DC), 45
Bell, Nelson, 110
Bellamy, Ralph, 105
Benchley, Robert C., 38, 41
Bennett College, 74
Bentley, Walter Edmund, 98
Bergman, Ingrid, 87
Berry, Marilyn, 81
The Birth of a Nation (film), 3, 19
Bishop, Jane, 257
Black Arts Movement, 11, 166, 216, 223, 231, 270
Blackface performances, 3, 29–30, 32, 34, 97
Blackfriars Guild, 94, 99–102, 103
Blackfriars Institute of Dramatic Arts, 100, 101
Blackfriars Theatre (New York), 99, 101
Black Liberation Movement, 234
Black Nationalism, 213
Black Nativity (Hughes), 12, 236, 237, 248
The Blacks (Genet), 161, 219, 237–39, 252
Black Theatre Alliance, 196
Blake, Eubie, 35
Bledsoe, Harold, 42, 285n76

Blitzstein, Marc: *The Cradle Will Rock,* 58
Blueblood (Johnson), 69
Blues for Mr. Charlie (Baldwin), 76
Blues People: Negro Music in White America (Baraka), 214
Bogart, Humphrey, 105
Bolm, Adolph, 75
Bond, Sadie, 180
Bonner, Marita, 68
The Book Club Play (Zacarías), 273
Books, Gwendolyn, 248
Borchert, James, 24
Bosco, Phillip, 7
Boseman, Chadwick, 76
Boskoff, Alexander, 238
Boucicault, Dion, 95; *Arrah-na-Pogue,* 96; *The Colleen Bawn,* 96; *The Octoroon,* 96; *The Shaughraun,* 96
Bowie, David: *Lazarus,* 195
Bowie State University, 232
Bowser, Muriel E., 212, 218
Boyd, Wesley, 200
Brady, Adah May, 101, 103, 107, 109
Brady, Leo, 101, 103, 107, 109–10, 123, 126–27; *Brother Orchid,* 105; *Yankee Doodle Boy,* 106–7
Brady, Roger, 270–71
Braham, David, 96, 97
Brawley, Benjamin, 26
Brecht, Bertolt, 150; *The Caucasian Chalk Circle,* 148, 153
Breuer, Lee: *The Gospel at Colonus,* 199–201
Briggs-Hall, Austin, 77
Broadway productions, 65, 120, 150, 156, 162, 164, 219, 236, 246. *See also specific productions and participants*
The Broken Banjo (Richardson), 64, 65–66

Brooks, Avery, 194, 221
Brother Orchid (Brady), 105
Brougham, John, 95, 96
Broun, Heywood, 38, 45
Brown, Charles, 71
Brown, Chuck, 217
Brown, Graham, 81
Brown, J. Carter, 231
Brown, Joe, 198
Brown, Oscar, Jr., 253
Brown, Ralph, 107, 109, 110; *Sanctuary DC,* 198
Brown, Rhozier H. "Roach," 187
Brown, Sterling A., 50, 54, 59–60, 68–69, 71, 77; "Negro Character as Seen by White Authors," 31, 68–69
Brown, Tamara Lizette, 72, 73, 228, 250
Brown, William Alexander, 30–31, 81
Browne, Roscoe Lee, 161, 221, 238
The Brownies' Book (magazine), 64
Brown-Terrell, Angela, 244
Brustein, Robert, 164
Buchanan, Cynthia, 180
Bunche, Ralph, 54
Bureau of Engraving and Printing (US), 61–62, 63
Burke, Inzes M., 64
Burleigh, Alston, 42
Burleigh, Harry T., 33, 43
Burnett, Leonie, 73
Burns, Tommy, 158
Burrill, Mary, 19
Burroughs, Eric, 58
Bushman, Francis X., 93
Bushnell, William, 164
Butcher, James W., Jr., 69, 80; *Milk and Honey,* 69

Cagney, James, 107
Callan, Josephine, 6–8, 100–106, 109–10, 114, 123
Calloway, Earl, 245
Cambridge, Godfrey, 161, 221, 238
Cameron, David, 232
Campbell, Kenneth, 121–22
Campbell, Sylvester, 75
Cane (Toomer), 26, 49
Capitol Ballet, 75, 247
Carew, Topper, 11–12, 13, 218, 226–27, 230–31. *See also* New Thing Art and Architecture Center
Carey, Bernadette, 193
Carey, Fabian, 99, 101–2
Carey, Thomas, 94
Carmichael, Stokely, 230
Carmody, Jay, 71, 78–79, 110, 111, 135
Carolina Playmakers, 36, 40
Carroll, John, 91
Carroll, Leo G., 110
Carroll, Pat, 7
Carter, Jack, 58
Carter, Philip D., 226–27
Casino Theatre (New York), 33
Catanese, Brandi Wilkins, 196
Catholic Actors Guild of America, 97–98
Catholic Theatre Movement (CTM), 98
Catholic University drama program: African Americans and, 85–86, 309n216; Blackfriars Guild and, 94, 99–102, 103; celebrities and, 125–27; history of, 6–8, 89–91; Irish stage presence and, 95–99; National Catholic Theatre Conference and, 99; Olney Theatre and, 116–18; productions by, 102–11, 122–25;

touring by, 111–15; Washington's Catholic heritage and, 91–93. *See also* Hartke, Gilbert V.
Cato (play), 28
The Caucasian Chalk Circle (Brecht), 148, 153
Ceremonies in Dark Old Men (play), 219
Chagrin, Claude, 124
Changes (Motojicho), 240
Chaplin, Charlie, 93
Chappelle, Dave, 259
Charles Playhouse (Boston), 141–42
Chekov, Anton, 44; *The Proposal,* 69
Cherry Lane Theater (New York), 76, 215, 221
The Cherry Orchard (play), 171
Chesley, Lorene, 197
Chestnut Street Theatre (Philadelphia), 28–29
Chicago World's Fair (1893), 32, 33
Childress, Alice, 59
The Chip Woman's Fortune (Richardson), 26, 62, 64–65
"Chocolate City," 143–47, 150, 190, 216–18
Chopin, Frederic, 252
Churchill, Sarah, 117
Churchill, Winston, 38
civil service, segregation policies in, 18–19
Clark, Stephanie, 234
Clarke, David A., 224
Cleage, Pearl, 180
Clef Club, 34
Cleveland, Grover, 90
Clifford, Carrie, 2, 68, 212
Clorindy; or the Origin in the Cakewalk (Cook & Dunbar), 33–34
Cochran, Stephen E., 117
Coconut Grove Playhouse (Florida), 111, 121, 150, 152

Coda (Walker), 232, 234
Coe, Richard: Arena Stage and, 135; awards for, 175; on DCBRC productions, 234, 242–43; on Hooks, 212, 239; on Howard Players, 71, 78; on Hyman, 78; on Motojicho, 240; on The Rep, Inc., 254
Cohan, George M., 97, 98, 106–7
Cole, Bob: *A Trip to Coontown,* 21, 34
Cole, Olivia, 156, 157, 192
Coleridge-Taylor, Samuel, 43
Coles, Zaida, 81
The Collection (Pinter), 151
The Colleen Bawn (Boucicault), 96
The Comedian (Gheon), 106
The Comedy of Errors (Shakespeare), 65
Communist Party, 219
Compromise (Richardson), 63, 64, 65–66, 69
Compton, Gardner, 246
Connelly, Marc: *Green Pastures,* 43, 82
Cook, Charles Lee, 42
Cook, Will Marion, 26, 32–33; *Clorindy; or the Origin in the Cakewalk,* 33–34; *In Dahomey,* 26, 34; *Jes' Lak White Fo'ks,* 21; *A Lucky Coon,* 34; *Senegambian Carnival,* 34
Cook, Will Mercer, 35
Cooke, Anne, 70, 77, 80
Cools, George Cram "Jig," 36
Cooper, Anna Julia, 2, 28, 82, 212
Cooper, Peggy, 231, 232, 237, 245–46, 257–59
Copland, Aaron: *The Second Hurricane,* 194
Corbin, John, 65
Corrigan, Joseph, 108

Costello, Charles, 99
The Cradle Will Rock (Blitzstein), 58
Craven, Franc, 104
Cronyn, Hume, 117, 151
Crouch, Donald, 161
CTM (Catholic Theatre Movement), 98
Cuffrey, Anthony, 91
Cuney-Hare, Maud, 64
Cyrano de Bergerac (Rostand), 104

Dafora, Asadata, 58
dance: African Heritage Dancers and Drummers, 228–29; DCBRC and, 244–48; Howard University Dance Group, 72–75, 246–47
Dance Theater of Harlem, 247
Da Silva, Howard, 58
Davies, Robertson, 63
Davis, Angela, 190
Davis, Chuck, 74
Davis, Clinton Turner, 196–97
Davis, Miles, 214
Davis, Ossie, 60, 76, 190
Day, Mary, 247
Day of Absence (Ward), 248
DC Black Repertory Company (DCBRC), 231–45; Arena Stage and, 222; closing of, 248–49, 255; establishment of, 218; financial challenges, 241, 250; legacy of, 249–52; music and dance in productions of, 244–48
DC Cab (film), 226
DC Home Rule Bill (1973), 11, 14, 217
DC Public Schools, 188, 223, 259; Duke Ellington School for the Arts, 12, 237, 246, 248, 258–59; Dunbar High School, 68; M Street High School, 23, 61
The Deacon's Awakening (Richardson), 63

Deal, Melvin, 74, 228–29
Dee, Ruby, 190, 194
Deferrari, Roy J., 100, 101, 113
De Lanux, Pierre Combret, 43
Dellums, Ron, 234
Dennis, Ralph, 102, 105, 125
desegregation, 75–76
Det Nye Teater (Oslo), 81
The Devil's Discipline (Shaw), 124
Dickerson, Glenda, 197, 232; *Owen's Song*, 242–44
Dillon, Melinda, 151
Dinkins, David, 54
The Disappointment or The Force of Credulity (play), 29
District of Columbia Teachers College, 224
Dixwell Players (New Haven), 39
Dr. Faustus (Marlowe), 106
Dr. Strangelove (film), 161
Dodson, Owen, 69–71, 76–80, 197, 242–43; *Bayou Legend*, 71
Donaldson, Ivanhoe, 224
Donnelly, Tom, 135, 162
Doris W. Jones School of Dance (DC), 75
Dorsey, Earle, 46
Dostert, Leon, 103
Douglas, Aaron, 68
Douglass, Frederick, 32
Douglass, Joseph, 32
Dove, Ulysses, 74
Drake, Alfred, 88
Dramatists' Guild, 7, 87
Dreiser, Theodore, 40
Drew, Charles R., 54
Dreyfus, Joel, 241
Du Bois, W. E. B.: Cooke and, 70; Grimké's *Rachel* and, 4; Howard Players and, 20, 22–23, 38, 46; Krigwa Players and, 59, 66, 68; legacy of, 82; Little Negro

Theatres and, 56; Locke and, 55; Richardson and, 64, 65–66; Saturday Night Salons and, 68; *Souls of Black Folk*, 245
Dukakis, Olympia, 118, 190
Duke Ellington School for the Arts (DC), 12, 237, 246, 248, 258–59
Dumbarton College, 103, 107
Dunbar, Paul Laurence, 24, 26, 32, 64; *Clorindy; or the Origin in the Cakewalk*, 33–34; *In Dahomey*, 26, 34; *A Lucky Coon*, 34; *Senegambian Carnival*, 34
Dunbar High School (DC), 68. *See also* M Street High School
Dunbar-Nelson, Alice, 19
Duncan, Thelma Myrtle, 64
Dunsany, Lord, 47; *The Lost Silk Hat*, 69
Dupont, Gerald E., 115
Durkee, J. Stanley, 42, 47–48, 53–54, 65
The Dutchman (Baraka), 76, 214–15, 219
Dvořák, Antonin, 32–33
Dyson, Ernest, 225
Dyson, Lyn, 253–54

Eastman, Max, 20
Edmonds, Randolph, 68
Egypt, Ophelia S., 168
Eliot, Samuel L., Jr., 38
Eliot, T. S., 21, 119; *Murder in the Cathedral*, 106
Ellington, Duke, 26, 34; *Sophisticated Ladies*, 199
The Emperor Jones (O'Neill), 43–47
Enclave (Laurents), 176
England, Lois, 247
Ethiopian Art Players, 56, 62, 65
Europe, Jim Reese, 34
Everyman Street Theatre (DC), 236
Ewell, Tom, 121, 152

Fainson, George, 74
Fairbanks, Henry, 115
Faison, George, 75
The Fall of British Tyranny (play), 29
Farley, James A., 108
Farrow, Charles, 235, 240–41
Fauntroy, Walter, 224
Federal City College, 211, 224–25, 231
Federal Theatre Project, 57, 58–59, 133
Feigan, Norman, 234
Felder, Robert, 225
Fences (Wilson), 157, 194
Feng, Hsi Yun, 21
Ferrel, Conchata, 180
Ferris, George Washington Gale, Jr., 33
Fichandler, Thomas: African Americans and, 155–59, 167, 168–72, 191–99; Alexander (Robert) and, 189; Arena Stage community and, 177; Foggy Bottom transition and, 138–40; founding of Arena Stage, 8–10, 131–34; Hartke and, 127–28; Hippodrome acquisition and, 134–36; Hooks and, 222; Kreeger Theater and, 178–81; League of Regional Theatres and, 142, 164; Living Stage and, 190–91; new building construction and, 148–50; transition to not-for-profit theater, 140–43
Fichandler, Zelda Diamond: African Americans and, 155–59, 167, 168–72, 191–99; Alexander (Robert) and, 187–89; *The Arena Adventure: The First Forty Years,* 10; Arena Stage community and, 177; awards for Arena and, 201–2; Foggy Bottom transition and, 138–40; founding of Arena Stage, 8–10, 131–34; Hartke and, 127–28; Hippodrome acquisition and, 134–36; Hooks and, 222; Kreeger Theater and, 178–81; Living Stage and, 190–91; new building construction and, 148–50; Schneider and, 151; "Towards a Deepening Aesthetic," 158; transition to not-for-profit theater, 140–43; Wager replacing as artistic director, 195
Fiedler, Arthur, 73
"Fine Clothes to the Jew" (Hughes), 26
Fish, Hamilton, Jr., 21
Fishburne, Laurence, 221
Flack, Roberta, 227
Flanagan, Hallie, 57, 134
Fleisher, Leon, 175
Fletcher, Jay, 156, 157
Foch, Ferdinand, 42
Foggy Bottom (DC): Arena Stage transition to, 138–40; gentrification of, 207; redevelopment of, 143–47
Fokine, Mikhail, 75
Folger Theater Company, 271
Ford Foundation: Arena Stage and, 141–42, 149, 156, 179, 192–93; Negro Ensemble Company and, 219
Fordham University, 89
Ford's Theatre (DC), 123, 127
For One Night Only (Baker), 27
Foster, Stephen, 30
Fountain, Clarence, 200, 201
Foxworth, Robert, 160, 184
Franklin, Aretha, 247
Franklin, John Hope, 54
Franklin-Cook, Coralie, 27

Frazee Theater (New York), 65
Frazier, E. Franklin, 46, 54
Freedman's Bureau, 25
Freeman, Mabel Jones, 74
Freeman, Morgan, 194, 200
Fribert, Christen, 81
Front Theatre (Memphis), 141
Frye, Christopher: *The Lady's Not for Burning,* 77
Funk, Jacob, 139

Gaines-Carter, Patrice, 245
GALA (Grupo de Artistas Latino-americanos), 261–63
Galella, Donatella, 157, 159, 166, 193, 202–3, 208, 250; *America in the Round,* 143
García Lorca, Federico, 184
Gardner, R. H., 193
Gaxton, William, 104
Gee, Richard L., 248
Geer, Will, 58
General Education Board, 70
Genesis: Juba and Other Jewels, a Song-Step of Black America (documentary), 245–46
Genet, Jean: *The Blacks,* 161, 219, 237–39, 252
gentrification: in Adams Morgan, 13–14, 227; backlash against, 217; in Foggy Bottom, 207; in U Street neighborhood, 190. *See also* Southwest Redevelopment Project
Georgetown University, 89, 91
George Washington University, 139
Gerald, Melvin D., Jr., 256
Gershwin, George: *Porgy and Bess,* 33
Gheon, Henri: *The Comedian,* 106
Gibson, Al, 169

Gibson, Henry, 7, 116
Gibson, James O., 231–32
Gielgud, John, 77, 78–79, 112
Gilpin, Charles S., 44–46
Gilpin Players (Cleveland), 56
The Gingham Dog (Wilson), 176
Gjesdahl, Paul, 81
A Glance at New York (Baker), 95
Glaspell, Susan, 36
The Glass Menagerie (Williams), 71, 154, 194
Glover, Danny, 221
God's Stage (Kerr), 112
Goettelmann, Paul, 103, 124
Goetz, Ruth and Augustus: *The Heiress,* 197
Gogol, Nikolai: *The Inspector General,* 160
go-go music, 198, 217–18
Goldsmith, Oliver: *She Stoops to Conquer,* 27, 132, 135
Good Morning, Miss Dove (McCleery), 125–26
Gordone, Charles, 161, 238; *No Place to Be Somebody,* 176
The Gospel at Colonus (Breuer & Telson), 199–201
Gossett, Louis, Jr., 161, 219, 221, 238
Gottfried, Martin, 121, 165
Graham, Bill, 116, 123
Graham, Gilbert, 107
Graham, Martha, 73, 184
Graham, Ottie, 42
Graves, Denyce, 259
Gray, Christine Rauchfuss, 61, 62
The Great Macdaddy (Harrison), 221
The Great White Hope (Sackler), 158–72
Green, Constance McLaughlin, 82
Green, Paul, 36, 40; *In Abraham's Bosom,* 69

Green, Petey, 222
Greenberg, Stanley R.: *Pueblo,* 177
Green Pastures (Connelly), 43, 82
Gregory, Dick, 231
Gregory, Lady, 5, 36, 263
Gregory, Thomas Montgomery:
    acting in productions at How-
    ard Theatre, 28; appointment
    to Howard University, 21–22;
    departure from Howard Uni-
    versity, 49; Dodson and, 71; *The
    Emperor Jones* production and,
    45–46; Grimké's *Rachel* and, 5;
    Locke and, 50; NAACP and, 2,
    5, 212; National Negro The-
    atre and, 17, 36, 76–77; in New
    Jersey, 49–50; playbill collection
    of, 43–44; World Disarmament
    Conference and, 41–43. *See also*
    Howard Players
Griffin, Eleanor, 126
Griffith, D. W., 3, 19
Grimké, Angelina Weld, 3–4, 61;
    Rachel, 4–5, 19, 21
Grimké, Archibald, 3
Grimké, Francis, 3
Grizzard, George, 118, 132, 151
Gross, Clay, 197
Grupo de Artistas Latinoamerica-
    nos (GALA), 261–63
Guest, Mrs. Polk, 234
Guillaume, Paul, 52
Guinn, Dorothy C., 64
Gunner, Frances, 64
Guy, Nathaniel, 4

Haddock, Frances, 73
Hadestown (Mitchell), 195
Hagan, Fannie Emma, 22
Hagen, Uta, 151
Hall, Adelaide, 35
Hall, Arthur, 228

Hall, Juanita, 88
Hall, Leonard, 35–36
Hallam, Lewis, 29
Hallam, Lewis, Jr., 29
Hamilton, Brian, 208
Hamlet (Shakespeare), 77–79
Hammerstein, Oscar, II, 7
Hammond, Bernice, 74–75
Hammond, Percy, 65
Hampton Institute, 228
Hanley, William: *Slow Dance on a
    Killing Ground,* 176
Hansberry, Lorraine, 76; *A Raisin
    in the Sun,* 199, 219
Happy Journey (Wilder), 106
Harding, Warren G., 41
Harlem Renaissance. *See* New Ne-
    gro (Harlem) Renaissance
Harlem Suitcase Theatre, 59
Harman, Sidney, 207
Harrigan, Edward, 95, 96; *The Mul-
    ligan Guard,* 96–97; *The Mulligan
    Guard Picnic,* 97
Harriman, Averell, 126
Harris, Abram, 54
Harrison, Paul Carter: *The Great
    Macdaddy,* 221
Harrison, Richard B., 43
Hart, Tony Cannon, 96; *The Mulli-
    gan Guard,* 96–97; *The Mulligan
    Guard Picnic,* 97
Hartke, Emil, 93
Hartke, Gilbert V.: biographical
    background, 93–94; Blackfri-
    ars Guild and, 94, 99–102, 103;
    Catholic University drama
    productions and, 6–8, 102–15,
    122–25; celebrities and, 125–27;
    death of, 123; drama program
    founded by, 86; Fichandlers
    and, 132; Kennedy Center and,
    7, 122, 127, 270; in Kennedy's

funeral procession, 268; legacy of, 127–28; National Catholic Theater and, 88–89; Olney Theatre and, 116–18. *See also* Catholic University drama program

Harvard Dramatic Club, 37

Hassan, Rusty, 227

Hastie, William, 54

Haydon, Julie, 104

Hayes, Helen, 7, 94, 125–27

Hayes, Patrick, 128

Haywood, Claire, 247

The Heart of a Woman (Johnson), 67

Hecht, Ben, 93

Hedda Gabler (Ibsen), 69

The Heiress (Goetz & Goetz), 197

Helfen, Mathias, 98

Henig, Jeffrey, 13–14

Henry Street Playhouse (New York), 74

Herman, George, 7

Herod (Phillips), 27

Heurich, Christian, 138

Hewlett, James, 30–31

Heyman Foundation, 184

Heyward, Dorothy and duBose: *Mamba's Daughters*, 80, 81

Hill, Abram, 59

Hill, Arthur, 151

The Hip Hop Nightmares of Jujube Brown (Nelson), 256

Hippodrome (DC), 8–9, 132, 134–37, 181

Hitchcock, Alfred, 112

Hoban, James, 91–92

Hobson, Julius, 224

Hodge, Mike, 232

Hogan, Ernest, 33

Holland, Endesha, 180

Holliday, Kene, 232

Holman, M. Carl, 232

home rule, 11, 14, 217

Hook, James, 234

Hooker, Brian, 104

Hooks, Robert: as actor, 215, 219; DCBRC closing and, 12, 248–49; DCBRC established by, 12, 212, 218, 231–32; DCBRC productions and, 237–44; Howard Players and, 76; move to Washington, 222–23; Negro Ensemble Company and, 218–22

Hopper, Hedda, 112

Horn, Shirley, 227

Horne, Lena, 190, 197

Houseman, John, 57

Houston, Charles, 46, 54

Howard, Oliver Otis, 23, 25

Howard Players: in 1930s and 1940s, 68–71; in 1950s, 76–77; Brown (Sterling) and, 59–60, 68–69; Durkee and, 48, 65; *The Emperor Jones* production, 43–47; establishment and development of, 26–28, 35–40; evolution of, 68–71; *Hamlet* productions, 77–79; institutional challenges, 47–50; international tour (1949), 80–82; *Mortgaged* production, 65; music and dance incorporated in productions, 72–75; New Negro Renaissance and, 51–59; Richardson (Willis) and, 60–68; World Disarmament Conference performance (1921), 41–43

Howard Theatre, 26, 28, 35, 65, 76

Howard University: Black Arts Movement and, 231; commitment to drama, 26–28; Dance Group and Dance Ensemble, 72–75, 246–47; Drama Club, 26–28; Glee Club, 42–43; Gregory's appointment to, 21–22; neighborhood surrounding,

24–26, 63; Stylus Society, 36. *See also* Howard Players

Hughes, Charles Evans, 41

Hughes, Langston, 24, 43, 51, 59, 68, 82; *Black Nativity,* 12, 236, 237, 248; "Fine Clothes to the Jew," 26; *Mulatto,* 68; *Simply Heavenly,* 252; *Tambourines of Glory,* 257

Hume, Paul, 74

Hurston, Zora Neale, 36, 54, 68, 82

Hyacinth on Wheels (Kerr), 105, 106

Hyman, Earle, 71, 77, 78, 79

Hyra, Derek, 271

Ibsen, Henrik, 44; *Hedda Gabler,* 69; *Peer Gynt,* 109; *The Wild Duck,* 71, 80, 81

I'd Rather Be Right (play), 106

Imamu (Baraka), 232, 233

Immaculata College, 103, 107

In Abraham's Bosom (Green), 69

In Dahomey (Cook & Dunbar), 26, 34

Inherit the Wind (Lawrence & Lee), 154–55

The Inspector General (Gogol), 160

In the Heights (Miranda), 263

Ionesco, Eugène: *The Lesson,* 173

Irish immigrants, 95–97

Irish National Theater, 5, 36, 37, 40, 62, 88

Ives, Burl, 88

Jackson, Samuel L., 221

Jamal, Sati, 232

James, Henry: *Washington Square,* 197

Jaochim, Joseph, 32

Jar the Floor (West), 183, 194

jazz music, 214, 225, 227

Jeffries, James J., 158

Jenny Kissed Me (Kerr), 110

Jes' Lak White Fo'ks (Cook), 21

Jeyifous, Abiodun, 214

Jim Crow policies, 7–8, 19, 25, 85–86, 120, 173, 270

Jim Dandy (Saroyan), 108

Joan of Lorraine (play), 87

Joe Turner's Come and Gone (Wilson), 180

John F. Kennedy Center for the Performing Arts: African Heritage Dancers and Drummers, 229; Arena Stage and, 182; DCBRC's *The Blacks,* 237–38; DCBRC's *Owen's Song,* 243; Hartke and, 7, 122, 127, 270; role in DC's performing arts community, 269–70

Johns Hopkins University, 90

Johnson, Billy, 34

Johnson, Charles S., 52

Johnson, Georgia Douglas, 19, 20, 60, 67; *Blueblood,* 69; *The Heart of a Woman,* 67; *A Sunday Morning in the South,* 20

Johnson, Henry Lincoln, 67

Johnson, Jack, 158–59

Johnson, James Weldon, 32, 64, 68, 82

Johnson, Lady Bird, 148

Johnson, Louis, 12–13, 75, 223, 232–33, 236, 240, 246; *No Outlet,* 234

Johnson, Lyndon, 122, 268

Johnson, Mortdecai, 54

Johnson, Pat, 244

Johnson, Philip, 179

John Street Theatre (New York), 29

Jones, Davey Marlin, 174–75

Jones, Doris, 75, 247

Jones, James Earl, 159–63, 165, 169, 176, 219, 238

Jones, LeRoi. *See* Baraka, Imamu
   Amiri
Jones, Margo, 9, 131, 134
Jones, Robert Earl, 161, 200
Jones, Robert L., 38
Jones, William B., 238
Jones Haywood School of Ballet
   (DC), 75, 236, 247
Joplin, Scott, 33; *Treemonisha,* 246
Jordan, Barbara, 190
The Journal of Negro History (Wood-
   son), 63
Julian, Percy, 54
Junk Yard Band, 217
Just, Ernest Everett, 2, 26, 27, 82

Kahn, Michael, 271
Kaplan, Morris, 164
Karamu Theatre (Cleveland), 56
Karlweis, Ninow, 238
Katz, Vera, 197
Kaufman, George S., 317n22
Kazan, Elia, 57
Kennedy, John F., 122, 268
Kennedy Center. *See* John F. Ken-
   nedy Center for the Performing
   Arts
Kerner Commission (1968), 192,
   312n281
Kerr, Jean, 7; *Jenny Kissed Me,* 110
Kerr, Walter: awards for, 120;
   Catholic University drama pro-
   gram and, 6–8, 87–88, 101–10,
   113, 120–21; *God's Stage,* 112;
   Hyacinth on Wheels, 105, 106;
   on Negro Ensemble Company,
   220; on Sackler's *The Great White
   Hope,* 162; *Yankee Doodle Boy,*
   106–7
King, Martin Luther, Jr., 10–11,
   166, 169, 172, 192
King, Woodie, Jr., 232

Koch, Frederick, 36, 38, 40
Kociolek, Ted: *Abyssinia,* 194
Koston, Dina, 175
Kotto, Yaphet, 234
Krazy Kat Klub (DC), 48
Kreeger, David Lloyd, 179
Kreeger Theater (DC), 179–81, 204,
   222
Kriegsman, Alan, 234–35
Krigwa Players, 56, 59, 66, 68
Krone, Gerald S., 218–22
Kubrick, Stanley, 161

The Lady's Not for Burning (Frye),
   77
Lafayette Players (New York), 56,
   58
Lahr, Bert, 121, 152
Lahr, John, 121
La MaMa Experimental Theatre
   Club (New York), 199–200
Lamb, Thomas W., 262
Larson, Jonathan: *Rent,* 195
Last Colony Theater (DC), 233, 243,
   251, 252
Latimore, Joseph, 147, 206
Latin American community,
   260–63, 273
Laurents, Arthur: *Enclave,* 176
Lavery, Emmet, 98–99
Laves, Peggy, 149
Lawrence, Jacob, 229
Lawrence, Jerome: *Inherit the Wind,*
   154–55
Lawton, Jacqueline E., 257
Lazarus (Bowie), 195
Lead Belly (Huddie William Led-
   better): "The Bourgeois Blues,"
   24
League of Nations, 41
League of Regional Theatres, 142,
   164, 197, 243

Lee, Canada, 58, 59
Lee, Ming Cho, 152–53, 154, 155
Lee, Robert E.: *Inherit the Wind*, 154
Lee, Tunney, 230
Lenox, Adriane, 194
Leo XIII (pope), 90
Leon, Kenny, 257
Lescaze, William, 134
The Lesson (Ionesco), 173
Levenson, Steven, 204
Levey, Ethel, 106
Levin, Herman, 167–68
Levy, Jacques, 153
Lewis, Del, 190
Lewis, Grace Hegger, 38
Lewis, Sinclair, 38
Leyba, Claire, 77
Lillie, Frank R., 27
Lincoln, Abbey, 161, 238
Lincoln Theater (DC), 257
Linden, Hal, 176
Lippmann, Walter, 21
Lisner Auditorium (George Washington University), 7, 87
Little, Cleavon, 221
Little Negro Theatres, 56
Little Theatre Movement, 39, 94, 133
Living Stage, 184–94, 256
Livingston, Myrtle Smith, 19
Locke, Alain LeRoy: departure from Howard University, 50; Gregory and, 50; Grimké's *Rachel* and, 4–5; Howard Players and, 22, 47; NAACP and, 2, 5, 212; Negro National Theater and, 36–37, 38–39, 43, 77; *The New Negro: An Interpretation*, 53, 54, 65; New Negro Renaissance and, 50–56; "Steps Toward a Negro Theatre," 38
Logan, Belina, 232

Logan, Rayford, 54
Long Day's Journey into Night (O'Neill), 125, 126–27
Longworth, Alice Roosevelt, 126
Look Back in Anger (Osborne), 160
Lorton Correctional Center, 187
The Lost Silk Hat (Dunsany), 69
Lowery, W. McNeil "Mac," 142
Loyola Community Theatre (Chicago), 99, 100
Luckinbill, Larry, 116
A Lucky Coon (Cook & Dunbar), 34
Lumbly, Carl, 200
Lummis, Eliza O'Brien, 98
Lyles, Aubrey, 35

Macgowan, Kenneth, 38, 45
Mackaye, Percy, 38
MacMachon, Aline, 114
The Magic Door (television show), 50
Mallard, Carol, 244
Malone, Mike, 12, 223, 231–33, 236–37, 240, 247–48, 259; *Genesis: Juba and Other Jewels, a Song-Step of Black America* (documentary) and, 245–46; *Owen's Song*, 242–44; *Spirit*, 234
Mamba's Daughters (Heyward & Heyward), 80, 81
Mangum, Ed, 8–9, 127–28, 132–36, 205
Manning's Minstrels, 96
Marie H. Reed Recreation Center, 230
Marks, Peter, 263
Marlowe, Christopher: *Dr. Faustus*, 106
Marriott, John, 156, 194
Marshall, Thurgood, 54
Martyn, Edward, 5, 36, 263
Matheus, John, 64

Matura, Mustafa: *Playboy of the West Indies,* 194
Maynard, Dorothy, 128
McAllister, Marvin, 22
McCarthy, Joseph, 114
McCleery, William: *Good Morning, Miss Dove,* 125–26
McConnell, Bernard, 103
McCoo, Edward J., 64
McCue, Lori, 273
McDonald, William Joseph, 124
McGee, Thomas D'Arcy, 95
McGiver, John, 7, 118
McLaughlin, Leonard B., 117
McMahon, Ed, 7, 124
McMillan, John, 217
McPherson, Cynthia, 156, 157, 192
Mead Center for American Theater, 204
Medrano, Hugo, 260–63
Mencken, H. L., 57
The Merchant of Venice (Shakespeare), 27, 28
The Merry Wives of Windsor (Shakespeare), 27
Metheny, Russell, 271
Meyer, Eugene, 124
Meyer Foundation, 143, 149, 179, 184, 223
Meyers, Patrick, 153
Mfume, Kweisi, 190
Midsummer Night's Dream (Shakespeare), 28
Migliaccio, Donna, 271
Milk and Honey (Butcher), 69
Miller, Arthur, 8, 57; *All My Sons,* 71
Miller, Ethelbert, 190
Miller, Fournoy, 35
Miller, Henry D., 4; *Theorizing Black Theatre,* 21
Miller, James A., 53

Miller, Kelly, 21, 37
Miller, May, 64, 68, 71
Milloy, Courtland, 201
Mills, Florence, 35
Milwaukee Repertory Company, 141
Miner, Myrtilla, 224
minstrel shows, 18, 29–30, 32, 246
Miranda, Lin-Manuel: *In the Heights,* 263
The Miser (Molière), 106
Mitchell, Abbie, 33
Mitchell, Anaïs: *Hadestown,* 195
Mitchell, Arthur, 247
Mitchell, Koritha, 19–20
Molière: *The Miser,* 106; *School for Wives,* 114
Monk, Isabell, 200
Montgomery County Recreation Department, 260
Moore, Douglas, 224
Moore, George, 5, 36
Moore, John L., III, 255
Moore, Robert, 118
Moore, William H., 225
Moore-Forrest, Marie, 26, 43, 77
Moorland, Jesse E., 48, 54
Morris, Byron, 227
Morrison, Toni, 54
Mortgaged (Richardson), 48, 64, 65
Mortimer, John: *What Shall We Tell Caroline?,* 154
Morton, Jelly Roll, 252
Motojicho (Vantile Whitfield), 12–13, 223, 232–33, 250, 255; *Changes,* 240
M Street High School (DC), 23, 61
Mulatto (Hughes), 68
The Mulligan Guard (Harrigan & Hart), 96–97
The Mulligan Guard Picnic (Harrigan & Hart), 97

Multi-Media Training Institute, 253
Mummers Theatre (Oklahoma
    City), 141
A Murder Has Been Arranged (Wil-
    liams), 69
Murder in the Cathedral (Eliot), 106
Murray, Peg, 176
music: African Heritage Dancers
    and Drummers, 228–29; Arena
    Stage and, 200–201; in DCBRC
    productions, 244–48; GALA
    and, 262; go-go music, 198,
    217–18; Howard Players and,
    42–43, 60, 72–75; jazz music,
    214, 225, 227; Living Stage and,
    187; in Motojicho's *Changes,* 240;
    New Thing Art and Architec-
    ture Center and, 226; The Rep,
    Inc. and, 254. *See also specific*
    artists
Myerberg, Michael, 121
Myrtilla Miner Normal School
    (DC), 4, 45, 224

NAACP, 2–4, 5, 56, 86, 212
Nagel, Urban E., 94, 99, 101–2
Nalle, David, 155
National Advisory Commission
    on Civil Disorders (1968), 192,
    312n281
National Capital Planning Com-
    mission, 146
National Catholic Theatre Confer-
    ence, 6, 99, 100, 102
National Conservatory (New
    York), 32–33
National Endowment for the Arts,
    122–23, 124, 184, 193, 233
National Park Service, 241–42
National Players Program, 113
National Theatre (DC), 7, 82,
    86–87, 107, 133

National Urban League, 49
National Women's Party, 43
Native Gardens (Zacarías), 273
Native Son (Wright), 59
Ndegeocello, Meshell, 259
Neal, Gaston, 230–31
Neal, Larry, 215
Neale, Francis Ignatius, 91
Neglected Neighbors (Weller), 24
Negro Dramatists' Laboratory, 59
Negro Ensemble Company (NEC),
    12, 197, 218–22
Negro Playwrights Company, 59
Negro Repertory Players of Wash-
    ington, 69
Negro Theatre Unit, 57–58, 59
Neiiendam, Henrik, 81
Nelson, Jennifer, 255–56; *The Hip*
    Hop Nightmares of Jujube Brown,
    256
Nelson, Stanley, 245
Nentoff, Nat, 221
Nevinson, Henry, 43
Nevius, Gilbert, 101
New Deal programs, 57, 139, 268
The New Negro: An Interpretation
    (Locke), 53, 54, 65
New Negro (Harlem) Renaissance,
    4, 31, 50–59, 66–68, 216
New School of Afro-American
    Thought, 230–31
New Theater (New York), 28
New Thing Art and Architecture
    Center, 11–12, 218, 224, 226–29,
    231, 261
The New Yorker's Stratagem, or Ba-
    nana's Wedding (play), 29
New York Harmonic Society, 28
New York Public Library, 57
Nicola, Jim, 195
Nixon, Richard, 176
No-Neck Monsters Theatre Com-
    pany, 198

nontraditional casting, 176, 191, 195–98, 211
Non-Traditional Casting Project, 196
No Outlet (Johnson), 234
No Place to Be Somebody (Gordone), 176
Northeast Academy of Dance (DC), 75
Norton, Eleanor Holmes, 190
Nottage, Lynn, 317n22

The Octoroon (Boucicault), 96
Old Dominion Fund, 143, 149, 179
Olde Heurich Brewery (DC), 138
Olney Summer Theater, 7, 87
Olney Theatre Center, 113, 117–18
O'Neill, Eugene, 38, 40, 317n22; *The Emperor Jones*, 43–47; *Long Day's Journey into Night*, 125, 126–27
O'Neill, James, 96
O'Neill, Raymond, 62, 65
Opera Society of Washington, 241
Opportunity (journal), 49, 52
Orton, Joe, 6
Osborne, John: *Look Back in Anger*, 160
Our Town (Wilder), 154–55, 156–57
Owen's Song (Dickerson & Malone), 242–44

The Padlock (play), 28–29, 30
Paige, Jerome, 145–46
Papp, Joseph, 161, 219–20
Parks, Suzan-Lori, 180
Parson, Louella, 93
Pasek, Benj, 204
Patton, Frances Gray, 126
Paul, Justin, 204
Paul Robeson Center (DC), 253

Pavlova, Anna, 75
Peer Gynt (Ibsen), 109
Pei, I. M., 140, 143
Pekin Theatre (Chicago), 56
Performing Arts Society of Los Angeles, 233
Period of Adjustment (Williams), 173–74
Perry, Shauneille, 81
The Persecution and Assassination of Jean-Paul Marat (Weiss), 177
Perseverance Theatre (Juneau), 204
Peters, Brock and DiDi, 167, 238
Phillips, Stephen: *Herod*, 27
Picket, Jessye, 33
Pierce, Neal, 147, 206
Pinkett, Flaxie, 232
Pinter, Harold, 6, 150; *The Collection*, 151
Pittsburgh Cycle (Wilson), 62, 215–16
Pius XI (pope), 86
Playboy of the Western World (Synge), 115
Playboy of the West Indies (Matura), 194
Players, Incorporated, 113, 115–18, 122
Plays and Pageants from the Life of the Negro (Richardson), 64
Plays of Negro Life: A Source-Book of Native American Drama (Gregory & Locke), 50
Plummer, Christopher, 201
Poe, Harry, 197
Poitier, Sidney, 59
The Politicians (play), 29
Porgy and Bess (Gershwin), 33, 43
Powell, Matthew Donald, 6, 102
Prince, Sabiyha, 271
The Prince of Parthia (play), 28
"propaganda" plays, 20

The Proposal (Chekov), 69
Prosky, Robert, 155, 160, 184
Providence College, 94
Provincetown Players, 36, 39–40, 43, 44, 48
Pueblo (Greenberg), 177
Pyles, Raymond S., 174

Quill Club (Boston), 39

Racheff, James: *Abyssinia,* 194
Rachel (Grimké), 4–5, 19, 21
racial presence, 17–82; African American community and, 24–26; Gregory's return to Howard University, 21–22; history of African Americans on stage, 28–31; Howard University's commitment to drama and, 26–28; stage responses to Wilson's segregationist policies, 19–21; transcending division, 23–24. *See also* Howard Players
A Raisin in the Sun (Hansberry), 199, 219
Raitt, Bonnie, 200
Randall, Tony, 117
Randolph, Harland, 225
Rankin Chapel (Howard University), 27–28, 42–43
Rashad, Phylicia, 76, 197, 221
Rawlins, Lester, 132, 176
Read, Rebecca, 261
Reagon, Bernice, 12, 13, 223, 232, 244; *Upon This Rock,* 234–37
Reed, John, 21, 40
Reid, Louise, 252
Reinisch, Linda, 270–71
Rent (Larson), 195
The Rep, Inc., 252–54
Reuss, Margaret, 145–46
Revere, Anne, 173

Revolutionary Music Collective, 200
Rhodes, George R., 259
Rice, Dan, 30
Richards, Dave, 153, 200
Richards, Lloyd, 180
Richards, Scott, 198
Richardson, Willis, 60–68; *The Broken Banjo,* 64, 65–66; *The Chip Woman's Fortune,* 26, 62, 64–65; *Compromise,* 63, 64, 65–66, 69; *The Deacon's Awakening,* 63; *Mortgaged,* 48, 64, 65; *Plays and Pageants from the Life of the Negro,* 64
Rider of the Dream (Torrence), 69
Ring, Montague, 43
Ritchard, Cyril, 124
The Rivals (Sheridan), 27, 28
Rivera, Chita, 75
The River Niger (Walker), 76, 119, 219
Roach, Hildred, 225
Robbins, Jerome, 12, 223, 236
Roberts, Pernell, 132
Robeson, Paul, 35, 46
Robinson, Edward G., 105
Robinson, Renee, 75
Robinson Crusoe and Harlequin Friday (play), 29
Rockefeller, John D., 70
Rockefeller Foundation, 143, 149, 192
Roker, Roxie, 71, 81, 221
Rolle, Esther, 221
Roney, Wallace, 259
Roosevelt, Eleanor, 80
Roosevelt, Franklin D., 268
Rose McClendon Players, 59
Ross, Elizabeth, 110
Rostand, Edmond: *Cyrano de Bergerac,* 104

Round House Theater (Silver Spring), 260, 271
Ruby, James, 103

Sackler, Howard, 161, 164–65; *The Great White Hope,* 158–72
St. Jacques, Raymond, 161, 238
St. Mary's University, 89
St. Matthew's Cathedral (DC), 92
St. Patrick's Church (DC), 91
St. Vincent Millay, Edna, 40
Saint Augustine's Church (DC), 92
Saint Malachy's Church (New York), 98
Saint Margaret's Episcopal Church (DC), 227
Saint Martin de Porrer Church (DC), 92
Saint Michael's College, 115–16, 117
Salomé (Wilde), 65
Sanctuary DC (Brown), 198
Sanders, Don, 239
Santo Pietro, Mary Jo, 87–88, 107–8, 123
Sarah Lawrence College, 74
Sarandon, Susan, 7
Saroyan, William, 112, 150; *Jim Dandy,* 108
Saunders, Garrett, 156, 157, 192
Schaeffer, Eric, 271
Schick, George, 77
Schier, Ernie, 135
Schmigelsky, Ruth, 109
Schneider, Alan: African American actors used by, 156; Arena Stage and, 135, 148, 150–54; Catholic University drama program and, 6–7, 108–11, 114, 121; Fichandlers and, 128; Moscow tour, 154–55
Schneider, Roy, 118

Schomburg Center for Research in Black Culture, 57
School for Wives (Molière), 114
School of American Ballet (New York), 12, 236
Scott, Emmett J., 42, 50
Scott-Heron, Gil, 1, 211, 225, 277n1
Scribblers (Baltimore), 39
The Second Hurricane (Copland), 194
Seeger, Pete, 184
segregation. *See* Jim Crow policies
Sellars, Peter, 182
Senegambian Carnival (Cook & Dunbar), 34
Shaftsbury Theatre (London), 34
Shakespeare, William, 119; *The Comedy of Errors,* 65; *Hamlet,* 77–79; *The Merchant of Venice,* 27, 28; *The Merry Wives of Windsor,* 27; *Midsummer Night's Dream,* 28; *The Tempest,* 176
Shales, Tom, 241
Shalwitz, Howard, 175, 270–71
Shapiro, Mel, 149
The Shaughraun (Boucicault), 96
Shaw, George Bernard: *The Devil's Discipline,* 124
Sheridan, Richard Brinsley: *The Rivals,* 27, 28
Sherin, Edwin, 149, 159, 160, 162, 170
Sherwood, Robert E., 317n22
She Stoops to Conquer (Goldsmith), 27, 132, 135
Shipp, Jesse A., 34
Show Boat (play), 43
Shuffle Along (play), 35
Signature Theater (DC), 271
Silvera, Frank, 233
Simms, Hilda, 59
Simon, the Cyrenian (Torrence), 42

Simply Heavenly (Hughes), 252
Sinclair, William A., 49
Sing Out, Sweet Land (play), 87–88
Sissle, Noble, 35
Skinner, Cornelia Otis, 7
The Skin of Our Teeth (Wilder), 110, 150
Slaiman, Marjorie, 149
Slezak, Erica, 116
Slow Dance on a Killing Ground (Hanley), 176
Smith, Anna Deveare, 180
Smith, Cecil, 220
Smith, Dick, 208
Smith, Frank, 224
Smith, Harold C., 117
Smith, John Talbot, 98
Smith, Lane, 180
Smith, Molly, 166, 194, 203–5, 267, 274
Smith, Valerian E., 240
Smithsonian Folklife Festival, 242
SNCC (Student Nonviolent Organizing Committee), 224, 235
Snotherly, Rett, 272
A Soldier's Play (play), 219
Sons of Ham (play), 34
Sophisticated Ladies (Ellington), 199
Sothern, Ann, 105
Souls of Black Folk (Du Bois), 245
Source Theater (DC), 256
Southwest Neighborhood Assembly, 147, 183
Southwest Redevelopment Project, 140, 143, 145, 181, 206
Spalding, John Lancaster, 90
Speaight, Robert, 106
Spence, Eulalie, 68; *Undertow,* 69
Spingarn, Joel E., 22, 38
Spirit (Malone), 234
Stage Directors and Choreographers Society, 142

Stanislavski, Konstantin, 184
Starks, Tia Juana, 244
Step Afrika! International Cultural Festival (1994), 229
Stephens, C. Y., 117
Sternhagen, Frances, 7, 118
Stevens, George, Jr., 231
Stevens, Roger, 182, 223, 234, 249
Stevens, Wallace, 40
Stewart, Carolyn Hill, 77, 79
Stewart, Jaye, 232, 253–54
Stewart, Jeffrey C., 53, 55
Strathotte, Maurice Arnold, 33
Student Nonviolent Organizing Committee (SNCC), 224, 235
Studio Theater (DC), 271
The Stylus (magazine), 36
suburbanization, 144–45
A Sunday Morning in the South (Johnson), 20
Swanson, Gloria, 93, 117
Sweet Honey in the Rock (musical group), 13, 244–45
Sylvan Theater (DC), 106
Synge, John Millington: *Playboy of the Western World,* 115

Taft, William Howard, 67
Tambourines of Glory (Hughes), 257
Tandy, Jessica, 117, 151
Tarkington, Booth, 47
Taylor, Lois, 79
Teatro Doble (children's theater company), 260–61
Telson, Bob: *The Gospel at Colonus,* 199–201
The Tempest (Shakespeare), 176
Terrell, Mary Church, 46, 68
Terry, W. Benson "Bill," 168–71
Theater Chamber Players, 175
theater-in-the-round, 9, 131–32, 134–35, 178

Theatre Comique (New York), 96
Theatre '47 (Dallas), 134
Theorizing Black Theatre (Miller), 21
Thimey, Erika, 73
Thom, Bing, 204–5
Thomas, Edna, 58
Thompson, Tazewell, 183, 194–95
Throckmorton, Cleon, 42, 45, 48
Tibbs, Roy W., 42
Tiger, Tiger Burning Bright (play), 219
Tivoli Theater (DC), 262–63
Tomlin, Lily, 180
Toomer, Jean, 26, 68; *Cane,* 26, 49
Torrence, Ridgely, 38, 47; *Rider of the Dream,* 69; *Simon, the Cyrenian,* 42
Traylor, Eleanor, 30, 197
Treemonisha (Joplin), 246
Trinity College, 103, 107
A Trip to Coontown (Cole), 21, 34
The Triumph of Love (play), 29
True Colors Theater Company, 257
Tucker, Iantha, 72
Turpin, Ben, 93
Twentieth Century Fund, 143, 148, 149, 179
Tyler, Aisha, 50
Tyrone, Mary Cavan, 126
Tyson, Cicely, 161, 238

Undertow (Spence), 69
Unitarian Players, 173
United Scenic Artists, 142
University of Dayton, 89
University of District of Columbia, 224
University of Maryland, 232
University of North Carolina, 36, 40, 55
University of Notre Dame, 89
Upon This Rock (Reagon), 234–37

US Conference of Catholic Bishops, 90, 123
US Information Service, 81

Vallila, Marja, 259
Venture, Richard, 184
Voight, Jon, 7, 116, 160
Von Eckardt, Wolf, 145
Voodoo Macbeth (Welles), 58

Wade, Stephen, 180
Wager, Doug, 193–95, 196, 202–3
Wagner, Robin, 149
Waiting for Godot (Beckett), 111, 121, 150
Walker, Aida Overton, 34
Walker, Evan: *Coda,* 232, 234
Walker, George, 33, 34
Walker, Joseph A.: *The River Niger,* 76, 119, 219
Walton, Lester Aglar, 17–18, 35
Wanamaker, Sam, 87
Ward, Douglas Turner, 12, 218–22; *Day of Absence,* 248
Ward, Lillian, 93
Warfield, Violet, 72–73
Waring, James, 109–11, 113, 118, 124
Warren, Ed, 116
Washington, Booker T., 23, 49
Washington, Denzel, 221
Washington, Fredi, 35
Washington, Walter, 14, 222, 259
Washington Drama Center, 173
Washington Drama Society, Inc., 140–43
Washington Dramatic Club, 28
Washington Naval Conference (1921), 41–43
Washington Nontraditional Casting Conference, 195
Washington Shakespeare Theater Company, 271

Washington Square (James), 197
Washington Technical Institute, 224
Washington Theatre Club, 9–10, 172–76, 241, 253
Wayans, Marlon, 76
Weese, Harry, 143, 148, 179
Weiss, Peter: *The Persecution and Assassination of Jean-Paul Marat,* 177
Weller, Charles Frederick: *Neglected Neighbors,* 24
Welles, Orson, 57, 59, 104; *Voodoo Macbeth,* 58
Wells, H. G., 43
Wells, James Lesesne, 64
Wentworth, Hazel and John, 9–10, 172–76
Wesley, Richard, 71
West, Cheryl, 180; *Before It Hits Home,* 194; *Jar the Floor,* 183, 194
West, Jennifer, 215
Wharton, Diana, 244
What Shall We Tell Caroline? (Mortimer), 154
White, Andrew, 227
White, Miles, 254
Whitfield, Lynn, 232
Whitfield, Vantile. *See* Motojicho
Who's Afraid of Virginia Woolf? (Albee), 150–51
The Wild Duck (Ibsen), 71, 80, 81
Wilde, Oscar: *Salomé,* 65
Wilder, Thornton, 112, 119, 317n22; *Happy Journey,* 106; *Our Town,* 154–55, 156–57; *The Skin of Our Teeth,* 110, 150
Wiley, Dennis, 242, 243
Wilkerson, Frederick, 77
Williams, Bert, 32, 33, 34
Williams, Billy Dee, 176, 219
Williams, Brian, 229

Williams, Charles, 228
Williams, Edward Christopher, 2, 23, 68, 212
Williams, Emlyn: *A Murder Has Been Arranged,* 69
Williams, George D., 45
Williams, Rosalyn Coleman, 259
Williams, Tennessee, 119, 317n22; *The Glass Menagerie,* 71, 154, 194; *Period of Adjustment,* 173–74
Wilson, August: *Fences,* 157, 194; *Joe Turner's Come and Gone,* 180; *Pittsburgh Cycle,* 62, 215–16
Wilson, George W., 42
Wilson, John A., 224
Wilson, Landford: *The Gingham Dog,* 176
Wilson, Woodrow, 18–19
Wolfe, Thomas, 40
Wolff, Geoffrey A., 76
Wolman, Jerry, 124
Woodson, Carter G., 48, 64, 68, 82; *The Journal of Negro History,* 63
Woollcott, Alexander, 45
Woolly Mammoth Theater (DC), 175, 203, 271
Workshop 47 (Harvard University), 37, 40
Works Progress Administration, 57, 58
World Disarmament Conference (1921), 41–43
Wright, Richard: *Native Son,* 59

Xu, Guo, 18–19

Yankee Doodle Boy (Brady & Kerr), 106–7
Yeats, W. B., 5, 36, 263
Yordan, Philip: *Anna Lucasta,* 59
Young, Stark, 38
Young Playwrights' Theater (DC), 272

Zacarías, Karen, 272–73; *The Book Club Play,* 273; *Native Gardens,* 273
Zacarías, Miguel, 272

Zeisler, Peter, 164
Zinoman, Joy, 271
Zolotow, Sam, 164